THE POETICAL WORKS

OF

ALEXANDER POPE

EDITED

WITH NOTES AND INTRODUCTORY MEMOIR

BY

ADOLPHUS WILLIAM WARD, M.A., Litt.D.

FROM THE GLOBE EDITION
REVISED AND ENLARGED

VOL. I

WILDSIDE PRESS

PREFACE TO ENGLISH EDITION.

IN the *Text* of this edition, Warburton's arrangement has (with a single unimportant exception) been maintained ; the remaining pieces have been added from subsequent editions, or, where possible, from earlier sources. Throughout, I have endeavoured to preserve Pope's use of capital letters, and of apostrophised syllables ; of the former, lest his intentions of emphasis, — of the latter, lest his metrical accuracy, should be unnecessarily obscured. His uncertain spelling, and his frequently perplexing interpunctuation, it seemed useless to reproduce with religious fidelity.

Among the *Notes* will be found all Pope's own (marked '*P.*'), except in the case of the *Dunciad*, where curtailment was unavoidable. I have not, so far as I am aware, transcribed anything from previous editors without acknowledgment. The extent of my obligations to Mr. Carruthers' edition (the only edition of Pope which has any claim to completeness) will therefore be apparent on the surface. For everything enclosed within [ ]'s I am myself responsible ; and the quotations which previous editors have successively transcribed I have taken care to verify.

In conclusion, I cannot forbear from thanking my accomplished friend, the Rev. Alfred Ainger, for many suggestions whereby he has aided me during pleasant hours spent in common over the following pages.

A. W. W.

OWENS COLLEGE, MANCHESTER,
April 30th, 1869.

PREFACE TO AMERICAN EDITION.

EXCEPT for the correction of obvious misprints, the text of the present edition is practically a reprint of the "Globe" edition. A few brief notes bracketed and marked *Am. Ed.* have been here and there inserted. And the fragment entitled Sylvia, and the reprint of the first edition of the *Rape of the Lock* and that of the *Dunciad* taken from the ten-volume edition of Elwin and Courthope, have been included in the Appendix. An index of first lines also adds completeness to the volume, which it is hoped will be found both accurate and singularly well adapted for library and school use.

THE PUBLISHERS.

Sept. 1, 1896.

CONTENTS.

	Page		Page
INTRODUCTORY MEMOIR	ix–lii	Moral Essays.	
PREFACE	1	Epistle IV. (to the Earl of Burlington):	
JUVENILE POEMS	5	of the Use of Riches	262
Pastorals	5	Epistle V. (to Mr. Addison. Occasioned	
A Discourse on Pastoral Poetry	6	by his Dialogues on Medals)	269
Spring	10	SATIRES	273
Summer	14	Epistle to Dr. Arbuthnot, being the Prologue to the Satires	274
Autumn	17	Satires and Epistles of Horace Imitated	289
Winter	20	The First Satire of the Second Book	291
Messiah	24	The Second Satire of the Second Book	296
Windsor Forest	28	The First Epistle of the First Book	301
Odes	40	The Sixth Epistle of the First Book	306
Ode for Music on St. Cecilia's Day	40	The First Epistle of the Second Book	309
Two Chorus's to the Tragedy of Brutus	44	The Second Epistle of the Second Book	323
Ode on Solitude	46	Satires of Dr. Donne versified	331
The Dying Christian to his Soul	47	Satire II.	332
Essay on Criticism	48	Satire IV.	335
The Rape of the Lock	72	Epilogue to the Satires in Two Dialogues	342
Elegy to the Memory of an Unfortunate Lady	93	Dialogue I.	342
		Dialogue II.	347
Prologue to Mr. Addison's Tragedy of Cato	95	THE DUNCIAD	356
		Preface (1727)	360
Epilogue to Mr. Rowe's Jane Shore	97	Advertisement (1729)	362
TRANSLATIONS AND IMITATIONS	99	A Letter to the Publisher	363
Sappho to Phaon	99	Advertisement (1742)	366
Eloisa to Abelard	105	Advertisement (1743)	367
The Temple of Fame	113	Advertisement (Printed in the Journals, 1730)	367
January and May	129		
The Wife of Bath	146	Martinus Scriblerus of the Poem	368
The First Book of Statius his Thebais	155	By Authority	370
The Fable of Dryope	173	The Dunciad: Book I.	370
Vertumnus and Pomona	176	Book II.	384
Imitations of English Poets	179	Book III.	400
Chaucer	179	Book IV.	413
Spenser (The Alley)	180	Imitations	435
Waller	182	By the Author: a Declaration	441
(Of a Lady singing to her Lute)	182	A List of Books, Papers, and Verses, &c.	442
(On a Fan of the Author's Design)	182	Index of Persons celebrated in this Poem	444
Cowley	182	Index of matters contained in this Poem and Notes	445
(The Garden)	182		
(Weeping)	183	MISCELLANEOUS PIECES IN VERSE	451
Earl of Rochester (On Silence)	184	Imitations of Horace	451
Earl of Dorset	186	Book I. Epistle VII.	451
(Artemisia)	186	Book II. Satire VI.	453
(Phryne)	186	Book IV. Ode I.	458
Dr. Swift (The Happy Life of a Country Parson)	187	Part of the Ninth Ode of the Fourth Book	459
		Epistles	460
MORAL ESSAYS	188	To Robert Earl of Oxford	460
Essay on Man	192	To James Craggs, Esq.	461
Epistle I.	194	To Mr. Jervas, with Mr. Dryden's Translation of Fresnoy's *Art of Painting*	462
Epistle II.	202		
Epistle III.	210	To Miss Blount, with the Works of Voiture	464
Epistle IV.	219		
The Universal Prayer	230	To the Same, on her leaving the Town after the Coronation	466
Moral Essays in Four Epistles to several Persons)	232		
		On receiving from the Right Hon. the Lady Frances Shirley a Standish and two Pens	467
Epistle I. (to Lord Cobham): of the Knowledge and Characters of Men	232		
		Epitaphs	469
Epistle II. (to a Lady): of the Characters of Women	240	I. On Charles Earl of Dorset	469
		II. On Sir William Trumbal	470
Epistle III. (to Lord Bathurst): of the Use of Riches	248	III. On the Hon. Simon Harcourt	470

CONTENTS.

Epitaphs.

	Page
IV. On James Craggs, Esq.	471
V. Intended for Mr. Rowe	471
VI. On Mrs. Corbet	472
VII. On the Monument of the Hon. Robert Digby and of his Sister Mary	472
VIII. On Sir Godfrey Kneller	473
IX. On General Henry Withers	473
X. On Mr. Elijah Fenton	474
XI. On Mr. Gay	474
XII. Intended for Sir Isaac Newton	475
XIII. On Dr. Francis Atterbury	475
XIV. On Edmund D. of Buckingham	476
XV. For one who would not be buried in Westminster Abbey	476
Another, on the same	476
Miscellaneous	477
A Paraphrase on Thomas à Kempis	477
To the Author of a Poem entitled *Successio*	478
Argus	479
Imitation of Martial	479
Occasioned by some Verses of His Grace the Duke of Buckingham	480
On Mrs. Tofts	480
Epigram on the Feuds about Handel and Bononcini	480
Epigram (You beat your pate, &c.)	480
Epitaph (Well, then, poor G—, &c.)	480
Epitaph (Here Francis C— lies, &c.)	481
The Balance of Europe	481
To a Lady with 'The Temple of Fame'	481
Impromptu to Lady Winchilsea	481
Epigram on the Toasts of the Kit-Cat Club	482
A Dialogue (Pope and Craggs)	482
On Drawings of the Statues of Apollo, Venus, and Hercules, made by Sir G. Kneller	482
Prologue to the 'Three Hours after Marriage'	482
Prologue designed for Mr. D'Urfey's last Play	484
A Prologue by Mr. Pope to a Play for Mr. Dennis's Benefit	484
Macer: a Character	485
Umbra	486
To Mr. John Moore, Author of the Celebrated Worm-Powder	487
Sandys' Ghost	488
The Translator	490
The Three Gentle Shepherds	490
Lines written in Windsor Forest	491
To Mrs. M. B. on her Birth-Day	491
The Challenge, a Court Ballad	492
Answer to a Question of Mrs. Howe	494
Song, by a Person of Quality	494
On a certain Lady at Court	495
A Farewell to London	496
The Basset-Table, an Eclogue	497
To Lady Mary Wortley Montagu	501
Extemporaneous Lines, on the Picture of Lady M. W. Montagu	502
Imitation of Tibullus	502
Epitaphs on John Hughes and Sarah Drew	502
On the Countess of Burlington cutting Paper	503
On a Picture of Queen Caroline	504

Miscellaneous.

	Page
The Looking-Glass: on Mrs. Pulteney	504
On certain Ladies	504
Celia	504
Epigram, engraved on the Collar of a Dog which I gave to H.R.H.	505
Lines sung by Durastanti	505
On his Grotto at Twickenham	505
Verses to Mr. C.	506
To Mr. Gay, who had congratulated Mr. Pope on finishing his House and Gardens	506
Upon the Duke of Marlborough's House at Woodstock	507
On Beaufort House Gate at Chiswick	507
Lines to Lord Bathurst	508
Inscription on a Punch-Bowl	508
Verbatim from Boileau	508
Epigram (My Lord complains, &c.)	509
Epigram (Yes, 'tis the time, &c.)	509
Occasioned by reading the Travels of Captain Lemuel Gulliver	509
I. To Quinbus Flestrin, the Man-Mountain	510
II. The Lamentation of Glumdalclitch for the Loss of Grildrig	510
III. To Mr. Lemuel Gulliver from the Houyhnhnms	512
IV. Mary Gulliver to Captain Lemuel Gulliver	513
Lines on Swift's Ancestors	516
From the Grub-street Journal	516
I. Epigram: occasioned by seeing some Sheets of Bentley's Edition of Milton's *Paradise Lost*	516
II. Epigram (Should D—s print, &c.)	516
III. Mr. J. M. S—e catechised on his one Epistle to Mr. Pope	517
IV. Epigram: on Mr. M—re's going to law with Gilliver	517
V. Epigram (A Gold Watch found, &c.)	517
VI. Epitaph (Here lies what had no Birth, &c.)	517
VII. A Question by Anonymous	518
VIII. Epigram (Great G—, &c.)	518
IX. Epigram (Behold! ambitious of the British Bays, &c.)	518
On seeing the Ladies at Crux-Easton walk in the Woods by the Grotto	518
Inscription on a Grotto, the Work of Nine Ladies	518
Verses left by Mr. Pope, on his lying in Rochester's Bed at Adderbury	519
To the Right Hon. the Earl of Oxford	519
Translation of a Prayer of Brutus	520
Lines written in Evelyn's Book on Coins	520
To Mr. Thomas Southern, on his Birth-Day	520
Bishop Hough	521
Prayer of St. Francis Xavier	521
Appendix I. 1740: a Poem	523
II. Sylvia: a Fragment	526
III. The Rape of the Lock: Reprint of First Edition	527
IV. The Dunciad: Reprint of First Edition	537
Index to First Lines	571

INTRODUCTORY MEMOIR.

VERY wonderful is the vitality of names; and there is reason to believe that books and essays continue to this day to make their appearance, in which the period of our literary history coinciding with the literary life of Pope is spoken of as our Augustan age. Were this transfer of title intended to imply the existence during the period in question of any royal patronage of letters such as the first of the legitimate Cæsars was too prudent absolutely to neglect, it would condemn itself at once. The English Augustans were not warmed by the favour of any English Augustus. William the Deliverer, in whose reign they had grown up, had been without stomach for the literature of a nation with whose tastes and habits he had never made it part of his political program to sympathise. Queen Anne's very feeble light of personal judgment was easily kept under by the resolute will of her favourites, or flickered timidly under cover of the narrowest orthodoxy. Of the first two Georges the former, indifferent to an unpopularity which never seemed to endanger his tenure of the throne, neither possessed an ordinary mastery of the English tongue nor manifested even a transient desire to acquire it. His successor had no objection to be considered, in virtue of his mistress rather than his wife, the patron of the literary adherents of a political party, until, on mounting the throne, he blandly disappointed the hopes of that party itself. The epoch of our Augustans had all but closed, when the death of Frederick, Prince of Wales, put an absolute end to the nominal hopes in the advent of a golden age for the liberal arts, by averting the accession of a Patriot King.

Neither was the defect of royal patronage supplied by any genuine Mæcenas from among the great ones of the realm. The traditions in this respect of the Stuart period — traditions doubtless exaggerated in the age of Pope, yet not wholly baseless — had barely survived the expulsion of the last Stuart King. Of King William's Batavian comrades, none had sought to grace their newly-acquired dignities and incomes by fostering the efforts of genius in the country which they had consented to adopt. Among the chief English-born noblemen and gentlemen of this reign those of the older generation were too intently engaged in picking their path through events and eventualities to find time for dallying with the delights of literature and art. One only of their number, the sage whom all parties honoured because he so circumspectly abstained from being of vital service to any, Sir William Temple, alone had a thought for literature, and horticulture, and other liberal amusements. With Queen Anne's accession commenced among the leaders of political and social life a period of eager speculation as to the contingencies which might supervene on her decease. Parties within parties, and factions within factions, battled over their living sovereign because it seemed that everything must depend upon the hands into which the power should fall when she should lie dead.

In a time of national abasement foreign intellectual fashions and the patronage of such fashions may prevail; and such had been actually the case in the reigns of both the Charles's. In a time of national elevation a national literature will find its patrons; nor had such been wanting to our Elizabethans, nor were they (though in a different fashion) to fail English writers in subsequent times. But amidst the cynically selfish party-warfare which degraded our political life in the reign of Queen Anne, the value of literature was depreciated in accordance with the general decay of national feeling. For it was an age in which all things were viewed in their relation to the main issue upon which men's thoughts were fixed. Church and crown, freedom of action and of speech, the rights of the citizen at home and the glories of the nation abroad, were freely and fiercely tossed about in the caldron where the political future was believed to be brewing. Where the national honour was hardly taken into account as a secondary consideration, and the national wishes so little consulted that in the eyes of history they to this day frequently remain obscure, a national literature could obviously have no intrinsic cause for existence in the eyes of either Tories or of Whigs. It is for the parties that the nation and its feelings have been created; its traditions, its sympathies are so many adventitious aids, its foremost men so many candidates for partisan employment. The Whigs will crown Addison the laureate of their party; but not till he has sung the glories of its acknowledged hero. Bolingbroke, who liked to compare himself to Alcibiades, and Oxford, in whom the oblique vision of some party adulator discerned a Pericles to match, repaid their literary henchmen in the coin dearest to the frugal souls of literary men, and cheapest to the condescending great, a social familiarity at times facilitated by the bottle. Their literary assailants they were eager to imprison and pillory and utterly extinguish. Pegasus was always welcome if he would run in harness; otherwise away with him to the pound. Queen Anne's reign came to an end; and under the administration which supervened, a yet more practical method of reducing literature to her level was consistently adopted. No minister has probably ever expended so large a sum upon the hire of pens as Sir Robert Walpole. The consent of contemporaries and posterity stigmatises him as the poet's foe. The warmth of his patronage elicited the grubs from the soil, and bred dunces faster than Swift and Pope could destroy them.

INTRODUCTORY MEMOIR. xi

Still, if the world of politics pursued its own ends, the world of society, never wholly absorbed in political life, might have essayed to offer its pleasing aid. It is true that in England, happily perhaps for our political development, the social life of the upper classes has generally found its centre in the political life of their times. Even after the Restoration society had only exaggerated, not distorted, the political tendencies of the age. Fashion in England has always driven ideas and notions to extremes; it has rarely or never invented them for itself. Thus, at the close of the Protectorate, society had anticipated the restoration of the Stuarts by taking the drama into favour once more. The stage seemed to feed the imagination by a tragedy chiefly of rant and fustian, national in its grossness if foreign in its form; while for an enforced period of spiritual austerity society found its revenge in a comedy of something more than flesh and blood. But every debauch has its limit; and the generation amidst which Pope grew up was growing weary of the boisterous sensuality as well as of the furious bombast which had intoxicated its predecessors. Dryden had sickened over the abominations to which he had prostituted his Muse; and though Congreve still remained an authority on account of the wit with which he had relieved the sameness of his dramatic fare, the ruder, but equally creative, Wycherley was fain to make a desperate attempt to eke out his withering wreath by a leaf or two of lyric laurels. Society had ceased to care for literature other than dramatic, unless recommended by an authority other than its own; and where was it to seek for such an authority except in the world of politics?

For our so-called Augustan age might indeed in one sense have asserted its claim to the title with which it was credited, had the Varros and Pollios revived a learning whence literature might have drawn the nourishing sap of a new and more luxuriant development. Our ancient seats of learning were identified with the national church; and it was in them that she must count at once her chief ornaments and her surest supports. But they had in truth suffered with her. In religious matters, the great Revolutionary struggle had come to represent itself to the inheritors of its achievements under the aspect of its extremes. Oxford the descendant of a Presbyterian, Bolingbroke the scion of a Puritan family, availed themselves of the reaction and cold-bloodedly stood forward as the instigators of a High-Church mob. The Church had saved its connexion with the state by what was, unjustly in many cases but not unnaturally upon the whole, regarded as a compromise with opinions formerly elevated to the place of principles. The result was inevitable, that the moral influence of the clergy had fallen from its original height. The Universities throughout the first half of the century swarmed with the worst class of political malcontents, — those who acquiesce and remain disloyal; for few priests and no prelates followed Atterbury into exile. Among the educated classes, indifference, veiled under the thin disguise of a philosophy hardly rising above the superficial deductions of common sense, had become the prevailing note in views of religion; and in morality, a code found ready acceptance which accommodated itself without difficulty even to slippery shoulders. This general tone of feeling communicated itself even to members of a creed protected as it were by the consolidating influences of continued persecution; and a sense of decency sufficed to recommend an outward attitude dependent on no deep-seated convictions of heart and mind. The discipline of the Universities was still struggling among the folds of an apparently immortal scholasticism. The new Oxford scholarship was that of *dilettanti;* and Cambridge was only gradually reconstructing her system of teaching on the basis of the writings of Locke, and under the surviving influence of the devoted life of her unforgotten Barrow. Yet in those branches of study which most closely connect themselves with the progress of literature, though Bentley had taken the field, his services were hardly appreciated by his own generation. Free translation, the enemy of accurate scholarship, was adapting the classics to modern tastes rather than raising the latter to an earnest contemplation of the ancient models. And a critical knowledge, or even a faithful study of the national literature, had been scarcely begun by one or two enthusiasts; Shakspeare, mutilated on the stage, still awaited his first competent editor. Criticism, insisting upon rules the meaning of which it blindly ignored, lost itself in empty dogmatism, or strayed into the exchange of sheer personalities. The true critic and the true student were rare among the children of our Augustan age.

For in this age literature is in the main regarded under two aspects — as a political instrument and as an intellectual stimulant. The literary hero of these times will therefore not be a mind intent upon pondering and revealing the depths of human nature; nor a poet who from out of the turmoil of political conflicts or social distractions betakes himself into the secrecy of lyrical composition; not even the singer who recounts or inspires to great national actions. He will rather be the writer whose point pierces just as deeply as suffices for the insight which society desires to enjoy into the characters of men and women, and who never forgets the special in the general. He will be, in form, an eclectic of eclectics, sworn to fidelity to no school, and founding none, but like the society with which he accords, correct within the limits of a self-formed taste. From ancients and moderns, from French and Italian and our own interesting literature, he will circumspectly choose the most attractive models to adorn the grotto in which he receives the visits of his Muse. He will write to please, but to please a difficult public. He will therefore be master of that nicely chosen kind of allusions which is transparent to the educated intelligence; avoiding illustrations either commonplace or far-fetched, sparing no pains to sustain the attention which he arouses, and to make sure of the effect which it is his purpose to create. Whether his theme be love or hate, he will not forget the hearers for whose benefit he discourses upon it; and when he is most in earnest, he will be least liable to forget the eyes which are watching his conduct of the enterprise.

Controversy is the very breath in the nostrils of such a writer and such an age. Society must be in a state of suspense, of secret intrigues, of envy and malice beneath and an artificial politeness on the surface, if it is thoroughly to relish a literature combative in its most reflexive moments, and polished in the very crisis of the combat. The age was a great age of clubs; of associations, large or small, of men bound together by the spirit of common antagonism or hatred towards this or that political or literary counter-coterie. Just as the world of politics in this age was limited to a very small numerical proportion of the nation whose affairs it swayed, so the world of literature, extremely confined in comparison to that of only a generation or two later, was clearly and definitely marked off into the fractions which composed it. Political and literary clubs were alike characterised by a single-mindedness of antipathies which the lower orders were not slow to burlesque in the confraternities of the tap-room.[1] Kit-Cat and Calves-head, Beefsteak and October, may have occasionally drowned even their party-feelings in the oblivion ensured by an unflinching devotion to the club-rules. But the Brothers' Club founded by Bolingbroke in 1711 was a kind of backstairs Cabinet of the Tory party; while the literary champions of the latter (including the professedly neutral Pope) met in the Scribblerus Club to pulverise in a common mortar the small fry of their literary adversaries. At all these clubs (and the 'Brothers' occasionally admitted their 'Sisters') a rivalry in abuse was one of the unwritten laws of the fraternity.[2]

Our Augustan age was not the most immoral which court and society in England have known (at least it may be said that the profligacy of the Restoration period, arrested by the reaction under William III., was not to revive in its fulness till after the death of Queen Anne); but it was assuredly the most scandalous. And its peculiarity was this, that while evil speaking, even in the age of the Regency, was as a rule left as an unenvied privilege to the lowest hangers-on of literature, or to those members of society whom age and sex or constitutional vacuity include in a licensed category, the practice was assiduously cultivated by the leaders in society and literature of our Augustan age. Horace Walpole lived almost a generation too late. Far happier in this respect was the lot of one with whom an elective affinity at all events connected him, of Lord Hervey, who found a fellow-railer in Lady Mary Wortley Montagu, and but too willing an adversary in Pope. It was in literature as in politics. If a man avowed himself, or caused himself to be supposed, the opponent of another, or of his coterie, or the supporter of a coterie opposed to the latter, any means of bringing his face to the grindstone was accounted within the limits of legitimate warfare. To blacken his character, to blast his reputation, to defile his grandfather's grave, all these things followed as a matter of course. An aspersion of venom was held a justifiable addition to the point of the foil; and the slightest sign of hostility, an unfavourable criticism, a line in a farce, was pursued with Corsican persistency of vengeance. How unnatural in the eyes of a more self-possessed posterity seems this age: when great poets made war upon women, when no enemy was deemed too

[1] [The so-called *mug-houses* were frequented by Whig Societies who in 1715 and 1716 came to frequent blows with Tory mobs. See Wright's *Caric. Hist. of the Georges*, chap. i.]

[2] This subject is treated with his usual incisiveness by M. Ch. de Rémusat in his admirable essay on Bolingbroke.

weak to be worthy of the most practised steel. What a lack of dignity as well as of good sense, corresponding to that which a House of Commons endeavoured to hunt down a pulpit Xanthippe, and a Secretary of State entered upon a crusade against the pygmies of the press. Statesman and man of letters — there was little as to true generosity of spirit to choose between the two.[1] The comparative smallness of the literary world may help to account for the importance with which its members invested even their most trivial disputes. But few escaped the taint of their age, and nothing in the life of Addison strikes his contemporaries as so remarkable, as the fact that he forgives his enemies before composing himself for an exemplary death. The commonest courtesies of literary life which even Bavius and Mavius would not have permitted themselves to neglect, are defiantly violated by our Augustans. Anonymity, far from serving as a cover against nominal recriminations, is in truth resorted to only as an evasion of an uncertain law; and cowardice too frequently skulks behind a lampoon, as a literary weapon no more fitting than the bludgeons hired by Rochester for his Rose Alley ambuscade. How imperfectly had Dryden's successors learnt to imitate the example of one who truthfully declared that 'he had seldom answered any scurrilous lampoon, and,' though 'naturally vindictive, had suffered in silence, and possessed his soul in quiet.'

That a healthy current of life was still flowing in the nation's veins, in despite of the vices which seemed to pervade society, is of course a fact to which our literature alone bears sufficient testimony. From out of the sphere of the middle classes a reaction had been preparing itself. Its direction was towards that close obedience to the divine law as a practical, if possible a literal, fingerpost in all relations of life which is in accordance with the Puritan spirit of the nation, and which was in due time to force itself upon the classes long in their own opinion practically emancipated from its control. De Foe and his lineal literary descendants, the essayists and novelists, succeeded in saving its national character to our literature. But an examination of their influence and the gradual progress of its operation would be out of place here. As the age appears to us in the mirror of the literature which professedly and unhesitatingly attached itself to the world of politics, fashion and learning, it is an unnatural age, because licentious in every direction except that of the form which by its own authority it has chosen as the exponent of its very spirit and essence. All the emotions of the Augustans, except their hatreds, seem shallow and transitory, and most of all so in their literary expression. Men who estimate their neighbours according to a selfish standard, necessarily adjust to it their measures of praise as well as of blame. Queen Anne, whose childish dependence upon others was no secret even to herself, is addressed in strains of uncom-

---

[1] Bolingbroke, as Secretary of State, writes to the Queen in 1711: 'I have discovered the author of another scandalous libel, who will be in custody this afternoon; he will make the 13th I have seized, and the 15th I have found out.' Swift writes in his Journal to Stella of the same year: 'One Boyer, a French dog, has abused me in a pamphlet, and I have got him up in a messenger's hands; the Secretary promises me to swinge him. I must make that rogue an example for warning to others.' See Macknight's *Life of Bolingbroke*.

INTRODUCTORY MEMOIR. xv

promising panegyric before which even the tributes of the Cavaliers to the Rose of Bohemia grow pale. Even Prior is recklessly dull when he begins to flatter [1] *ex officio;* even Young's unctuous religiosity adapts itself to the exigencies of a courtly veneration.[2] Nor was it only loyalty which was thus galvanised into a spasmodic existence. Dryden had scattered panegyrics with the profuse vigour belonging to his genial *abandon;* his successors swung their censers in honour of their minor divinities with the measured oscillations of drilled acolytes; and even a Wharton had his poet-in-ordinary. The amatory verse of the age is perhaps the most unnatural that has ever been written; instead of exhausting itself on even ruby lips and dainty feet, it hovers with inquisitive placidity round ladies' fans or lapdogs or paper-knives. The ladies themselves could hardly be natural without falling into downright cynicism; and passed an existence as unreal as their outward selves, made up as they were of powders and patches, and fenced in with hurdles of whalebone. The real epos of society under Queen Anne, though designed as a burlesque, is Pope's *Rape of the Lock.* Under the first two Georges the coating of varnish grew thinner and thinner; but the material remained equally rotten beneath.

Such as these were, if I rightly estimate the characteristics of the age in so far as he was brought into contact with it, the conditions under which Pope entered upon and led his literary life. Its course could not fail to be affected and in some degree determined by them. Yet the chief element in the story of his life, as in the stories of all human lives, remains of course the gradual development of his own individuality, and the unconscious compromise ultimately effected between it and the influences which surrounded him. Of his triumphant struggle against difficulties of no ordinary significance, and of his single-minded devotion to the task which his genius hand marked out for him, his life, however imperfectly told, cannot fail to offer clear and abundant testimony. It intertwines itself almost inseparably with his works; for Pope, as has been well said,[3] was a literary man, as Garrick was an actor, pure and simple. And life and works viewed together will, I think, irresistibly lead to the conclusion that Pope belonged to that second order of great writers, who return to their age the seeds which it has sown in them, grown and tended into magnificent fruits; not to that other and assuredly higher order, whose genius is not receptive and reproductive only, but creative, and of whom England was barren in its so-called Augustan age.

---

[1] See, besides his well-known Ode to the Queen, the Epistle desiring the Queen's picture, characteristically 'left unfinished, by the sudden news of H. M. death.'

[2] See above all the exordium of his *Last Day;* besides his poems on the accession of George I. and II. respectively.

[3] By Dibdin, in his *History of the Stage.* In this sense Warburton might justly write to Garrick: 'Nobody but you and Pope ever knew how to preserve the dignity of your respective employments.' Fitzgerald's *Life of Garrick,* chap. v.

I.

Much that is peculiar in the life and literary career of Pope is accounted for by the circumstances of his birth and education.

Alexander Pope was born on the twenty-first of May of the year 1688, in Lombard Street in the city of London. Of his father and namesake it is known with certainty that he realised in the linen-trade a fortune sufficient to enable him to retire from business at a comparatively early period in life, and at his death to leave behind him an income which has been variously estimated, but which at all events sensibly added to the worldly ease of his son. That the elder Pope was a devoted member of the Church of Rome, is equally undoubted; we find his son in his earlier letters referring to the pious habits prevailing in his family; and passages in the poetry of the son[1] picture the father's life as spent in cheerful resignation to the lot in those days incumbent upon adherents to the persecuted ancient faith. That Pope's father was a convert to the Church in which he lived and brought up his son, is a mere piece of hearsay built upon another piece of hearsay to the effect that the poet's grandfather was a clergyman of the Church of England. Though antiquarian zeal has sought to identify this supposed Anglican clerical grandsire in the person of an Alexander Pope, rector of Thruxton in Hampshire, who died in the year 1645, there is nothing beyond a mere conjecture to justify the application of an intrinsically uninteresting discovery. The poet no doubt claimed kindred with the family bearing his name formerly ennobled as earls of Downe; but as the family in question was entirely extinct in the male line, it is at best possible that the two families had at some former period been more or less closely connected. There is just as much and as little reason to assume that the poet was descended from a Scotch branch of the Popes; the foundation of the claim resting chiefly on the two facts that there have been Catholic Popes in Scotland, and that an enthusiastic Presbyterian namesake of the poet vaguely asserted a kind of kinsmanship with the latter in his lifetime.

The maiden name of Pope's mother was Edith Turner. She was the daughter of William Turner, a Roman Catholic gentleman of good position, and lord of the manor of Towthorpe in Yorkshire. He was the father of no less than seventeen children, of whom Pope's mother survived all the rest. She died at the age of 93, in 1733, affectionately mourned in death as she had been tenderly cherished throughout his life by her son. On a monument which he erected to her he recorded her character as that of the best of mothers and most loving of women.[2] Dr. Johnson, in whose large heart the sentiment of piety sat enthroned, generously observes of Pope under this aspect, that 'life has, among its soothing and quiet comforts, few things better to give than such a son.' Of William Turner's children some were

---

[1] *Epistle to Arbuthnot*, vv. 394 ff. *Imit of Hor.* bk. II. Ep. II. vv. 54 ff.

[2] No attention need be paid to Mrs. Piozzi's statement that Pope's mother was 'a poor feebleminded thing, unworthy anyone's care or esteem.' Hayward, *Autobiography and Remains of Mrs. Piozzi*, II. 154.

INTRODUCTORY MEMOIR. xvii

brought up as Protestants and some Catholics; but it cannot be doubted that Pope's mother was among the latter number. Her attachment to the Catholic faith seemed to her son a sufficient argument to outweigh all the inducements to conversion urged upon him, after his father's death, by Atterbury. Thus his attitude towards the church in which he was nurtured invariably remained that of a cheerful outward acquiescence, whatever at times may have been his views in regard to creeds and churches in general.[1]

On retiring from business, the elder Pope, after residing for a time at Kensington, finally took up his abode at Binfield, on the border of Windsor Forest, and about nine miles distant from the royal castle and town. Here he remained in modest but comfortable circumstances until the year 1716, when the family removed to Chiswick, little more than a year before his death. Whatever may have been his own earlier history, he was a kind and indulgent parent to his precocious only son, the development of whose tastes and tendencies the father seems at times to have been fain to moderate, but never to check. When the son affected the art of painting, his father placed no obstacles in his way; when he adopted literature as the calling of his life, his father with equal readiness acquiesced in this hazardous choice. He never appears to have intended that his son should engage in trade; and even had the delicate and sickly nature of the latter admitted of his following one of the learned professions, all were closed to him by the circumstance of his creed. With his father Pope shared the love of gardening, which, notwithstanding many absurd excrescences, was one of the healthiest tastes of the times, and in which he was afterwards, after a fashion of his own, to indulge in the fantastic laying-out of his Twickenham villa.

Among the many precocious children of whom we read in literary and artistic biography (and precocity is as frequent here as it is rare in the case of future great statesmen; for talents unfold themselves amidst tranquil surroundings, but to fashion a character are needed the storms of the world [2]), Pope was assuredly one of the most precocious. At five years of age he had already displayed sufficient signs of promise to be chosen by an aunt as the reversionary legatee of all her books, pictures and medals. His education in its beginnings and progress corresponds very closely with its ultimate results. Pope was by necessity rather than choice a self-educated man; and he never became a scholar. Science may number self-taught geniuses among her chief luminaries; of scholarship, as the term implies, discipline is an indispensable element. Pope taught himself writing by copying from printed books, and hence acquired at least one external mark of scholarly habits, the practice of minute calligraphy crowded into nooks and corners of paper — a practice which afterwards in Pope's case almost developed itself into a mania and obtained for him from Swift the epithet of 'paper-sparing' Pope. And as he passed onward

---

[1] The above summary is based on a comparison of Carruthers with various antiquarian tracts on the parentage and family of Pope by J. Hunter and R. Davies.
[2] Goethe's *Tasso*.

from the first rudiments, his education remained very much a matter of chance. From the family priest (it is very touching to find how few of these Roman Catholic families lacked the ministration of one of the persecuted servants of their Church), whose name was Banister, he learnt the accidence of Latin and Greek, when eight years of age; and afterwards successively attended two small Catholic schools, one at Twyford near Winchester, which he is said to have left in disgrace after fleshing upon its master the youthful weapon of his satire, the other in London, kept by a convert of the name of Deane, whose principle of education seems to have been as far as possible removed from that of unremitting personal superintendence. About this time must be dated the famous incident of the boy Pope's visit to Will's Coffee-house, the sole occasion (according to his account to Spence) on which he ever beheld Dryden.

Quitting Mr. Deane's seminary for his father's house at Binfield, Pope, now twelve or thirteen years of age, brought with him little or no accurate learning, but tastes already developed and a literary ambition already active. At about eight years of age he had translated part of Statius, who next to Virgil continued through life his favourite Latin poet; and at twelve he had composed a play founded on the *Iliad*. At Twyford he had prepared himself for this effort by the study of Ogilby's Homer, followed by that of Sandys' Ovid; and now that he was left to follow the bent of his own inclinations, his studies continued to pursue the same direction. 'Considering,' he told Spence, 'how very little I had when I came from school, I think I may be said to have taught myself Latin, as well as French, or Greek; and in all these my chief way of getting them was by translation.'[1] Translation without guidance is the ruin of accurate scholarship; but it is not Pope or his father, it is the penal statutes against Catholic teachers which are to be held accountable for his having availed himself of the only method left open to his use.

It is to this period that we must ascribe the first of his preserved juvenile pieces. Though he had no public, the tonic of common sense appears to have been occasionally administered by his father; and the sense of rhythm was a gift which had been bestowed upon him by nature, together with a general correctness of taste in the choice of words and expressions which his preference for poetical over prose reading could not fail to heighten. To these causes must be ascribed the extraordinary and perhaps unparalleled fact that there is little vital difference, so far as form is concerned, between some of the earliest and some of the latest of Pope's productions. His early pieces lack the vigour of wit and the brilliancy of antithesis of his later works; but they have the same felicity of expression, and the same easy flow of versification. It is only in the management of rhymes that Pope's earliest productions are comparatively negligent. We have it on Pope's own authority, as related by Spence, that some of the couplets in an epic poem on the subject of Alcander, prince of Rhodes, which he begun soon after his twelfth birthday, were

[1] Even the Latin scholarship of Pope accordingly appears to have been of a somewhat unsound description. See e.g. the strange quotation from Horace among the 'Imitations,' noted by Pope in his *Temple of Fame* (p. 127 of the present edition).

afterwards inserted by him without alteration not only in the *Essay on Criticism*, but in the *Dunciad*. Alcander, after having progressed to the number of 4000 lines, and though uniting in itself specimens of every style admired by its author — Milton and Cowley and Spenser, Homer and Virgil, Ovid and Claudian and Statius — was left uncompleted and ultimately perished in the flames, to which this juvenile *magnum opus* seems to have been sentenced by the author himself, and not, as has been stated, by Bishop Atterbury.[1]

In his fifteenth year Pope went to London to learn French and Italian; but there is no evidence, either in his letters or in his works, that he ever attained to any real familiarity with either of these languages. French he seems to have learnt to read with ease; whether he conversed in it may be doubted, and his invariable habit in his poetry of accentuating French words according to the English rule would seem to lead to a contrary conclusion. As to Italian, he is said to have preferred Ariosto to Tasso; but translations existed of both; and the circumstance that in his *Essay on Criticism* he unjustifiably singles out Vida for an unmerited eminence among the Italian writers of the renaissance proves less than nothing as to Pope's knowledge either of that language or its literature; inasmuch as the work of Vida to which special allusions are made in the *Essay* was written in Latin. After a few months in London we find him once more returned to the retirement of Binfield; and hereupon ensues a period of five or six years' close application to study. As with Pope everything was precocious, so during this early period of his life he is overtaken by that phase of despondency and seemingly uncontrollable melancholy which work engenders in those of sedentary, as it cures in those of active habits of life, but which has tried few at so premature a point of their careers. In Pope's case the friendly advice of a priest named Southcote prescribed the obvious remedy, moderation in study combined with regular bodily exercise, and it is touching to find the poet in the days of his prosperity mindful of the inestimable service rendered him by the good father, and obtaining for the latter, at the hands of the obnoxious Walpole, a comfortable abbacy in France.

It was not till a much later period of his life, that under the influence of minds, foreign in their constitution to his own, Pope's studies ever seriously deviated from the narrow course which they had taken in his boyhood. Ancient and English poets nearly monopolised his attention; translation and imitation helping him to familiarise himself by practice with the styles of his favourite authors. He translated that part of Statius which he subsequently published with the corrections of his friend and adviser Walsh; as well as Cicero's *De Senectute*, an isolated juvenile effort in prose which chance has continued to hide from the eyes of posterity. Among English writers he was attracted in a far higher degree by the poets than by the prosaists. Yet he read Locke's *Essay*, though not without effort; and Sir William Temple's *Varia*, though without sympathy. His own prose style can

---

[1] See Roscoe's *Life*, pp. 19-20.

hardly be said to have suffered from his study of the latter author; and from his earlier letters, as well as from his *Discourse on Pastoral Poetry*, it is manifest that as a prose-writer he only lost the art of writing naturally by slow degrees. Of his appreciation of the distinctive styles of several English poets his *Imitations* offer sufficient proofs; that the genius of Chaucer only in part, and that of Spenser hardly at all, revealed itself to him, seems equally clear, if equally natural. His brief apprenticeship was already drawing towards its close; and he became an author before he had found time or opportunity to exchange dilettantism for scholarship.

II.

A kindly remembrance will ever be due to the friendly circle whose encouragement first launched Pope upon his literary life. Yet it required no extraordinary penetration to recognise in the gifted and studious boy the promise of brilliant original workmanship, even when he was most intent upon reproducing in juvenile clay of his own such monuments of past masters as had attracted his attention. Pope's parental home was far enough removed from the busy city to enable him to become one of the wonders of his vicinity; and at East Hamstead near Binfield dwelt an old gentleman well qualified by shrewdness and experience to become the earliest patron of youthful merit. The retirement of diplomatists has frequently been of service to literature; and Sir William Trumball, as his letters prove, well merited the encomium which Pope bestowed upon him in his Epitaph, that he was at once 'fill'd with the sense of age' and 'the fire of youth.' 'Give me leave to tell you,' he wrote to Pope as early as 1705, 'that I know nobody so likely to equal' Milton as the author of his earlier poems 'even at the age he wrote most of them, as yourself.' It was Trumball who introduced his protégé to Wycherley, the veteran of many a literary campaign. 'Manly' Wycherley, though he could look back upon a series of comedies unsurpassed in brutal vigour, was now in his old age collecting and revising the more innocent, if less powerful, efforts of his lyric moments. To Pope, however, he could at first hardly fail to be a literary hero, until at a rather later period familiarity with the old man's poems (submitted by him for the correction of the tiro) bred its inevitable consequence, and a too literal interpretation on Pope's part of a proverbially delicate request caused a coolness which prevented a continuance of friendly intercourse on the old terms. To Trumball in the first instance, and then to Wycherley, Pope had communicated a copy of his first completed effort, the *Pastorals*. Wycherley in his turn sent them to Walsh, who was himself not unknown as a poet, but enjoyed a still higher reputation as a critic. He received the juvenile poems favourably and returned a gratifying verdict upon them: 'It is not flattery at all to say that Vergil had written nothing so good at his age.'[1] He then extended his personal patronage to the young aspirant after

---

[1] Referring of course to the 'juvenile poems' of Vergil now universally regarded as spurious. The first of his *Eclogues* were certainly written at a later age than the *Pastorals* of Pope.

poetic fame, and invited him to his seat of Abberley in Worcestershire. Walsh died in 1708, a year before the *Pastorals* were actually published; but he lived to point out to his young friend the path from which the latter never swerved during his literary career; he bade him be a 'correct poet,' or in other words, desired to limit the excursions of Pope's muse to regions already meted out by trustworthy predecessors, 'prescribed her heights and pruned her tender wing.'[1] 'The best of the modern poets in all languages,' wrote Walsh to Pope in 1706, 'are those that have the nearest copied the ancients,' a maxim sufficiently characteristic of his critical standpoints. Another friend with whom Pope at this time became intimate and to whom he addressed many letters (published surreptitiously in 1727 by the mistress of his correspondent) was Henry Cromwell. Of the latter personally little is known; except that he was slovenly in his person and 'rode a hunting in a tye-wig;'[2] but his letters to Pope show him to have been an amateur critic as well as student, and he seems to have largely contributed to introduce Pope and his writings to the knowledge of society in town, where Cromwell was a resident.

And thus among these patrons and friends the *Pastorals* during four years or thereabouts passed from hand to hand, and were again shown to other personages prominent in society or letters: — to George Granville afterwards Lord Lansdowne, a poet and patron of poets, modest on the head of his own performances, eager for the success of those of others; — to Lord Halifax who afterwards when first lord of the Treasury was to honour himself by offering a pension to Pope which the latter, equally to *his* honour, declined; — to Lord Somers, a venerated chief of the same party, the Whigs; — and among the acknowledged leaders of literature to the popular Garth, and to Congreve the all-admired, the inimitable, who could afford to beam benignantly upon rising talent, though avowing himself careless of his own literary fame.

Fortified by the approval of such patrons as these, the young poet could have no difficulty in finding an opportunity for ushering into the world his poetic offspring. Its sponsors had been secured beforehand; and the necessary midwife appeared in the person of the famous bookseller Jacob Tonson,[3] who expressed his desire to include Pope's *Pastorals* in the forthcoming volume of his Poetic Miscellany. Tonson and his brother-publisher Lintot were the Bacon and Bungay of our Augustan age; enterprising men whose rivalry was of high significance to the literary men of their times. If the one produced a poetic miscellany, the other was sure to outbid it by a miscellany to match; if the one rode down to Oxford to gather in the slowly-ripening fruits of academic leisure, his rival might be safely sought on the way to Cambridge; and thus to those authors whose name was not known enough to ensure a subscription-list, to poets, critics and translators they were the best of friends.

---

[1] *Essay on Criticism*, v. 736.   [2] Johnson.
[3] See the 2d Book of the *Dunciad, passim*.

They kept their hands free from the lawless audacity of their contemporary Curll; and though the confraternity of authors was too small and weak to enable them to hold their own in a bargain, it cannot be doubted that the enterprise of these publishers helped to transfer much of the public attention from the stage to the bookseller's counter. Lintot soon afterwards became Pope's usual publisher; but the mysterious vagaries in which he loved to indulge in bringing out his works frequently led him to avail himself of other and inferior channels.

In 1709, then, Pope's *Pastorals* saw the light of publicity; and as the same volume of *Miscellanies* (which included a few other of Pope's early pieces) commenced with the Pastorals of Ambrose Phillips (afterwards mercilessly burlesqued by Gay) the young poet found himself on his first appearance before the world unintentionally furnished with that invaluable aid towards a literary success — a foil.

III.

Between the years 1709 and 1715 falls the most varied and active period of Pope's personal life and literary career. It extends from the publication of the *Pastorals* to that of the first volume of his *Iliad*. As it was the latter work which established him as a Classic in the eyes of his contemporaries, and the proceeds of which furnished him with the means of leading a life congenial to his disposition and suitable to his temperament and health, so its publication marks the conclusion of his brief period of journeymanship in the world of literature. It was during this period too that after a few oscillations he finally determined the circle of his intimacy, and secured for himself the lasting enmity of some amongst his most persevering opponents.

The literary world which Pope entered as the author of poems full of promise, but betraying no special mark such as to range him at once among the adherents of any particular school or coterie, was, as has been already sufficiently indicated, divided into two camps. Parnassus was split from summit to base; and it was upon the Tory half that the sun of Royal and government favour had just begun to shine with concentrated warmth. The Tory wits were accordingly with hardly an exception politicians above all; while the Whig writers ranged with greater freedom through more various walks of literature. Whig patronage has perhaps at other times been distributed among literary men with a less immediate expectation of a *quid pro quo* than that of their opponents. At all events, Pope's early patrons had been chiefly connected with the former party; and, averse by nature from busying himself with political questions,[1] he was more likely to be drawn into

---

[1] Whenever as a boy, in reading Sir Wm. Temple's writings, he found anything political in them he had no manner of feeling for it. (Spence, quoted by Roscoe.) In 1714 he writes to Edward Blount that he is, 'thank God, below all the accidents of state-changes by his circumstances, and above them by his philosophy.' And to this indifference he adhered so consistently throughout life that Ruffhead (*Life of Pope*, p. 45) declares himself warranted by the best authorities in stating that Pope never wrote a single political paper. In his writings he can hardly be said to

the wider circle of which Addison was the centre than among the fiery band where Swift loved to lord it over peers and prelates. Pope was both young enough and sympathetic enough to seek and find friends on either side; but it was with the Whig writers that during his visits to town in 1710 and the following year he appears to have principally associated. When in 1711 he published his *Essay on Criticism*, it was at once commended by Addison in the *Spectator* to the favour of a discerning public; Steele brimmed over with eager requests for contributions to the same paper from so accomplished a hand, and, about the commencement of the year 1712, appears to have introduced the young author to Addison himself.

Unhappily it was not long before a relation thus auspiciously commenced was to be enveloped in a network of petty clouds, until it ended in the most pitiable, though far from the most violent, of Pope's literary quarrels. The quarrel — if a series of unreturned attacks can be called a quarrel — did not actually explode till the time of the publication of the *Iliad*. Yet its origin dates almost from the commencement of Pope's acquaintance with Addison, and connects itself with that *Essay on Criticism* by which Pope took rank among the most brilliant writers of his age.

In his friendly notice of that poem Addison had taken exception to the attacks which it contains upon Blackmore and Dennis; but the praise bestowed upon the entire work had been too cordial to allow this exception to rankle in Pope's mind. In 1712 appeared in a volume of miscellanies published by Lintot the first edition of the young poet's fresh and sparkling *Rape of the Lock*. Addison's notice of this poem in the *Spectator* had been favourable, but not enthusiastic; while his own avowed followers Tickell and Ambrose Phillips had, as contributors to the same Miscellany, received a measure of eulogy which Pope might justly regard as excessive. When he informed Addison of his design to enlarge the *Rape of the Lock* by introducing the machinery of the Sylphs, Addison pronounced against the proposed addition. According to Warburton, Pope discerned (and as Warburton implies, truly discerned) in this advice the insidious intention of preventing an improvement sure of success. There is no reason for accepting Warburton's insinuation at more than its worth; and at best, therefore, this interpretation on the part of Pope of a very natural and plausible counsel must be viewed as an afterthought. For in April 1713 we find Pope furnishing Addison's tragedy of *Cato* with a prologue, which was duly printed with an encomium by Steele in Addison's new paper, the *Guardian*, to which Pope was himself an occasional contributor.[1] Dennis in his character of devil's advocate made a furious, though not wholly inept, onslaught upon the popular tragedy; and Pope took upon himself to stand forth as its defender.

---

have ever manifested any political opinions genuinely his own; he took his party preferences and dislikes at second hand, and was at heart about as fervent a Jacobite as Oliver Goldsmith, who also at times affected to coquet with extreme views.

[1] He wrote eight papers in it.

In 1713 was published a pamphlet entitled *The Narrative of Dr. Robert Norris on the Frenzy of J. D.* It contained an imaginary report pretending to be written by a notorious quack mad-doctor of the day; and was anonymous. It cannot be assumed with certainty that Addison was at first aware of the identity of its real author. In any case he directed Steele to write a note to its publisher, expressing Mr. Addison's disapproval of the treatment to which Dennis had been subjected. Thus to his inexpressible mortification, Pope found himself placed in the intolerable position of a disavowed champion, reprimanded for his officiousness by the very individual whom he had put himself forward to serve.

The pamphlet itself is, in my opinion at least, quite unworthy of Pope. It is a palpable imitation of Swift's immortal hoax upon Partridge the prophet; but the extravagance of its supposition falls far short of that in the latter, and the commonplace character of the joke is unredeemed by any genuine humour in its execution. In any case Addison was fully justified in disavowing a proceeding otherwise certain to be attributed in some degree to his own inspiration, abhorrent though it was from every principle observed by him in the conduct of his literary life. On the other hand, if he was aware that Pope was the author, Addison showed at once timidity and discourtesy in the indirect method of blame adopted by him. But whether he was so aware, remains very uncertain.[1] A painful soreness was naturally enough created in Pope's mind. But before Addison's conduct in the transaction is stigmatised as it has been, it should be shown that an interpretation which leaves it unimpeachable deserves to be rejected.

This episode produced a twofold result. Although Pope continued to remain on friendly terms with Addison (his Epistle to the latter, occasioned by his *Dialogues on Medals*, was written in 1715), yet an angry feeling had been aroused against the latter in Pope's mind which, if charged with the sense of any additional energy, could not fail to explode. He was thus naturally rendered more amenable to the attractions of another coterie to which Addison gave no laws, and where his satellites were treated with open scorn. And, in the second place, it established Dennis in the position of a foe with a grievance quite sufficient in his case to lead to permanent hostility.

John Dennis was one of those old campaigners who can boast more scars than laurels; but with whom a long experience in the wars goes to supply the want of regular training or native capacity. As an original author, he occupied a place among the rank and file of his contemporaries. He wrote or altered nine dramatic pieces, among which two comedies are said by an indefatigable and conscientious searcher of such wares[2] to display considerable merit. As a critic, he undoubtedly possessed certain characteristics which would have ensured him the prominence he coveted even in our own times. He was free from that sentiment which with the

---

[1] Dennis made two statements on the subject, thoroughly contradictory to one another. See Carruthers' *Life of Pope*, where an opposite conclusion is suggested to that preferred above.
[2] Geneste.

generality of critics so fatally interferes with a due exercise of the judicial faculty
— a respect for success. Indeed he avowed it as his guiding principle in the choice
of his victims, to select leading instances of unmerited popularity. His *Remarks on
Cato* had not failed to exemplify his ability of occasionally hitting the nail on the
head amidst a series of random blows. Pope's burlesque of his characteristics had
failed to crush him by its exaggerated ridicule. In 1716 Dennis retorted by his
Character of Mr. Pope, in which the latter was abused for an imitation of Horace
which he had never published; and in 1720 he saluted the completion of Pope's
Iliad by a discharge of minute cavils, of which as usual a certain proportion were
by no means defective in point. Finally (for it is necessary to omit the subsidiary
passes in this prolonged duel) Dennis found his place in the *Dunciad*, and lived
to receive from Pope the sneeringly-bestowed alms of a prologue written for his
benefit in his blind old age. He died shortly afterwards in 1734, secure of a certain kind of immortality.

Pope's first acquaintance with Swift, destined to ripen into an intimacy of paramount influence upon the younger of the pair, connects itself with the publication
of *Windsor Forest* early in 1713. In the summer of the same year Swift returned
to Ireland, after performing services of inestimable value to the Tory party, but
disappointed in his just hopes of episcopal preferment. Later in the year he paid
another visit to England, in order to heal if he could the breach widening from
day to day between the Tory chiefs Oxford and Bolingbroke. In the succeeding
winter commenced a correspondence between him and Pope which was continued
for a quarter of a century, until Swift's mind was at last overwhelmed by the dark
cloud of which it had long foreseen and dreaded the approach. In 1713 Swift was
at the height of his influence among the party to whose side personal resentment
had originally driven him over. But if the subtle flattery conveyed in the courtesy,
frequently descending even to obsequiousness, of his lordly friends had helped to
attach him to their service, yet when they fell it was his own proud nature which
caused him to adhere with equal stedfastness to a hopeless cause. Swift gradually
introduced Pope to the entire clique of politicians and writers who were deluding
themselves by the intricacies of their own devices. Thus Pope became acquainted
with Robert Harley Earl of Oxford, the lord treasurer, an arch-intriguer who had
only attained to power in order to prove his incapacity for its exercise, and whose
supporters had begun to doubt the political sagacity with which they had credited
his artful manipulation of national difficulties. Thus too he was made known to
one whom he was afterwards to venerate as his guide and philosopher, — to Henry
St. John Viscount Bolingbroke. Pope's literary conscience prevented him from accepting Bolingbroke as a brother poet; in every other capacity he was willing to
offer homage to this dazzling and unsafe leader. Connected with both Dean and
Secretary, though by a courageous consistency of character elevated above either,
was Atterbury bishop of Rochester, the representative scholar of Oxford University;
the one Jacobite who was found ready for action at the critical moment of Queen

Anne's death; and afterwards (in 1722) the principal conspirator in a desperate plot. Among the literary notabilities of the same circle were, besides their leader Swift, Thomas Parnell, an apostate from the Whigs and a lyrical poet of genuine merit, whom intemperate habits were believed to have hurried into a premature grave (in 1718),[1] and Matthew Prior; but the latter was at this time absent as ambassador at Paris from the meetings of his friends and boon-companions. A higher esteem was justly enjoyed by Arbuthnot, a man of principle as well as wit, a physician who in Swift's phrase 'knew his art but not his trade,' and a satirist who could work with Swift and Pope on their own ground, and be acknowledged as their equal by both. With Gay, who cheerfully oscillated between political camps as to whose tenets he was indifferent, while his vivacious satire was of inestimable advantage to those at whose service it was placed, Pope had already become intimate in 1711; and their friendship continued unabated[2] till Gay's death in 1732, which was mourned by Pope with a depth of feeling such as he rarely cared to manifest.[3]

Most of these men, both politicians and authors, had long associated together in clubs where the political element predominated — above all in the October Club; but as the party became disorganised by the rivalry of Oxford and Bolingbroke, the harmony of these meetings suffered, and the establishment of a pre-eminently literary club seemed to offer the means of easier converse. The Scribblerus Club was so named in honour of Swift, for whose name *Martin* had been substituted as a humorous synonym by Lord Oxford, whence the appellation of *Martinus Scribblerus*.[4] The burlesque writings with which this club amused itself were subordinated to a very felicitous design, that of parodying all the vagaries of literature in the form of the memoirs of a representative Dunce. Swift (the original notion of whose Gulliver is contained in the *Memoirs of Scriblerus*), Arbuthnot and others contributed with Pope to the execution of the scheme, which afterwards suggested to Pope his *Treatise on the Bathos* (1727), and thus connects itself with the great satire of the *Dunciad* itself.

But the indulgencies of club life as it was then conducted were ill-suited to the delicate constitution of Pope, and threatened at one time seriously to interfere with the project of a literary *magnum opus* with which he had already familiarised himself. For his experiment of becoming a painter, under the tuition of Jervas, had been soon abandoned after its commencement in 1713; and he had returned with renewed energy to his proper studies. It was Swift who encouraged him to persevere in the arduous undertaking of translating the *Iliad*, and who, before the hopeless collapse of the Tory party in 1714, had by his personal exertions

---

[1] This is Pope's own account: Johnson had heard Parnell's death attributed to grief for the loss of his son, or of his wife.

[2] On the strength of a caricature it has been supposed that Pope was jealous of the success of the *Beggar's Opera!* See Wright's *Caric. Hist. of the Georges*, Chap. III.

[3] *Epistle to Arbuthnot*, vv. 255 ff.

[4] Carruthers.

INTRODUCTORY MEMOIR. xxvii

obtained for him a subscription-list of unprecedented length and splendour. Yet Pope had never sufficiently identified himself with the Tory party to forfeit the encouragement of the Opposition magnates as well. When the Tories had fallen, when Bolingbroke after his ephemeral tenure of supreme power had fled in disgrace, when Oxford was under arrest, and Swift had retreated with dignified slowness into his Irish deanery, Pope was courteously entreated by one of the Whig ministers of the new sovereign, Lord Halifax, to accept a pension at his hands. This offer, as we have seen, Pope declined; and the brilliant success of his *Iliad*, of which the first four books appeared in the summer of 1715, rendered him for the future absolutely independent of patronage.

IV.

The publication of Pope's Homer constitutes one of the most noteworthy episodes of his entire career. It thoroughly established him in the foremost rank among the writers of his age, it brought him a competent fortune, it secured him a circle of friends which he could henceforth widen at his own choice, it involved him in the bitterest and most lamentable dispute of his life. Anticipating, therefore, in some points the regular order of this sketch, I place together at once such circumstances as it seems desirable to recal in connexion with the various stages of the publication. Gay, in a charming occasional poem *Alexander Pope his safe return from Troy* (which will be found in nearly all the biographies of Pope and to which frequent reference is made in the notes of the present edition) congratulated his friend upon the completion of the *Iliad* in the name of a host of sympathising associates and admirers; but even then the Homer was only half complete, and a second equally prosperous voyage awaited the poet, though on this his vessel was to be partly worked by hired mariners.

In 1714 Pope had published specimen passages from the *Odyssey* in one of Lintot's *Miscellanies;* and soon afterwards, and during the greater part of the following year, he was engaged upon the translation of the *Iliad.* In the autumn of 1714 he visited Oxford in order to benefit by her libraries, and in 1715 the subscribers received their copies of the first four books. The volumes completing the *Iliad* were published in 1717, '18 and '20; and the stamp of completeness set upon the whole by the well-known dedication to Congreve. The translation of the *Odyssey* occupied Pope and his conductors from 1723 to '5, by which latter year the whole work (including the *Batrachomyomachia* by Parnell) had been absolved. The proceeds of the *Iliad* brought to Pope a sum exceeding £5000, even after deducting the payments for the assistance which he had received in the notes. The *Odyssey* produced between £3000 and £4000 in addition, in which are not comprehended the sums paid to Fenton and Broome, who had contributed half the work. Pope's dealings with his coadjutors, like most of the pecuniary transactions of his life, have been exposed to much angry comment, and even later writers have echoed the exaggeration according to which Fenton was requited only by a small gratuity and a stolen epitaph. These squabbles concerning literary *honoraria* rarely admit, and are still more rarely deserving, of being decided by posterity. Whether Fenton and Broome were sufficiently paid or not, their names may be without danger forgotten in connexion with Pope's Homer. To their employer they were absolutely indebted for manner and style; and Fenton's verse is in reality as much Pope's as Pope's own. For (as will be suggested below) Pope was imitable; and herein he offers a salient contrast to Dryden, whose own touches in the second part of *Absalom and Achitophel* in every case are distinctly discernible as they diversify a dead level of Tate.

Such was the gradual progress towards completion of Pope's famous work. But the publication of its first instalment was attended by an event for ever memorable in our literary history. At the same time as the version by Pope of the first four books of the Iliad, appeared another of the first book by Tickell.

Thomas Tickell was known as an Oxonian and man of letters who had after a youth of very unripe Toryism developed into a full-blown Whig. In former days he had ventured to produce a rival play to Addison's *Cato;* but the success and virtue of the great Whig author had in the end made a complete conquest of the honest man. Though it is inadmissible on the strength of Pope's unproved insinuations to describe him as Addison's dummy, he shared with Ambrose Phillips the distinction of being universally regarded as one of the *âmes damnées* of the dictator at Button's. It might fairly be supposed that nothing which he now undertook was undertaken without the sanction of his acknowledged leader. Otherwise his venture might have been regarded as nothing more than an ordinary instance of the competition common among the publishers of the day (particularly as it only consisted of a single book, to which Tickell never added any more, though his workmanship is not without decided merit of its own). But Pope, who professed to have undertaken his own translation at the instigation of Addison's most intimate friend, Steele, and whose mind was only too ready to admit any apparent confirmation of the suspicion which it harboured against Addison himself, was enraged beyond all bounds. His wrath increased when he was told that Addison had declared Tickell's translation to be the best ever put forth in any language. His indignation, accountable indeed, but wholly inexcusable in the wilfulness of its conclusions and the licence of its expression, first found vent in a letter to Secretary Craggs, a common friend of Addison and himself. In this he declared Tickell to be the 'humblest slave' among Addison's followers at Button's. And then his fury found a wider outlet in the famous lines which were afterwards, with revisions and omissions, inserted in the *Epistle*

INTRODUCTORY MEMOIR. xxix

to Dr. Arbuthnot.[1] It was the first, as it was the most brilliant, of those satiric sketches of character upon which Pope's genius was to expend its most consummate efforts; so that from hatred, that most powerful passion of the age, was born a species of composition in which its representative poet has excelled all other writers.

In the earlier version of these immortal lines occurs a passage showing clearly enough the source of the taunts which Pope allowed himself to launch against one to whom he was yet,[2] happily for his reputation, to live to make partial amends:

'Who, if two wits on rival themes contest,
Approves of both, but likes the worst the best.'

His resentment further blinded him into charging Addison with the real authorship of Tickell's Homer; but this charge was soon dropped. Meanwhile Addison remained serenely imperturbable, replying to Pope's satire by a more than complimentary reference to his Homer in the *Freeholder*, where he ranked it on a level with Dryden's Vergil. And thus, the quarrel, like all quarrels conducted on one side only, could proceed no further. Yet (as the republication, so late as 1735, of the verses upon Addison proves) the offence, whether real or imaginary, long continued to rankle in Pope's breast. Was it real, or was it imaginary? Allowing Addison to have been fully responsible for Tickell's proceeding, we are not obliged as a necessary consequence to condemn him for having permitted it. Nor can he as a critic who, like few in his age, was anxious to discover beauties rather than detect flaws, be blamed for having praised both Tickell's and Pope's translations in accordance with his high opinion of either. In neither case, as modern critics are fain to agree, was that high opinion wholly undeserved, though in either it was exaggerated. On the other hand there is much significance in the observations on this subject of one of the most penetrating students of literary men and manners. 'It was natural,' writes Thackeray,[3] 'that Pope and Pope's friends should believe that this counter-translation, suddenly advertised and so long written,—though Tickell's college-friends had never heard of it, though when Pope first wrote to Addison regarding his scheme Addison knew nothing of the similar projects of Tickell's,—it was natural that Pope and his friends, having interests, passions, and prejudices of their own, should believe that Tickell's translation was but an act of opposition against Pope, and that they should call Tickell's emulation Addison's envy,'—'if envy,' adds the same writer, 'it were.' The solution of the last query must be found in our estimate of the character of Addison; a character the whiteness of which, after annoying generation after generation of sceptics, rests as unstained as if it had never been subjected to examination at their pains-taking hands. But what-

[1] vv. 193-214.
[2] In the *Imitation of Horace*, Bk. I. Ep. II. (vv. 215-220), published in 1737.
[3] In his *Lectures on the English Humourists*.

ever the character of Addison, Pope and his age at all events preferred to judge it according to their own standard.

V.

We turn for a moment from the progress of Pope's literary career to the circumstances of his personal life, though indeed it would be a futile attempt to endeavour to dissociate the two. Soon after the publication of the first volume of Pope's Homer, he removed with his parents from Binfield to Chiswick, where they settled in the spring of 1716, for a sojourn which was not to extend over more than a couple of years. By this time Pope had already become a welcome guest in the fashionable circles of the metropolis and its vicinity; nor could it be otherwise than that the influence of female fascination should be brought to bear upon his susceptible nature. It was very well for Walsh to have admonished him, as an author of sixteen, to take occasion (in his Fourth Pastoral) 'to shew the difference between Poets' mistresses and other men's;'[1] but such problems require, even in the case of poets, to be worked out by experience; and Pope was not anxious to avoid the opportunities with which he met.

Before his admission into the fashionable life of the Town, his personal acquaintances had been chiefly restricted to the Catholic gentry of the counties around Windsor. Among these were the Carylls of Sussex, of whom John Caryll (formerly secretary to the Consort of James II.) became one of Pope's most favoured correspondents. Among the members of this family who in Gay's congratulatory poem 'come by dozens' to grace the Translator's triumph, was the 'Unhappy Lady,' whose melancholy story has been mingled up with that of the 'Unfortunate Lady' whose case gave rise to Pope's beautiful elegy. Another of these Families was that of the Fermors of Tusmore in Oxfordshire, of whom Miss Arabella Fermor was immortalised as Belinda in the *Rape of the Lock*. But a closer interest attached Pope to a third Catholic family, the Blounts of Mapledurham in Oxfordshire, near Reading. The head of this family, Mr. Lister Blount, had two daughters named Teresa and Martha, born respectively in the years 1688 and 1690. Both these ladies had received part of their education at Paris, where the natural vivacity of their dispositions had been heightened, and the charm of their manners had received an additional piquancy. Scandal afterwards busied itself with the progress of the relations between Pope and these ladies, in which however there seems nothing either unnatural or unparalleled.[2] It seems clear that as Pope's acquaintance with the Miss Blounts ripened into intimacy, he came to admire them both; that his attentions, poetic and other, were at first chiefly addressed to the elder sister, but that in the end the younger Martha became the object of a lifelong sentiment, oscillating between friendship and a deeper feeling,

---

[1] See Walsh's letter to Pope, dated Sept. 9th, 1796.

[2] The well known instance of Schiller's relations towards the sisters of whom one became his wife, may be cited in illustration of part of a very easy psychological problem.

INTRODUCTORY MEMOIR. xxxi

but tinged to the last with the warm hues of an unselfish devotion. Whether Pope was ever in love with Martha Blount is a question of terms rather than of facts. The report that, when almost at the point of death he offered her marriage, seems nothing more than a baseless invention. The feeling which he entertained towards her might have operated differently in the case of a different man. It is certain that his regard, both for herself and for her sister, involved him in a desperate broil with a volatile fopling (James Moore Smythe) who had ventured upon a pastoral flirtation with the lively sisters. It is more than probable that for Martha's sake he descended to an action which cast the worst of stains upon his literary honour.[1] And to Martha Blount, on his decease, Pope bequeathed 'out of a sincere regard and long friendship for her' the largest share of his personal property.

It was hardly however to be expected that Pope's affection towards the Miss Blounts should preclude him from offering the incense of his adoration from time to time to other beauties. Scandal alone (or hyperconscientious biography) has contrived to pervert the character of his relations towards the ladies of Mapledurham;[2] but scandal itself must allow the innocence of his admiration for Lady Mary Wortley Montagu. To this celebrated personage he was introduced through the medium of Mrs. Howard, afterwards Countess of Suffolk, a lady to whose influence over the Prince of Wales (afterwards George II.) no bounds existed, until they were imposed by his political sagacity. With Lady Mary love of admiration had been a passion ever since the day when her father had introduced her as a child to the boisterous attentions of the Kit-Cat Club;[3] and she devoted herself to literary pursuits and studies with an energy unusual among ladies of rank since the days of Queen Elizabeth. It was therefore not wonderful that she should be gently attracted by the pronounced homage of an already fashionable author. Nor was there anything in the nature of the attentions she received and permitted, to arouse the suspicions of her even-minded husband, or to offer materials sufficient at a later date to exercise the malice with which Horace Walpole endeavoured to colour all her actions. During her absence with her husband in the East (from 1716 to '18) Lady Mary allowed Pope to address her in the strains of a masquerade lover, but her replies are characterised by a cool irony which even her correspondent cannot have deluded himself into interpreting as self-restraint. After her return, when she became his near neighbour at Twickenham, his vanity seems to have been ultimately wounded by some instance of the equanimity to which she had from the first done her best to accustom him. For there is no reason to believe that a fancied jealousy had anything to do with the offence. Gradually they

---

[1] By consenting, in order to obtain the capital for an investment for her benefit, to accept a large sum from the Duchess of Marlborough in return for the suppression of a satirical attack upon her character.

[2] It is difficult, notwithstanding the indignant *Reply* of Bowles (printed in Vol. xvii. of the *Pamphleteer*) to acquit him of the attempt, in his biography of Pope, to charge the 'licentiousness of the man' with an offence imputable to the 'grossness of the times.'

[3] See the well known story in Lord Wharncliffe's *Introductory Anecdotes* to the *Letters of Lady M. W. M.*

became bitter enemies; and, together with her favourite associate Lord Hervey, Lady Mary came to be included in the category of the best-abused victims of Pope's vindictive satire. His specific charges against her have been satisfactorily disproved; but such was Pope's satirical genius that Sappho is no more than any of his other characters of women or men a mere caricature. Lady Mary was unwise enough to venture upon retorts which have by no means added to her literary fame. As she ceased to reside in England from the summer of 1739, the most ignoble warfare of Pope's literary life then came to a natural end.

No other similar relation added its perturbation to the agitations of Pope's life. The bevy of beautiful maids of honour who adorned the court of the Princess of Wales (where he was a frequent visitor at the time of his residence at Chiswick) were delighted by the flatteries of his versatile wit. And rather later, from 1722 to '3, a passing attachment seems to have occupied his imagination towards Miss Judith Cowper, which appropriately came to an end with her marriage towards the close of the latter year.[1]

Nor were brilliant friendships of another kind formed by Pope during the period of his residence at Chiswick, able to detach him from the serious business of his life. The heroes of fashion, such as Lord Peterborough, the hero of Barcelona, and the dictators of taste, such as Lord Burlington, made him welcome in town and country; and he followed the fashion of his day by summer excursions to the Bath. Yet it was far from an idle period of his literary life. For besides carrying on his translation of the *Iliad*, he found time to produce some of his most finished poetic efforts, among them the *Epistle of Eloïsa to Abelard* (of which the address appears in the course of composition to have been transferred from Martha Blount to Lady Mary Wortley Montagu) and the exquisite *Elegy to the Memory of an Unfortunate Lady*.

As no period of Pope's life was without its quarrels, so that of his residence at Chiswick was disturbed by two at least which may not be passed over in a narrative of his career. In 1716 he first came into the hostile contact which it was, indeed, difficult for any author of note to avoid, with the notorious pirate-publisher Edmund Curll. It was the invariable practice of this individual to publish any piece popularly attributed to an eminent name, in an unauthorised edition with that name attached to it. He had adopted this course with a series of very common-place burlesque poems called the *Town-Eclogues*, of which only one had been actually written by Pope himself. The latter, as usual irretentive of his dignity, wrote several pamphlets against Curll, of which the first is the *Account of the Poisoning of Edmund Curll;* a coarse burlesque narrative of the effects produced upon the bookseller by a half-pint of wine drunk by him in Pope's company,

---

[1] She was the daughter of Judge Spencer Cowper, and the niece of the great Chancellor; she married Colonel Madan; and to their daughter Frances Maria, afterwards wife of Major Cowper and the friend and correspondent of her cousin the poet, she transmitted her own poetical and devout spirit. See Hayley's *Life of William Cowper*.

INTRODUCTORY MEMOIR. xxxiii

effects actually attributed by the sufferer to the malice of the poet. It was to guard themselves against the indefatigable activity of Curll that Pope and Swift afterwards published their Miscellanies in an authorised form; and the same publisher afterwards put forth the surreptitiously obtained correspondence of Pope with Cromwell, and at a later date engaged in the publication of his letters to various friends, abstracted, as Pope declared, by equally nefarious means.[1]

Early in the following year (1717) the production of the farce of *Three Hours after Marriage*, in which Gay had been assisted by Arbuthnot and Pope, occasioned the outbreak of a quarrel between the latter and Colley Cibber. The farce itself (Pope's co-operation in which constituted his solitary dramatic effort) is beneath contempt. Pope, as Gay afterwards admitted, 'never heartily approved of' the piece. Nor can the wit of those parts in which the hand of Pope is clearly discernible, and where Dennis is caricatured as Sir Tremendous, and literary ladies of the day under other names, be fairly said to rise above the level of the remainder. The play was however damned on account of the extravagant nonsense of its last act, in which two lovers insert themselves respectively into the skins of a mummy and a crocodile. The *Rehearsal*, a play always used (like its successor the *Critic*) as an opportunity for introducing gag on popular topics of the day, happened to be performed shortly afterwards. Colley Cibber on this occasion introduced an allusion to the unhappy mummy and crocodile. Pope, whose presence in the theatre may have added to the effect of the allusion, sharply inveighed against the actor behind the scenes; and the latter not unnaturally swore to repeat the joke on every future occasion. To this episode Cibber in his *Apology* attributes the origin of Pope's animosity against him. There can be little doubt that the production towards the close of the year of Cibber's *Non-Juror* (so successful an attack upon Jacobites and concealed Papists that a patriotic pamphlet of the day desired to see it as common in every house as a Prayer-book or *Whole Duty of Man*) added a worthier cause of anger in Pope's mind against the future laureate of King George II.

Thus, amidst studies and diversions Pope's life continued until the death of his father, which took place at Chiswick in October 1717. The blow was keenly felt by the son whom he left to mourn his loss. To his father, as we have seen, Pope owed much beyond the discreet liberality which had allowed him to choose his own path in life, and enabled him in his early years to pursue his favourite studies. For to his father he was indebted for the example of a moral uprightness which in the main he endeavoured faithfully to follow; and for the noble lesson of adherence to a persecuted creed. After his father's death Pope might have abandoned the profession of the Catholic faith; and exchanged a Church with whose tenets he can hardly be supposed to have entertained an intellectual sympathy, for one towards which he was urged by the representations of venerated friends. But in answer to Atterbury's arguments he simply appealed to his consideration for his remaining

---

[1] See below, p. xl.

parent; and honoured himself by maintaining a consistent attitude of respectful submission to the Church of his father and mother, in which there was perhaps more true philosophy than in the indignation expressed by Bolingbroke when immediately after his friend's death he learnt that the latter had accepted the ministrations of a priest. 'I am,' Pope writes to Swift in 1729, 'of the religion of Erasmus, a Catholic; so I live, so I shall die; and hope one day to meet you, Bishop Atterbury, the younger Craggs, Dr. Garth, Dean Berkeley, and Mr. Hutchenson in heaven.' No fuller exposition seems required, after this, of his religious views.

Very soon after his father's death Pope, whose means were now ample for one who had to provide only for the maintenance of himself and his mother, removed with her from Chiswick to Twickenham. In the latter place, whose name will ever be associated with his own, he passed the remainder of his life.

VI.

Pope took up his residence at Twickenham early in 1718, after purchasing the lease of a house and five acres of land on the banks of the Thames. The house itself he left very much the simple habitation he had found it; but the garden and grounds he laid out with enthusiastic care. Landscape gardening was one of the passions of the age; and for horticulture in general Pope had conceived a taste from the days of his childhood on the borders of Windsor Forest. But Le Nôtre or Capability Brown himself would have found their genius cramped by the dimensions of Pope's estate; and the dream of his youth for 'woods, gardens, rookeries, fish-ponds, arbours' had to be satisfied with the fulfilment of its more modest items. Yet he contrived, according to the enumeration of one of his biographers,[1] to introduce into his five acres 'a shell temple, a large mount, a vineyard, two small mounts, a bowling-green, a wilderness, a grove, an orangery, a garden-house, and kitchen-garden.' The favourite object of his efforts however was the famous 'grotto,' in reality a tunnel beneath the turnpike road which divided the two parts of the garden. It contained a spring and could accordingly be credited with a nymph; and in its diminutive recesses were distributed a variety of eccentric ornaments such as are in our own day reserved for the admiration of children in seaside lodging-houses: shells and spars and what Dr. Johnson calls 'fossil bodies,' and a hundred natural curiosities with which the master of the grotto was gratified by his friends and admirers.

The Twickenham grotto and gardens became one of the delights of Pope's life; here he received the visits of his friends and dispensed his temperate hospitality. The convenient situation of Twickenham made it unnecessary for him to vary the even tenour of his outward life by more than occasional visits to his friends in town and country; he was at no great distance from Mapledurham, the Wortley

[1] Carruthers.

Montagus took up their residence at Twickenham itself; Lord Peterborough was resting from his labours at Fulham, Lord Burlington owned a box at Chiswick, and after a time Bolingbroke was to settle at Dawley near Uxbridge. That in his rural retreat Pope was not out of the world, he proved in 1720, the year of the South Sea bubble. There seems every reason to conclude that he withdrew his investments in time to save part of his gains. He could not, indeed, rest doubly content, like Sir Robert Walpole, at having condemned the scheme from the outset and afterwards sold out at the highest price.[1] But he had no reason to lament for himself the effects of a catastrophe which brought ruin to some among his friends, and dishonour to others.

At Twickenham the *Iliad* was completed; and henceforth Pope's name was eagerly sought by the booksellers. Before he had commenced the translation of the *Odyssey*, he was induced to undertake an edition of Shakspere which was published by Tonson in 1725. Its failure was perhaps more decided than it deserved; but its defects were sufficient to warrant many of the cavils advanced against it in haste by Lewis Theobald, who thereby established himself as one of Pope's adversaries, and brought down upon himself the most signal vengeance ever inflicted upon an unfriendly critic. He was soon afterwards made the hero of the *Dunciad*.

For the number of Pope's assailants had increased with his fame; and it only needed encouragement from without to induce him to give vent to the wrath which had long been accumulating in his sensitive mind. He entertained a genuine hatred of the petty scribblers who infested the literary atmosphere; no less than a personal feeling of vengefulness against many of their number. In 1726 Swift spent four months with Pope at Twickenham, and repeated his visit in 1727. Swift's genius was at this time at its height. His mind was already oppressed by the presentiment of its coming overthrow; and his heart torn by the constant ill health of Stella, which early in 1728 was to terminate in her death. Yet in the midst of his gloom and of the bitterness arising from the certainty that no hopes existed for his preferment in England, he was elated by the triumphant results of his self-sustained campaign against the oppressors of Ireland, and strong in the sense of a power more real than that which he had possessed when he believed himself to be dictating the policy of the Oxford ministry. Gloom, anger and pride combined to inspire the greatest of Swift's — the greatest of modern, — satires; and in the late autumn of 1726 *Gulliver's Travels* took the world by storm. In the same year and in the following Swift and Pope brought out three volumes of their Miscellanies; and during his converse with his friends the former suggested the idea of the *Beggar's Opera* to Gay, and encouraged Pope to proceed with the *Dunciad*.[2]

The Miscellanies contained, among many of Pope's pieces which he had better

---

[1] See Lord Stanhope's *History of England from the Peace of Utrecht*, chap. XI.

[2] Swift, who was entirely above literary envy, writes to Gay (Nov. 23, 1727): 'The Beggar's Opera hath knocked down Gulliver; I hope to see Pope's Dulness knock down the Beggar's Opera, but not till it hath fully done its job.'

have left in the obscurity of unauthorised publications, his *Treatise on the Bathos* or *Art of Sinking in Poetry*, which was founded on the old idea of the Scribblerus club. It is in my opinion by far the most successful of Pope's prose satires, and evinces the extraordinary facility with which he was able to develop ideas originally suggested to him by other minds. It pilloried the whole tribe of poetasters whose names the *Dunciad* was afterwards to preserve, nailed to the post by quotations from their own works. The chief, or at all events, the tenderest victim was Ambrose Phillips, who resorted to the cautious revenge of hanging up a rod in the Whig sanctum at Button's for the chastisement of the offender, should he ever make his appearance there. The *Treatise on the Bathos* would be more frequently read and enjoyed than it is, had not its victims soon afterwards been subjected to another, and yet more classical castigation. The *Dunciad* seems to have been first published in May 1728; and the enlarged edition which followed a few months later was dedicated to the true foster-father of the work, to Swift.[1]

There is no necessity for entering at length into the effect which this unparalleled satire created, and the endless warfare into which by its publication Pope had with full consciousness plunged. He had proposed to himself to lash unmercifully all the bad writers of the day, and among their number he included all his personal enemies or those whom he accounted as such. The wasps whose nests he had thus heroically stirred were around his head at once; Theobald more like a humble-bee than a wasp, with a heavy but honest protest; Dennis and his peers with an avowed intention to infuse into their stings all the venom which their natures could spare. Inferior but equally irrepressible combatants each contributed his buzz to the general sabbath of the Dunces. And Lady Mary Wortley Montagu, by this time unhappily included in the ever extending canon of Pope's adversaries, was believed to have contributed the feeblest retort of all, a silly squib entitled a *Pop upon Pope*, containing an account of an imaginary whipping administered to the poet at Twickenham, with the feminine adjunct of a sneer at his friendship with Martha Blount.

The conflict which Pope had provoked, it was in accordance with his nature to prolong almost indefinitely. The *Dunciad*, instead of remaining his last word against the Dunces, was supplemented by a series of lighter attacks in the *Grubstreet Journal*, which for eight years (1730–7) made war upon the enemies of true literature and Pope. Many of the epigrams which he furnished to this weekly periodical will be found among the *Miscellanies* at the close of the present volume; several other pieces are with much probability, though not with absolute certainty, attributed to him. At all events he directed the judgments of the 'Knights of the Bathos,' as the critics of this journal called themselves, who turned their more or less righteous indignation against the victims of the *Dunciad*, down to Henley the butchers' lecturer and Ward the quack. In one case only, that of Aaron Hill, the

---

[1] See Introductory Remarks to the *Dunciad*.

dramatist whom Pope had correctly attacked in the *Dunciad*, was a reconciliation brought about by the determination of the former, and an instance afforded of the timidity occasionally displayed by Pope when driven home by a resolute opponent.

VII.

But while these petty combats still continued to occupy a share of the poet's time and attention, he was already passing under the new influence of an old acquaintance, into what may be termed the third phase of his literary life. In the school of Addison Pope had learnt to cultivate that correctness of form which accorded with the leanings of his own mind and the influences of his boyish studies; and gracefully to mingle the reminiscences of a classical education with a careful observation of the characteristics of existing society. In the school of Swift, again assimilating the influences which he admitted to the tendencies of his own individuality, he had imbibed that bitter hatred of the petty and trivial, and adopted that principle of conducting every personal dispute as if its end must be the extinction of his adversary, which had substituted for the elegant refinements of the *Essay on Criticism* and the suave irony of the *Rape of the Lock* the scathing invectives of the *Dunciad*. From Bolingbroke he believed that he learnt the secrets of a philosophy of which he had long been a half-conscious adherent; what he really gained, was a habit of closer and more accurately classified observation, a nearer acquaintance with the machinery rather than the principles of political life, and a fuller insight into the characters of public men.

Pope had seen little personally of Bolingbroke before the flight of the latter into France, in 1715. On the exile's first return in 1723 the only members of the old literary circle whom he found in England, were Pope, Congreve, Arbuthnot and Gay.[1] This short stay sufficed to disabuse Bolingbroke of his hopes of immediate political rehabilitation; and he accordingly writes to Swift from London to assure him that 'his philosophy grew confirmed by habit,' and that he considers himself a hermit in comparison with Pope. Upon the latter this lofty resignation, with which Bolingbroke at times imposed upon himself as well as his friends, must have made a deep impression. In 1725 Bolingbroke was again in England, this time (according to his own expression) 'two-thirds restored.'[2] As his father still persisted in remaining alive, he purchased a house for himself at Dawley near Uxbridge in Middlesex. Thus it came to pass that Swift on his visit to England in 1726 found the most brilliant members of his ancient clique once more in familiar union, and Bolingbroke and Pope, with Gay and Arbuthnot, passing to and fro between Dawley and Twickenham.

[1] Swift was in Ireland; Atterbury was exiled in this year; 'it is sure my ill fate,' writes Pope to Swift in announcing Bolingbroke's return, 'that all those I most loved, and with whom I most lived, must be banished.' Of lesser men, Prior had died in 1721 and Parnell in 1718.

[2] He was enabled to hold his estates, but not freed from the consequences of the Act of Attainder which prevented his taking public office or his seat in the House of Lords. His father, an old roué of the Restoration, lived to the age of ninety.

To us the delusiveness of Bolingbroke's repeated observations, that he had now become a retired philosopher, are transparent enough. '*Satis beatus ruris honoribus*' was the inscription over the porch of the house in which he dispensed his rural hospitality. But we know that Bolingbroke had only applied himself to philosophical studies as alternatives to the tedium of his enforced leisure in France. In the more stirring atmosphere of his native country he soon re-assumed a more familiar character, and began to contribute partisan papers to the *Craftsman* and to intrigue for the overthrow of Walpole. But in Pope's eyes an indescribable charm attached to the society and personality of this unrepentant Alcibiades. As Bolingbroke discoursed to him on his system of natural theology, clear and shallow as the streamlet in the grotto where they sat, and communicated to him those Essays which he never had the courage to publish, the mind of his friend became imbued with enough of the facile lesson to make him in his own belief the disciple of an exhaustive system, while he was in reality only the acolyte of a sophist and a man of the world. Thus Bolingbroke devised for Pope, or Pope devised with Bolingbroke's direct aid, the scheme of his *Essay on Man*. It was published in instalments of four epistles during the years 1732–4; and already, under the same influence, Pope was contemplating the development of the plan of which the *Essay* formed part, and into which Warburton was ultimately to help him to fit in his other epistles, partly subsequent in date, but partly also antecedent, to the *Essay*. The dates of these Epistles are given in their place; among the personages to whom they were addressed are most of the noblemen and gentlemen with whom Pope, at his own house or in visits to their seats, enjoyed the pleasure of friendly intercourse: Lords Burlington, Bathurst and Cobham, all in politics opposed to the existing administration, and rising lawyers like Fortescue and Murray.

He had now at last found the species of composition best adapted to his literary genius. The satire of characters, not the direct inculcation of philosophical principles, continued to employ his pen, when, in consequence of a suggestion of Bolingbroke's, he began his *Imitations of Horace*, in which the brilliancy of his *Moral Essays* was equalled and their pungency sustained. In all these productions he was once more able to range his friends and foes opposite to one another like the children of light and the children of darkness; but his attacks were no longer directed against Grubstreet and Newport-market, but boldly ranged to the highest in the land. Personal enemies such as Lady Mary Wortley Montagu and Lord Hervey were tortured in the presence of their peers; and where his own political indifference might have left him silent, the disappointments of Swift and Bolingbroke, and the traditional hatreds of a party with which he had unconsciously identified himself, inspired him to Alcæic invective. The old Duchess of Marlborough, it can hardly be doubted, had to buy off his attacks upon the memory of her husband, if not upon her own character and antecedents. The omnipotent minister himself was only spared after he had rendered a personal service to the poet. As his shafts flew higher and higher, they ventured to touch the sacred personages of royalty itself. With the court of King George II. or Queen Caroline, Pope (though no hopes of his own had ever been disappointed by them) had long ceased to be on friendly terms; and now he dared to deride the one as a mock Augustus, and pursue the other with his sneers even to her deathbed.[1] At last he contrived to bring upon himself the danger, or at all events the menace, of a prosecution. Possibly the timidity which he sometimes exhibited in the face of extreme measures may have been judiciously worked upon; at all events he abandoned all further exploration of this vein with the year 1738; and the fragment called '1740,' supposing it to have been his own, was hardly destined for other than private or posthumous circulation. Being in disfavour with the Court of St. James', Pope was of course in favour with that of Leicester House, where Frederick Prince of Wales cast around him dubious shadows of a future golden age. But the latter relation exercised no influence upon the remaining phases of his poetic productivity. Prince Frederick sent busts for the Twickenham library, and urns for the Twickenham grounds; and his suite were civil to the writer who had known how to annoy their master's father; and this, said Pope, 'is all I ask from courtiers, and all a wise man will expect from them.'

In noting some of the circumstances connected with Pope's activity as a satirist of men and women in exalted spheres, we have, however, anticipated the few events which interfered with the even tenour of his private life between the years 1730 and '40. This life was neither that of a man of fashion nor that of a recluse. Visits to the friends already mentioned, and to Lord Peterborough at Bevis Mount, and to the worthy Ralph Allen at Widcombe near Bath, merely diversified the tranquillity of his life at home, where till 1733 he tended the old age of his mother. In a postscript to one of Bolingbroke's letters to Swift, written in 1731, Pope speaks in touching terms of her gradual decline, and of his gratitude to Heaven for having preserved her to him so long. She died in 1733, in the ninety-third year of her age. In the following year Pope had to mourn the loss of his dearly-loved friend Arbuthnot, to whom he had only shortly before addressed the *Epistle* which, published after Arbuthnot's death, bore public record to the friendship which united them. The generation of the Augustans was rapidly passing away; and Pope, whose literary career had commenced at so precocious a date in his life, might feel himself old before his time. With the younger poets he showed much kindly sympathy; upon Thomson he bestowed a friendly patronage;[2] Young whose earlier poems had displayed many characteristics common to his own genius had commended himself by two Epistles published in 1730 against the assailants of the *Dunciad;* and to a very different poet, the unhappy Savage, Pope at a somewhat later date (1742) proved himself a generous benefactor. But his old friendships were being fast extinguished in death; and his last letter to Swift was written

---

[1] *Epil. to Satires Dial.* I. vv. 79—81.
[2] On the occasion of the production of Thomson's tragedy of *Agamemnon* in 1738.

early in 1740. Even before that time the mind of the latter had been so darkened as to make a regular continuance of the correspondence impossible. In his great friend's unhappy mind the stronger demon had at last laid the weaker; and Pope was no longer to be invigorated by the intellectual embrace of the greatest of his associates. Swift remained a hopeless lunatic till his death in 1745.

As Pope gradually saw the last of those who had encouraged his juvenile efforts and welcomed the triumphs of his early manhood, passing away before him, it is not strange that he should have thought of collecting the memorials of a brilliant past, in the shape of such of his correspondence as he had preserved, or could contrive to recover. His letters to Cromwell, as we have seen, had already been published without his consent by the unscrupulous Curll in 1726. They had not, we may rest assured, been intended by Pope for publication; and as this proceeding had been effected without his consent, no opportunity had been afforded him for controlling the arrangement of the letters. But in 1735, when Pope had collected a large number of letters of himself and his friends and deposited them in his friend Lord Oxford's library, the literary world was startled by the publication, again through Curll's agency, of a collection of Pope's correspondence with various personages, including several of noble rank. These letters Curll declared to have been delivered to him by an unknown personage, attired half as a clergyman half as a lawyer, who had without stating his authority offered them for sale, and had after receiving the price, departed without further parley. Great indignation was manifested by several of Pope's noble correspondents at the announcement of this publication; and the printer and publisher were summoned before the House of Lords and examined before a committee. Pope offered a trifling reward (£20) for the discovery of any person engaged in the transaction, and published in the *London Gazette* of July 15th, 1735, a statement to the effect that he found himself driven in self-defence to publish on his own account such of the letters as were genuine. The authorised edition accordingly made its appearance in 1737. In its preface and in the 'True Narrative of the method by which Pope's letters have been published' (a paper doubtless drawn up by Pope at the same time) it was stated that he had recalled from his several correspondents the letters formerly written to them and caused MS. copies of these to be drawn up and deposited in Lord Oxford's library. (According to the *True Narrative* these copies were interspersed with some of the originals themselves.)

But since, on a comparison of Curll's with the authorised edition, it becomes evident that both were made from the same original, both presenting in certain cases the same variations from the letters as originally addressed to Pope's correspondents, a choice between two alternatives is left to us. Either Curll's mysterious purveyor had obtained access to Lord Oxford's library and transcribed the letters *en masse;* or, Pope himself had supplied Curll with copies. On the latter supposition, the entire proceeding was one of his intricate manœuvres in order to obtain notoriety for his letters, and by the spurious publication to benefit the sale of the intended genuine one. The former alternative involves an obvious improbability; the latter is supported by the circumstance since ascertained,[1] that Pope had withdrawn the letters from Lord Oxford's library in the spring of 1735. This discovery seems at first sight to tend towards the conclusion that Pope had entertained the idea of publishing the letters *before* Curll's venture saw the light. In this case Pope's edition of his letters cannot have been brought out in sheer self-defence.

The question (which continues to constitute one of the *cruces* of which the life of Pope is so prolific) remains in its original difficulty. It is certain that Pope had allowed himself to alter the letters in every possible way from the form in which they were originally written, by additions and omissions and variations. Yet this is insufficient to prove his intention of publishing them. He could not at any time keep any printed or written thing by him without revising it and altering it for the better or the worse; whether it was his own (as in the case of the *Rape of the Lock* and the *Dunciad*, and numerous passages afterwards incorporated in his Satires), or whether it was another man's, (as in the notable case, to be mentioned below, of Bolingbroke's letters *On the Spirit of Patriotism* &c.). A grave suspicion rests however upon the straightforward character of his conduct in this transaction; unhappily not the only case connected with the publication of his works which continues obscure and doubtful.

As Pope's letters remain to us, they are not, with the exception of those to Cromwell and of those which have been preserved in MS., spontaneous effusions. His letters to Lady Mary at the same time prove that even as he wrote at the time, he wrote with affectation. But in editing his correspondence, he succeeded in depriving it of every vestige of natural freshness. A letter which is written with one eye to the person addressed, and the other to the public beyond, possesses no charm apart from all other literary compositions. Yet it may be doubted whether Pope could ever have excelled in a branch of writing where genius can claim no monopoly of excellence. His pen could have never strayed into the 'little language' of Swift; or rushed along with the reckless vigour of Byron; still less could it have matched in sweet simplicity the epistolary style of Cowper; but he was even without Horace Walpole's ability for telling a story. Yet his prose in itself is unaffected and clear; and though far from approaching that of Swift in strength or that of Addison in beauty, is free from an undue affectation of classicisms, and from other peculiarities of an impotent grandiloquence.

[1] See Johnson's *Lives of the Poets*, Cunningham's edition, Vol. III. p. 13, cited by Carruthers.

VIII.

In 1739 Bolingbroke sold Dawley; and though he continued in frequent connexion with the Marcellus of his hopes at Leicester House, and with Pope at Twickenham, he was frequently absent in France. It was not till 1742 that the death of Bolingbroke's father established him in his paternal domain at Battersea; while the overthrow of Walpole in the same year caused him for the last time to hope for an after-summer of political power. It was perhaps the bitterest drop in the full cup of the ambitious intriguer's disappointments, to find that his own party treated him with respectful neglect, and that he was politely set aside as an interesting but useless specimen of 'narrative old age.'

Although after Bolingbroke's removal from Dawley his friendship with Pope continued unbroken, the latter was gradually passing under the influence of another mind. Warburton, the presiding genius of the closing period of Pope's life, had approached him in the humble attitude of an interpreter offering his services to a misunderstood philosopher. The career of Warburton offers a cheering instance of the success of a man determined from the first to succeed. He had marked out the English Church and English literature as the avenues likely to lead to eminence and emolument; and both were opened to him in accordance with his speculations. By asserting himself as one of the pillars of orthodoxy, and coming forward as an aid to faith just at the close of the struggle between the Church and her deistical opponents, he ultimately obtained the bishopric of Gloucester as his temporal reward. In literature he knew how to claim saints as well as to expose sinners; and thus he had, at an early point of his career, recommended himself to Pope's notice by a volunteer attempt to bring the author of the *Essay on Man* and pupil of Bolingbroke into harmony with orthodox Anglicanism, and to defend him against the arguments of a French professor (de Crousaz) who had maintained Spinozism to be the logical outcome of the poet's system. Pope gratefully accepted the service; and his slight personal acquaintance with Warburton soon developed into a close intimacy. Warburton played a far more important part in connexion with Pope than that which men of genius in their decline have frequently permitted to assiduous admirers. He not only proclaimed, but interpreted, the utterances of his oracle. By him all Pope's later works were arranged under a neat and comprehensive system; and so well was the poet contented with this re-arrangement of himself, that he entrusted to one who understood him almost better than himself the collected edition of his works commenced towards the close of his life. And in his will he left to Warburton the property of all such of his works as the former had furnished, or *should furnish*, with commentaries.

Yet even a righteous victory is not always gained at once. Pope seems to have oscillated between the influence exerted over him by Warburton and the still unexhausted fascination of Bolingbroke. The indefatigable activity of Warburton, and the nervous weakness of Pope's declining health, were in favour of the former.

An attempt on the part of Murray (in the style of the late Mr. Rogers) to reconcile the two conflicting influences by inviting Warburton and Bolingbroke to meet at his table, led to no result except agitating Pope, who was of the party. 'He was obliged,' he exclaimed, after listening to an animated contest between the two, 'to be of the opinion of both the antagonists, since the one was his teacher and the other his apologist; since the one thought, and the other answered for him.'[1]

But this incident occurred only a few months before the death of Pope. However much he may have fallen under the influence of Warburton (and such was the value which he set upon his friend that he refused an honorary degree offered to him by the University of Oxford, because it was not offered to Warburton, who accompanied him on his visit to the University, at the same time), upon the literary activity of Pope's closing years it acted as a stimulant. The fourth book of the *Dunciad*, which Pope published in 1741, would, as he expressly declared, never have been written but for the suggestive influence of his friend. It betrayed no falling off in power of expression; but to Warburton's influence must be ascribed the direction which Pope's invective, unhappily for his reputation for moral justice, took in this his last important production. The adaptation, which followed, of the entire *Dunciad* to a new hero was, as will be observed elsewhere, an unfortunate attempt to gratify personal spleen at the expense of poetic consistency. Colley Cibber, finding himself suddenly re-introduced to public ridicule in the new edition of the *Dunciad*, had very naturally raised his arm in self-defence; and had published a letter to Pope endeavouring to account for the genesis and growth of the enmity of the latter against the writer. Pope intended a revenge, as crushing as it was unexpected, by the bold step of dethroning Theobald as hero of the poem in favour of Cibber. Cibber was not slow with a retort; although Warburton had as usual evolved the fitness of an adventitious personality out of the entire scheme of the poem. But the ill-directed shaft of the revised *Dunciad* had fallen harmless; and thus Pope's last literary effort unfortunately produced no effect beyond that of marring one of his most brilliant poems.

But towards the close of his life Pope had lost most of his literary enemies, as he had been deprived of most of his intimate associates and friends. On the other hand, popular fame surrounded him with a halo to which his general absence from public haunts lent something mysterious. When curiosity drew him to the theatre to witness one of the first performances of Garrick, the knowledge of his presence filled the confident actor with an anxiety approaching to awe.[2] The veneration with which his name for some time continued to inspire rising poets of a school which could have little sympathy with his own, is evinced by such expressions as those in Mason's juvenile monody of *Musæus*. But gradually the end was

---

[1] The anecdote is told by M. Ch. de Rému- sat, *u. s.*

[2] The incident is mentioned in Mr. Fitzgerald's recent *Life of Garrick*. For instances of the reverential awe with which Pope was towards the close of his life regarded by such men as Johnson and Reynolds, see Forster's *Life and Times of Goldsmith*, 1. 373, note.

approaching, when nothing but the society of old friends could cheer the decline of health and spirits, until even affections such as these should lose their power. The last months of Pope's life were passed chiefly in the society of Warburton, though he was still occasionally able to visit his older friends, Lords Bolingbroke and Marchmont, at Battersea: while Martha Blount, towards whom his affection remained unabated, solaced him by her occasional presence in his own home. At last came that sense of the insufficiency of all human affections which to all except vulgar minds heralds the near approach of death. Pope died after an open and free acknowledgment of the faith from the profession of which he had never swerved, and in a calm tranquillity offering a consoling contrast to the turbulence of his intellectual life. The date of his death was the 30th of May, 1744. He was buried, according to the directions of his will, in Twickenham church, near the monument which his filial piety had erected to his parents. He desired no inscription on his tomb; but the officious devotion of Warburton, seventeen years later, placarded a tasteless monument with an epigram written by Pope himself, but never, we may be sure, designed by him to degrade his resting-place.[1] His will is only interesting in so far as ample provision was made in it for Martha Blount, to whom the principal part of the poet's property was bequeathed for her life. To his literary friends he made many bequests of books and statues. The legacy to Warburton has been already mentioned; but as literary executor he named Lord Bolingbroke, or (in case he should not survive the testator,) Lord Marchmont. To Bolingbroke's hands were to be committed all MS. and unprinted papers; and thus it came to pass that even after his death Pope's name and fame were involved in two of those literary imbroglios to which he had too frequently exposed them in his lifetime.

Bolingbroke made the discovery that shortly before his death Pope had caused to be printed off, in readiness for publication in his Epistle *on the Characters of Women*, that satiric sketch of the Duchess of Marlborough, under the name of Atossa, which he had formerly been induced to suppress. It has already been stated that there is too little room for doubt that Pope, in order to secure an independence for Martha Blount, had accepted from the Duchess the sum of £1000; but the extent of the undertaking which he had made in return must ever remain unknown. The existence both of the problem and of the certainty, casts an unwelcome shadow on Pope's character. Another grievance, which stung Bolingbroke to allow the bitterest reproaches to be uttered in writing, and virtually in his name, against Pope, was intrinsically of less moment. It concerned the unwarranted printing by Pope's directions, five years before his death, of Bolingbroke's Letters *on the Spirit of Patriotism, on the Idea of a Patriot King,* and *on the State of Parties,* with alterations in the arrangements and omissions never sanctioned by their author. Pope seems in this instance to have been guilty of an inexcusable offence

---

[1] See the *Epitaph*, No. xv.

against his friend; but as, the letters being kept private, no evil result had followed, Bolingbroke would have shown no more than ordinary generosity in remaining silent as to the practically harmless affront. But there was no generosity in his nature; and instead of contenting himself with burning the offensive copies, he ordered his editor, Mallet, to revile Pope for his breach of trust in terms which reflect even less credit upon the offended than upon the offender.

'There is nothing easier,' it has been remarked by the most generous, as he is the most refined, of living critics,[1] 'than to make a caricature of Pope.' Hogarth and his public contemporaries never lighted upon a more facile task; and it needs no genius for description to reproduce with telling elaboration the familiar outlines. But little is gained by intermingling personalities from which Dennis might have shrunk with an estimate of intellectual characteristics; and a very few facts suffice to change into infinite pity the curiosity with which his bodily and mental sufferings have been exhibited, like the contortions of a marionette.

From the day of his birth Pope was weak and sickly in body; and the extreme sensibility of his nerves, the feebleness of his digestive organs, and the general fragility of his constitution, made his life, in Dr. Johnson's phrase, a long disease. In boyhood he nearly sank under the influence of an uncontrollable hypochondria; such indulgences of town life as he afterwards permitted himself had speedily to be relinquished; in middle age he was dependent for ordinary comfort on the constant care of women. He was bald and deformed and almost a dwarf; his wearing-apparel had to be stiffened here and padded there; and his bodily wants were in consequence those of a child, and his habits those of a valetudinarian. If his treatment of his maladies was sometimes petulant and sometimes unwise, his friends might have spared posterity their anecdotes of these inevitable failings; nor need Dr. Johnson, of all men, have gravely recorded the fact that Pope 'loved too well to eat.'

'It might well be expected,' observes a brilliant critic, whose cruelty in dwelling upon Pope's physical infirmities has rarely been surpassed,[2] that such a man would be 'capricious and susceptible.' Upon Pope's sensitive nature every spoken or written word, and every event in which he was interested, operated with thrilling effect. Martha Blount often saw him weep, in reading very tender and melancholy passages; he told Spence that he could never peruse Priam's lament for Hector without tears. This would not have astonished the generation of Sterne and Mackenzie; but Pope's age was not given to sensibility. On the other hand, Pope had, like a child, no judgment of the relative importance of injuries; his anger was uncontrollable, and with the passionate petulance of childhood he combined the resentfulness of a mind unable to forgive till it forgets. In his vanity I see nothing superlative. For him, wholly wrapped up in the progress of his

[1] M. Ste. Beuve, in his *Nouveaux Lundis* (T. VIII.).   [2] M. Taine.

literary career, every incident apparently advancing or retarding its progress, assumed an exceptional importance; and in order to keep himself before the public he frequently condescended to doubtful stratagems. But it was restlessness rather than a false estimate of his own value which prompted him to these steps. He never exalted himself above those whom his literary consciousness had taught him to venerate. He never courted the great for other than an equal friendship, or sought favours which he was unable to return.

He has been frequently charged with an inordinate love of money; a supposed weakness on which Lady Mary, in the days of her enmity with Pope, was especially glad to descant. Johnson noted his extreme talkativeness on this subject; but there is little in his actual proceedings to warrant the main accusation. Swift (who resigned to Pope the profits of their *Miscellanies*) would not have objected to be paid in *place* for the services for which he scornfully spurned any other return. But Pope was a literary man — a name which Swift would have despised — and on his literary earnings built up his literary independence. His parsimony in small matters savours rather of a habit than a vice; nor is there reason to disbelieve his statement that of his modest income he expended one-eighth in alms.

In compensation for his bodily infirmities, nature had bestowed upon him a brilliant eye and a melodious voice. To counteract the debilitating effects of his miserable health, he had been gifted with an indefatigable activity of mind, aided by an extraordinary memory. But he also possessed an affectionate heart, to whose promptings he listened in all the dearest relations of life. He was the best of sons to both his parents, a kind brother, and to those who had once engaged his affections, a faithful and devoted friend. No suspicion perverted the attachment which united him to the associates of his youth, to the Carylls and Cromwells and Blounts, and to the friends of his manhood, to Swift and Arbuthnot and Gay, and to Bolingbroke, whom he thought 'superior to anything he had seen in human nature.' Nor was he a friend in sunshine only; the exile of many was cheered by his sympathy; and Swift predicted that among all his friends Pope would grieve longest for his death. His relations to women were those of tender friendship or affected gallantry, but they exercised no momentous influence upon his life. Had he not occasionally allowed his pen to pander to the profligacy of the age, we might regard with unmixed pity the fate which condemned him to an unmarried life. Lastly, a true generosity of spirit held him fast to his father's faith; and as he became the tool of no political faction, so he permitted no arguments of self-interest to weigh against the dictates of an unaffected piety.

Yet there remains the fact that Pope's real life lay in his literary labours. He quitted them indeed from time to time, but they never quitted him. His social gifts were small; and in conversation he never shone.[1] 'As much company as I

---

[1] On this point *Spence's Anecdotes* must remain the chief evidence. It is true that Pope's conversation could have gained nothing in Spence's hands, whose note-book is without a spark of dra-

INTRODUCTORY MEMOIR. xlvii

have kept, and as much as I love it, I love reading better. I would rather be employed in reading than in the most agreeable conversation.' From reading he passed to writing, without the interval of experience of the world which might have saved him many false steps and many empty griefs. But nothing that arose out of the circumstances of his literary life was empty to him. As a boy he had determined to devote himself to literature. Neither the cruel law which deprived him of the opportunity of a regular education, nor the weakness of his health, nor the knowledge that his success must depend upon himself alone, could stop his prosecution of this resolve. He had faith in himself; and this faith, justified by his achievements, stamps him a great man. No self-delusion diverted him from the path which he had chosen. Brought up under the influences of a narrow taste, and in an age when literature was used rather than honoured, he devoted himself to her service as an end, and not as a mean. His age welcomed him as one of its children; but by what he achieved in and for the national literature his true fame must endure.

The time has gone by for Pope to be ranked among the master-geniuses of our literature. In the last of his uncompromising devotees, Lord Byron, we already recognise the note of half-conscious exaggeration usual in the defenders of a no longer tenable cause. "Neither time, nor distance, nor age," writes Lord Byron in 1821, "can ever diminish my veneration for him who is the great moral poet of " all times, of all climes, of all feelings, and of all stages of existence. The delight " of my boyhood, the study of my manhood, perhaps (if allowed to me to attain to " it) he may be the consolation of my age. His poetry is the book of life. Without " canting and yet without neglecting religion, he has assembled all that a good and " great man can gather together of moral wisdom clothed in consummate beauty. " Sir Wm. Temple observes, 'That of all the members of mankind that live within " the compass of a thousand years, for one man that is capable of making a *great* "*poet*, there may be a *thousand* born capable of making as great generals or minis- " ters of state as any in story.' Here is a statesman's opinion of poetry; it is " honourable to him and to the art. Such a 'poet of a thousand years' was Pope. " A thousand years will roll away before such another can be hoped for in our " literature. But it can *want* them. He is himself a literature."

Such an avalanche of enthusiasm in Lord Byron can sometimes be traced to provocation; and the cause of the above extravagant burst was the edition of Pope by Bowles, which had far the first time brought under active debate Pope's claims to a place among the greatest names of English literature. For Johnson had cavilled rather than protested; and Warton's doubts had, in the opinion of the public, met with a satisfactory reply. Bowles's edition is not without its faults, it

---

matic vitality. (Joseph Spence first became acquainted with Pope in 1725, by publishing a criticism on the translation of the *Odyssey*. Afterwards, through the influence of Pope's friends, he was appointed a prebend of Durham and Professor of Modern History in the University of Oxford.)

is indeed not without its vices; for it displays an *animus* against Pope which makes the editor unfair in his judgment of biographical details, as well as ungenerous in the picture which he draws of his author as a man. Yet Bowles has been justly termed the most poetical editor of Pope; and it was he who, under the influences of a new current in English literature with which Byron had more in common than he cared to know, first succeeded in establishing those defects in his author which no candid criticism can since pretend to overlook.

Pope is the foremost of our classical poets, if the term be correctly applied to a school which sought in the masterpieces of ancient times the starting-point of their own literary development. But a national literature cannot engraft itself upon a foreign trunk; and England already possessed a national literature. Moreover, the classical taste which prevailed in Pope's youth was not the result of another *Renaissance*, of another movement towards intellectual freedom through genuine culture. English society and its handmaid, English literature, had in the days of the Restoration, recklessly seized upon what seemed most attractive in the social and literary activity of our nearest and most influential neighbours — the French. Foreign literary models had thus been thoughtlessly adopted by our own writers, and by one great genius, Dryden, amongst their number. French classicism, a bastard birth, had been transplanted to our soil; and though it could not be acclimatised without undergoing many modifications in accordance with our national peculiarity, yet it remained an exotic and unnatural growth. Already Dryden, when in the hot haste of his literary life his better genius had found time to take counsel with itself, had recognised the truth that the French classical school was merely a French adaptation of classical rules — and supposed classical rules — into a code which was French rather than classical. He had turned from the French to the ancients themselves, but he could not shake off the influence to which he had allowed himself to be subjected. Pope was less immediately under the influence of French models than Dryden; but, on the other hand, the influence of the latter exerted itself in its turn upon his successor. Hence it was impossible that Pope should approach such a classic as Homer with the freshness of original appreciation; and hence, in his own original poetry, he naturally formed his taste among the moderns, upon those in whom he found the so-called classical element in predominance, and among the ancients in those most capable of assimilation to the conception of classical poetry which the age of his predecessors had derived at second-hand. But the models which he consistently followed were recommended to him by more than an ordinary acceptance of the prevailing canons of taste. He was even as a boy too quick-witted not to perceive many of the characteristic features of such writers as Chaucer and Spenser; yet we seek in vain for any influence of these upon the writings either of his youth or of his maturity. He thought Statius the best of all the Latin poets after Vergil; and perhaps even the exception of the latter was merely conventional. Among the Italians he preferred Tasso to Ariosto; and the preference is equally significant.

Pope had been told by Walsh to be a correct poet, and such he became. Including his very first publications, everything he wrote in verse was invariably, to use a homely but expressive phrase, excellent as far as it went. The *Pastorals*, the *Messiah*, *Windsor Forest*, continue to give the pleasure which finished copies of verse can never fail to afford to an educated ear. *Eloisa to Abelard* is an equally felicitous imitation of a long-accepted style. *The Rape of the Lock* was a novelty in English, but not in general, literature; in execution, though made up out of two sets of materials, it nearly approaches perfection. In all these efforts he had shown mastery of form, but no original power marking out any species of poetic composition as signally his own.

He was not to find it in lyric, or dramatic, or epic poetry. The first two of these he barely attempted; his *Ode on St. Cecilia's Day* is only a feeble duplicate of Dryden, his share in Gay's farce is not to be included in any summary of his serious performances. For epic poetry he lacked the historic sense; had he ever ventured upon an attempt in this direction it would have been, like his juvenile *Alcander*, a slavish imitation of the ancients, such as they appeared to his eyes. A plan for an epic on *Brutus*, the mythical grandson of Æneas, was found among his papers after his death.

There remains didactic poetry in both its direct and indirect form; the poetry which has for its express object the inculcation of principles, and which must be primarily judged according to its success in teaching the lessons which it intends to convey. The *Essay on Criticism* is a series of detached precepts, not the development of a complete system. Apart from its marvellous finish as a juvenile effort, it succeeds in enforcing many truths in a form of which the incisiveness has rarely been surpassed. For the development of a philosophical system, such as that propounded in the *Essay on Man*, Pope was imperfectly qualified, because, in Lessing's simple words, he was no philosopher. But here again he succeeds, by his mastery of form, in impressing upon the mind many of the precepts incidental to his system; and produces a string of poetic proverbs which will serve for many a future text. Pope's satirical poetry is also didactic in its aim. It has a positive purpose; it contrasts excellence and virtue with dulness and vice; and its examples are illustrations of its precepts. Here Pope is master; his ability in representing types of character is unsurpassed. Personal spleen may have generally suggested their selection, but this fact fails to interfere with the triumphant success of the result. The men and women of his Satires and Epistles, his Atticus and Atossa, and Sappho and Sporus, are real types, whether they be more or less faithful portraits of Addison and the old Duchess, of Lady Mary and Lord Hervey. His Dunces are the Dunces of all times; his orator Henley the mob-orator, and his awful Aristarch the don, of all epochs; though there may have been some merit in Theobald, some use even in Henley, and though in Bentley there was undoubted greatness. But in Pope's hands individuals become types; and his creative power in this respect surpasses that of the Roman satirists, and leaves Dryden himself behind.

Pope's fame as a translator was ranked by Addison on a level with that of Dryden, but even Addison can in this case be hardly admitted as a competent judge. If the art of translation consists not in carrying into an author the characteristics of the translator and his age, but in reproducing at all events the leading characteristics of that author himself, Pope's Homer must be accounted a failure. It is a noble achievement as an English poem; but it resembles those efforts in landscape-gardening which require to he surveyed from particular points of view, unless their artificiality is to betray itself at once. Pope has not caught, — he could not catch, — the manner of Homer. Had he succeeded in this, he might be forgiven a thousand inaccuracies more glaring than those which he has actually committed. A scholar's hand might make Dryden's Juvenal Juvenal, but to be made Homer Pope's translations need not to be revised, but recast. This is not a mere question of metre. Garrick wore a wig in *Macbeth*, but he moved the passions of his audience by the spirit of Shakspere. Pope had not caught that Homeric spirit which has communicated itself to at least one later translator, even when imprisoned by his own wilfulness in the machinery of a modern stanza.

As a writer of prose Pope had no ambition to achieve eminence. The majority of his prose satires are mere lampoons; the conception of the *Treatise on the Bathos* is that of an excursus from the leading idea of the *Dunciad*. His edition of Shakspere was undertaken as booksellers' work; it is in many respects a careless performance; but his ingenuity is apparent in his abundant emendations, many of which have since met with universal acceptance. Had he carried out the scheme which he entertained towards the close of his life, of writing a history of English poetry, he could hardly have produced more than an interesting, but radically imperfect performance.[1]

Of his poetic form Pope was master. He perfected an English metre, the heroic couplet, which for the purposes of didactic and satirical poetry has since remained the chosen vehicle of expression in our language. To his command over this metre he had attained rapidly, though not at once. His earlier poems are not free from false rhymes,[2] and display that free introduction of an Alexandrine line which Cowley had first among English poets permitted himself, but which Pope afterwards abandoned. Whether Pope could have attained to equal mastery over other metres, seems an idle question; for none could have equally suited the peculiarity of his genius. Lady Mary was of opinion that Pope must have failed in blank verse, just as Dryden declared that Milton would have written *Paradise Lost* in rhymed couplets if he *could*. But the heroic couplet, and no other form of verse, was that adapted to the genius of Pope. He once observed that one of the great conditions of writing well is 'to know thoroughly what one writes about.' The clear conception of a thought was in each case his first step; next came the inde-

---

[1] So I judge from the scheme itself, which was first published by Ruffhead, and is given at length in Roscoe, Vol. 1.
[2] [Pope to the end persisted in making false rhymes. *Am. Ed.*]

fatigable labour of condensing and compressing it into the form in which its expression, most finished in form, is at the same time most convenient to the memory. Thus he, as it were, engraved ideas; and his poems are full of those couplets which can cleanly and without damage to themselves be taken out of their setting.[1] In versification Pope was, as he often said, a pupil of Dryden; but he far surpassed his master. Dryden's verse is often slovenly, and abounds in weak lines. In Pope there is never a syllable, hardly ever a line, too much. On the other hand, Pope might, with advantage to the effect of his poems as a whole, have departed more frequently from the ordinary rule as to the position of the *cæsura* in the verse. The ear is delighted after listening to a page of Pope; an entire poem is apt to weary by the regularity of the cadence, resembling the march-past of column after column of perfectly-drilled troops. It would be difficult to point out any other defect in Pope's versification. To this day, except in a few instances where the pronunciation of a diphthong or the accentuation of a word has changed, it remains a classic model. And Johnson was guilty of no Byronic extravagance when he told Boswell that 'a thousand years may elapse before there shall appear another man with a power of versification equal to that of Pope.'

Such were, as far as I can judge, the principal achievements of Pope during his life of devotion to literature. But English literature owes him more than these — she owes him the effects of that devotion itself. It was not only that he made war upon those who degraded an art into a trade, and into the vilest of trades. The infirmity of his temper, which charity will judge with gentleness in consideration of the miserable frailty of his bodily health, led him into many self-degradations. But the master passion in his breast was not his vanity; it was his veneration for what is great and noble in intellectual life, and his loathing for what is small and mean and noxious. He could not exterminate Grub-street; but as long as he lived and battled against it, it felt that it was only Grub-street, and the world around was conscious of the fact. He served literature neither for power, like Swift; nor, like nearly all his contemporaries, for place and pay; not even for fame chiefly; but for her own sake. And the acknowledgment due to a noble and lifelong self-devotion should not be grudged to Pope, even by those who perceive his shortcomings and lament his faults.

---

[1] The late Lord Carlisle, in a *Lecture on Pope*, gave a long but not exhaustive list of these familiar gems.

CHRONOLOGICAL TABLE.

1688. (MAY 21.) Birth of Pope.

1700. (*Circ.*) Pope takes up his residence with his father at Binfield.

1704. Commencement of intimacy with Sir Wm. Trumball,

1705. and Walsh.

1707. First acquaintance with the Blount family.

1709. *Pastorals* published.

1711. *Essay on Criticism* p. Pope introduced to Gay,

1712. and Addison. *Rape of the Lock* (original edition) p. *The Messiah* p.

1713. (APRIL.) Addison's *Cato* first acted. *Prologue to Cato* p.

Pope's attack on Dennis reproved by Addison.

Windsor Forest p. Pope introduced to Swift. *Ode on St. Cecilia's Day* p.

Pope studies painting under Jervas.

(NOVEMBER.) Subscription for *Translation of Iliad* opened.

1713-4. Meetings of the Scriblerus Club.

1714. Death of Queen Anne. *Rape of the Lock* (enlarged). *Temple of Fame* p.

1715. *Iliad* (Vol. I.) p.

1715-6. Quarrel with Addison.

1716. (APRIL.) Pope settles with his parents at Chiswick.

Departure for the East of Lady Mary Wortley Montagu.

1717. *Elegy to the Memory of an Unfortunate Lady* p. *Epistle of Eloisa to Abelard* p. *Three Hours after Marriage* produced. First quarrel with Cibber.

(OCTOBER.) Death of Pope's father.

1718. Pope settles with his mother at Twickenham.

Return from the East of Lady Mary Wortley Montagu.

1720. South-Sea Year. *Iliad* (last volume) p.

1722. Correspondence with Judith Cowper.

1723. First return of Bolingbroke. Banishment of Atterbury.

1725. Edition of *Shakspere* p. Pope attacked by Theobald.

Odyssey (Vols. I.-III.) p. Second return of Bolingbroke, who settles at Dawley.

1726. *Letters to Cromwell* (Curll) p. Swift pays a long visit to Twickenham.

1727. (JUNE.) Death of George I. *Miscellanies* (Vols. I. and II.) p.; containing, among other pieces by Pope, the *Treatise on the Bathos*.

1728. *The Dunciad* (Books I.-III.) p.

1730. *Grub-street Journal* (continued by Pope and others till 1737). Quarrels with Aaron Hill and others.

1731. *Epistle on Taste* p. The remaining *Moral Essays* up to 1735.

1732. *Essay on Man* (Ep. I.) p. The remaining Epistles up to 1734.

(DECEMBER.) Death of Gay.

1733. Quarrel with Lord Hervey.

(JUNE.) Death of Pope's mother.

1735. *Epistle to Arbuthnot* p. Death of Arbuthnot.

Pope's *Correspondence*. (Curll.)

1736. Pope's *Correspondence* (authorised edition).

1737. *Imitations of Horace* p.

1738. *Epilogue to Satires* p.

1740. (MARCH.) Close of correspondence with Swift.

First meeting with Warburton.

1742. *The New Dunciad* (in four books) p.

1743. *The Dunciad* (with Cibber as hero) p.

1744. (MAY 30.) Death of Pope.

THE AUTHOR'S PREFACE.

I AM inclined to think that both the writers of books, and the readers of them, are generally not a little unreasonable in their expectations. The first seem to fancy that the world must approve whatever they produce, and the latter to imagine that authors are obliged to please them at any rate. Methinks, as on the one hand, no single man is born with a right of controuling the opinions of all the rest; so on the other, the world has no title to demand, that the whole care and time of any particular person should be sacrificed to its entertainment. Therefore I cannot but believe that writers and readers are under equal obligations, for as much fame, or pleasure, as each affords the other.

Every one acknowledges, it would be a wild notion to expect perfection in any work of man: and yet one would think the contrary was taken for granted, by the judgment commonly past upon Poems. A Critic supposes he has done his part, if he proves a writer to have failed in an expression, or erred in any particular point:[1] and can it then be wondered at, if the Poets in general seem resolved not to own themselves in any error? For as long as one side will make no allowances, the other will be brought to no acknowledgements.

I am afraid this extreme zeal on both sides is ill-placed; Poetry and Criticism being by no means the universal concern of the world, but only the affair of idle men who write in their closets, and of idle men who read there.

Yet sure upon the whole, a bad Author deserves better usage than a bad Critic: for a Writer's endeavour, for the most part, is to please his Readers, and he fails merely through the misfortune of an ill judgment; but such a Critic's is to put them out of humour; a design he could never go upon without both that and an ill temper.

I think a good deal may be said to extenuate the fault of bad Poets. What we call a Genius, is hard to be distinguished by a man himself, from a strong inclination: and if his genius be ever so great, he cannot at first discover it any other way, than by giving way to that prevalent propensity which renders him the more liable to be mistaken. The only method he has, is to make the experiment by writing, and appealing to the judgment of others: now if he happens to write ill (which is certainly no sin in itself) he is immediately made an object of ridicule. I wish we had the humanity to reflect that even the worst authors might, in their endeavour to please us, deserve something at our hands. We have no cause to quarrel with them but for their obstinacy in persisting to write; and this too may admit of alleviating circumstances. Their particular friends may be either igno-

[1] [Cf. *Essay on Criticism*, 265.]

rant, or insincere; and the rest of the world in general is too well bred to shock them with a truth, which generally their Booksellers are the first that inform them of. This happens not till they have spent too much of their time, to apply to any profession which might better fit their talents; and till such talents as they have are so far discredited as to be but of small service to them. For (what is the hardest case imaginable) the reputation of a man generally depends upon the first steps he makes in the world, and people will establish their opinion of us, from what we do at that season when we have least judgment to direct us.

On the other hand, a good Poet no sooner communicates his works with the same desire of information, but it is imagined he is a vain young creature given up to the ambition of fame; when perhaps the poor man is all the while trembling with the fear of being ridiculous. If he is made to hope he may please the world, he falls under very unlucky circumstances: for, from the moment he prints, he must expect to hear no more truth, than if he were a Prince, or a Beauty. If he has not very good sense (and indeed there are twenty men of wit, for one man of sense) his living thus in a course of flattery may put him in no small danger of becoming a Coxcomb: if he has, he will consequently have so much diffidence as not to reap any great satisfaction from his praise; since, if it be given to his face, it can scarce be distinguished from flattery, and if in his absence, it is hard to be certain of it. Were he sure to be commended by the best and most knowing, he is as sure of being envied by the worst and most ignorant, which are the majority; for it is with a fine Genius as with a fine fashion, all those are displeased at it who are not able to follow it: and it is to be feared that esteem will seldom do any man so much good, as ill-will does him harm. Then there is a third class of people who make the largest part of mankind, those of ordinary or indifferent capacities; and these (to a man) will hate, or suspect him: a hundred honest Gentlemen will dread him as a Wit, and a hundred innocent Women as a Satirist. In a word, whatever be his fate in Poetry, it is ten to one but he must give up all the reasonable aims of life for it. There are indeed some advantages accruing from a Genius to Poetry, and they are all I can think of: the agreeable power of self-amusement when a man is idle or alone; the privilege of being admitted into the best company; and the freedom of saying as many careless things as other people, without being so severely remarked upon.

I believe, if any one, early in his life, should contemplate the dangerous fate of authors, he would scarce be of their number on any consideration. The life of a Wit is a warfare upon earth;[1] and the present spirit of the learned world is such, that to attempt to serve it (any way) one must have the constancy of a martyr, and a resolution to suffer for its sake. I could wish people would believe what I am pretty certain they will not, that I have been much less concerned about Fame than I durst declare till this occasion, when methinks I should find more credit than I could heretofore: since my writings have had their fate already, and it is too late to think of prepossessing the reader in their favour. I would plead it as some merit in me, that the world has never been prepared for these Trifles by Prefaces, byassed by recommendations, dazled with the names of great Patrons, wheedled with fine reasons and pretences, or troubled with excuses. I confess it was want

---

[1] [Cf. *Essay on Criticism*, 494, ff.]

THE AUTHOR'S PREFACE.

of consideration that made me an author; I writ because it amused me; I corrected because it was as pleasant to me to correct as to write; and I published because I was told I might please such as it was a credit to please. To what degree I have done this, I am really ignorant; I had too much fondness for my productions to judge of them at first, and too much judgment to be pleased with them at last. But I have reason to think they can have no reputation which will continue long, or which deserves to do so: for they have always fallen short not only of what I read of others, but even of my own Ideas of Poetry.

If any one should imagine I am not in earnest, I desire him to reflect, that the Ancients (to say the least of them) had as much Genius as we: and that to take more pains, and employ more time, cannot fail to produce more complete pieces. They constantly apply'd themselves not only to that art, but to that single branch of an art, to which their talent was most powerfully bent; and it was the business of their lives to correct and finish their works for posterity. If we can pretend to have used the same industry, let us expect the same immortality: Tho' if we took the same care, we should still lie under a farther misfortune: they writ in languages that became universal and everlasting, while ours are extremely limited both in extent and in duration. A mighty foundation for our pride! when the utmost we can hope, is but to be read in one Island, and to be thrown aside at the end of one Age.

All that is left us is to recommend our productions by the imitation of the Ancients: and it will be found true, that, in every age, the highest character for sense and learning has been obtain'd by those who have been most indebted to them. For, to say truth, whatever is very good sense, must have been common sense in all times; and what we call Learning, is but the knowledge of the sense of our predecessors. Therefore they who say our thoughts are not our own, because they resemble the Ancients, may as well say our faces are not our own, because they are like our Fathers: And indeed it is very unreasonable, that people should expect us to be Scholars, and yet be angry to find us so.

I fairly confess that I have serv'd myself all I could by reading; that I made use of the judgment of authors dead and living; that I omitted no means in my power to be inform'd of my errors, both by my friends and enemies: But the true reason these pieces are not more correct, is owing to the consideration how short a time they, and I, have to live: One may be ashamed to consume half one's days in bringing sense and rhyme together; and what Critic can be so unreasonable, as not to leave a man time enough for any more serious employment, or more agreeable amusement?

The only plea I shall use for the favour of the public, is, that I have as great a respect for it, as most authors have for themselves; and that I have sacrificed much of my own self-love for its sake, in preventing not only many mean things from seeing the light, but many which I thought tolerable. I would not be like those Authors, who forgive themselves some particular lines for the sake of a whole Poem, and *vice versa* a whole Poem for the sake of some particular lines. I believe no one qualification is so likely to make a good writer, as the power of rejecting his own thoughts; and it must be this (if any thing) that can give me a chance to be one. For what I have published, I can only hope to be pardon'd;

but for what I have burn'd, I deserve to be prais'd. On this account the world is under some obligation to me, and owes me the justice in return, to look upon no verses as mine that are not inserted in this collection. And perhaps nothing could make it worth my while to own what are really so, but to avoid the imputation of so many dull and immoral things, as partly by malice, and partly by ignorance, have been ascribed to me. I must farther acquit myself of the presumption of having lent my name to recommend any Miscellanies or Works of other men; a thing I never thought becoming a person who has hardly credit enough to answer for his own.

In this office of collecting my pieces, I am altogether uncertain, whether to look upon myself as a man building a monument, or burying the dead.

If Time shall make it the former, may these Poems (as long as they last) remain as a testimony, that their Author never made his talents subservient to the mean and unworthy ends of Party or Self-interest; the gratification of public prejudices, or private passions; the flattery of the undeserving, or the insult of the unfortunate. If I have written well, let it be consider'd that 't is what no man can do without good sense, a quality that not only renders one capable of being a good writer, but a good man. And if I have made any acquisition in the opinion of any one under the notion of the former, let it be continued to me under no other title than that of the latter.

But if this publication be only a more solemn funeral of my Remains, I desire it may be known that I die in charity, and in my senses; without any murmurs against the justice of this age, or any mad appeals to posterity. I declare I shall think the world in the right, and quietly submit to every truth which time shall discover to the prejudice of these writings; not so much as wishing so irrational a thing, as that every body should be deceived merely for my credit. However, I desire it may then be considered, That there are very few things in this collection, which were not written under the age of five and twenty : so that my youth may be made (as it never fails to be in executions) a case of compassion. That I was never so concerned about my works as to vindicate them in print, believing, if any thing was good, it would defend itself, and what was bad could never be defended. That I used no artifice to raise or continue a reputation, depreciated no dead author I was obliged to, bribed no living one with unjust praise, insulted no adversary with ill language; or when I could not attack a Rival's works, encouraged reports against his Morals. To conclude, if this volume perish, let it serve as a warning to the Critics, not to take too much pains for the future to destroy such things as will die of themselves; and a *Memento mori* to some of my vain contemporaries the Poets, to teach them that, when real merit is wanting, it avails nothing to have been encouraged by the great, commended by the eminent, and favoured by the public in general.

P.

Nov. 10, 1716.

JUVENILE POEMS.

PASTORALS,

WITH A DISCOURSE ON PASTORAL.

WRITTEN IN THE YEAR 1704.

> Rura mihi et rigui placeant in vallibus amnes,
> Flumina amem, sylvasque, inglorius! — VIRG.

[IF the pastoral poetry with which English literature is overloaded may with propriety be divided into real and sham, there is little doubt but that the following juvenile productions of Pope, written by him in 1704 at the age of sixteen, must be included in the latter and larger category. The two main objections which have been raised against Pope's *Pastorals*, viz. the barrenness of invention and the mixture of modern and antique ideas and associations displayed in them, apply with more or less force to all efforts in this branch of poetical composition which are purely and avowedly artificial and imitative. In an ironical criticism of his Pastorals sent anonymously by Pope to the *Guardian*, he avows both characteristics; and takes credit for having abstained from the rustic nomenclature adopted by Phillips, who had in this respect followed the precedent of Spenser, and was accordingly ridiculed in the burlesque *Shepherd's Week*, by Gay. Dr. Johnson has said all that needs to be said as to the absolute and relative value belonging to these poetic exercises in English literature generally, and among the works of Pope in particular, when he observes that 'to charge these Pastorals with want of invention, is to require what never was intended. The imitations are so ambitiously frequent, that the writer evidently means rather to shew his literature than his wit. It is surely sufficient for an author of sixteen not only to be able to copy the poems of antiquity with judicious selection, but to have obtained sufficient power of language, and skill in metre, to exhibit a series of versification, which had in English poetry no precedent, nor has since had an imitation.' It may, however, be remarked that these poems contain a number of doubtful rhymes — an objection which is not to be made to the author's maturer pieces.

The arrangement of the four Pastorals under the names of the four seasons of the year, while scarcely meriting praise due to an exceptionally bold originality, is more convenient than that of Spenser's *Shepherd's Kalendar*, in which, as has been pointed out, it was impossible to sustain in each case the character attaching or supposed to attach to each particular month. Such as it is, Pope's arrangement was stated by Thomson to have given him the first hint and idea of writing his *Seasons*.

The scenery of the Pastorals is in the main that of Windsor Forest, where (at Binfield) the poet had from the age of twelve resided with his father; but, in accordance with the nature of these compositions, there is no attempt to keep up a very distinct local colouring.

These productions obtained for the young poet immediate and cordial recognition from many eminent men. By Sir William Trumball they were shown to Wycherley, and by the latter to Walsh, and subsequently communicated to Lord Lansdowne, Dr. Garth, Lords Halifax and Somers, Mr. Mainwaring, and others.]

A DISCOURSE ON PASTORAL POETRY.[1]

THERE are not, I believe, a greater number of any sort of verses, than of those which are called Pastorals; nor a smaller, than of those which are truly so. It therefore seems necessary to give some account of this kind of Poem, and it is my design to comprize in this short paper the substance of those numerous dissertations the Criticks have made on the subject, without omitting any of their rules in my own favour. You will also find some points reconciled, about which they seem to differ, and a few remarks, which, I think, have escaped their observation.

The original of Poetry is ascribed to that Age which succeeded the creation of the world: and as the keeping of flocks seems to have been the first employment of mankind, the most ancient sort of poetry was probably *pastoral*.[2] It is natural to imagine, that the leisure of those ancient shepherds admitting and inviting some diversion, none was so proper to that solitary and sedentary life as singing; and that in their songs they took occasion to celebrate their own felicity. From hence a Poem was invented, and afterwards improved to a perfect image of that happy time; which by giving us an esteem for the virtues of a former age, might recommend them to the present. And since the life of shepherds was attended with more tranquillity than any other rural employment, the Poets chose to introduce their Persons, from whom it received the name of Pastoral.

A Pastoral is an imitation of the action of a shepherd, or one considered under that character. The form of this imitation is dramatic, or narrative, or mixed of both;[3] the fable simple, the manners not too polite nor too rustic: the thoughts are plain, yet admit a little quickness and passion, but that short and flowing: the expression humble, yet as pure as the language will afford; neat, but not florid; easy, and yet lively. In short, the fable, manners, thoughts, and expressions are full of the greatest simplicity in nature.

---

[1] Written at sixteen years of age. P.   [2] Fontenelle's *Disc. on Pastorals.* P.
[3] Hensius in Theocr. P.

A DISCOURSE ON PASTORAL POETRY.

The complete character of this poem consists in simplicity,[1] brevity, and delicacy; the two first of which render an eclogue natural, and the last delightful.

If we could copy Nature, it may be useful to take this Idea along with us, that Pastoral is an image of what they call the golden age. So that we are not to describe our shepherds as shepherds at this day really are, but as they may be conceived then to have been; when the best of men followed the employment. To carry this resemblance yet farther, it would not be amiss to give these shepherds some skill in astronomy, as far as it may be useful to that sort of life. And an air of piety to the Gods should shine through the Poem, which so visibly appears in all the works of antiquity: and it ought to preserve some relish of the old way of writing; the connection should be loose, the narrations and descriptions short,[2] and the periods concise. Yet it is not sufficient, that the sentences only be brief, the whole Eclogue should be so too. For we cannot suppose Poetry in those days to have been the business of men, but their recreation at vacant hours.

But with a respect to the present age, nothing more conduces to make these composures natural, than when some Knowledge in rural affairs is discovered.[3] This may be made to appear rather done by chance than on design, and sometimes is best shewn by inference; lest by too much study to seem natural, we destroy that easy simplicity from whence arises the delight. For what is inviting in this sort of poetry proceeds not so much from the Idea of that business, as of the tranquillity of a country life.

We must therefore use some illusion to render a Pastoral delightful; and this consists in exposing the best side only of a shepherd's life, and in concealing its miseries.[4] Nor is it enough to introduce shepherds discoursing together in a natural way; but a regard must be had to the subject; that it contain some particular beauty in itself, and that it be different in every Eclogue. Besides, in each of them a designed scene or prospect is to be presented to our view, which should likewise have its variety.[5] This variety is obtained in a great degree by frequent comparisons, drawn from the most agreeable objects of the country; by interrogations to things inanimate; by beautiful digressions, but those short; sometimes by insisting a little on circumstances; and lastly, by elegant turns on the words, which render the numbers extremely sweet and pleasing. As for the numbers themselves, though they are properly of the heroic measure, they should be the smoothest, the most easy and flowing imaginable.

It is by rules like these that we ought to judge of Pastoral. And since the instructions given for any art are to be delivered as that art is in perfection, they must of necessity be derived from those in whom it is acknowledged so to be. It is therefore from the practice of Theocritus and Virgil, (the only undisputed authors of Pastoral) that the Criticks have drawn the foregoing notions concerning it.

Theocritus excels all others in Nature and simplicity. The subjects of his Idyllia are purely pastoral; but he is not so exact in his persons, having intro-

---

[1] Rapin, *de Carm. Past.* p. 2. P.
[2] Rapin, *Réflex. sur l'Art Poët. d'Arist.* p. 2. Refl. xxvii. P.
[3] Pref. to Virg. Past. in Dryd. Virg. P.
[4] Fontenelle's *Disc of Pastorals.* P.
[5] See the forementioned Preface. P.

duced reapers[1] and fishermen as well as shepherds. He is apt to be too long in his descriptions, of which that of the Cup in the first pastoral is a remarkable instance. In the manners he seems a little defective, for his swains are sometimes abusive and immodest, and perhaps too much inclining to rusticity; for instance, in his fourth and fifth Idylli. But 't is enough that all others learnt their excellencies from him, and that his Dialect alone has a secret charm in it, which no other could ever attain.

Virgil, who copies Theocritus, refines upon his original: and in all points where judgment is principally concerned, he is much superior to his master. Though some of his subjects are not pastoral in themselves, but only seem to be such; they have a wonderful variety in them, which the Greek was a stranger to.[2] He exceeds him in regularity and brevity, and falls short of him in nothing but simplicity and propriety of style; the first of which perhaps was the fault of his age, and the last of his language.

Among the moderns, their success has been greatest who have most endeavoured to make these ancients their pattern. The most considerable Genius appears in the famous Tasso, and our Spenser. Tasso in his Aminta has as far excelled all the Pastoral writers, as in his Gierusalemme he has out-done the Epic Poets of his country. But as this Piece seems to have been the original of a new sort of poem, the pastoral Comedy, in Italy, it cannot so well be considered as a copy of the ancients. Spenser's Calendar, in Mr. Dryden's opinion, is the most complete work of this kind which any Nation has produced ever since the time of Virgil.[3] Not but that he may be thought imperfect in some few points. His Eclogues are somewhat too long, if we compare them with the ancients. He is sometimes too allegorical, and treats of matters of religion in a pastoral style, as the Mantuan had done before him. He has employed the Lyric measure, which is contrary to the practice of the old Poets. His Stanza is not still the same, nor always well chosen. This last may be the reason his expression is sometimes not concise enough: for the Tetrastic has obliged him to extend his sense to the length of four lines, which would have been more closely confined in the Couplet.

In the manners, thoughts, and characters, he comes near to Theocritus himself; tho', notwithstanding all the care he has taken, he is certainly inferior in his Dialect: For the Doric had its beauty and propriety in the time of Theocritus; it was used in part of Greece, and frequent in the mouths of many of the greatest persons: whereas the old English and country phrases of Spenser were either entirely obsolete, or spoken only by people of the lowest condition. As there is a difference betwixt simplicity and rusticity, so the expression of simple thoughts should be plain, but not clownish. The addition he has made of a Calendar to his Eclogues, is very beautiful; since by this, besides the general moral of innocence and simplicity, which is common to other authors of Pastoral, he has one peculiar to himself; he compares human Life to the several Seasons, and at once exposes to his readers a view of the great and little worlds, in their various changes and aspects. Yet the scrupulous division of his Pastorals into months, has obliged

---

[1] ΘΕΡΙΣΤΑΙ Idyl. x. and ΆΛΙΕΙΣ Idyl. xxi. P.

[2] Rapin, *Refl. on Arist.*, part II. refl. xxvii. Pref. to the Ecl. in Dryden's Virg. P.

[3] Dedication to Virg. Ecl. P.

him either to repeat the same description, in other words, for three Months together; or, when it was exhausted before, entirely to omit it: whence it comes to pass, that some of his Eclogues (as the sixth, eighth, and tenth for example) have nothing but their Titles to distinguish them. The reason is evident, because the year has not that variety in it to furnish every month with a particular description, as it may every season.

Of the following Eclogues I shall only say, that these four comprehend all the subjects which the Criticks upon Theocritus and Virgil will allow to be fit for pastoral: That they have as much variety of description, in respect of the several seasons, as Spenser's: that in order to add to this variety, the several times of the day are observ'd, the rural employments in each season or time of day, and the rural scenes or places proper to such employments; not without some regard to the several ages of man, and the different passions proper to each age.

But after all, if they have any merit, it is to be attributed to some good old Authors, whose works as I had leisure to study, so I hope I have not wanted care to imitate.

SPRING.[1]

THE FIRST PASTORAL,

OR

DAMON.

TO SIR WILLIAM TRUMBAL.[2]

FIRST in these fields I try the sylvan strains,
 Nor blush to sport on Windsor's blissful plains:
Fair Thames, flow gently from thy sacred spring,
While on thy banks Sicilian Muses sing;

---

[1] These Pastorals were written at the age of sixteen, and then passed through the hands of Mr. Walsh, Mr. Wycherley, G. Granville afterwards Lord Landsdown, Sir William Trumbal, Dr. Garth, Lord Hallifax, Lord Somers, Mr. Mainwaring, and others. All these gave our author the greatest encouragement, and particularly Mr. Walsh (whom Mr. Dryden, in his postscript to Virgil, calls the best critic of his age). "The author (says he) seems to have a particular genius for this kind of poetry, and a judgment that much exceeds his years. He has taken very freely from the ancients. But what he has mixed of his own with theirs is no way inferior to what he has taken from them. It is not flattery at all to say that Virgil had written nothing so good at his age. His preface is very judicious and learned." Letter to Mr. Wycherley, Ap. 1705. The Lord Lansdown about the same time, mentioning the youth of our poet, says (in a printed letter of the character of Mr. Wycherley) "that if he goes on as he has begun in the pastoral way, as Virgil first tried his strength, we may hope to see English poetry vie with the Roman," etc. Notwithstanding the early time of their production, the author esteemed these as the most correct in the versification, and musical in the numbers, of all his works. The reason for his labouring them into so much softness, was, doubtless, that this sort of poetry derives almost its whole beauty from a natural ease of thought and smoothness of verse; whereas that of most other kinds consists in the strength and fulness of both. In a letter of his to Mr. Walsh about this time we find an enumeration of several niceties in versification, which perhaps have never been strictly observed in any English poem, except in these Pastorals. They were not printed till 1709. P.

[2] *Sir William Trumbal.*] Our author's friendship with this gentleman commenced at very unequal years: he was under sixteen, but Sir William above sixty, and had lately resigned his employment of Secretary of State to King William. P. [Sir William Trumball, whom Macaulay (chap. xxi) characterises as "a learned civilian and an experienced diplomatist, of moderate opinions and of temper cautious to timidity," was appointed Secretary of State in 1691 and resigned in 1697 to make way for a more zealous partisan. He died at his native place of East Hamstead near Binfield, and Pope honoured his memory by an epitaph (II). Trumball was the first to recognise the merits of the *Essay on Criticism*, and to induce its author to publish it; he also eulogised the *Rape of the Lock* and encouraged the translation of the *Iliad*. Of Trumball it is related that being in 1687 appointed ambassador to the Ottoman Porte, he performed the journey on foot, thus outdoing by anticipation the German poet's *Promenade to Syracuse*.]

ALEXANDER POPE.
(From the painting by Richardson, in the possession of Lord Lyttelton, at Hagley.)

SPRING.

Let vernal airs thro' trembling osiers play,   5
And Albion's cliffs resound the rural lay.
You, that too wise for pride, too good for pow'r,
Enjoy the glory to be great no more,
And carrying with you all the world can boast,
To all the world illustriously are lost!   10
O let my Muse her tender reed inspire,
Till in your native shades[1] you tune the lyre:
So when the Nightingale to rest removes,
The Thrush may chant to the forsaken groves,
But, charm'd to silence, listens while she sings,   15
And all th' aërial audience clap their wings.
  Soon as the flocks shook off the nightly dews,
Two Swains, whom Love kept wakeful, and the Muse,
Pour'd o'er the whitening vale their fleecy care.
Fresh as the morn, and as the season fair: 20
The dawn now blushing on the mountain's side,
Thus Daphnis spoke, and Strephon thus reply'd.

DAPHNIS.

Hear how the birds, on ev'ry bloomy spray,
With joyous musick wake the dawning day!
Why sit we mute when early linnets sing,   25
When warbling Philomel salutes the spring?
Why sit we sad when Phosphor shines so clear,
And lavish nature paints the purple Year?[2]

STREPHON.

Sing then, and Damon shall attend the strain,
While yon' slow oxen turn the furrow'd Plain.   30
Here the bright crocus and blue vi'let glow;
Here western winds on breathing roses blow.
I'll stake yon' lamb, that near the fountain plays,
And from the brink his dancing shade surveys.

DAPHNIS.

And I this bowl, where wanton Ivy twines,   35
And swelling clusters bend the curling vines:
Four figures rising from the work appear,
The various seasons of the rolling year;
And what is that, which binds the radiant sky,
Where twelve fair Signs in beauteous order lie?   40

---

[1] *In your native shades.*] Sir W. Trumbal was born in Windsor-Forest, to which he retreated, after he had resigned the post of Secretary of State to King William III. P.

[2] *purple year?*] Purple here used in the Latin sense, of the brightest, most vivid colouring in general, not of that peculiar tint so called. *Warburton.* [Ver purpureum. Verg. *Ecl.* ix. 40.]

DAMON.

Then sing by turns, by turns the Muses sing,
Now hawthorns blossom, now the daisies spring,
Now leaves the trees, and flow'rs adorn the ground,
Begin, the vales shall ev'ry note rebound.

STREPHON.

Inspire me, Phœbus, in my Delia's praise   45
With Waller's[1] strains, or Granville's[2] moving lays!
A milk-white bull shall at your altars stand,
That threats a fight, and spurns the rising sand.

DAPHNIS.

O Love! for Sylvia let me gain the prize,
And make my tongue victorious as her eyes;   50
No lambs or sheep for victims I'll impart,
Thy victim, Love, shall be the shepherd's heart.

STREPHON.

Me gentle Delia beckons from the plain,
Then hid in shades, eludes her eager swain;
But feigns a laugh, to see me search around,   55
And by that laugh the willing fair is found.

DAPHNIS.

The sprightly Sylvia trips along the green,
She runs, but hopes she does not run unseen;
While a kind glance at her pursuer flies,
How much at variance are her feet and eyes!   60

STREPHON.

O'er golden sands let rich Pactolus flow,
And trees weep amber on the banks of Po;[3]
Blest Thames's shores the brightest beauties yield,
Feed here my lambs, I'll seek no distant field.

---

[1] [Edmund Waller born 1605, died, 1687.]

[2] *Granville* —] George Granville, afterwards Lord Landsdown, known for his poems, most of which he composed very young, and proposed Waller as his model. P.

[Born about 1667 and connected by descent with the Stuart cause, George Granville remained in retirement during the reign of William III.; but entered Parliament in the reign of Queen Anne, and on the accession to power of the Tories in 1710 took office as secretary at war. In 1711 he was created Lord Lansdowne of Bideford; and after undergoing temporary imprisonment for supposed connection with the Scottish insurrection of 1715, died in 1735. His poems, of which he says that they "seem to begin where Mr. Waller left off, though far unequal and short of so unimitable an original," contain little or nothing deserving to be read; but though his *Myra* is forgotten, his own modest estimate of his poetic merits deserves to be remembered by the side of Pope's praises in the Dedication to *Windsor Forest*.]

[3] [See Ov. *Metam.* II. 364-6.]

SPRING.

DAPHNIS.

Celestial Venus haunts Idalia's groves;
Diana Cynthus, Ceres Hybla loves;
If Windsor-shades delight the matchless maid,
Cynthus and Hybla yield to Windsor-shade.

STREPHON.

All nature mourns, the Skies relent in show'rs,
Hush'd are the birds, and clos'd the drooping flow'rs;
If Delia smile, the flow'rs begin to spring,
The skies to brighten, and the birds to sing.

DAPHNIS.

All nature laughs, the groves are fresh and fair,
The Sun's mild lustre warms the vital air;
If Sylvia smiles, new glories gild the shore,
And vanquish'd nature seems to charm no more.

STREPHON.

In spring the fields, in autumn hills I love,
At morn the plains, at noon the shady grove,
But Delia always; absent from her sight,
Nor plains at morn, nor groves at noon delight.

DAPHNIS.

Sylvia 's like autumn ripe, yet mild as May,
More bright than noon, yet fresh as early day;
Ev'n spring displeases, when she shines not here;
But blest with her, 't is spring throughout the year.

STREPHON.

Say, Daphnis, say, in what glad soil appears,
A wond'rous Tree that sacred Monarchs bears:[1]
Tell me but this, and I'll disclaim the prize,
And give the conquest to thy Sylvia's eyes.

DAPHNIS.

Nay tell me first, in what more happy fields
The Thistle springs, to which the Lily yields:[2]
And then a nobler prize I will resign;
For Sylvia, charming Sylvia, shall be thine.

---

[1] *A wond'rous Tree that sacred Monarchs bears.*] An allusion to the Royal Oak, in which Charles II. had been hid from the pursuit after the battle of Worcester. P.

[2] *The Thistle springs, to which the Lily yields,*] alludes to the device of the Scots monarchs, the thistle worn by Queen Anne; and to the arms of France, the fleur de lys. P. [In the

DAMON.

Cease to contend, for, Daphnis, I decree,
The bowl to Strephon, and the lamb to thee:
Blest Swains, whose Nymphs in ev'ry grace excel;   95
Blest Nymphs, whose Swains those graces sing so well!
Now rise, and haste to yonder woodbine bow'rs,
A soft retreat from sudden vernal show'rs,
The turf with rural dainties shall be crown'd,
While op'ning blooms diffuse their sweets around.   100
For see! the gath'ring flocks to shelter tend,
And from the Pleiads fruitful show'rs descend.

SUMMER.

THE SECOND PASTORAL,

OR

ALEXIS.

TO DR. GARTH.

A SHEPHERD'S Boy (he seeks no better name)
Led forth his flocks along the silver Thame,[1]
Where dancing sun-beams on the waters play'd,[2]
And verdant alders form'd a quiv'ring shade.
Soft as he mourn'd, the streams forgot to flow,   5
The flocks around a dumb compassion show,
The Naiads wept in ev'ry wat'ry bow'r,
And Jove consented in a silent show'r.
  Accept, O GARTH,[3] the Muse's early lays,

---

early part of Queen Anne's reign the royal arms were the same as those of her father. The union with Scotland occasioned a change of armorial bearings; and they then appeared, England and Scotland impaled in the first and fourth quarter; France in the second; and Ireland in the third. On the great seal prepared in the year of the union (1706) we have England and Scotland only, and a new badge, the rose and thistle conjoined. The Scottish order of the Thistle was re-established Dec. 31, 1703. *Annals of England*, III. 173-4, and 182.]

[1] [*Thame.* Spenser repeatedly uses this form.]

[2] The scene of this pastoral by the river's side; suitable to the heat of the season; the time noon. P.

[3] Dr. Samuel Garth, author of *The Dispensary*, was one of the first friends of the author, whose acquaintance with him began at fourteen

SUMMER.   15

That adds this wreath of Ivy to thy Bays;   10
Hear what from Love unpractis'd hearts endure,
From Love, the sole disease thou canst not cure.
Ye shady beeches, and ye cooling streams,
Defence from Phœbus', not from Cupid's beams,
To you I mourn, nor to the deaf I sing,   15
The woods shall answer, and their echo ring.[1]
The hills and rocks attend my doleful lay,
Why art thou prouder and more hard than they?
The bleating sheep with my complaints agree,
They parch'd with heat, and I inflam'd by thee.   20
The sultry Sirius burns the thirsty plains,
While in thy heart eternal winter reigns.
Where stray ye, Muses, in what lawn or grove,
While your Alexis pines in hopeless love?
In those fair fields where sacred Isis glides,   25
Or else where Cam his winding vales divides?[2]
As in the crystal spring I view my face,
Fresh rising blushes paint the wat'ry glass;
But since those graces please thy eyes no more,
I shun the fountains which I sought before.   30
Once I was skill'd in ev'ry herb that grew,
And ev'ry plant that drinks the morning dew;
Ah wretched shepherd, what avails thy art,
To cure thy lambs, but not to heal thy heart!
Let other swains attend the rural care,   35
Feed fairer flocks, or richer fleeces shear:
But nigh yon' mountain let me tune my lays,
Embrace my Love, and bind my brows with bays.
That flute is mine which Colin's[3] tuneful breath
Inspir'd when living, and bequeath'd in death;   40
He said: Alexis, take this pipe, the same
That taught the groves my Rosalinda's name:
But now the reeds shall hang on yonder tree,
For ever silent, since despis'd by thee.
Oh! were I made by some transforming pow'r   45
The captive bird that sings within thy bow'r!

or fifteen. Their friendship continued from the year 1703 to 1718, which was that of his death. P. [Dr. afterwards Sir Samuel Garth, the author of the above-mentioned mock-heroic poem and a distinguished physician, died in 1718. Pope, who in his *Epistle to Dr. Arbuthnot*, speaks of 'well-natured' Garth as one who 'inflam'd him with early praise,' bestows a similar epithet upon him in a letter regretting his death, where he also pays him the singular compliment that 'if ever there was a good Christian without knowing himself to be so, it was Dr. Garth.']

[1] *The woods shall answer, and their echo ring*] is a line out of Spenser's *Epithalamion*. P. [It is the refrain of that poem.]

[2] [The Cam, as well as many other rivers whose names are formed from the same Celtic root, derives his appellation from the tortuousness of his course. See Isaac Taylor's *Words and Places*, p. 217.]

[3] *Colin.*] The name taken by Spenser in his *Eclogues*, where his mistress is celebrated under that of Rosalinda. P. [Colin in the *Shepherd's Kalendar* generally, but not always, appears to stand for Spenser. The ingenious author of the life prefixed to Church's edition of Spenser has

Then might my voice thy list'ning ears employ,
And I those kisses he receives, enjoy.

And yet my numbers please the rural throng,
Rough Satyrs dance, and Pan applauds the song: 50
The Nymphs, forsaking ev'ry cave and spring,
Their early fruit, and milk-white turtles bring;
Each am'rous nymph prefers her gifts in vain,
On you their gifts are all bestow'd again.
For you the swains the fairest flow'rs design, 55
And in one garland all their beauties join;
Accept the wreath which you deserve alone,
In whom all beauties are compris'd in one.

See what delights in sylvan scenes appear!
Descending Gods have found Elysium here. 60
In woods bright Venus with Adonis stray'd,
And chaste Diana haunts the forest-shade.
Come, lovely nymph, and bless the silent hours,
When swains from shearing seek their nightly bow'rs,
When weary reapers quit the sultry field, 65
And crown'd with corn their thanks to Ceres yield.
This harmless grove no lurking viper hides,
But in my breast the serpent Love abides.
Here bees from blossoms sip the rosy dew,
But your Alexis knows no sweets but you. 70
Oh deign to visit our forsaken seats,
The mossy fountains, and the green retreats!
Where'er you walk, cool gales shall fan the glade;
Trees, where you sit, shall crowd into a shade;
Where'er you tread, the blushing flowers shall rise, 75
And all things flourish where you turn your eyes.[1]
Oh! how I long with you to pass my days,
Invoke the Muses, and resound your praise!
Your praise the birds shall chant in ev'ry grove,[2]
And winds shall waft it to the pow'rs above, 80
But would you sing, and rival Orpheus' strain,
The wond'ring forests soon should dance again;
The moving mountains hear the pow'rful call,
And headlong streams hang list'ning in their fall!

But see, the shepherds shun the noonday heat, 85
The lowing herds to murm'ring brooks retreat,

---

invented a Kentish lady, Miss Rose Lynde, for the original of Rosalind.]

[1] Very much like some lines in *Hudibras*, but certainly no resemblance was intended.

[2] Your praise the tuneful birds to heav'n shall bear,
And list'ning wolves grow milder as they hear.

So the verses were originally written. But the author, young as he was, soon found the absurdity which *Spenser* himself overlooked, of introducing wolves into England. P. [e.g. in *Sheph. Kal.* July.]

Where'er you tread, your feet shall set
The primrose and the violet;
Nature her charter shall renew,
And take all lives of things from you.
                            Bowles.

[The familiar original of the familiar idea is of course in *Persius* II. 38.]

To closer shades the panting flocks remove;
Ye Gods! and is there no relief for Love?
But soon the sun with milder rays descends
To the cool ocean, where his journey ends.   90
On me love's fiercer flames for ever prey,
By night he scorches, as he burns by day.

AUTUMN.[1]

THE THIRD PASTORAL,

OR

HYLAS AND ÆGON.

TO MR. WYCHERLEY.

BENEATH the shade a spreading Beech displays,
Hylas and Ægon sung their rural lays,
This mourn'd a faithless, that an absent Love,
And Delia's name and Doris' fill'd the Grove.
Ye Mantuan nymphs, your sacred succour bring;   5
Hylas and Ægon's rural lays I sing.
Thou, whom the Nine[2] with Plautus' wit inspire,
The art of Terence, and Menander's fire;[3]

---

[1] This Pastoral consists of two parts, like the viiith of Virgil: the Scene, a Hill; the Time, at Sun-set. P.

[2] *Thou, whom the Nine*] Mr. Wycherley, a famous author of comedies; of which the most celebrated were the *Plain-dealer* and *Country-Wife*. He was a writer of infinite spirit, satire, and wit. The only objection made to him was that he had too much. However he was followed in the same way by Mr. Congreve; though with a little more correctness. P.

[William Wycherley (born 1640, died 1715) was in the 64th year of his age at the time when he was thus addressed by Pope. In the following year Wycherley submitted his poems to the correction of his youthful friend; but the 'honest freedom' with which the latter exercised his office of censor, produced a coolness between the pair which prevented a renewal of friendly intercourse. The judgments of Pope's and Wycherley's biographers as to the amount of blame to be respectively attached to their heroes, vary considerably.]

[3] *The art of Terence, and Menander's fire;*] This line evidently alludes to that famous character given of Terence, by Cæsar,

Tu quoque, tu in summis, ô dimidiate Menander,

Pomeris, et merito, puri sermonis amator;
Lenibus atque utinam scriptis adjuncta foret *vis Comica*.

So that the judicious critic sees he should have said — *with Menander's fire*. For what the poet meant, in this line, was, that his friend had joined to Terence's art what Cæsar thought wanting in Terence, namely the *vis comica* of Menander. Besides, — *and Menander's fire* is making that the characteristic of Menander which was not. His character was the having art and *comic spirit* in perfect conjunction, of which Terence having only the first, he is called the *half of Menander*. *Warburton.*

Whose sense instructs us, and whose humour charms,
Whose judgment sways us, and whose spirit warms! 10
Oh, skill'd in Nature! see the hearts of Swains,
Their artless passions, and their tender pains.
  Now setting Phœbus shone serenely bright,
And fleecy clouds were streak'd with purple light;
When tuneful Hylas with melodious moan, 15
Taught rocks to weep, and made the mountains groan.
  Go, gentle gales, and bear my sighs away!
To Delia's ear, the tender notes convey.
As some sad Turtle his lost love deplores,
And with deep murmurs fills the sounding shores; 20
Thus, far from *Delia*, to the winds I mourn,
Alike unheard, unpity'd, and forlorn.
  Go, gentle gales, and bear my sighs along!
For her, the feather'd quires neglect their song;
For her, the limes their pleasing shades deny; 25
For her, the lilies hang their heads and die.
Ye flow'rs that droop, forsaken by the spring,
Ye birds that, left by summer, cease to sing,
Ye trees that fade when autumn-heats remove,
Say, is not absence death to those who love? 30
  Go, gentle gales, and bear my sighs away!
Curs'd be the fields that cause my Delia's stay;
Fade ev'ry blossom, wither ev'ry tree,
Die ev'ry flow'r, and perish all, but she.
What have I said? where'er my Delia flies, 35
Let spring attend, and sudden flow'rs arise:
Let op'ning roses knotted oaks adorn,
And liquid amber drop from ev'ry thorn.
  Go, gentle gales, and bear my sighs along!
The birds shall cease to tune their ev'ning song, 40
The winds to breathe, the waving woods to move,
And streams to murmur, e'er[1] I cease to love.
Not bubbling fountains to the thirsty swain,
Not balmy sleep to lab'rers faint with pain,
Not show'rs to larks, nor sun-shine to the bee, 45
Are half so charming as thy sight to me.
  Go, gentle gales, and bear my sighs away!
Come, Delia, come; ah, why this long delay?
Thro' rocks and caves the name of Delia sounds,
Delia, each cave and echoing rock rebounds. 50
Ye pow'rs, what pleasing frenzy sooths my mind!
Do lovers dream, or is my Delia kind?
She comes, my Delia comes!—Now cease my lay,
And cease, ye gales, to bear my sighs away!

---

[1] [Pope's spelling of *e'er*, which Warton and subsequent editors have altered into *ere*, was probably due to a reminiscence of the phrase *or e'er*, incorrectly spelt by Shakspere *or ere*, made up of *or*, a corruption of *ere* (= *ær*, before) and *e'er*, an abbreviation of *ever*.]

AUTUMN.

Next Ægon sung, while Windsor groves admir'd;   55
Rehearse, ye Muses, what yourselves inspir'd.
   Resound, ye hills, resound my mournful strain!
Of perjur'd Doris, dying I complain:
Here where the mountains less'ning as they rise
Lose the low vales, and steal into the skies: 60
While lab'ring oxen, spent with toil and heat,
In their loose traces from the field retreat:
While curling smokes from village-tops are seen,
And the fleet shades glide o'er the dusky green.
   Resound, ye hills, resound my mournful lay!   65
Beneath yon' poplar oft we past the day:
Oft' on the rind I carv'd her am'rous vows,
While she with garlands hung the bending boughs:
The garlands fade, the vows are worn away;
So dies her love, and so my hopes decay.   70
   Resound, ye hills, resound my mournful strain!
Now bright Arcturus glads the teeming grain,
Now golden fruits on loaded branches shine,
And grateful clusters[1] swell with floods of wine;
Now blushing berries paint the yellow grove;   75
Just Gods! shall all things yield returns but love?
   Resound, ye hills, resound my mournful lay!
The shepherds cry, "Thy flocks are left a prey"—
Ah! what avails it me, the flocks to keep,
Who lost my heart while I preserv'd my sheep.   80
Pan came, and ask'd, what magic caus'd my smart,
Or what ill eyes malignant glances dart?
What eyes but hers, alas, have pow'r to move!
And is there magic but what dwells in love?
   Resound, ye hills, resound my mournful strains!   85
I'll fly from shepherds, flocks, and flow'ry plains.—
From shepherds, flocks, and plains, I may remove,
Forsake mankind, and all the world—but love!
I know thee, Love! on foreign Mountains bred,
Wolves gave thee suck, and savage Tigers fed.   90
Thou wert from Ætna's burning entrails torn,
Got by fierce whirlwinds, and in thunder born!
   Resound, ye hills, resound my mournful lay!
Farewell, ye woods! adieu the light of day!
One leap from yonder cliff shall end my pains,   95
No more, ye hills, no more resound my strains!
   Thus sung the shepherds till th' approach of night,

---

[1] *And grateful clusters etc.* The scene is in Windsor-forest. So this image is not so exact. *Warburton.*
[The grapes are doubtful; but Mr. Jesse mentions, in his *Summer's Day at Windsor*, that what are now called the *Slopes*, extending into the Home Park, are in Norden's Map (1607) described as 'the Deanes Orcharde' &c.]

The skies yet blushing with departing light,[1]
When falling dews with spangles deck'd the glade,
And the low sun had lengthen'd ev'ry shade.   100

———oo᠄o᠄oo———

WINTER.[2]

THE FOURTH PASTORAL,

OR

DAPHNE.

TO THE MEMORY OF MRS. TEMPEST.[3]

LYCIDAS.

THYRSIS, the music of that murm'ring spring,
  Is not so mournful as the strains you sing.
Nor rivers winding thro' the vales below,
So sweetly warble, or so smoothly flow.
Now sleeping flocks on their soft fleeces lie,   5
The moon, serene in glory, mounts the sky,
While silent birds forget their tuneful lays,
Oh sing of Daphne's fate, and Daphne's praise!

THYRSIS.

Behold the groves that shine with silver frost,
Their beauty wither'd, and their verdure lost.   10
Here shall I try the sweet Alexis' strain,
That called the list'ning Dryads to the plain?
Thames heard the numbers as he flow'd along,
And bade his willows learn the moving song.

---

[1] There is a little inaccuracy here; the first line makes the time after sunset; the second, before. *Warburton.*

[2] This was the poet's favourite pastoral. *Warburton.*

[3] *Mrs. Tempest.*] This lady was of an ancient family in Yorkshire, and particularly admired by the author's friend Mr. Walsh, who, having celebrated her in a pastoral elegy, desired his friend to do the same, as appears from one of his letters, dated Sept. 9, 1706: 'Your last eclogue being on the same subject with mine on Mrs. Tempest's death, I should take it very kindly in you to give it a little turn as if it were to the memory of the same lady.' Her death having happened on the night of the great storm in 1703, gave a propriety to this eclogue, which in its general turn alludes to it. The scene of the pastoral lies in a grove, the time at midnight. P. [Walsh's elegy is that entitled '*Delia;*' an insignificant piece.]

LYCIDAS.

So may kind rains their vital moisture yield, 15
And swell the future harvest of the field.
Begin; this charge the dying Daphne gave,
And said; "Ye shepherds, sing around my grave!
Sing, while beside the shaded tomb I mourn,
And with fresh bays her rural shrine adorn." 20

THYRSIS.

Ye gentle Muses, leave your crystal spring,
Let Nymphs and Sylvans cypress garlands bring;
Ye weeping Loves, the stream with myrtles hide,
And break your bows, as when Adonis died;
And with your golden darts, now useless grown, 25
Inscribe a verse on this relenting stone:
"Let nature change, let heav'n and earth deplore,
Fair Daphne's dead, and love is now no more!"
'T is done, and nature's various charms decay,
See gloomy clouds obscure the cheerful day! 30
Now hung with pearls the dropping trees appear,
Their faded honours scatter'd on her bier.
See, where on earth the flow'ry glories lie,
With her they flourish'd, and with her they die.
Ah what avails the beauties nature wore? 35
Fair Daphne's dead, and beauty is no more!
For her the flocks refuse their verdant food,
Nor thirsty heifers seek the gliding flood.
The silver swans her hapless fate bemoan,
In notes more sad than when they sing their own; 40
In hollow caves sweet Echo [1] silent lies,
Silent, or only to her name replies;
Her name with pleasure once she taught the shore,
Now Daphne's dead, and pleasure is no more!
No grateful dews descend from ev'ning skies, 45
Nor morning odours from the flow'rs arise;
No rich perfumes refresh the fruitful field,
Nor fragrant herbs their native incense yield.
The balmy Zephyrs, silent since her death,
Lament the ceasing of a sweeter breath; [2] 50
Th' industrious bees neglect their golden store;
Fair Daphne's dead, and sweetness is no more!
No more the mounting larks, while Daphne sings,
Shall list'ning in mid air suspend their wings;
No more the birds shall imitate her lays, 55

---

[1] 'This expression of *sweet Echo* is taken from *Comus;* as is another expression, *loose traces*, Third Past. v. 62.' *Warton.*

[2] 'I wish that his fondness had not overlooked a line in which the zephyrs are made to lament in silence.' *Johnson.*

Or hush'd with wonder, hearken from the sprays:
No more the streams their murmur shall forbear,
A sweeter music than their own to hear,
But tell the reeds, and tell the vocal shore,
Fair Daphne's dead, and music is no more! 60
  Her fate is whisper'd by the gentle breeze,
And told in sighs to all the trembling trees;
The trembling trees, in ev'ry plain and wood,
Her fate remurmur to the silver flood;
The silver flood, so lately calm, appears 65
Swell'd with new passion, and o'erflows with tears;
The winds and trees and floods her death deplore,
Daphne, our grief! our glory now no more!
  But see! where Daphne wond'ring mounts on high
Above the clouds, above the starry sky![1] 70
Eternal beauties grace the shining scene,
Fields ever fresh, and groves for ever green!
There while you rest in Amaranthine bow'rs,
Or from those meads select unfading flow'rs,
Behold us kindly, who your name implore, 75
Daphne, our Goddess, and our grief no more!

LYCIDAS.

How all things listen, while thy Muse complains!
Such silence waits on Philomela's strains,
In some still ev'ning, when the whisp'ring breeze
Pants on the leaves, and dies upon the trees. 80
To thee, bright goddess, oft a lamb shall bleed,
If teeming ewes increase my fleecy breed.
While plants their shade, or flow'rs their odours give,
Thy name, thy honour, and thy praise shall live!

THYRSIS.

But see, Orion sheds unwholesome dews, 85
Arise, the pines a noxious shade diffuse;
Sharp Boreas blows, and Nature feels decay,
Time conquers all, and we must Time obey.
Adieu, ye vales, ye mountains, streams and groves,
Adieu, ye shepherd's rural lays and loves; 90
Adieu, my flocks, farewell ye sylvan crew,
Daphne, farewell, and all the world adieu![2]

---

[1] [Warton naturally compares the 'same beautiful change of circumstances' in Spenser's *November* (S. K.) and Milton's *Lycidas*, from line 165.]

[2] These four last lines allude to the several subjects of the four Pastorals, and to the several scenes of them, particularized before in each. P.

IMITATIONS.

SPRING.

Ver. 1.
'Prima Syracosio dignata est ludere versu,
Nostra nec erubuit sylvas habitare Thalia.'
This is the general exordium and opening of the Pastorals, in imitation of the 6th of Virgil, which some have therefore not improbably thought to have been the first originally. In the beginnings of the other three Pastorals, he imitates expressly those which now stand first of the three chief poets in this kind, Spenser, Virgil, Theocritus.
' A Shepherd's Boy (he seeks no better name) '—
' Beneath the shade a spreading beech displays,'—
'Thyrsis, the musick of that murm'ring spring,'—
are manifestly imitations of
— ' A Shepherd's Boy (no better do him call) '
—' Tityre, tu patulæ recumbans sub tegmine fagi '
—''Αδύ τι τὸ ψιθύρισμα καὶ ἁ πίτυς, αἰπόλε, τήνα.' P.

Ver. 35, 36.
' Lenta quibus torno facili superaddita vitis,
Diffusos hedera vestit pallente corymbos.'
Virg. P.

Ver. 38. *The various seasons.*] The subject of these Pastorals engraven on the bowl is not without its propriety. The shepherd's hesitation at the name of the Zodiac, imitates that in Virgil.
' Et quis fuit alter,
Descripsit radio totum qui gentibus orbem?' P.

Ver. 41. *Then sing by turns.*] Literally from Virgil,
' Alternis dicetis, amant alterna Camænæ:
Et nunc omnis ager, nunc omnis parturit arbos,
Nunc frondent sylvæ, nunc formosissimus annus.' P.

Ver. 47. *A milk-white bull.*] *Virg.*
' Pascite taurum,
Qui cornu petat, et pedibus jam spargat arenam.'

Ver. 58. *She runs, but hopes.*] Imitation of Virgil,
' Malo me Galatea petit, lasciva puella,
Et fugit ad salices, sed se cupit ante videri.' P.

Ver. 69. *All nature mourns.*] *Virg.*
' Aret ager, vitio moriens sitit aeris herba, &c.
Phyllidis adventu nostræ nemus omne virebit.' P.

Ver. 90. The two riddles are in imitation of those in Virg. *Ecl.* iii.
' Dic quibus in terris inscripti nomina Regum
Nascantur flores, et Phillida solus habeto.' P.

SUMMER.

Ver. 8. *And Jove consented.*]
' Jupiter et læto descendet plurimus imbri.'
Virg. P.

Ver. 15. *Nor to the deaf I sing.*]
' Non canimus surdis, respondent omnia sylvæ.'
Virg. P.

Ver. 23. *Where stray ye Muses, etc.*]
' Quæ nemora, aut qui vos saltus habuere, puellæ
Naiades, indigno cum Gallus amore periret?
Nam neque Parnassi vobis juga, nam neque Pindi
Ulla moram fecere, neque Aonia Aganippe.'
Virg. out of Theocr. P.

Ver. 27. Virgil again from the *Cyclops* of Theocritus,
' nuper me in littore vidi
Cum placidum ventis staret mare, non ego Daphnim,
Judice te, metuam, si nunquam fallat imago.' P.

Ver. 40. *bequeath'd in death; etc.*] Virg. *Ecl.* ii.
' Est mihi disparibus septem compacta cicutis
Fistula, Damœtas dono mihi quam dedit olim,
Et dixit moriens, te nunc habet ista secundum.'
P.

Ver. 60. *Descending gods have found Elysium here.*]
——' Habitarunt di quoque sylvas '—— *Virg.*
' Et formosus oves ad flumina pavit Adonis.'
Idem. P.

Ver. 80. *And winds shall waft, etc.*]
' Partem aliquam, venti, divum referatis ad aures!' *Virg.* P.

Ver. 88. *Ye gods! etc.*]
' Me tamen urit amor, quis enim modus adsit amori?' *Idem.* P.

AUTUMN.

Ver. 37. 'Aurea duræ
Mala ferant quercus, narcisso floreat alnus,
Pinguia corticibus sudent electra myricæ.'
Virg. *Ecl.* viii. P.

Ver. 43, *etc.*]
'Quale sopor fessis in gramine, quale per æstum
Dulcis aquæ saliente sitim restinguere rivo.'
Ecl. v. P.

Ver. 52. 'An qui amant, ipsi sibi somnia fingunt?' Virg. *Ecl.* v. P.

Ver. 82. *Or what ill eyes.*]
'Nescio quis teneros oculus mihi fascinat agnos.'
P.

Ver. 89. 'Nunc scio quid sit Amor: duris in cotibus illum,' etc. P. This from Virgil is much inferior to the passage in Theocritus, whence it is taken. *Warton.*

WINTER.

Ver. 1. *Thyrsis, the music, etc.*]
Ἁδύ τι, etc. Theocr. *Id.* i.

Ver. 13. *Thames heard, etc.*]
'Audiit Eurotas, jussitque ediscere lauros.'
Virg. P.

Ver. 23, 24, 25.
'Inducite fontibus umbras —
Et tumulum facite, et tumulo superaddite carmen.'
P.

Ver. 69, 70. 'miratur limen Olympi,
Sub pedibusque vidit nubes et sydera Daphnis.'
Virg. P.

Ver. 81.
'illius aram
Sæpe tener nostris ab ovilibus imbuet agnus.'
Virg. P.

Ver. 86. 'solet esse gravis cantantibus umbra, Juniperi gravis umbra.' Virg. P.

Ver. 88. *Time conquers all, etc.*]
'Omnia vincit amor, et nos cedamus amori.'
Vid. etiam Sannazarii Ecl. et Spenser's Calendar. *Warburton.*

MESSIAH,

A SACRED ECLOGUE.

In Imitation of VIRGIL'S POLLIO.

ADVERTISEMENT.

IN reading several passages of the Prophet Isaiah, which foretell the coming of Christ and the felicities attending it, I could not but observe a remarkable parity between many of the thoughts, and those in the Pollio of Virgil. This will not seem surprising, when we reflect, that the Eclogue was taken from a Sibylline prophecy on the same subject. One may judge that Virgil did not copy it line by line, but made use of such ideas as best agreed with the nature of pastoral poetry, and disposed them in that manner which served most to beautify his piece. I have endeavoured the same in this imitation of him, though without admitting any thing of my own; since it was written with this particular view, that the reader, by comparing the several thoughts, might see how far the images and descriptions of the Prophet are superior to those of the Poet. But as I fear I have prejudiced them by my management, I shall subjoin the passages of Isaiah, and those of Virgil, under the same disadvantage of a literal translation. P.

[Dr. Johnson, who translated this poem into Latin verse as a college exercise, in his *Life of Pope* observes, 'That the *Messiah* excels the *Pollio* is no great praise, if

MESSIAH.

it be considered from what original the improvements are derived.' Many may, however, be indisposed to agree with the assumption for which so triumphant an explanation is found in the above remark. Whilst it is by no means improbable (see Merivale's *Romans under the Empire*, ch. XXVII, referred to by Conington) that 'Virgil was acquainted with the prophetic portions of the Jewish Scriptures, if not directly, at least through the medium of the so-called Sibylline oracles,' these references are in the Roman poet after all only ornaments of an offering distinctly intended to celebrate by anticipation the birth of a Roman child. In Pope these ornaments become the subject-matter of the poem, which is thus merely the paraphrase of an authoritative prophecy on the same subject.]

YE Nymphs of Solyma![1] begin the song:
  To heav'nly themes sublimer strains belong.
The mossy fountains, and the sylvan shades,
The dreams of Pindus and th' Aonian maids,
Delight no more — O thou my voice inspire   5
Who touch'd Isaiah's hallow'd lips with fire!
  Rapt into future times, the Bard begun:
A Virgin shall conceive, a Virgin bear a Son!
From Jesse's[2] root behold a branch arise,
Whose sacred flow'r with fragrance fills the skies: 10
Th' Æthereal spirit o'er its leaves shall move,
And on its top descends the mystic Dove.
Ye Heav'ns![3] from high the dewy nectar pour,
And in soft silence shed the kindly show'r!
The sick[4] and weak the healing plant shall aid,   15
From storms a shelter, and from heat a shade.
All crimes shall cease, and ancient fraud[5] shall fail;
Returning Justice[6] lift aloft her scale;
Peace o'er the World her olive wand extend,
And white-rob'd Innocence from heav'n descend.   20
Swift fly the years, and rise th' expected morn!
Oh spring to light, auspicious Babe, be born!
See Nature hastes her earliest wreaths to bring,
With all the incense of the breathing spring:
See lofty[7] Lebanon his head advance,   25
See nodding forests on the mountains dance:
See spicy clouds from lowly Saron rise,
And Carmel's flow'ry top perfumes the skies!
Hark! a glad voice the lonely desert cheers;
Prepare the way![8] a God, a God appears: 30
A God, a God! the vocal hills reply,
The rocks proclaim th' approaching Deity.
Lo, earth receives him from the bending skies!
Sink down ye mountains, and ye valleys rise,
With heads declin'd, ye cedars homage pay;   35
Be smooth ye rocks, ye rapid floods give way!
The Saviour comes! by ancient bards foretold:

---

[1] [Hierosolyma, Jerusalem.]
[2] Isa. xi. 1.   [3] ch. xlv. 8.
[4] ch. xxv. 4.
[5] *ancient fraud* i.e. the fraud of the Serpent. Warburton.   [6] ch. ix. 7.
[7] ch. xxxv. 2.   [8] ch. xl. 3, 4.

Hear him,[1] ye deaf, and all ye blind, behold!
He from thick films shall purge the visual ray,[2]
And on the sightless eye-ball pour the day: 40
'T is he th' obstructed paths of sound shall clear,
And bid new music charm th' unfolding ear:
The dumb shall sing, the lame his crutch forego,
And leap exulting like the bounding roe.
No sigh, no murmur the wide world shall hear, 45
From ev'ry face he wipes off ev'ry tear.
In adamantine [3] chains shall Death be bound,
And Hell's grim Tyrant feel th' eternal wound.
As the good shepherd [4] tends his fleecy care,
Seeks freshest pasture and the purest air, 50
Explores the lost, the wand'ring sheep directs,
By day o'ersees them, and by night protects,
The tender lambs he raises in his arms,
Feeds from his hand, and in his bosom warms;
Thus shall mankind his guardian care engage, 55
The promis'd father [5] of the future age.
No more shall nation [6] against nation rise,
Nor ardent warriours meet with hateful eyes,
Nor fields with gleaming steel be cover'd o'er,
The brazen trumpets kindle rage no more; 60
But useless lances into scythes shall bend,
And the broad fa̍lchion in a plough-share end.
Then palaces shall rise; the joyful Son [7]
Shall finish what his short-liv'd Sire begun;
Their vines a shadow to their race shall yield, 65
And the same hand that sow'd, shall reap the field.
The swain in barren deserts [8] with surprise
See lilies spring, and sudden verdure rise;
And starts, amidst the thirsty wilds to hear
New falls of water murm'ring in his ear. 70
On rifted rocks, the dragon's late abodes,
The green reed trembles, and the bulrush nods.
Waste sandy valleys,[9] once perplex'd with thorn,
The spiry fir and shapely box adorn:
To leafless shrubs the flow'ring palms succeed, 75
And od'rous myrtle to the noisome weed.
The lambs [10] with wolves shall graze the verdant mead,
And boys in flow'ry bands the tiger lead;
The steer and lion at one crib shall meet,
And harmless serpents [11] lick the pilgrim's feet. 80
The smiling infant in his hand shall take
The crested basilisk and speckled snake,

[1] ch. xlii. 18; xxxv. 5, 6.
[2] *He from thick films shall purge the visual ray,*] The sense and language shew, that, by *visual ray*, the poet meant the *sight*, or, as Milton calls it, *the visual nerve. Warburton.*
[3] ch. xxv. 8.
[4] ch. xl. 11.
[5] ch. ix. 6.
[6] ch. ii. 4.
[7] ch. lxv. 21, 22.
[8] ch. xxxv. 1, 7.
[9] ch. xli. 19; lv. 13.
[10] ch. xi. 6, 7, 1.
[11] ch. lxv. 25.

Pleas'd the green lustre of the scales survey,
And with their forky tongues shall innocently play.
Rise, crown'd with light, imperial Salem,[1] rise! 85
Exalt thy tow'ry head, and lift thy eyes!
See, a long race [2] thy spacious courts adorn;
See future sons, and daughters yet unborn,
In crowding ranks on ev'ry side arise,
Demanding life, impatient for the skies! 90
See barb'rous nations [3] at thy gates attend,
Walk in thy light, and in thy temple bend;
See thy bright altars throng'd with prostrate kings,
And heap'd with products of Sabæan [4] springs!
For thee Idume's spicy forests blow, 95
And seeds of gold in Ophir's mountains glow.
See heav'n its sparkling portals wide display,
And break upon thee in a flood of day!
No more the rising Sun [5] shall gild the morn,
Nor ev'ning Cynthia fill her silver horn; 100
But lost, dissolv'd in thy superior rays,
One tide of glory, one unclouded blaze
O'erflow thy courts: the light himself shall shine
Reveal'd, and God's eternal day be thine!
The seas [6] shall waste, the skies in smoke decay, 105
Rocks fall to dust, and mountains melt away;
But fix'd his word, his saving pow'r remains; —
Thy realm for ever lasts, thy own MESSIAH reigns!

[1] ch. lx. 1. [3] ch. lx. 3. [5] ch. lx. 19, 20.
[2] ch. lx. 4. [4] ch. lx. 6. [6] ch. li. 6; liv. 10.

IMITATIONS.

Ver. 8. *A virgin shall conceive — All crimes shall cease, etc.*]
Virg. E. iv. 6.
'Jam redit et Virgo, redeunt Saturnia regna;
Jam nova progenies cælo demittitur alto.
Te duce, si qua manent sceleris vestigia nostri,
Irrita perpetua solvent formidine terras —
Pacatumque reget patriis virtutibus orbem.'

'Now the virgin returns, now the kingdom of Saturn returns, now a new progeny is sent down from high heaven. By means of thee, whatever reliques of our crimes remain, shall be wiped away, and free the world from perpetual fears. He shall govern the earth in peace, with the virtues of his father.'

Isaiah, ch. vii. 14. — 'Behold a virgin shall conceive and bear a son.' Ch. ix. v. 6, 7. —
'Unto us a child is born, unto us a Son is given; the Prince of Peace: of the increase of his government, and of his peace, there shall be no end: Upon the throne of David, and upon his kingdom, to order and to establish it, with judgment, and with justice, for ever and ever.' P.

Ver. 23. *See Nature hastes, etc.*]
Virg. E. iv. 18.
'At tibi prima, puer, nullo munuscula cultu,
Errantes hederas passim cum baccare tellus,
Mixtaque ridenti colocasia fundet acantho —
Ipsa tibi blandos fundent cunabula flores.'

'For thee, O child, shall the earth, without being tilled, produce her early offerings; winding ivy, mixed with Baccar, and Colocasia with smiling Acanthus. Thy cradle shall pour forth pleasing flowers about thee.'

Isaiah, ch. xxxv. 1.—'The wilderness and the solitary place shall be glad, and the desart shall rejoice and blossom as the rose.' Ch. lx. 13.—'The glory of Lebanon shall come unto thee, the fir-tree, the pine-tree, and the box together, to beautify the place of thy sanctuary.' P.

Ver. 29. *Hark! a glad voice, etc.*]
Virg. *E.* iv. v. 46.

'Aggredere o magnos, aderit jam tempus, honores,
Cara deum soboles, magnum Jovis incrementum—
Ipsi lætitia voces ad sydera jactant
Intonsi montes, ipsæ jam carmina rupes,
Ipsa sonant arbusta, Deus, deus ille Menalca!'
                                        E. v. v. 62.
'Oh come and receive the mighty honours: the time draws nigh, O beloved offspring of the gods, O great encrease of Jove! The uncultivated mountains send shouts of joy to the stars, the very rocks sing in verse, the very shrubs cry out, A god, a god!'

Isaiah, ch. xl. 3, 4.—'The voice of him that crieth in the wilderness, Prepare ye the way of the Lord! make strait in the desart a high way for our God! Every valley shall be exalted, and every mountain and hill shall be made low, and the crooked shall be made strait, and the rough places plain.' Ch. xliv. 23.—'Break forth into singing, ye mountains! O forest, and every tree therein! for the Lord hath redeemed Israel.' P.

Ver. 67. *The swain in barren deserts, etc.*]

Virg. *E.* iv. v. 28.

'Molli paulatim flavescet campus arista,
Incultisque rubens pendebit sentibus uva,
Et duræ quercus sudabunt roscida mella.'

'The fields shall grow yellow with ripen'd ears, and the red grape shall hang upon the wild brambles, and the hard oaks shall distill honey like dew.'

Isaiah, ch. xxxv. 7.—'The parched ground shall become a pool, and the thirsty land springs of water: In the habitations where dragons lay, shall be grass, and reeds, and rushes.' Ch. lv. 13.—'Instead of the thorn shall come up the fir-tree, and instead of the briar shall come up the myrtle-tree.' P.

Ver. 77. *The lambs with wolves, etc.*]
Virg. *E.* iv. v. 21.

'Ipsæ lacte domum referent distenta capellæ
Ubera, nec magnos metuent armenta leones—
Occidet et serpens, et fallax herba veneni
Occidet.'—

'The goats shall bear to the fold their udders distended with milk; nor shall the herds be afraid of the greatest lions. The serpent shall die, and the herb that conceals poison shall die.'

Isaiah, ch. xi. 6, etc.—'The wolf shall dwell with the lamb, and the leopard shall lie down with the kid, and the calf and the young lion and the fatling together: and a little child shall lead them.—And the lion shall eat straw like the ox. And the sucking child shall play on the hole of the asp, and the weaned child shall put his hand on the den of the cockatrice.' P.

Ver. 85. *Rise, crown'd with light, imperial Salem, rise!*] The thoughts of Isaiah, which compose the latter part of the poem, are wonderfully elevated, and much above those general exclamations of Virgil, which make the loftiest parts of his *Pollio*:

'Magnus ab integro sæclorum nascitur ordo!
— toto surget gens aurea mundo!
— incipient magni procedere menses!
Aspice, venturo lætentur ut omnia sæclo!' etc.

The reader needs only to turn to the passages of Isaiah, here cited. P. [Cited at bottom of text.]

WINDSOR FOREST.

To the Right Honourable George, Lord Lansdown.[1]

Non injussa cano: Te nostræ, *Vare*, myricæ,
Te *Nemus* omne canet; nec Phœbo gratior ulla est
Quam sibi quæ *Vari* præscripsit pagina nomen. Virg. [*Ecl.* vi. 10-12.]

[The design of this poem is universally allowed to have been derived from Denham's *Cooper's Hill*, the first specimen in English literature of what Johnson denominates 'local poetry.' As a descriptive poem, *Windsor Forest* has the merits both of dignity

[1] [See note to p. 12.]

and of variety; though the sense of the picturesque is a discovery which had dawned neither upon the age nor upon the individual genius of Pope. Perhaps the most ambitious passage, in which the river Thames is introduced and personified, is only a weak imitation of greater models. As proceeding from an inhabitant of the immediate neighbourhood of Windsor Castle, the treatment of the historical associations connected with it is remarkably loose and incomplete. Otway's *Windsor Castle*, though in execution infinitely inferior to Pope's, is superior to the latter in the unity of its conception, which is that of a threnody on the recent death of Charles II., naturally suggested by the royal abode.]

This poem was written at two different times: the first part of it, which relates to the country, in the year 1704, at the same time with the Pastorals: the latter part was not added till the year 1713, in which it was published. P. [The division is at line 289.]

    THY forests, Windsor! and thy green retreats,
       At once the Monarch's and the Muse's seats,
Invite my lays. Be present, sylvan maids!
Unlock your springs, and open all your shades.
GRANVILLE commands; your aid, O Muses, bring!   5
What Muse for GRANVILLE can refuse to sing?
    The Groves of Eden, vanish'd now so long,
Live in description, and look green in song:
These, were my breast inspir'd with equal flame,
Like them in beauty, should be like in fame.   10
Here hills and vales, the woodland and the plain,
Here earth and water seem to strive again;
Not Chaos-like together crush'd and bruis'd,
But, as the world, harmoniously confus'd:
Where order in variety we see,   15
And where, tho' all things differ, all agree.
Here waving groves a chequer'd scene display,
And part admit, and part exclude the day;
As some coy nymph her lover's warm address
Nor quite indulges, nor can quite repress.   20
There, interspers'd in lawns and op'ning glades,
Thin trees arise that shun each other's shades.
Here in full light the russet plains extend:
There wrapt in clouds the blueish [1] hills ascend.
Ev'n the wild heath displays her purple dyes,   25
   And 'midst the desert fruitful fields arise,
That crown'd with tufted trees and springing corn,
Like verdant isles the sable waste adorn.
Let India boast her plants, nor envy we
The weeping amber or the balmy tree,   30
While by our oaks the precious loads are born,
And realms commanded which those trees adorn
Not proud Olympus [2] yields a nobler sight,

---

[1] *blueish*. [The word has the authority of both Shakspere and Dryden.]

[2] *Not proud Olympus, etc.*] Sir J. Denham, in his *Cooper's Hill*, had said,

'Than which a nobler weight no mountain bears,
But Atlas only, which supports the spheres.'

The comparison is childish, for the story of Atlas being fabulous, leaves no room for a compliment. *Warburton.*

Tho' Gods assembled grace his tow'ring height,
Than what more humble mountains offer here,
Where, in their blessings, all those Gods appear.
See Pan with flocks, with fruits Pomona crown'd,
Here blushing Flora paints th' enamel'd ground,[1]
Here Ceres' gifts in waving prospect stand,
And nodding tempt the joyful reaper's hand;
Rich Industry sits smiling on the plains,
And peace and plenty tell, a STUART reigns.
  Not thus the land appear'd in ages past,
A dreamy desert, and a gloomy waste,
To savage beasts and savage laws[2] a prey,
And kings more furious and severe than they;
Who claim'd the skies, dispeopled air and floods,
The lonely lords of empty wilds and woods:
Cities laid waste, they storm'd the dens and caves,
(For wiser brutes were backward to be slaves:)
What could be free, when lawless beasts obey'd,
And ev'n the elements a tyrant sway'd?
In vain kind seasons swell'd the teeming grain,
Soft show'rs distill'd, and suns grew warm in vain;
The swain with tears his fustrate labour yields,
And famish'd dies amidst his ripen'd fields.
What wonder then, a beast or subject slain
Were equal crimes in a despotic reign?
Both doom'd alike, for sportive Tyrants bled,
But while the subject starv'd, the beast was fed.
Proud Nimrod first the bloody chase began,
A mighty hunter, and his prey was man:
Our haughty Norman boasts that barb'rous name,
And makes his trembling slaves the royal game.
The fields are ravish'd[3] from th' industrious swains,
From men their cities, and from Gods their fanes:
The levell'd towns with weeds lie cover'd o'er;
The hollow winds thro' naked temples roar;
Round broken columns clasping ivy twin'd;
O'er heaps of ruin stalk'd the stately hind;
The fox obscene to gaping tombs retires,
And savage howlings fill the sacred quires.
Aw'd by his Nobles, by his Commons curst,
Th' Oppressor rul'd tyrannic where he durst,
Stretch'd o'er the Poor and Church his iron rod,
And serv'd alike his Vassals and his God.

---

[1] [A tautology.]

[2] [The Forest Laws. 'Amabat rex,' says the Saxon chronicle quoted by Thierry, 'ferus feras tanquam esset pater earum.']

[The allusion, after a compliment to the Stuarts, to laws which a Stuart attempted in part to revive, is unintentionally infelicitous.]

[3] *The fields are ravish'd, etc.*] Alluding to the destruction made in the New Forest, and the tyrannies exercised there by William I. P. [Warton and Bowles have sufficiently pointed out the exaggerated character of this description.]

Whom ev'n the Saxon spar'd the bloody Dane,
The wanton victims of his sport remain.
But see, the man who spacious regions gave
A waste for beasts, himself deny'd a grave![1]   80
Stretch'd on the lawn his second hope[2] survey,
At once the chaser, and at once the prey:
Lo Rufus, tugging at the deadly dart,
Bleeds in the Forest[3] like a wound'd hart.
Succeeding monarchs heard the subjects' cries,   85
Nor saw displeas'd the peaceful cottage rise.
Then gath'ring flocks on unknown mountains fed,
O'er sandy wilds were yellow harvests spread,
The forests wonder'd at th' unusual grain,
And secret transport touch'd the conscious swain.   90
Fair Liberty, Britannia's Goddess, rears
Her cheerful head, and leads the golden years.

   Ye vig'rous swains! while youth ferments your blood,
And purer spirits swell the sprightly flood,
Now range the hills, the gameful woods beset,   95
Wind the shrill horn, or spread the waving net.
When milder autumn summer's heat succeeds,
And in the new-shorn field the partridge feeds,
Before his lord the ready spaniel bounds,
Panting with hope, he tries the furrow'd grounds;   100
But when the tainted gales the game betray,
Couch'd close he lies, and meditates the prey:
Secure they trust th' unfaithful field beset,
'Till hov'ring o'er 'em sweeps the swelling net.
Thus (if small things we may with great compare)   105
When Albion sends her eager sons to war,
Some thoughtless Town, with ease and plenty blest,
Near, and more near, the closing lines invest;
Sudden they seize th' amaz'd, defenceless prize,
And high in air Britannia's standard flies.[4]   110
   See! from the brake the whirring pheasant springs,
And mounts exulting on triumphant wings:
Short is his joy; he feels the fiery wound,
Flutters in blood, and panting beats the ground.
Ah! what avail his glossy, varying dyes,   115
His purple crest, and scarlet-circled eyes,

---

[1] *himself deny'd a grave!*] The place of his interment at Caen in Normandy was claimed by a gentleman as his inheritance, the moment his servants were going to put him in his tomb: so that they were obliged to compound with the owner before they could perform the king's obsequies. *Warburton.*

[The gentleman's name was Asselin; and the story, with additional details, is told from Ordericus Vitalis by Thierry.]

[2] [Richard duke of Bernay, said to have been killed by a stag in the New Forest.]

[3] The oak under which Rufus was shot was standing till within a few years. *Bowles.* (1806.)

[4] [The allusion may be to the capture of Gibraltar, easily effected by Rooke with his sailors and marines in the year (1704) in which the earlier part of this poem was written.]

The vivid green his shining plumes unfold,
His painted wings, and breast that flames with gold?
  Nor yet, when moist Arcturus clouds the sky,
The woods and fields their pleasing toils deny. 120
To plains with well-breath'd [1] beagles we repair,
And trace the mazes of the circling hare:
(Beasts, urg'd by us, their fellow-beasts pursue,
And learn of man each other to undo).
With slaught'ring guns th' unwearied fowler roves, 125
When frosts have whiten'd all the naked groves;
Where doves in flocks the leafless trees o'ershade,
And lonely woodcocks haunt the wat'ry glade.
He lifts the tube, and levels with his eye;
Straight a short thunder breaks the frozen sky: 130
Oft, as in airy rings they skim the heath,
The clam'rous lapwings feel the leaden death:
Oft, as the mounting larks their notes prepare,
They fall, and leave their little lives in air.
  In genial spring, beneath the quivering shade, 135
Where cooling vapours breathe along the mead,
The patient fisher takes his silent stand,
Intent, his angle trembling in his hand:
With looks unmov'd, he hopes the scaly breed,
And eyes the dancing cork, and bending reed. 140
Our plenteous streams a various race supply,
The bright-ey'd perch with fins of Tyrian dye.
The silver eel, in shining volumes roll'd,
The yellow carp, in scales bedropp'd with gold,
Swift trouts, diversified with crimson stains, 145
And pikes, the tyrants of the wat'ry plains.
  Now Cancer glows with Phœbus' fiery car:
The youth rush eager to the sylvan war,
Swarm o'er the lawns, the forest walks surround,
Rouse the fleet hart, and cheer the opening hound. 150
Th' impatient courser pants in every vein,
And, pawing, seems to beat the distant plain:
Hills, vales, and floods appear already cross'd,
And ere he starts, a thousand steps are lost.
See the bold youth strain up the threat'ning steep, 155
Rush thro' the thickets, down the valleys sweep,
Hang o'er their coursers' heads with eager speed,
And earth rolls back beneath the flying steed.
Let old Arcadia boast her ample plain,
Th' immortal huntress, and her virgin train; 160
Nor envy, Windsor! since thy shades have seen
As bright a Goddess, and as chaste a Queen; [2]

---

[1] [i.e. well-exercised, cf. ' ' breathed stags.' Shaksp. *Taming of the Shrew*, Intr.]
[2] Queen Anne.
[A statue of this sovereign still standing at Windsor has an inscription conveying the same measured compliment:
    Annæ vis similem sculpere? Sculpe *Deam*.]

Whose care, like hers, protects the sylvan reign,
The Earth's fair light, and Empress of the main.
  Here too, 't is sung, of old Diana stray'd,   165
And Cynthus' top forsook for Windsor shade:
Here was she seen o'er airy wastes to rove,
Seek the clear spring, or haunt the pathless grove;
Here arm'd with silver bows, in early dawn,
Her buskin'd Virgins trac'd the dewy lawn.   170
  Above the rest a rural nymph was fam'd,
Thy offspring, Thames! the fair Lodona nam'd;
(Lodona's fate, in long oblivion cast,
The Muse shall sing, and what she sings shall last).
Scarce could the Goddess from her nymph be known,   175
But by the crescent and the golden zone.
She scorn'd the praise of beauty, and the care;
A belt her waist, a fillet binds her hair;
A painted quiver on her shoulder sounds,
And with her dart the flying deer she wounds.   180
It chanc'd, as eager of the chase, the maid
Beyond the forest's verdant limits stray'd,
Pan saw and lov'd, and, burning with desire,
Pursued her flight; her flight increas'd his fire.
Not half so swift the trembling doves can fly,   185
When the fierce eagle cleaves the liquid sky;
Not half so swiftly the fierce eagle moves,
When thro' the clouds he drives the trembling doves;
As from the god she flew with furious pace,
Or as the god, more furious, urg'd the chase.   190
Now fainting, sinking, pale, the nymph appears;
Now close behind, his sounding steps she hears;
And now his shadow reach'd her as she run,
His shadow lengthen'd by the setting sun;
And now his shorter breath, with sultry air,   195
Pants on her neck, and fans her parting hair.
In vain on father Thames she calls for aid,
Nor could Diana help her injur'd maid.
Faint, breathless, thus she pray'd, nor pray'd in vain;
"Ah, Cynthia! ah—tho' banish'd from thy train,   200
Let me, O let me, to the shades repair,
My native shades—there weep, and murmur there."
She said, and melting as in tears she lay,
In a soft, silver stream dissolv'd away.
The silver stream her virgin coldness keeps,   205
For ever murmurs, and for ever weeps;
Still bears the name [1] the hapless virgin bore,
And bathes the forest where she rang'd before.
In her chaste current oft the goddess laves,
And with celestial tears augments the waves.   210

---

[1] *Still bears the name*] The river Loddon. *Warburton.*

Oft in her glass[1] the musing shepherd spies
The headlong mountains and the downward skies,
The wat'ry landscape of the pendant woods,
And absent trees that tremble in the floods;
In the clear azure gleam the flocks are seen,   215
And floating forests paint the waves with green,
Thro' the fair scene roll slow the lingering streams,
Then foaming pour along, and rush into the Thames.
  Thou, too, great father of the British floods!
With joyful pride survey'st our lofty woods;   220
Where tow'ring oaks their growing honours rear,
And future navies on thy shores appear.
Not Neptune's self from all her streams receives
A wealthier tribute than to thine he gives.
No seas so rich, so gay no banks appear,   225
No lake so gentle, and no spring so clear.
Nor Po so swells the fabling Poet's lays,
While led along the skies his current strays,
As thine, which visits Windsor's fam'd abodes,
To grace the mansion of our earthly Gods: 230
Nor all his stars above a lustre show,
Like the bright Beauties on thy banks below,
Where Jove, subdued by mortal Passion still,
Might change Olympus for a nobler hill.
  Happy the man whom this bright court approves,   235
His Sov'reign favours, and his Country loves:
Happy next him, who to these shades retires,
Whom Nature charms, and whom the Muse inspires:
Whom humbler joys of home-felt quiet please,
Successive study, exercise, and ease.   240
He gathers health from herbs the forest yields,
And of their fragrant physic spoils the fields:
With chymic art exalts the min'ral pow'rs,
And draws the aromatic souls of flow'rs:
Now marks the course of rolling orbs on high;   245
O'er figur'd worlds now travels with his eye;
Of ancient writ unlocks the learned store,
Consults the dead, and lives past ages o'er:
Or wand'ring thoughtful in the silent wood,
Attends the duties of the wise and good,   250
T' observe a mean, be to himself a friend,
To follow nature, and regard his end;
Or looks on heav'n with more than mortal eyes,
Bids his free soul expatiate in the skies,
Amid her kindred stars familiar roam,   255
Survey the region, and confess her home!
Such was the life great Scipio once admir'd:—

---

[1] *Oft in her glass, etc.*] These six lines were added after the first writing of this poem. P.

WINDSOR FOREST.

Thus Atticus, and Trumbal thus retir'd.[1]
Ye sacred Nine! that all my soul possess,
Whose raptures fire me, and whose visions bless, 260
Bear me, O bear me to sequester'd scenes,
The bow'ry mazes, and surrounding greens:
To Thames's banks, which fragrant breezes fill,
Or where ye Muses sport on Cooper's Hill.
(On Cooper's Hill eternal wreaths shall grow, 265
While lasts the mountain, or while Thames shall flow.)
I seem thro' consecrated walks to rove,
I hear soft music die along the grove.
Led by the sound, I roam from shade to shade,
By god-like Poets venerable made: 270
Here his first lays majestic Denham sung;[2]
There the last numbers flow'd from Cowley's tongue.[3]
Oh early lost! what tears the river shed,
When the sad pomp along his banks was led?
His drooping swans on every note expire, 275
And on his willows hung each muse's lyre.
    Since fate relentless stopp'd their heavenly voice,
No more the forests ring, or groves rejoice;
Who now shall charm the shades where Cowley strung
His living harp, and lofty Denham sung? 280
But hark! the groves rejoice, the forest rings!
Are these reviv'd? or is it Granville sings?[4]
'T is yours, my Lord, to bless our soft retreats,
And call the Muses to their ancient seats;
To paint anew the flow'ry sylvan scenes, 285
To crown the forests with immortal greens,
Make Windsor-hills in lofty numbers rise,
And lift her turrets nearer to the skies;
To sing those honours you deserve to wear,
And add new lustre to her silver star![5] 290
    Here noble Surrey felt the sacred rage,
Surrey, the Granville of a former age:
Matchless his pen, victorious was his lance,
Bold in the lists, and graceful in the dance:
In the same shades the Cupids tun'd his lyre,[6] 295

---

[1] [The parallel between Scipio and Sir William Trumball is complete; for the retirement of neither was voluntary.]

[2] [Sir John Denham was born in 1615 and died in 1688; and was buried by the side of Cowley.]

[3] *There the last numbers flow'd from Cowley's tongue.*] Mr. Cowley died at Chertsey, on the borders of the Forest, and was from thence conveyed to Westminster. P.
[Born 1618, died 1667.]

[4] [See note to p. 2.]

[5] *Her silver star!*] All the lines that follow were not added to the poem till the year 1710.

What immediately followed this, and made the conclusion, were these,
    My humble muse in unambitious strains, &c. P.

[6] *Here noble Surrey*] Henry Howard, Earl of Surrey, one of the first refiners of the English poetry; who flourished in the time of Henry VIII. P.
[Born in 1517; died 1547. In the famous sonnet in 'Description and Praise of his love Geraldine' he sings that 'Windsor, alas! doth chase me from her sight.' All the conjectures concerning the lady are based upon this sonnet.]

To the same notes, of love, and soft desire:
Fair Geraldine, bright object of his vow,
Then fill'd the groves, as heav'nly Mira now.[1]
  Oh wouldst thou sing what heroes Windsor bore,
What Kings first breath'd upon her winding shore, 300
Or raise old warriors, whose ador'd remains
In weeping vaults her hallow'd earth contains!
With Edward's acts[2] adorn the shining page,
Stretch his long triumphs down through every age,
Draw monarchs chain'd, and Cressi's glorious field, 305
The lilies blazing on the regal shield:
Then, from her roofs when Verrio's colours fall,
And leave inanimate the naked wall;[3]
Still in thy song should vanquish'd France appear,
And bleed for ever under Britain's spear. 310
  Let softer strains ill-fated Henry mourn,[4]
And palms eternal flourish round his urn.
Here o'er the martyr-king the marble weeps,
And, fast beside him, once-fear'd Edward sleeps:[5]
Whom not th' extended Albion could contain, 315
From old Belerium[6] to the northern main,
The grave unites; where e'en the great find rest,
And blended lie th' oppressor and th' opprest!
  Make sacred Charles's tomb for ever known[7]
(Obscure the place, and uninscrib'd the stone), 320
Oh fact accurst! what tears has Albion shed,
Heav'ns, what new wounds! and how her old have bled!
She saw her sons with purple deaths expire,
Her sacred domes involv'd in rolling fire,
A dreadful series of intestine wars, 325
Inglorious triumphs and dishonest scars.
At length great Anna said, "Let Discord cease!"
She said! the world obey'd, and all was Peace!
  In that blest moment from his oozy bed
Old father Thames advanc'd his reverend head. 330
His tresses dropp'd with dews, and o'er the stream

---

[1] The Mira of Granville was the countess of Newburgh. Towards the end of her life Dr. King, of Oxford, wrote a very severe satire against her, in three books, 4to, called 'The Toast.' *Warton.*

[2] *Edward's acts*] Edward III. born here. P.

[In the year 1312. It was in 1340 that he first quartered the arms of France with his own.]
I have sometimes wondered that Pope did not mention the building of Windsor Castle by Edward III. His architect was William of Wykeham. *Warton.*

[3] [Verrio's ceilings, enumerated at length in Jesse's *Eton and Windsor*, pp. 51, 2, are severely criticised by Horace Walpole. See Bowles *ad loc.* They were painted temp. Carol. II.]

[4] *Henry mourn*] Henry VI. P.

[5] *once-fear'd Edward sleeps:*] Edward IV. P.

[Both are buried in St. George's chapel.]

[6] *Belerium.* [The Land's End.]

[7] [The grave of Charles I., of which, owing to the confusion which had attended his interment, the locality was unknown at the Restoration, though one of the witnesses, Mr. Herbert, declared himself certain as to its precise situation, was discovered in 1813 in the locality indicated. See Sir Henry Halford's account, quoted by Jesse, *u.s.*]

WINDSOR CASTLE FROM THE RIVER

WINDSOR FOREST.

His shining horns diffus'd a golden gleam:
Grav'd on his urn appear'd the moon, that guides
His swelling waters and alternate tides;
The figur'd streams in waves of silver roll'd,   335
And on their banks Augusta rose in gold.
Around his throne the sea-born brothers stood,
Who swell with tributary urns his flood;
First the fam'd authors of his ancient name,[1]
The winding Isis, and the fruitful Thame: 340
The Kennet swift, for silver eels renown'd;
The Loddon slow, with verdant alders crown'd;
Cole, whose dark streams his flowery island lave;
And chalky Wey, that rolls a milky wave:
The blue, transparent Vandalis appears;   345
The gulfy Lee his sedgy tresses rears;
And sullen Mole, that hides his diving flood;[2]
And silent Darent, stain'd with Danish blood.[3]

High in the midst, upon his urn reclin'd
(His sea-green mantle waving with the wind),   350
The god appear'd: he turn'd his azure eyes
Where Windsor-domes and pompous turrets rise;
Then bow'd and spoke; the winds forget to roar,
And the hush'd waves glide softly to the shore.

Hail, sacred peace! hail, long-expected days,[4]   355
That Thames's glory to the stars shall raise!
Tho' Tiber's streams immortal Rome behold,
Tho' foaming Hermus swells with tides of gold,
From heav'n itself though sev'nfold Nilus flows,
And harvests on a hundred realms bestows;   360
These now no more shall be the Muse's themes,
Lost in my fame, as in the sea their streams.
Let Volga's banks with iron squadrons shine,
And groves of lances glitter on the Rhine,
Let barb'rous Ganges arm a servile train;   365
Be mine the blessings of a peaceful reign.
No more my sons shall dye with British blood
Red Iber's sands, or Ister's foaming flood:
Safe on my shore each unmolested swain
Shall tend the flocks, or reap the bearded grain; 370
The shady empire shall retain no trace

---

[1] He has copied, and equalled, the Rivers of Spenser, Drayton and Milton. *Warton.* [viz. in the *Faërie Queen*, bk. iv. canto xi, the *Polyolbion*, and the *Vacation exercise anno ætatis xix.*]

[2] The Mole sinks through its sands, in dry summers, into an invisible channel under ground at Mickleham, near Dorking, Surrey. *Bowles.*

[3] [Not Danish, but Saxon. The Britons under Vortimer the son of Vortigern are said to have repulsed the Saxon invaders on the Darent.]

[4] [The allusions are of course to the expected peace, for which the conferences were opened in January 1711 at Utrecht; to the previous campaigns in Spain and Germany; to the war between Peter the Great and Charles XII.; and to the early difficulties of our East India settlements.]

Of war or blood, but in the sylvan chase;
The trumpet sleep, while cheerful horns are blown,
And arms employ'd on birds and beasts alone.
Behold! th' ascending Villas on my side 375
Project long shadows o'er the crystal tide.
Behold! Augusta's glitt'ring spires increase,
And Temples rise,[1] the beauteous works of Peace.
I see, I see, where two fair cities bend
Their ample bow, a new Whitehall ascend![2] 380
There mighty Nations shall inquire their doom,
The World's great Oracle in times to come;
There Kings shall sue, and suppliant States be seen
Once more to bend before a BRITISH QUEEN.
Thy trees, fair Windsor! now shall leave their woods, 385
And half thy forests rush into thy floods,
Bear Britain's thunder, and her Cross display,
To the bright regions of the rising day;
Tempt icy seas, where scarce the waters roll,
Where clearer flames glow round the frozen Pole: 390
Or under southern skies exalt their sails,
Led by new stars, and borne by spicy gales!
For me the balm shall bleed, and amber flow,
The coral redden, and the ruby glow,
The pearly shell its lucid globe infold, 395
And Phœbus warm the ripening ore to gold.
The time shall come, when, free as seas or wind,
Unbounded Thames[3] shall flow for all mankind,
Whole nations enter with each swelling tide,
And seas but join the regions they divide; 400
Earth's distant ends our glory shall behold,
And the new world launch forth to seek the old.
Then ships of uncouth form shall stem the tide,
And feather'd people crowd my wealthy side,
And naked youths and painted chiefs admire 405
Our speech, our colour, and our strange attire!
O stretch thy reign, fair Peace! from shore to shore,
Till Conquest cease, and Slav'ry be no more;
Till the freed Indians in their native groves
Reap their own fruits, and woo their sable loves, 410
Peru once more a race of kings behold,
And other Mexico's be roof'd with gold.
Exil'd by thee from earth to deepest hell,
In brazen bonds shall barbarous Discord dwell;
Gigantic Pride, pale Terror, gloomy Care, 415
And mad Ambition, shall attend her there:
There purple Vengeance bath'd in gore retires,

---

[1] *And temples rise,*] The fifty new churches.   [2] [Designs for a new palace of Whitehall had
P.   been commenced by Inigo Jones.]

[3] *Unbounded Thames, etc.*] A wish that London may be made a free port. P.

Her weapons blunted, and extinct her fires:
There hateful Envy her own snakes shall feel,
And Persecution mourn her broken wheel: 420
There Faction roar, Rebellion bite her chain,
And gasping Furies thirst for blood in vain.
Here cease thy flight, nor with unhallow'd lays
Touch the fair fame of Albion's golden days:
The thoughts of gods let Granville's verse recite,   425
And bring the scenes of op'ning fate to light.
My humble Muse, in unambitious strains,
Paints the green forests and the flow'ry plains,
Where Peace descending bids her olives spring,
And scatters blessings from her dovelike wing.   430
Ev'n I more sweetly pass my careless days,
Pleas'd in the silent shade with empty praise;
Enough for me, that to the list'ning swains
First in these fields I sung the sylvan strains.

IMITATIONS.

Ver. 6. 'neget quis carmina Gallo?' *Virg. Warburton.*

Ver. 65. The fields were ravish'd from th' industrious swains, From men their cities, and from Gods their fanes:]
Translated from,
' Templa adimit divis, fora civibus, arva colonis,'
an old monkish writer, I forget who. P.

Ver. 89. ' Miraturque novas frondes et non sua poma.' *Virg. Warburton.*

Ver. 134. ' Præcipites alta vitam sub nube relinquunt.' *Virg. Warburton.*

Ver. 151. *Th' impatient courser, etc.*] Translated from Statius,
' Stare adeo miserum est, pereunt vestigia mille
Ante fugam, absentemque ferit gravis ungula campum.'
These lines Mr. Dryden, in his preface to his translation of Fresnoy's Art of Painting, calls *wonderfully fine*, and says *they would cost him an hour, if he had the leisure to translate them, there is so much of beauty in the original;* which was the reason, I suppose, why Mr. P. tried his strength with them. *Warburton.*

Ver. 158. *and earth rolls back*] He has improved his original,
' terræque urbesque recedunt.'
Virg. Warburton.

Ver. 183, 186.
'Ut fugere accipitrem penna trepidante columbæ,
Ut solet accipiter trepidas agitare columbas.'
Ovid. Warburton.

Ver. 191, 194.
' Sol erat a tergo: vidi præcedere longam
Ante pedes umbram: nisi si timor illa videbat.
Sed certe sonituque pedum terrebar; et ingens
Crinales vittas afflabat anhelitus oris.'
Most of the circumstances in this tale are taken from Ovid. *Warton.*

Ver. 249, 50.
    Servare modum finemque tenere.
    Naturamque sequi.' *Luc.*

Ver. 259. ' O qui me gelidis, etc.'
Virg. Warburton.

Ver. 421.
' Quo, Musa, tendis ? desine pervicax
    Referre sermones Deorum et
    Magna modis tenuare parvis.'
Hor. Warburton.

ODE ON ST. CECILIA'S DAY,

MDCCVIII.

AND OTHER PIECES FOR MUSIC.

ODE FOR MUSIC ON ST. CECILIA'S DAY.

[This famous Ode, written by Pope in the year 1708 at Steele's desire, in praise of an art 'of the principles of which he was ignorant, while to its effects he was insensible,' has been naturally compared by successive generations of critics to Dryden's master-piece on the same subject. A superiority which few will be disposed to deny has been generally claimed for *Alexander's Feast;* but it may be questioned whether in this class of poetry either the choice of historical instead of mythological illustrations, or the unity of the action represented, is to be regarded as an absolute merit. A more tenable objection to Pope's Ode is the circumstance that in his endeavour to vary expressively the versification, he has in Stanza IV. and in the second part of Stanza V. permitted himself the use of metres which mar the dignity of the poem.

This Ode was set to music as an exercise for his degree of *doct. mus.* by Maurice Greene, and performed at the Public Commencement at Cambridge, on July 6th, 1730. The text of the Ode as sung on this occasion contains in the first four stanzas many variations introduced by Pope; and the following stanza is inserted as the third of the Ode:

> Amphion thus bade wild dissension cease,
> And softened mortals learn'd the Arts of Peace —
>   Amphion taught contending Kings
>   From various discords to create
>   The Musick of a well tun'd State,
> Nor slack nor strain the tender Strings;
>   Those useful touches to impart
>   That strike the Subject's answ'ring heart;
> And the soft silent Harmony that springs
> From sacred union and consent of Things.]

I.

DESCEND, ye Nine! descend and sing;
  The breathing instruments inspire,
Wake into voice each silent string,
And sweep the sounding lyre!
  In a sadly-pleasing strain   5
  Let the warbling lute complain:
    Let the loud trumpet sound,
    Till the roofs all around
    The shrill echoes rebound:
While in more lengthen'd notes and slow,   10
The deep, majestic, solemn organs blow.
  Hark! the numbers soft and clear,
  Gently steal upon the ear;

Now louder, and yet louder rise
And fill with spreading sounds the skies;   15
Exulting in triumph now swell the bold notes,
In broken air, trembling, the wild music floats;
   Till, by degrees, remote and small,
     The strains decay,
     And melt away,   20
   In a dying, dying fall.

II.

By Music, minds an equal temper know,
Nor swell too high, nor sink too low.
If in the breast tumultuous joys arise,
Music her soft, assuasive voice applies;   25
   Or when the soul is press'd with cares,
   Exalts her in enlivening airs.
Warriors she fires with animated sounds;
Pours balm into the bleeding lover's wounds:
   Melancholy lifts her head,   30
   Morpheus rouses from his bed,
   Sloth unfolds her arms and wakes,
   List'ning Envy drops her snakes;
Intestine war no more our Passions wage,
And giddy Factions hear away their rage.   35

III.

But when our Country's cause provokes to Arms,
How martial music ev'ry bosom warms!
So when the first bold vessel dar'd the seas,
High on the stern the Thracian rais'd his strain,
   While Argo saw her kindred trees   40
   Decend from Pelion to the main.
   Transported demi-gods stood round,[1]
   And men grew heroes at the sound,
   Enflam'd with glory's charms:
Each chief his sev'nfold shield display'd,   45
And half unsheath'd the shining blade:
And seas, and rocks, and skies rebound,
To arms, to arms, to arms!

IV.

But when thro' all th' infernal bounds,
Which flaming Phlegethon surrounds,   50

---

[1] Few images in any poet, ancient or modern, are more striking than that in Apollonius, where he says, that when the Argo was sailing near the coast where the Centaur Chiron dwelt, he came down to the very margin of the sea, bringing his wife with the young Achilles in her arms, that he might shew the child to his father Peleus, who was on his voyage with the other Argonauts. Apollon. Rhod. v. 553. *Warton.*

Love, strong as Death, the Poet led
To the pale nations of the dead,
What sounds were heard,
What scenes appear'd,
  O'er all the dreary coasts!   55
    Dreadful gleams,
    Dismal screams,
    Fires that glow,
    Shrieks of woe,
    Sullen moans,   60
    Hollow groans,
And cries of tortur'd ghosts!
But hark! he strikes the golden lyre;
And see! the tortur'd ghosts respire,
  See, shady forms advance!   65
Thy stone, O Sisyphus, stands still,[1]
Ixion rests upon his wheel,
  And the pale spectres dance!
The Furies sink upon their iron beds,
And snakes uncurl'd hang list'ning round their heads. 70

V.

By the streams that ever flow,
By the fragrant winds that blow
  O'er th' Elysian flow'rs;
By those happy souls who dwell
In yellow meads of Asphodel,   75
  Or Amaranthine bow'rs;
By the hero's armed shades,
Glitt'ring thro' the gloomy glades,
By the youths that died for love,
Wand'ring in the myrtle grove,   80
Restore, restore Eurydice to life:
Oh take the husband, or return the wife!
He sung, and hell consented
  To hear the Poet's prayer:
Stern Proserpine relented,   85
  And gave him back the fair.
    Thus song could prevail
    O'er death, and o'er hell,
A conquest how hard and how glorious!
  Tho' fate had fast bound her   90
  With Styx nine times round her,[2]
Yet music and love were victorious.

---

[1] This line is taken from an ode of Cobb. *Warton.*

[2] [Warton justly observes that these numbers are of so burlesque, so low, and ridiculous a kind, and have so much the air of a vulgar drinking song, that one is amazed and concerned to find them in a serious ode.]

VI.

But soon, too soon, the lover turns his eyes:
Again she falls, again she dies, she dies!
How wilt thou now the fatal sisters move? 95
No crime was thine, if 't is no crime to love.
   Now under hanging mountains,
   Beside the fall of fountains,
   Or where Hebrus wanders,
   Rolling in Mæanders, 100
     All alone,
   Unheard, unknown,
   He makes his moan;
   And calls her ghost,
For ever, ever, ever lost! 105
Now with Furies surrounded,
Despairing, confounded,
He trembles, he glows,
Amidst Rhodope's snows;
See, wild as the winds, o'er the desert he flies; 110
Hark! Hæmus resounds with the Bacchanals' cries —
    Ah see, he dies!
Yet ev'n in death Eurydice he sung,
Eurydice still trembled on his tongue,
   Eurydice the woods, 115
   Eurydice the floods,
Eurydice the rocks, and hollow mountains rung.

VII.

   Music the fiercest grief can charm,
   And fate's severest rage disarm:
   Music can soften pain to ease, 120
   And make despair and madness please:
     Our joys below it can improve,
     And antedate the bliss above.
   This the divine Cecilia found,
And to her Maker's praise confin'd the sound. 125
When the full organ joins the tuneful quire,
   Th' immortal pow'rs incline their ear,
Borne on the swelling notes our souls aspire,
While solemn airs improve the sacred fire;
   And Angels lean from heav'n to hear. 130
Of Orpheus now no more let Poets tell,
To bright Cecilia greater power is giv'n;
   His numbers rais'd a shade from hell,
     Hers lift the soul to heav'n.

TWO CHORUS'S

TO THE TRAGEDY OF BRUTUS.[1]

[*Julius Cæsar*, after undergoing a previous process of emasculation, was converted by the Duke of Buckinghamshire into two five act tragedies, entitled respectively *Julius Cæsar* and *Marcus Brutus*, each being supplied with a Prologue and choruses between the acts. They were published in 1722. Pope's choruses occur after the Ist and the IInd Act of *Brutus* respectively. The best excuse for Buckinghamshire's attempt lies in what is really a fault in Shakspere's work — its duality of heroes; but the manner in which he executed this task speaks ill for the judgment of one who himself avers that the hope of mending Shakspere is 'such a jest would make a stoic smile.' The concluding lines of his *Cæsar* may be quoted as a specimen of his additions:

'Ambition, when unbounded, brings a curse,
But an assassinate deserves a worse.'

As to John Sheffield Duke of Buckinghamshire see note to *Essay on Crit.* v. 724.]

CHORUS OF ATHENIANS.[2]

STROPHE I.

YE shades, where sacred truth is sought;
  Groves, where immortal Sages taught;
Where heav'nly visions Plato fir'd,
And Epicurus lay inspir'd![3]
In vain your guiltless laurels stood   5
Unspotted long with human blood.
War, horrid war, your thoughtful walks invades,
And steel now glitters in the Muses' shades.

ANTISTROPHE I.

Oh heav'n-born sisters! source of art!
Who charm the sense, or mend the heart;   10
Who lead fair Virtue's train along,
Moral Truth, and mystic Song!
To what new clime, what distant sky,
Forsaken, friendless shall ye fly?

---

[1] Altered from Shakespear by the Duke of Buckingham, at whose desire these two Chorus's were composed to supply as many wanting in his play. They were set many years afterwards by the famous Bononcini, and performed at Buckingham-house. P.

[2] [In the play this chorus is composed 'of Athenian Philosophers,' and succeeds a scene at Athens between Brutus and Cassius, founded in part on Shaksp. — Act. IV. Sc. 3.]

[3] *Where heavenly visions Plato fired, And Epicurus lay inspired!*] The propriety of these lines arises from hence, that *Brutus*, one of the heroes of this play, was of the old Academy; and *Cassius*, the other, was an Epicurean; but, this had not been enough to justify the poet's choice, had not Plato's system of *Divinity*, and Epicurus's system of *Morals*, been the most rational amongst the various sects of Greek philosophy. *Warburton.*

I cannot be persuaded that Pope thought of Brutus and Cassius as being followers of different sects of philosophy. *Warton.*

[In the play we read 'godlike Zeno,' instead of 'Epicurus.']

Say, will you bless the bleak Atlantic shore? 15
Or bid the furious Gaul be rude no more?

Strophe II.

When Athens sinks by fates unjust,
When wild Barbarians spurn her dust;
Perhaps ev'n Britain's utmost shore
. Shall cease to blush with stranger's gore, 20
See Arts her savage sons control,
And Athens rising near the pole!
'Till some new Tyrant lifts his purple hand,
And civil madness tears them from the land.

Antistrophe II.

Ye Gods! what justice rules the ball? 25
Freedom and Arts together fall;
Fools grant whate'er Ambition craves,
And men, once ignorant, are slaves.
Oh curs'd effects of civil hate,
In ev'ry age, in ev'ry state! 30
Still, when the lust of tyrant power succeeds,
Some Athens perishes, some Tully bleeds.

CHORUS OF YOUTHS AND VIRGINS.[1]

Semichorus.

OH Tyrant Love! hast thou possest
The prudent, learn'd, and virtuous breast?
Wisdom and wit in vain reclaim,
And Arts but soften us to feel thy flame.
Love, soft intruder, enters here, 5
But ent'ring learns to be sincere.
Marcus with blushes owns he loves,
And Brutus tenderly reproves.
Why, Virtue, dost thou blame desire,[2]
Which Nature has imprest? 10
Why, Nature, dost thou soonest fire
The mild and gen'rous breast?

---

[1] [This chorus follows a scene in which Varius, a young Roman bred at Athens, has confessed to Brutus his hopeless passion for the sister of the latter, Junia, the wife of Cassius.]

[2] *Why, Virtue, etc.*] In allusion to that famous conceit of Guarini, "Se il peccare è si dolce, etc." — *Warburton*.

Chorus.

Love's purer flames the Gods approve;
The Gods and Brutus bend to love:
Brutus for absent Portia sighs, 15
And sterner Cassius melts at Junia's eyes.
What is loose love? a transient gust,
Spent in a sudden storm of lust,
A vapour fed from wild desire,
A wand'ring, self-consuming fire, 20
  But Hymen's kinder flames unite;
  And burn for ever one;
  Chaste as cold Cynthia's virgin light,
  Productive as the Sun.

Semichorus.

Oh source of ev'ry social tie, 25
United wish, and mutual joy!
What various joys on one attend,
As son, as father, brother, husband, friend?
Whether his hoary sire he spies,
While thousand grateful thoughts arise; 30
Or meets his spouse's fonder eye;
Or views his smiling progeny;
  What tender passions take their turns,
  What home-felt raptures move?
  His heart now melts, now leaps, now burns, 35
  With rev'rence, hope, and love.

Chorus.

Hence guilty joys, distastes, surmises,
Hence false tears, deceits, disguises,
Dangers, doubts, delays, surprises;
  Fires that scorch yet dare not shine, 40
Purest love's unwasting treasure,
Constant faith, fair hope, long leisure,
Days of ease, and nights of pleasure;
  Sacred Hymen! these are thine.

ODE ON SOLITUDE.[1]

HAPPY the man whose wish and care
  A few paternal acres bound,
Content to breathe his native air,
    In his own ground.

[1] This was a very early production of our Author, written at about twelve years old. P.
Though this Ode ... is said to be his earliest production, yet Dodsley, who was honoured with his intimacy, had seen several pieces of a still earlier date. *Roscoe.*

Whose herds with milk, whose fields with bread, 5
   Whose flocks supply him with attire,
Whose trees in summer yield him shade,
   In winter fire.

Blest, who can unconcern'dly find
   Hours, days, and years slide soft away, 10
In health of body, peace of mind,
   Quiet by day,

Sound sleep by night; study and ease,
   Together mixt; sweet recreation;
And Innocence, which most does please 15
   With meditation.

Thus let me live, unseen, unknown,
   Thus unlamented let me die,
Steal from the world, and not a stone
   Tell where I lie. 20

THE DYING CHRISTIAN TO HIS SOUL.

[WRITTEN 1712.]

THIS Ode was written, we find, at the desire of Steele; and our Poet, in a letter to him on that occasion, says,—'You have it, as Cowley calls it, just warm from the brain; it came to me the first moment I waked this morning; yet, you'll see, it was not so absolutely inspiration, but that I had in my head, not only the verses of Hadrian, but the fine fragment of Sappho.' It is possible, however, that our Author might have had another composition in his head, besides those he here refers to: for there is a close and surprising resemblance between this Ode of Pope, and one of an obscure and forgotten rhymer of the age of Charles the Second, Thomas Flatman. *Warton.*
[The following was Pope's first 'notion of the last words to Adrian,' sent to Steele for insertion in the *Spectator:*

Ah fleeting Spirit! wand'ring fire,	Whither, ah whither art thou flying!
That long hast warm'd my tender breast,	To what dark, undiscover'd shore?
Must thou no more this frame inspire	Thou see'st all trembling, shiv'ring, dying,
No more a pleasing, cheerful guest?	And Wit and Humour are no more!]

Prior also translated this little Ode, but with manifest inferiority to Pope. *Bowles.*
[Mrs. Piozzi, in a letter to Sir James Fellowes (Hayward's *Autobiography, Letters and Literary Remains of* Mrs. Piozzi, II. 287) declares it odd that her correspondent should prefer *her* version of Hadrian's lines to those of better poets.]

ODE.[1]

I.

VITAL spark of heav'nly flame!
   Quit, oh quit this mortal frame:
Trembling, hoping, ling'ring, flying,
Oh the pain, the bliss of dying!

[1] This ode was written in imitation of the famous sonnet of Hadrian to his departing soul; but as much superior in sense and sublimity to his original, as the Christian religion is to the

> Cease, fond Nature, cease thy strife, 5
> And let me languish into life.
>
> II.
>
> Hark! they whisper; Angels say,
> Sister Spirit, come away.
> What is this absorbs me quite?
> Steals my senses, shuts my sight, 10
> Drowns my spirits, draws my breath?
> Tell me, my Soul, can this be Death?
>
> III.
>
> The world recedes; it disappears!
> Heav'n opens on my eyes! my ears
> With sounds seraphic ring: 15
> Lend, lend your wings! I mount! I fly!
> O Grave! where is thy Victory?
> O Death! where is thy Sting?

AN ESSAY ON CRITICISM.

[Written in the Year M.DCC.IX.]

[Considered solely as a phenomenon in literary history, the *Essay on Criticism* is doubtless one of the most remarkable instances of precocious genius which the annals of English or of any other literature afford. Pope was in his twentieth year when he produced this work, one of the masterpieces of a class of poetry associated rather with the ripeness of experience than with the eager productivity of youth. The *Ars Poetica* of Horace with which it is naturally common to compare Pope's Essay, was, if not the last, at all events one of the last works of the Roman poet; and even the *Art Poétique* of Boileau was at least composed in manhood, being published in the writer's 33rd year (1674). But in the case of Pope, nothing beyond imitative attempts (among which we are justified in including the *Pastorals*) and a few trifling original pieces, had preceded a production which was at once hailed by the most judicious and cool-headed of contemporary critics, by Addison (in the *Spectator*, No. 253), as a masterpiece of its kind, and worthy to rank as an equal with its few distinguished predecessors in the same department, predecessors whose reputation has long been obscured by the fame of their panegyrist and rival. Of this phenomenon the secondary causes are no doubt to be sought in the facts that from his earliest days the studies of Pope had by preference as well as circumstance been directed to the best classical models; that his chief delights when a mere boy had been Homer and Ovid; and that among the English poets

---

Pagan. *Warburton.* [For Pope's very sensible criticism of the Emperor Hadrian's lines, see his letter to Steele dated November 7th 1712.]

whom he read Spenser and Dryden and Waller were at once the earliest and the
most favoured. Thus a correct and discriminating taste was from the first formed
in a youth whose mind, moreover, was not distracted by the influences of any
particular calling or profession; and the singleness of purpose with which he de-
voted himself to the cultivation of an art which even as a boy he had already
made the business of his life, enabled him to be a critic in that art at an age
when few men are enabled to class themselves even as its professed votaries.

The *Essay on Criticism*, written in 1709, was first advertised for publication in
1711. In the concluding lines of the poem in which Pope sums up the claims of
his predecessors to the 'critic's ivy,' we have if not a complete and satisfactory
view of what before him had been actually done for poetic criticism, at all events
a summary of what *in his opinion* had been accomplished, in other words, a sur-
vey of the authors and works to whom he thought it right to make his acknowl-
edgments. He justly connects the revival of criticism with that second revival
of learning which is known as the *Renaissance*, and which though originally fos-
tered by Popes, soon intimately united itself with, and powerfully invigorated
itself by, the movement of the Reformation. Vida is perhaps scarcely entitled
to be selected as the representative at once of the critical and the literary
Renaissance and to be coupled with Raphael. As the movement passed the Alps
and spread from Italy into France and Germany and England, the fashion of so-
called critical discourses accompanied it. English literature abounds in well-meant
attempts, from Puttenham downwards through Sidney and Spenser and King
James I. himself, to discuss the *rationale* as well as to exemplify the particular
forms of the poetic art. Little valuable criticism was, however, to be expected in
a strongly creative age. 'In the England of Shakspere,' as Mr Matthew Arnold
has observed, 'the poet lived in a current of ideas in the highest degree animating
and nourishing to the creative power; society was, in the fullest measure, permeated
by fresh thought, intelligent and active; and this state of things is the true basis
for the *creative* power's exercise; in this it finds its data, its materials, truly ready
for its hand; all the books and reading in the world are only valuable as they are
helps to this.' Bacon recognised the existence of this current when he wrote in
the second Book of his *Advancement of Learning:* 'In this part of learning, which
is poesy, I can report no deficiency. For being as a plant that cometh of the lust
of the earth, without a formal seed, it hath sprung up and spread abroad more than
any kind.' English literature ran its vigorous course through the reign of Elizabeth
and the first part of that of James, accompanying and illustrating the national de-
velopment. But then, as the great separation of the nation into two camps
became more and more broadly marked, literature too ceased to be a common
possession of the whole nation; and as the Court party after its final victory in the
Restoration sold England to an anti-national policy and system of government, so
literature swerved aside from its onward course to coquet with foreign develop-
ments and to neglect its own. The elevation to which Milton had carried English
poetry was obscured by the clouds of prejudice and fashion; and instead of pro-
gressing from the point at which it had arrived it deviated into paths whence it
was not to return for a century in order to resume its onward course. It is at such
a period, when a nation has lost its true creative enthusiasm, that uncertain of

E

itself it turns its eyes to foreign developments or supposed developments. The influence of French upon English literature in the 18th century is accounted for by our weakness rather than our neighbours' strength. It was not that French rules prevailed over English love for the 'liberties of wit;' but that in the absence of creative genius our writers naturally and necessarily resorted to imitation of models rather than adoption of rules. Boileau was as little as Pope an apostle of the pseudo-classicism of the so-called Augustan age of French literature; he as well as Pope knew that nothing will make a man a poet 'si son astre en naissant ne l'a formé poète;' and the classical simplicity which he preached was not in his opinion attained by the sham revival of stock subjects of ancient poetry, Hectors and Andromaches and Iliums, in which as he says the actors unfortunately drop the antique mass while the fiddle plays the chorus. In England, amidst the chaos of imitations of foreign models, among the reckless or helpless follies to which even a Dryden prostituted his muse in her many weaker hours, criticism would have been best employed in recalling what English poetry had already achieved and shewing to what extent even in the midst of its present deviations it still held to the pursuit of a legitimate onward movement. The Earl of Roscommon, in his *Essay on Translated Verse*, at all events did good service in dwelling upon the merits of Milton, an endeavour in which he was afterwards more elaborately seconded by Addison himself. No such merit however attaches to the efforts of Walsh and the Duke of Buckinghamshire; and the praise which Pope thinks fit to bestow upon them must be attributed in the one case to the influence of grateful friendship, and in the other to that of courtly obsequiousness. Such being Pope's modern predecessors in poetic criticism, it is easy to perceive that his chief obligations lie to the ancients whom he enumerates in this Essay, rather than to the moderns, to whom at the most he owes particular felicitous thoughts and expressions.

The *Essay on Criticism* is beyond a doubt constructed on a fixed plan, of which the main features are clearly enough marked by the author, while we are by no means obliged to accept its evolution as stated by Warburton in his lengthy Commentary. The latter effort is indeed rather a monument of piety than a marvel of ingenuity. Pope's Essay is not an Art of Poetry, but, what it professes to be, a connected discourse on Criticism, in which, however, it was neither intended nor necessary to avoid the incidental introduction of precepts concerning the subject-matter as well as the manner of poetic criticism. It divides itself into three parts naturally and easily following one another: the foundation of true criticism; the causes preventing it; and the causes producing it and exemplified in its most eminent professors. But, as should always be the case in a readable essay whether in prose or verse, abruptness is avoided in the transitions, and the successive precepts are easily and happily linked together by examples which render this didactic work as entertaining as it is instructive. The errors of manner in composition, and particularly in versification, on which the Essay incidentally touches, are illustrated without effort in the verse itself; the open vowels, the monosyllables, the lagging Alexandrine, the regulation rhyme, — all these are not discussed at length, but each is instanced in passing with a single and effective touch.]

CONTENTS OF THE ESSAY ON CRITICISM.

PART I.

Introduction. That 'tis as great a fault to judge ill, as to write ill, and a more dangerous one to the public, v. 1.

That a true Taste is as rare to be found, as a true Genius, v. 9 to 18.

That most men are born with some Taste, but spoiled by false Education, v. 19 to 25.

The multitude of Critics, *and causes of them*, v. 26 to 45.

That we are to study our own Taste, *and know the* Limits *of it*, v. 46 to 67.

Nature *the best guide of Judgment*, v. 68 to 87.

Improv'd by Art *and* Rules, *which are but* methodis'd Nature, 88.

Rules *derived from the Practice of the* Ancient Poets, v. id. to 110.

That therefore the Ancients *are necessary to be studyd, by a Critic, particularly* Homer *and* Virgil, v. 120 to 138.

Of Licenses, *and the use of them by the* Ancients, v. 140 to 180.

Reverence due to the Ancients, *and praise of them*, v. 181, *etc.*

PART II. Ver. 203, etc.

Causes hindering a true Judgment. 1. Pride, v. 208. 2. Imperfect Learning, v. 215. 3. *Judging by parts, and not by the whole*, v. 233 to 288. *Critics in* Wit, Language, Versification, *only*, v. 288, 305, 399, etc. 4. *Being too hard to please, or too apt to admire*, v. 384. 5. Partiality — *too much Love to a Sect, — to the* Ancients *or* Moderns, v. 394. 6. Prejudice *or* Prevention, v. 408. 7. Singularity, v. 424, 8. Inconstancy, v. 430. 9. Party Spirit, v. 452, etc. 10. Envy, v. 466. *Against Envy, and in praise of Good-nature*, v. 508, etc. *When Severity is chiefly to be used by Critics*, v. 526, etc.

PART III. Ver. 560, etc.

Rules for the Conduct of Manners *in a Critic.* 1. Candour, v. 563. Modesty, v. 566. Good-breeding, v. 572. Sincerity, *and* Freedom *of advice*, v. 578. 2. *When one's Counsel is to be restrained*, v. 584. *Character of an* incorrigible Poet, v. 600. *And of an* impertinent Critic, v. 610, etc. *Character of a* good Critic, v. 629. *The* History *of* Criticism, *and Characters of the best Critics*, Aristotle, v. 645. Horace, v. 653. Dionysius, v. 665. Petronius, v. 667. Quintilian, v. 670. Longinus, v. 675. *Of the Decay of Criticism, and its Revival.* Erasmus, v. 693. Vida, v. 705. Boileau, v. 714. *Lord* Roscommon, *etc.*, v. 725. Conclusion.

AN ESSAY ON CRITICISM.

'TIS hard to say, if greater want of skill
Appear in writing or in judging ill;
But, of the two, less dang'rous is th' offence
To tire our patience, than mislead our sense.
Some few in that, but numbers err in this,   5
Ten censure wrong for one who writes amiss;
A fool might once himself alone expose,
Now one in verse makes many more in prose.
'T is with our judgments as our watches, none
Go just alike, yet each believes his own.   10
In Poets as true genius is but rare,
True Taste as seldom is the Critic's share;
Both must alike from Heav'n derive their light,
These born to judge, as well as those to write.

Let such teach others who themselves excel,[1] 15
And censure freely who have written well.[2]
Authors are partial to their wit,[3] 't is true,
But are not Critics to their judgment too?
 Yet if we look more closely, we shall find
Most have the seeds of judgment in their mind:[4] 20
Nature affords at least a glimm'ring light;
The lines, tho' touch'd but faintly, are drawn right.
But as the slightest sketch, if justly trac'd,
Is by ill-colouring but the more disgrac'd,
So by false learning is good sense defac'd:[5] 25
Some are bewilder'd in the maze of schools,[6]
And some made coxcombs Nature meant but fools.
In search of wit these lose their common sense,
And then turn Critics in their own defence:
Each burns alike, who can, or cannot write, 30
Or with a Rival's, or an Eunuch's spite.
All fools have still an itching to deride,
And fain would be upon the laughing side.
If Mævius scribble in Apollo's spite,[7]
There are who judge still worse than he can write. 35
 Some have at first for Wits, then Poets past,
Turn'd Critics next, and prov'd plain fools at last.
Some neither can for Wits nor Critics pass,
As heavy mules are neither horse nor ass.
Those half-learn'd witlings, num'rous in our isle, 40
As half-form'd insects on the banks of Nile;
Unfinish'd things, one knows not what to call,
Their generation 's so equivocal:
To tell 'em, would a hundred tongues require,
Or one vain wit's, that might a hundred tire. 45
 But you who seek to give and merit fame,
And justly bear a Critic's noble name,
Be sure yourself and your own reach to know,

---

[1] *Let such teach others*] 'Qui scribit artificiose, ab aliis commode scripta facile intelligere poterit.' Cic. *ad Herenn.* lib. IV. 'De pictore, sculptore, fictore, nisi artifex, judicare non potest.' *Pliny.* P.

[2] [Warton, who quotes Dryden's remark that none but a poet is qualified to judge of a poet, has an excellent illustrative note, too long for insertion, on the amount of truth contained in the observation. The relations between the creative and the critical power have perhaps rarely been more clearly pointed out than in Mr. Matthew Arnold's *Essay on the Function of Criticism at the present Time.*]

[3] [The word 'wit' is said to be used in Pope's Essay on Criticism in seven different senses. Bain's *Eng. Comp. and Rhetoric*, p. 57. Here it seems tantamount to 'creative power' or 'genius.']

[4] *Most have the seeds*] 'Omnes tacito quodam sensu, sine ulla arte, aut ratione, quæ sint in artibus ac rationibus recta et prava dijudicant.' Cic. *de Orat.* lib. III. P.

[5] *So by false learning*] 'Plus sine doctrina prudentia, quam sine prudentia valet doctrina.' *Quint.* P.

[6] *Some are bewilder'd*, &c.] This thought is taken from Lord Rochester, but more decently expressed:

'God never made a coxcomb worth a groat,
 We owe that name to industry and arts.'
Warburton.

[7] [Verg. *Buc.* III. 90. Hor. *Epod.* X. 2.]

ESSAY ON CRITICISM.

How far your genius, taste, and learning go;
Launch not beyond your depth, but be discreet, 50
And mark that point where sense and dulness meet.
Nature to all things fix'd the limits fit,
And wisely curb'd proud man's pretending wit.
As on the land while here the ocean gains,
In other parts it leaves wide sandy plains; 55
Thus in the soul while memory prevails,
The solid pow'r of understanding fails;
Where beams of warm imagination play,
The memory's soft figures melt away.
One science only will one genius fit; 60
So vast is art, so narrow human wit:
Not only bounded to peculiar arts,
But oft in those confin'd to single parts.
Like kings we lose the conquests gain'd before,
By vain ambition still to make them more; 65
Each might his sev'ral province well command,
Would all but stoop to what they understand.
First follow Nature, and your judgment frame
By her just standard, which is still the same:
Unerring NATURE, still divinely bright, 70
One clear, unchang'd, and universal light,
Life, force, and beauty, must to all impart,
At once the source, and end, and test of Art.
Art from that fund each just supply provides,
Works without show, and without pomp presides: 75
In some fair body thus th' informing soul
With spirits feeds, with vigour fills the whole,
Each motion guides, and ev'ry nerve sustains;
Itself unseen, but in th' effects, remains.
Some, to whom Heav'n in wit has been profuse,[1] 80
Want as much more, to turn it to its use;
For wit and judgment often are at strife,
Tho' meant each other's aid, like man and wife.
'T is more to guide, than spur the Muse's steed;
Restrain his fury, than provoke his speed; 85
The winged courser, like a gen'rous horse,
Shows most true mettle when you check his course.
Those RULES of old discover'd, not devis'd,[2]
Are Nature still, but Nature methodiz'd;

---

[1] (Variation:)
There are whom Heav'n has blest with store of wit,
Yet want as much again to manage it.

[2] *Those Rules of old*, &c.] Cicero has, best of any one I know, explained what that is which reduces the wild and scattered parts of human knowledge into *arts*. — 'Nihil est quod ad artem redigi posset, nisi ille prius, qui illa tenet, quorum artem instituere vult, habeat illam scientiam, ut ex iis rebus, quarum ars nondum sit, artem efficere possit. — Omnia fere, quæ sunt conclusa nunc artibus, dispersa et dissipata quondam fuerunt, ut in musicis, etc. Adhibita est igitur ars quædam extrinsecus ex alio genere quodam, quod sibi totum PHILOSOPHI assumunt, quæ rem dissolutam divulsamque conglutinaret, et ratione quadam constringeret.' *De Orat*. lib. 1. c. 41, 2. *Warburton*.

Nature, like liberty, is but restrain'd 90
By the same laws which first herself ordain'd.
  Hear how learn'd Greece her useful rules indites,
When to repress, and when indulge our flights:
High on Parnassus' top her sons she show'd,
And pointed out those arduous paths they trod; 95
Held from afar, aloft, th' immortal prize,
And urg'd the rest by equal steps to rise.
Just precepts thus from great examples giv'n,[1]
She drew from them what they deriv'd from Heav'n.
The gen'rous Critic fann'd the Poet's fire, 100
And taught the world with reason to admire.
Then Criticism the Muses handmaid prov'd,
To dress her charms, and make her more belov'd:
But following wits from that intention stray'd,
Who could not win the mistress, woo'd the maid; 105
Against the Poets their own arms they turn'd,
Sure to hate most the men from whom they learn'd.
So modern 'Pothecaries,[2] taught the art
By Doctor's bills to play the Doctor's part,
Bold in the practice of mistaken rules, 110
Prescribe, apply, and call their masters fools.
Some on the leaves of ancient authors prey,[3]
Nor time nor moths e'er spoil'd so much as they.
Some drily plain, without invention's aid,
Write dull receipts how poems may be made. 115
These leave the sense, their learning to display,
And those explain the meaning quite away.[4]
  You then whose judgment the right course would steer,
Know well each ANCIENT'S proper character;
His fable, subject, scope in ev'ry page; 120
Religion, Country, genius of his Age:
Without all these at once before your eyes,
Cavil you may, but never criticize.[5]

---

[1] *Just precepts*] 'Nec enim artibus editis factum est ut argumenta inveniremus, sed dicta sunt omnia antequam præciperentur; mox ea scriptores observata et collecta ediderunt.' *Quintil.* P.

[2] [This familiar abbreviation is sanctioned in poetry by early dramatic usage. The Poticary is one of the 'Four P's' of John Heywood's Interlude.]

[3] *Some on the leaves — Some drily plain.*] The first, the *apes* of those Italian critics, who at the restoration of letters having found the classic writers miserably mangled by the hands of monkish librarians, very commendably employed their pains and talents in restoring them to their native purity. The second, the *plagiaries* from the French, who had made some admirable commentaries on the ancient critics. *Warburton.*

[4] [A forward Critic often dupes us
  With sham quotations *Peri Hupsous;*
  And if we have not read *Longinus*,
  Will magisterially outshine us.
  Then, lest with *Greek* he overrun ye,
  Procure the Book for Love or Money
  Translated from Boileau's Translation,
  And quote *Quotation* on *Quotation*.
    Swift *On Poetry*.]

[5] *Cavil you may, but never criticize.*] The author after this verse originally inserted the following, which he has however omitted in all the editions:

'Zoilus*, had these been known without a name,

*[Zoilus, called *Homeromastix* from his petty criticisms of Homer.]

Be Homer's works your study and delight,
Read them by day, and meditate by night;   125
Thence form your judgment, thence your maxims bring,
And trace the Muses upward to their spring.
Still with itself compar'd, his text peruse;
And let your comment be the Mantuan Muse.
   When first young Maro in his boundless mind [1]   130
A work t' outlast immortal Rome design'd,
Perhaps he seem'd above the critic's law,
And but from Nature's fountains scorn'd to draw:
But when t' examine ev'ry part he came,
Nature and Homer were, he found, the same.   135
Convinc'd, amaz'd, he checks the bold design;
And rules as strict his labour'd work confine,
As if the Stagirite o'erlook'd each line. [2]
Learn hence for ancient rules a just esteem;
To copy nature is to copy them.   140
   Some beauties yet no Precepts can declare,
For there's a happiness as well as care.
Music resembles Poetry, in each
Are nameless graces which no methods teach, [3]
And which a master-hand alone can reach.   145
If, where the rules not far enough extend, [4]
(Since rules were made but to promote their end)
Some lucky Licence answer to the full
Th' intent propos'd, that Licence is a rule.
Thus Pegasus, a nearer way to take,   150
May boldly deviate from the common track;
From vulgar bounds with brave disorder part,
And snatch a grace beyond the reach of art,
Which without passing thro' the judgment, gains
The heart, and all its end at once attains.   155
In prospects thus, some objects please our eyes,
Which out of nature's common order rise,
The shapeless rock, or hanging precipice.

Had died, and Perault* ne'er been damn'd to
  fame;
The sense of sound Antiquity had reign'd,
And sacred Homer yet been unprophan'd.
None e'er had thought his comprehensive
  mind
To modern customs, modern rules confin'd;
Who for all ages writ, and all mankind. P.
   *[Perault, a Dominican writer of the 13th
century.]
   [1] *When first young Maro*, &c.] Virg.
Eclog. VI. 'Cum canerem reges et prælia, Cyn-
thius aurem Vellit.'
   It is a tradition preserved by Servius, that
Virgil began with writing a poem of the Alban
and Roman affairs: which he found above his
years, and descended first to imitate Theocritus
on rural subjects, and afterwards to copy Homer
in Heroic poetry. P.
   [2] [Dr. Aikin, quoted by Warton, justly points
out the inconsistency between this line and
v. 272.]
   [3] *Non ratione aliquâ, sed motu nescio an
inerrabili judicatur. Neque hoc ab ullo satis
explicari puto licet multi tentaverint.* Quintil.
lib. VI. *Warton.*
   [4] *If, where the rules,* &c.] 'Neque enim ro-
gationibus plebisve scitis sancta sunt ista Præ-
cepta, sed hoc, quicquid est, Utilitas excogitavit.
Non negabo autem sic utile esse plerumque; ve-
rum si eadem illa nobis aliud suadebit Utilitas,
hanc, relictis magistrorum autoritatibus, seque-
mur.' *Quintil.* lib. II. cap. 13. P.

Great wits sometimes may gloriously offend,[1]
And rise to faults true Critics dare not mend. 160
But tho' the Ancients thus their rules invade,
(As Kings dispense with laws themselves have made)
Moderns, beware! or if you must offend
Against the precept, ne'er transgress its End;
Let it be seldom, and compell'd by need; 165
And have, at least, their precedent to plead·
The Critic else proceeds without remorse,
Seizes your fame, and puts his laws in force.
 I know there are, to whose presumptuous thoughts
Those freer beauties, ev'n in them, seem faults. 170
Some figures monstrous and mis-shap'd appear,
Consider'd singly, or beheld too near,
Which, but proportion'd to their light, or place,
Due distance reconciles to form and grace.
A prudent chief not always must display[2] 175
His pow'rs in equal ranks, and fair array.
But with th' occasion and the place comply,
Conceal his force, nay seem sometimes to fly.
Those oft are stratagems which error seem,
Nor is it Homer nods, but we that dream.[3] 180
 Still green with bays each ancient Altar stands,
Above the reach of sacrilegious hands;
Secure from Flames, from Envy's fiercer rage,[4]
Destructive War, and all-involving Age.
See, from each clime the learn'd their incense bring! 185
Hear, in all tongues consenting Pæans ring!
In praise so just let ev'ry voice be join'd,
And fill the gen'ral chorus of mankind.
Hail, Bards triumphant! born in happier days;
Immortal heirs of universal praise! 190
Whose honours with increase of ages grow,
As streams roll down, enlarging as they flow;
Nations unborn your mighty names shall sound,
And worlds applaud that must not yet be found!
Oh may some spark of your celestial fire, 195
The last, the meanest of your sons inspire,
(That on weak wings, from far, pursues your flights;

[1] Dryden's *Aurungzebe*:
'Mean soul, and dar'st not gloriously offend!'
  Stevens.

[2] *A prudent chief*, &c.] Οἷόν τι ποιοῦσιν οἱ φρόνιμοι στρατηλάται κατὰ τὰς τάξεις τῶν στρατευμάτων. Dion. Hal. *De struct. orat. Warburton.*

[3] *Nor is it Homer nods, but we that dream.*]
'Modeste, ac circumspecto judicio de tantis viris pronunciandum est, ne quod (quod plerisque accidit) damnent quod non intelligunt. Ac si necesse est in alteram errare partem, omnia eorum legentibus placere, quam multa displicere maluerim.' *Quint.* P.

[4] *Secure from* flames, *from* envy's *fiercer rage, Destructive* war, *and all-involving* age.] The poet here alludes to the four great causes of the ravage amongst ancient writings. The destruction of the Alexandrine and Palatine libraries by *fire;* the fiercer rage of Zoilus and Mævius and their followers against wit; the irruption of the barbarians into the empire; and the long reign of ignorance and superstition in the cloisters. *Warburton.*

ESSAY ON CRITICISM.

Glows while he reads, but trembles as he writes)
To teach vain Wits a science little known,
T' admire superior sense, and doubt their own!   200

Of all the Causes which conspire to blind
Man's erring judgment, and misguide the mind,
What the weak head with strongest bias rules,
Is *Pride*, the never-failing voice of fools.
Whatever nature has in worth denied,   205
She gives in large recruits[1] of needful pride;
For as in bodies, thus in souls, we find
What wants in blood and spirits, swell'd with wind:
Pride, where wit fails, steps into our defence,
And fills up all the mighty Void of sense.   210
If once right reason drives that cloud away,
Truth breaks upon us with resistless day.
Trust not yourself; but your defects to know,
Make use of ev'ry friend — and ev'ry foe.
  A *little learning* is a dang'rous thing;   215
Drink deep, or taste not the Pierian spring.
There shallow draughts intoxicate the brain,[2]
And drinking largely sobers us again.
Fir'd at first sight with what the Muse imparts,
In fearless youth we tempt the heights of Arts,   220
While from the bounded level of our mind
Short views we take, nor see the lengths behind;
But more advanc'd, behold with strange surprise
New distant scenes of endless science rise!
So pleas'd at first the tow'ring Alps we try,   225
Mount o'er the vales, and seem to tread the sky,
Th' eternal snows appear already past,
And the first clouds and mountains seem the last;
But, those attain'd, we tremble to survey
The growing labours of the lengthen'd way,   230
Th' increasing prospects tires our wand'ring eyes,
Hills peep o'er hills, and Alps on Alps arise!
  A perfect Judge will read each word of Wit[3]
With the same spirit that its author writ:
Survey the WHOLE, nor seek slight faults to find   235
Where nature moves, and rapture warms the mind;
Nor lose, for that malignant dull delight,

---

[1] *recruits*] [i.e. supplies.]

[2] *There shallow draughts*, &c.] The thought was taken from Lord Verulam, who applies it to more serious inquiries. *Warburton.* [See *Advancement of L.* bk. 1. (*ad fin.*). See also Whately's annotation to Bacon's Essay *Of Studies;* ' But the poet's remedies for the dangers of a little learning are both of them impossible. None can " drink deep" enough to be, in truth, anything more than very superficial; and every human being, that is not a downright idiot, must *taste*.']

[3] *A perfect judge*, &c.] ' Diligenter legendum est, ac pæne ad scribendi sollicitudinem: Nec per partes modo scrutanda sunt omnia, sed perlectus liber utique ex integro resumendus.' *Quintil. Warburton.*

The gen'rous pleasure to be charm'd with Wit.
But in such lays as neither ebb, nor flow,
Correctly cold, and regularly low,   240
That shunning faults, one quiet tenour keep,
We cannot blame indeed —— but we may sleep.
In wit, as nature, what affects our hearts
Is not th' exactness of peculiar parts;
'T is not a lip, or eye, we beauty call,   245
But the joint force and full result of all.
Thus when we view some well-proportion'd dome,
(The world's just wonder,[1] and ev'n thine, O Rome!)
No single parts unequally surprize,
All comes united to th' admiring eyes;   250
No monstrous height, or breadth, or length appear;
The Whole at once is bold, and regular.

  Whoever thinks a faultless piece to see,
Thinks what ne'er was, nor is, nor e'er shall be.
In every work regard the writer's End,   255
Since none can compass more than they intend;
And if the means be just, the conduct true,
Applause, in spight of trivial faults, is due;
As men of breeding, sometimes men of wit,
T' avoid great errors, must the less commit: 260
Neglect the rules each verbal Critic lays,
For not to know some trifles, is a praise.
Most Critics, fond of some subservient art,
Still make the Whole depend upon a Part:
They talk of principles, but notions prize,   265
And all to one lov'd Folly sacrifice.

  Once on a time, La Mancha's Knight,[2] they say,
A certain bard encount'ring on the way,
Discours'd in terms as just, with looks as sage,
As e'er could Dennis[3] of the Grecian stage;   270
Concluding all were desp'rate sots and fools,
Who durst depart from Aristotle's rules.
Our Author, happy in a judge so nice,
Produc'd his Play, and begg'd the Knight's advice;
Made him observe the subject, and the plot,   275
The manners, passions, unities; what not?
All which, exact to rule, were brought about,
Were but a Combat in the lists left out.
"What! leave the Combat out?" exclaims the Knight;
Yes, or we must renounce the Stagirite.   280
"Not so by Heav'n" (he answers in a rage),
"Knights, squires, and steeds, must enter on the stage."

---

[1] The Pantheon, I would suppose; perhaps St. Peter's; no matter which; the observation is true of both. *Warburton.*

[2] The incident is taken from the Second Part of Don Quixote, first written by Don Alonzo Fernandez de Avellanada, and afterwards translated, or rather imitated and new-modelled, by no less an author than the celebrated Le Sage. *Warton.*

[3] *Dennis*], see *Introductory Memoir.*

So vast a throng the stage can ne'er contain.
" Then build a new, or act it in a plain."
Thus Critics, or less judgment than caprice, 285
Curious not knowing, not exact but nice,
Form short Ideas; and offend in arts
(As most in manners) by a love to parts.
   Some to *Conceit* alone their taste confine,
And glitt'ring thoughts struck out at ev'ry line; 290
Pleas'd with a work where nothing's just or fit;
One glaring Chaos and wild heap of wit.
Poets like painters, thus, unskill'd to trace
The naked nature and the living grace,
With gold and jewels cover ev'ry part, 295
And hide with ornaments their want of art.[1]
True Wit is Nature to advantage dress'd,
What oft was thought, but ne'er so well express'd;[2]
Something, whose truth convinc'd at sight we find,
That gives us back the image of our mind. 300
As shades more sweetly recommend the light,
So modest plainness sets off sprightly wit.
For works may have more wit than does 'em good,
As bodies perish thro' excess of blood.
   Others for *Language* all their care express, 305
And value books, as women men, for Dress:
Their praise is still, — the Style is excellent:
The Sense, they humbly take upon content.
Words are like leaves; and where they most abound,
Much fruit of sense beneath is rarely found, 310
False Eloquence, like the prismatic glass,
Its gaudy colours spreads on ev'ry place;
The face of Nature we no more survey,
All glares alike, without distinction gay:
But true expression, like th' unchanging Sun, ⎫ 315
Clears and improves whate'er it shines upon, ⎬
It gilds all objects, but it alters none. ⎭
Expression is the dress of thought, and still
Appears more decent, as more suitable;
A vile conceit in pompous words express'd, 320
Is like a clown in regal purple dress'd:
For diff'rent styles with diff'rent subjects sort,
As several garbs with country, town, and court.
Some by old words to fame have made pretence,[3]

---

[1] [This class of poets and style of poetry have probably never been so well illustrated and exposed, as, in the case of the English Fantastic school, by Dr. Johnson in his life of Cowley.]

[2] [Warburton commends, while Johnson with much success impugns, this definition. The term *wit*, as observed above, is very loosely and variously applied in this poem.]

[' Humour is all; wit should be only brought To turn agreeably some proper thought.'
Buckingham's *Essay on Poetry*.]

[3] *Some by old words*, &c.] ' Abolita et abrogata retinere, insolentiæ cujusdam est, et frivolæ in parvis jactantiæ.' *Quintil.* lib. 1. cap. 6. P.

'Opus est ut verba a vetustate repetita neque crebra sint, neque manifesta, quia nil est odio-

Ancients in phrase, mere moderns in their sense;   325
Such labour'd nothings, in so strange a style,
Amaze th' unlearn'd, and make the learned smile.
Unlucky, as Fungoso in the play,[1]
These sparks with awkward vanity display
What the fine gentleman wore yesterday;   330
And but so mimic ancient wits at best,
As apes our grandsires, in their doublets drest.
In words, as fashions, the same rule will hold;
Alike fantastic, if too new, or old:
Be not the first by whom the new are try'd,   335
Nor yet the last to lay the old aside.

But most by Numbers judge a Poet's song;[2]
And smooth or rough, with them is right or wrong:
In the bright Muse though thousand charms conspire,
Her voice is all these tuneful fools admire;   340
Who haunt Parnassus but to please their ear,
Not mend their minds; as some to Church repair,
Not for the doctrine, but the music there.
These equal syllables alone require,
Tho' oft the ear the open vowels tire;[3]   345
While expletives their feeble aid do join;[4]
And ten low words oft creep in one dull line:
While they ring round the same unvary'd chimes,
With sure returns of still expected rhymes;
Where-e'er you find "the cooling western breeze,"   350
In the next line, it "whispers through the trees:"
If crystal streams "with pleasing murmurs creep,"
The reader's threaten'd (not in vain) with "sleep:"
Then, at the last and only couplet fraught
With some unmeaning thing they call a thought,   355
A needless Alexandrine ends the song[5]

---

sius affectatione, nec utique ab ultimis repetita temporibus. Oratio cujus summa virtus est perspicuitas, quam sit vitiosa, si egeat interprete? Ergo ut novorum optima erunt maxime vetera, ita veterum maxime nova.' *Idem.* P.

[1] *Unlucky as Fungoso,* &c.] See Ben Jonson's *Every Man in his Humour.* P. [But the reference is really to *Every Man out of his Humour,* where Fungoso endeavours to translate himself into the likeness of Fastidious Brisk.]

[2] *But most by Numbers,* &c.]
'Quis populi sermo est? quis enim? nisi carmine molli
Nunc demum numero fluere, ut per læve severos
Effundat junctura ungues: scit tendere versum
Non secus ac si oculo rubricam dirigat uno.'
Pers. *Sat.* 1. P.

[3] *Though oft the ear,* &c.] 'Fugiemus crebras vocalium concursiones, quæ vastam atque hiantem orationem reddunt. Cic. *ad Heren.* lib. iv. *Vide etiam,* Quintil. lib. ix. c. 4. P.

[4] *While expletives their feeble aid do join,*
And ten low words oft creep in one dull line.]
From Dryden. "He *creeps* along with *ten little words* in every *line,* and helps out his numbers with [for] [to] and [unto] and all the pretty *expletives* he can find, while the sense is left half tired behind it." *Essay on Dramatic Poetry. Warburton.*

[The beauty of Waller's versification, as Dr. Johnson has pointed out, is impaired by the very frequent use of the expletive *do.*]

[5] [It has been pointed out that Pope's *Messiah* is open to the objection of the introduction of Alexandrines, at the close of the poem and elsewhere. His later poems contain very few Alexandrines. Dr. Johnson believes that 'Cowley was the first poet that mingled Alexandrines

That, like a wounded snake, drags its slow length along.
Leave such to tune their own dull rhymes, and know
What's roundly smooth or languishingly slow;
And praise the easy vigour of a line, 360
Where Denham's strength, and Waller's sweetness join.[1]
True ease in writing comes from art, not chance,
As those move easiest who have learn'd to dance.
'T is not enough no harshness gives offence,
The sound must seem an Echo to the sense:[2] 365
Soft is the strain when Zephyr gently blows,[3]
And the smooth stream in smoother numbers flows;
But when loud surges lash the sounding shore,[4]
The hoarse, rough verse should like the torrent roar:
When Ajax strives some rock's vast weight to throw,[5] 370
The line too labours, and the words move slow;
Not so, when swift Camilla scours the plain,[6]
Flies o'er th' unbending corn, and skims along the main.
Hear how Timotheus' varied lays surprize,[7]
And bid alternate passions fall and rise! 375
While, at each change, the son of Libyan Jove
Now burns with glory, and then melts with love,
Now his fierce eyes with sparkling fury glow,
Now sighs steal out, and tears begin to flow:
Persians and Greeks like turns of nature found, 380
And the world's victor stood subdu'd by Sound!
The pow'r of Music all our hearts allow,
And what Timotheus was, is DRYDEN now.[8]

at pleasure with the common heroic of ten syllables; and from him Dryden borrowed the practice, whether ornamental or licentious.']

[1] [The master-pieces of these two poets are similarly linked in Buckingham's *Essay on Poetry:*
'But not an Elegy, nor writ with skill,
No *Panegyrick*, nor a *Cooper's Hill.*']

[2] *The sound must seem an Echo to the sense,*]
Lord Roscommon says,
The sound is still a comment to the sense.
They are both well expressed: only *this* supposes the sense to be assisted by the sound; *that,* the sound assisted by the sense. *Warburton.*

[3] *Soft is the strain,* &c.]
'Tum si læta canunt,' &c.
Vida *Poet.* lib. III. v. 403.

[4] *But when loud surges,* &c.]
'Tum longe sale saxa sonant,' &c.
Vida *ib.* 838.

[5] *When Ajax strives,* &c.]
'Atque ideo si quid geritur molimine magno,' &c.
Vida *ib.* 417.

[6] *Not so, when swift Camilla,* &c.]

'At mora si fuerit damno, properare jubebo,' &c.
Vida *ib.* 420.
[Pope's lines are slightly altered from Dryden's version of the *Æneid,* VII. 808 ff.]

[7] *Hear how Timotheus,* &c.] See *Alexander's Feast,* or *the Power of Music;* an Ode by Mr. Dryden. P. [' What Timotheus was' Pope had hardly ascertained from a study of his Fragments. Timotheus the dithyrambic poet of Miletus really died three years before the birth of Alexander, in 359.]

[8] [Pope was from his earliest youth a constant reader and ardent admirer of Dryden. He used to say, that Dryden had improved the art of versification beyond any of the preceding poets, and that he would have been perfect in it, had he not been so often obliged to write with precipitation. Pope was introduced to Dryden, but the latter died before any intimacy could take place between them. See Ruffhead's *Life of Pope,* 22, 3. Johnson, commenting on Voltaire's comparison between Dryden and Pope, said, that 'they both drive coaches and six; but Dryden's horses are either galloping or stumbling: Pope's go at a steady even trot.' Boswell *ad ann.* 1766.]

Avoid Extremes; and shun the fault of such,
Who still are pleas'd too little or too much. 385
At ev'ry trifle scorn to take offence,
That always shows great pride, or little sense;
Those heads, as stomachs, are not sure the best,
Which nauseate all, and nothing can digest.
Yet let not each gay Turn thy rapture move; 390
For fools admire,[1] but men of sense approve:
As things seem large which we thro' mists descry,
Dulness is ever apt to magnify.

Some foreign writers, some our own despise;
The Ancients only, or the Moderns prize. 395
Thus Wit, like Faith, by each man is apply'd
To one small sect, and all are damn'd beside.
Meanly they seek the blessing to confine,
And force that sun but on a part to shine,
Which not alone the southern wit sublimes, 400
But ripens spirits in cold northern climes;
Which from the first has shone on ages past,
Enlights the present, and shall warm the last;
Tho' each may feel increases and decays,
And see now clearer and now darker days. 405
Regard not then if Wit be old or new,
But blame the false, and value still the true.

Some ne'er advance a Judgment of their own,
But catch the spreading notion of the Town;
They reason and conclude by precedent, 410
And own stale nonsense which they ne'er invent.
Some judge of author's names, not works, and then
Nor praise nor blame the writings, but the men.
Of all this servile herd the worst is he
That in proud dulness joins with Quality. 415
A constant Critic at the great man's board,
To fetch and carry nonsense for my Lord.
What woful stuff this madrigal would be,
In some starv'd hackney sonneteer, or me?
But let a Lord once own the happy lines, 420
How the wit brightens! how the style refines!
Before his sacred name flies ev'ry fault,
And each exalted stanza teems with thought!

The Vulgar thus through Imitation err;
As oft the Learn'd by being singular; 425
So much they scorn the crowd, that if the throng
By chance go right, they purposely go wrong;
So Schismatics the plain believers quit,
And are but damn'd for having too much wit.
Some praise at morning what they blame at night; 430

---

[1] [It need hardly be pointed out that the 'nil admirari' desiderated by Horace includes moral self-restraint as well as intellectual equanimity.]

ESSAY ON CRITICISM. 63

But always think the last opinion right.
A Muse by these is like a mistress us'd,
This hour she's idoliz'd, the next abus'd;
While their weak heads like towns unfortify'd,
'Twixt sense and nonsense daily change their side.   435
Ask them the cause; they're wiser still, they say;
And still to-morrow's wiser than to-day.
We think our fathers fools, so wise we grow,
Our wiser sons, no doubt, will think us so.
Once School-divines this zealous isle o'er-spread;   440
Who knew most Sentences, was deepest read;[1]
Faith, Gospel, all, seem'd made to be disputed,
And none had sense enough to be confuted:
Scotists and Thomists, now, in peace remain,[2]
Amidst their kindred cobwebs in Duck-lane.[3]   445
If Faith itself has diff'rent dresses worn,
What wonder modes in Wit should take their turn?
Oft', leaving what is natural and fit,
The current folly proves the ready wit;
And authors think their reputation safe,   450
Which lives as long as fools are pleas'd to laugh.
 Some valuing those of their own side or mind,
Still make themselves the measure of mankind:
Fondly we think we honour merit then,
When we but praise ourselves in other men.   455
Parties in Wit attend on those of State,
And public faction doubles private hate.
Pride, Malice, Folly, against Dryden rose,
In various shapes of Parsons, Critics, Beaus;[4]
But sense surviv'd, when merry jests were past;   460
For rising merit will buoy up at last.
Might he return, and bless once more our eyes,
New Blackmores[5] and new Milbourns[6] must arise:

---

[1] *Sentences*] [i.e. passages from the Fathers. Peter Lombard who made a collection of these which was to settle all disputed doctrines, hence received the name of 'the Master of the Sentences.']

[2] ['The greatest of the schoolmen were the Dominican Thomas Aquinas, and the Franciscan Duns Scotus. They were founders of rival sects which wrangled with each other for two or three centuries. But the authority of their writings, which were incredibly voluminous, impeded in some measure the growth of new men.' *Hallam*, whose account of the schoolmen (so severely judged by Bacon in the *Novum Organon*) will be found in the first chapter of his *Introd. to the Liter. of Eur.*

John Duns Scotus taught at Oxford and Paris, and died at Cologne in 1308; Thomas Aquinas was born at Rocca Sicca 1227, died 1274, and was canonized 1323.]

[3] *Duck-lane*]. A place where old and second-hand books were sold formerly, near Smithfield. P.

[4] The parson alluded to was Jeremy Collier [the author of *A Short View &c. of the English Stage*]; the critic [and beau] was the Duke of Buckingham [the author of the *Rehearsal*.] *Warton.*

[5] [Sir Richard Blackmore (born about 1652, died 1729) the author of a philosophical poem called *The Creation*, attacked the dramatic authors generally in the preface to his poem of *Prince Arthur*, and Dryden individually in *A Satire on Wit*. He is the Quack Maurus of

[6] *Milbourn*]. The Rev. Mr. Luke Milbourn. See Pope's note to *Dunciad*, bk. 1. ver. 349.

Nay should great Homer lift his awful head,
Zoilus again would start up from the dead. 465
Envy will merit, as its shade, pursue;
But like a shadow, proves the substance true;
For envy'd Wit, like Sol eclips'd, makes known
Th' opposing body's grossness, not its own,
When first that sun too pow'rful beams displays, 470
It draws up vapours which obscure its rays;
But ev'n those clouds at last adorn its way.
Reflect new glories, and augment the day.
  Be thou the first true merit to befriend;
His praise is lost, who stays, till all commend. 475
Short is the date, alas, of modern rhymes,
And 't is but just to let them live betimes.
No longer now that golden age appears,
When Patriarch-wits surviv'd a thousand years:
Now length of Fame (our second life) is lost, 480
And bare threescore is all ev'n that can boast;
Our sons their fathers' failing language see,
And such as Chaucer is, shall Dryden be.
So when the faithful pencil has design'd
Some bright Idea of the master's mind, 485
Where a new world leaps out at his command,
And ready Nature waits upon his hand;
When the ripe colours soften and unite,
And sweetly melt into just shade and light;
When mellowing years their full perfection give, 490
And each bold figure just begins to live,
The treach'rous colours the fair art betray,
And all the bright creation fades away!
  Unhappy Wit, like most mistaken things,
Atones not for that envy which it brings. 495
In youth alone its empty praise we boast,
But soon the short-liv'd vanity is lost:
Like some fair flow'r the early spring supplies,
That gaily blooms, but ev'n in blooming dies.
What is this Wit, which must our cares employ? 500
The owner's wife, that other men enjoy;
Then most our trouble still when most admir'd,
And still the more we give, the more requir'd;
Whose fame with pains we guard, but lose with ease,
Sure some to vex, but never all to please; 505
'T is what the vicious fear, the virtuous shun,
By fools 't is hated, and by knaves undone!
  If Wit so much from Ign'rance undergo,
Ah let not Learning too commence its foe!

Dryden's Prologue to *The Secular Masque;* and is referred to by Swift as one of the few who 'have reach'd the *low sublime*.' But he 'beat his painful way' in spite of critics great and small; and lived to be saluted by Dennis as the author of a poem equal to that of Lucretius in poetical beauty and superior to it in argumentative strength.]

ESSAY ON CRITICISM.

Of old, those met rewards who could excel, 510
And such were prais'd who but endeavour'd well:
Tho' triumphs were to gen'rals only due,
Crowns were reserv'd to grace the soldiers too.
Now, they who reach Parnassus' lofty crown,
Employ their pains to spurn some others down; 515
And while self-love each jealous writer rules,
Contending wits become the sport of fools:
But still the worst with most regret commend,
For each ill Author is as bad a Friend.
To what base ends, and by what abject ways, 520
Are mortals urg'd thro' sacred lust of praise!
Ah ne'er so dire a thirst of glory boast,
Nor in the Critic let the Man be lost.
Good-nature and good-sense must ever join;
To err is human, to forgive, divine. 525
　But if in noble minds some dregs remain
Not yet purg'd off, of spleen and sour disdain;
Discharge that rage on more provoking crimes,
Nor fear a dearth in these flagitious times.
No pardon vile Obscenity should find, 530
Tho' wit and art conspire to move your mind;
But Dulness with Obscenity must prove
As shameful sure as Impotence in love.
In the fat age of pleasure wealth and ease,
Sprung the rank weed, and thriv'd with large increase: 535
When love was all an easy Monarch's care;
Seldom at council, never in a war:
Jilts rul'd the state, and statesmen farces writ;
Nay wits had pensions, and young Lords had wit:[1]
The Fair sate panting at a Courtier's play, 540
And not a Mask went unimprov'd away:[2]
The modest fan was lifted up no more,
And Virgins smil'd at what they blush'd before.
The following licence of a Foreign reign[3]
Did all the dregs of bold Socinus drain; 545
[4] Then unbelieving priests reform'd the nation,[5]

---

[1] [The principal 'wits to be found 'mongst noblemen' and men of fashion in the reign of Charles II. were, besides the duke of Buckingham, the earl of Rochester, the earl of Roscommon, the earl of Dorset, the marquis of Halifax, Lord Godolphin and Sir Charles Sedley. Though Dryden was laureate under Charles II., he was long left in indigence by the king, and, in laying his case before the government, bitterly exclaimed ''Tis enough for one age to have neglected Mr. Cowley, and starved Mr. Butler.' See R. Bell's *Life of John Dryden* in *Poetical Works*, I. 53, ff.]

[2] Alluding to the custom in that age of ladies going in masks to the play. *Bowles.*

[3] [Of William III., Tutchin's 'Foreigner.'] Pope, *for obvious reasons*, seems to forget there was such a King as James II. *Bowles.*

[4] The author has omitted two lines which stood here, as containing a *national reflection*, which in his stricter judgment he could not but disapprove on any people whatever. P.

[5] [viz. the 'Latitudinarian' divines of the Low Church party, of whom bishop Burnet was the most prominent.]

And taught more pleasant methods of salvation;
Where Heav'n's free subjects might their rights dispute,
Lest God himself should seem too absolute:
Pulpits their sacred satire learn'd to spare, 550
And Vice admir'd to find a flatt'rer there!
Encourag'd thus, Wit's Titans brav'd the skies,
And the press groan'd with licens'd blasphemies.
These monsters, Critics! with your darts engage,
Here point your thunder, and exhaust your rage! 555
Yet shun their fault, who, scandalously nice,
Will needs mistake an author into vice;
All seems infected that th' infected spy,
As all looks yellow to the jaundic'd eye.

   Learn then what MORALS Critics ought to show, 560
For 't is but half a Judge's task, to know.
'T is not enough, taste, judgment, learning, join;
In all you speak, let truth and candour shine:
That not alone what to your sense is due
All may allow; but seek your friendship too. 565
   Be silent always when you doubt your sense;
And speak, tho' sure, with seeming diffidence:
Some positive, persisting fops we know,
Who, if once wrong, will needs be always so;
But you, with pleasure own your errors past, 570
And make each day a Critic on the last.
   'T is not enough, your counsel still be true;
Blunt truths more mischief than nice falsehoods do;
Men must be taught as if you taught them not,
And things unknown propos'd as things forgot. 575
Without Good Breeding, truth is disapprov'd;
That only makes superior sense belov'd.
   Be niggards of advice on no pretence;
For the worst avarice is that of sense.
With mean complacence ne'er betray your trust, 580
Nor be so civil as to prove unjust.
Fear not the anger of the wise to raise;
Those best can bear reproof, who merit praise.
   'T were well might critics still this freedom take,
But Appius reddens at each word you speak, 585
And stares, tremendous, with a threat'ning eye,[1]

---

[1] *And stares, tremendous,* &c.] This picture was taken to himself by John Dennis, a furious old critic by profession, who, upon no other provocation, wrote against this essay and its author, in a manner perfectly lunatic: for, as to the mention made of him in v. 270, he took it as a compliment, and said it was treacherously meant to cause him to overlook this *abuse* of his *person*. P. [Dennis is alluded to by the name of Appius in consequence of his tragedy of *Appius and Virginia* which was damned in 1709. The thunder employed in it being both good and expensive was to the author's indignation 'stolen' for the representation of *Macbeth*. See Dibdin's *History of the Stage*, IV. 357. He is the 'Sir Tremendous' of Pope and Gay's farce, *Three Hours after Marriage*.]

ESSAY ON CRITICISM.

Like some fierce Tyrant in old tapestry.
Fear most to tax an Honourable fool,
Whose right it is, uncensur'd, to be dull;
Such, without wit, are Poets when they please,   590
As without learning they can take Degrees.[1]
Leave dang'rous truths to unsuccessful Satires,
And flattery to fulsome Dedicators,[2]
Whom, when they praise, the world believes no more,
Than when they promise to give scribbling o'er.   595
'T is best sometimes your censure to restrain,
And charitably let the dull be vain:
Your silence there is better than your spite,
For who can rail so long as they can write?
Still humming on, their drowsy course they keep,   600
And lash'd so long, like tops, are lash'd asleep.
False steps but help them to renew the race,
As, after stumbling, Jades will mend their pace.
What crowds of these, impenitently bold,
In sounds and jingling syllables grown old,   605
Still run on Poets, in a raging vein,
Ev'n to the dregs and squeezings of the brain,
Strain out the last dull droppings of their sense,
And rhyme with all the rage of Impotence.
  Such shameless Bards we have; and yet 't is true, 610
There are as mad abandon'd Critics too.
The bookful blockhead, ignorantly read,
With loads of learned lumber in his head,
With his own tongue still edifies his ears,
And always list'ning to himself appears.   615
All books he reads, and all he reads assails,
From Dryden's Fables down to Durfey's Tales.[3]
With him, most authors steal their works, or buy;
Garth did not write his own Dispensary.[4]

---

[1] *As without learning they can take Degrees.*] [Referring to a barbarous privilege of which the relics still remain at our ancient Universities.]

[2] [See on this subject Bacon's maxims (contradicted by his practice) in the first book of the *Advancement of L.*]

[3] [Durfey or D'Urfey; a writer in whom the art of versification probably reached its nadir; one of those poets who in Pope's times usually attached themselves to the chariot-wheels of some noble patron, and in our own are occasionally provided for out of the Royal Bounty Fund. Durfey's Mæcenas was that Wharton to whom according to Pope the attachment of women and fools was a condition of existence. Besides a sequel in 5 acts to the *Rehearsal* and some 'original' dramas, elegies, and panegyrical pieces, D. wrote the *Tales* on which his literary infamy chiefly rests. These versified stories, partly 'comick' and partly 'moral,' abound in every description of offence against the laws of taste, grammar, and rhyme, but are otherwise comparatively harmless.]

[4] *Garth did not write*, &c.] A common slander at that time in prejudice of that deserving author. Our poet did him this justice, when that slander most prevailed; and it is now (perhaps the sooner for this very verse) dead and forgotten. P.

[So Johnson was publicly reported to be the author of a considerable part of Goldsmith's *Traveller*, of which he wrote exactly nine lines, and Goethe of a considerable part of Schiller's *Camp of Wallenstein*, of which he wrote two lines. But the crowning discovery of this class, that Shakspere did not write his own plays, has been reserved for the present generation.]

Name a new Play, and he's the Poet's friend, 620
Nay, show'd his faults — but when would Poets mend?
No place so sacred from such fops is barr'd,
Nor is Paul's church more safe than Paul's churchyard:[1]
Nay, fly to altars; there they'll talk you dead:
For Fools rush in where Angels fear to tread.[2] 625
Distrustful sense with modest caution speaks,
It still looks home, and short excursions makes;
But rattling nonsense in full volleys breaks,
And never shock'd, and never turn'd aside,
Bursts out, resistless, with a thund'ring tide. 630
　But where's the man, who counsel can bestow,
Still pleas'd to teach, and yet not proud to know?
Unbiass'd, or by favour, or by spite;
Not dully prepossess'd, nor blindly right;
Tho' learn'd, well-bred; and tho' well-bred, sincere, 635
Modestly bold, and humanly severe:
Who to a friend his faults can freely show,
And gladly praise the merit of a foe?
Blest with a taste exact, yet unconfin'd;
A knowledge both of books and human kind: 640
Gen'rous converse; a soul exempt from pride;
And love to praise, with reason on his side?
　Such once were Critics; such the happy few,
Athens and Rome in better ages knew.
The mighty Stagirite first left the shore, 645
Spread all his sails, and durst the deeps explore:
He steer'd securely, and discover'd far,
Led by the light of the Mæonian Star.
Poets, a race long unconfin'd, and free,
Still fond and proud of savage liberty, 650
Receiv'd his laws; and stood convinc'd 't was fit,[3]
Who conquer'd Nature, should preside o'er Wit.
　Horace still charms with graceful negligence,
And without method talks us into sense,
Will, like a friend, familiarly convey 655
The truest notions in the easiest way.
He, who supreme in judgment, as in wit,
Might boldly censure, as he boldly writ,
Yet judg'd with coolness, tho' he sung with fire;
His Precepts teach but what his works inspire. 660
Our Critics take a contrary extreme,
They judge with fury, but they write with fle'me:
Nor suffers Horace more in wrong Translations
By Wits, than Critics in as wrong Quotations.

---

[1] [Before the Fire of London, St. Paul's Churchyard was the headquarters of the booksellers, who have never wholly deserted it.]

[2] [Compare the noble passage in the *Dunciad* III. 213 ff. Johnson's famous line about the female atheist seems to have been suggested by the lines in the *Essay*.]

As to Garth v. *ante*, note to p. 17.

[3] [In his *Natural History* and in his *Poetic* respectively.]

ESSAY ON CRITICISM. 69

   See Dionysius Homer's thoughts refine,[1]   665
And call new beauties forth from ev'ry line!
Fancy and art in gay Petronius please,[2]
The scholar's learning, with the courtier's ease.
In grave Quintilian's copious work, we find[3]
The justest rules, and clearest method join'd: 670
Thus useful arms in magazines we place,
All rang'd in order, and dispos'd with grace,
But less to please the eye, than arm the hand,
Still fit for use, and ready at command.
   Thee, bold Longinus![4] all the Nine inspire,   675
And bless their Critic with a Poet's fire.
An ardent Judge, who zealous in his trust,
With warmth gives sentence, yet is always just;
Whose own example strengthens all his laws;
And is himself that great Sublime he draws.   680
   Thus long succeeding Critics justly reign'd,
Licence repress'd, and useful laws ordain'd.
Learning and Rome alike in empire grew;
And Arts still follow'd where her Eagles flew;
From the same foes, at last, both felt their doom,   685
And the same age saw Learning fall, and Rome.[5]
With Tyranny, then Superstition join'd,
As that the body, this enslav'd the mind;
Much was believ'd, but little understood,
And to be dull was constru'd to be good;   690
A second deluge Learning thus o'er-run,
And the Monks finish'd what the Goths begun.
   At length Erasmus, that great injur'd name,[6]
(The glory of the Priesthood, and the shame!)
Stemm'd the wild torrent of a barb'rous age,   695
And drove those holy Vandals off the stage.
   But see! each Muse, in LEO's golden days,[7]
Starts from her trance, and trims her wither'd bays,
Rome's ancient Genius, o'er its ruins spread,
Shakes off the dust, and rears his rev'rend head   700
Then Sculpture and her sister-arts revive;
Stones leap'd to form, and rocks began to live;
With sweeter notes each rising Temple rung;[8]

---

[1] *See Dionysius.*] Of Halicarnassus. P. B. C. 30 *circ.*, author of treatise *de compositione verborum* and *Ars Rhetorica.*]

[2] [T. Petronius Arbiter, the reputed author of he *Satiricon*, lived in the time of Nero, at whose ourt he was revered as *elegantiæ arbiter.*]

[3] [M. Fabius Quintilianus, author of the *Intitutiones Oratoriæ*, born 42 A. D.]

[4] [Cassius Longinus, author of the *Treatise n the Sublime*, born 210, put to death 273 A. D.]

[5] *Rome.*] [Shakspere used both pronunciaons of this word.]

[6] [Born at Rotterdam 1467; died at Basle 1536.] ·

[7] [The papacy of Leo X. lasted from 1513 to 1521. The rebuilding of St. Peter's was commenced under his predecessor Julius II.; for whom also some of Raphael's greatest works were executed.]

[8] ' I have the best authority, that of the learned, accurate, and ingenious Dr. Burney, for observing that, in the age of Leo X., music did not keep pace with poetry in advancing towards perfection. Costantio Festa was the

A Raphael painted, and a Vida sung.¹
Immortal Vida: on whose honour'd brow 705
The Poet's bays and Critic's ivy grow:
Cremona now shall ever boast thy name,
As next in place to Mantua, next in fame!²
  But soon by impious arms from Latium chas'd,³
Their ancient bounds the banish'd Muses pass'd; 710
Thence Arts o'er all the northern world advance,
But Critic-learning flourish'd most in France:
The rules a nation, born to serve, obeys;
And Boileau still in right of Horace sways.⁴
But we, brave Britons, foreign laws despis'd, 715
And kept unconquer'd, and unciviliz'd;
Fierce for the liberties of wit, and bold,
We still defy'd the Romans, as of old.
Yet some there were, among the sounder few
Of those who less presum'd, and better knew, 720
Who durst assert the juster ancient cause,
And here restor'd Wit's fundamental laws.
Such was the Muse, whose rules and practice tell,⁵
"Nature's chief Master-piece is writing well."

---

best Italian composer during the time of Leo, and Pietro Aaron the best theorist. Palestrina was not born till eight years after the death of Leo.' *Warton.*

¹ [Vida is as a critical writer chiefly known by his *Art of Poetry*, subsequently, and probably in consequence of Pope's encomium, translated into English by Christopher Pitt. This *Art of Poetry*, written about 1520, is chiefly directed to a consideration of the rules of Epic Poetry; and was the first of many similar discourses by Italian poets, Torquato Tasso among the number.]

² *As next in place to Mantua,*] Alluding to 'Mantua væ miseræ nimium vicina Cremonæ.' *Virg.*
This application is made in Kennet's edition of Vida. *Warton.*

³ [Referring to the sack of Rome by the duke of Bourbon in 1527.]

⁴ [Boileau's (1636-1711) *Art Poétique*, in four cantos, like Pope's essay itself, heralds no new literary era; it is rather a summary by an independent critic of precepts which apply to poetic literature in general, though they are frequently pointed by special and even personal application. Nicolas Despréaux Boileau was born in 1636 and lived till 1711. Besides the *A.P.* his *Epistles* and *Lutrin* are his most noteworthy productions; as a satirist he is of the school of Horace rather than of Juvenal; as a critic he is distinguished by incisiveness rather than breadth. His *Odes* have no exceptional merit.]

⁵ *Such was the Muse,*] — *Essay on Poetry* by the Duke of Buckingham. Our poet is not the only one of his time who complimented this *Essay*, and its noble author. Mr. Dryden had done it very largely in the dedication to his translation of the Æneid; and Dr. Garth in the first edition of the *Dispensary* says,

'The Tiber now no courtly Gallus sees,
But smiling Thames enjoys his Normanbys.'

Though afterwards omitted, when parties were carried so high in the reign of Queen Anne, as to allow no commendation to an opposite in politics. The Duke was all his life a steady adherent to the Church-of-England party, yet an enemy to the extravagant measures of the court in the reign of Charles II. On which account after having strongly patronized Mr. Dryden, a coolness succeeded between them on that poet's bsolute attachment to the court, which carried him some lengths beyond what the Duke could approve of. This nobleman's true character had been very well marked by Mr. Dryden before,

'the Muse's friend,
Himself a Muse. In Sanadrin's debate
True to his prince, but not a slave of state.'
                              Abs. and Achit.

Our Author was more happy, he was honour'd very young with his friendship, and it continued till his death in all the circumstances of a familiar esteem. P.

ESSAY ON CRITICISM. 71

Such was Roscommon,[1] not more learn'd than good, 725
With manners gen'rous as his noble blood;
To him the wit of Greece and Rome was known,
And ev'ry author's merit, but his own.
Such late was Walsh [2]— the Muse's judge and friend,
Who justly knew to blame or to commend; 730
To failings mild, but zealous for desert;
The clearest head, and the sincerest heart.
This humble praise, lamented shade! receive,
This praise at least a grateful Muse may give:
The Muse, whose early voice you taught to sing, 735
Prescrib'd her heights, and prun'd her tender wing,
(Her guide now lost) no more attempts to rise,
But in low numbers short excursions tries:
Content, if hence th' unlearn'd their wants may view,
The learn'd reflect on what before they knew: 740
Careless of censure, nor too fond of fame;
Still pleas'd to praise, yet not afraid to blame,
Averse alike to flatter, or offend;
Not free from faults, nor yet too vain to mend.[8]

---

[1] An Essay on Translated Verse, seems, at first sight, to be a barren subject; yet Roscommon has decorated it with many precepts in utility and taste, and enlivened it with a tale in imitation of Boileau. It is indisputably better written, in a closer and more vigorous style, than the last-mentioned essay. Roscommon was more learned than Buckingham. He was bred under Bochart, at Caen in Normandy. He had laid a design of forming a society for the refining and fixing the standard of our language; in which project his intimate friend Dryden was a principal assistant. *Warton.*

[Wentworth Dillon earl of Roscommon, nephew of the great earl of Strafford, was born about 1632 and died in 1684. His muse was chaste at a dissolute court; but in his habits of life he participated in one at least of the vices of the age. As to his design of founding an English Academy, it was revived by De Foe and probably plagiarized from the latter by Swift, and also found favour with Prior and Tickell. It has been again advanced, upon a broader basis, by a brilliant critic of our own days. See Matthew Arnold's essay on *The Literary Influence of Academies.*]

[John Sheffield earl of Mulgrave and marquis of Normanby by creation of William and Mary, and duke of Buckinghamshire by creation of Queen Anne, was born in 1649 and died in 1722. His *Essay on Poetry*, to which Pope has given an undeserved immortality, is a short and tolerably meagre performance, in which a variety of disjointed rules are applied to the principal species of poetic composition. It contains however some vigorous lines and some sensible observations of individual criticism. Compare note to p. 59.]

[2] If Pope has here given too magnificent an eulogy to Walsh, it must be attributed to friendship, rather than to judgment. Walsh was, in general, a flimsy and frigid writer. The *Rambler* calls his works pages of inanity. His three letters to Pope, however, are well written. . . . Pope owed much to Walsh; it was he who gave him a very important piece of advice, in his early youth; for he used to tell our author, that there was now any still left open for him by which he might excel any of his predecessors, which was, by correctness; that though, indeed, we had several great poets, we as yet could boast of none that were perfectly correct; and that therefore he advised him to make this quality his particular study. *Warton.*

[As to Walsh's suggestion with reference to the Fourth Pastoral, see Pope's note to p. 11. William Walsh was born in 1663 and died about 1709; his poems and imitations shew him to have been an elegant and pleasing writer, who, however, in Dr. Johnson's words, 'is known more by his familiarity with greater men, than by anything done or written by himself.']

[3] These concluding lines bear a great resemblance to Boileau's conclusion of his *Art of Poetry*, but are perhaps superior: [saire, 'Censeur un peu facheux, mais souvent nécesPlus enclin à blâmer, que savant à bien faire.'
Warton.

THE RAPE OF THE LOCK.

AN HEROI-COMICAL POEM.

[1] Nolueram, Belinda, tuos violare capillos;
Sed juvat, hoc precibus me tribuisse tuis. MART. [*Epigr.* XII. 84.]

TO MRS. ARABELLA FERMOR.[2]

MADAM,

It will be in vain to deny that I have some regard for this piece, since I dedicate it to You. Yet you may bear me witness, it was intended only to divert a few young Ladies, who have good sense and good humour enough to laugh not only at their sex's little unguarded follies, but at their own. But as it was communicated with the air of a Secret, it soon found its way into the world. An imperfect copy having been offer'd to a Bookseller, you had the good-nature for my sake to consent to the publication of one more correct: This I was forc'd to, before I had executed half my design, for the Machinery was entirely wanting to compleat it.

The Machinery, Madam, is a term invented by the Critics, to signify that part which the Deities, Angels, or Dæmons are made to act in a Poem: For the ancient Poets are in one respect like many modern Ladies: let an action be never so trivial in itself, they always make it appear of the utmost importance. These Machines I determined to raise on a very new and odd foundation, the Rosicrucian doctrine of Spirits.

I know how disagreeable it is to make use of hard words before a Lady; but 't is so much the concern of a Poet to have his works understood, and particularly by your Sex, that you must give me leave to explain two or three difficult terms.

The Rosicrucians are a people I must bring you acquainted with. The best account I know of them is in a French book call'd *Le Comte de Gabalis*, which both in its title and size is so like a Novel, that many of the Fair Sex have read it for one by mistake. According to these Gentlemen, the four Elements are inhabited by Spirits, which they call Sylphs, Gnomes, Nymphs, and Salamanders. The Gnomes or Dæmons of Earth delight in mischief; but the Sylphs, whose habitation is in the Air, are the best-condition'd creatures imaginable. For they say, any mortals may enjoy the most intimate familiarities with these gentle Spirits, upon a condition very easy to all true Adepts, an inviolate preservation of Chastity.

---

[1] It appears, by this Motto, that the following Poem was written or published at the Lady's request. But there are some further circumstances not unworthy relating. Mr. Caryll (a Gentleman who was Secretary to Queen Mary, wife of James II. whose fortunes he followed into France, Author of the Comedy of *Sir Solomon Single*, and of several translations in Dryden's Miscellanies) originally proposed the subject to him in a view of putting an end, by this piece of ridicule, to a quarrel that was risen between two noble Families, those of Lord Petre and of Mrs. Fermor, on the trifling occasion of his having cut off a lock of her hair. The Author sent it to the Lady, with whom he was acquainted; and she took it so well as to give about copies of it. That first sketch, (we learn from one of his Letters) was written in less than a fortnight, in 1711, in two Cantos only, and it was so printed [see Appendix III. page 527]; first, in a Miscellany of Bern. Lintot's, without the name of the Author. But it was received so well that he made it more considerable the next year by the addition of the machinery of the Sylphs, and extended it to five Cantos.... This insertion he always esteemed, and justly, the greatest effort of his *skill* and *art* as a Poet. *Warburton.*

[2] [Warton quotes a poem addressed to the same lady by Parnell, on her leaving London, commencing: 'From town fair Arabella flies.' Miss Arabella Fermor's niece, Prioress of the English Austin Nuns at the Fossée at Paris, told Mrs. Piozzi 'that she believed there was but little comfort to be found in a house that harboured *poets;* for that she remembered Mr. Pope's praise made her aunt very troublesome and conceited, while his numberless caprices would have employed ten servants to wait on him.' *Life and Writings of Mrs. Piozzi*, i. 329. Miss Arabella Fermor was, in 1714, married to Francis Perkins, Esq. of Ufton Court, Berks. Though her own and her father's family are both extinct, her portrait is still preserved at his earlier seat, Tusmore. See Carruthers, *Life of Pope*, 107.]

As to the following Canto's, all the passages of them are as fabulous, as the Vision at the beginning, or the Transformation at the end; (except the loss of your Hair, which I always mention with reverence). The Human persons are as fictitious as the airy ones; and the character of Belinda, as it is now manag'd, resembles you in nothing but in Beauty.

If this Poem had as many Graces as there are in your Person, or in your Mind, yet I could never hope it should pass thro' the world half so Uncensur'd as You have done. But let its fortune be what it will, mine is happy enough, to have given me this occasion of assuring you that I am, with the truest esteem, MADAM,

Your most obedient, Humble Servant,

A. POPE.

[The original idea of this delightful poem — *merum sal*, as Addison called it — was confessedly due to Pope's friend Caryll; and the characters which carry on its action all belong to the circle of Catholic families in which Pope at the time moved. The heroine and her assailant are identified by him in his note; Thalestris was Mrs. Morley, and Sir Plume her brother Sir George Brown, who not unnaturally resented the use to which his individuality was put in the poem. In its original form it was published in 1712, in its present complete form, containing the addition of the machinery of the Sylphs,[1] in 1714. The *Key to the Lock*, put forth in the following year by 'Esdras Barnevelt Apoth.,' which gravely explained the whole poem as a covert satire upon Queen Anne and the Barrier Treaty, was only one of those exegetical mystifications to which Pope was in the habit of treating his public — apparently at his own expense, in reality in order to attract an adventitious interest to his own productions.

The *Rape of the Lock* is correctly termed by its author a heroicomical poem, and belongs distinctly to that class of compositions which we call *burlesque*. In other words, it applies a peculiar kind of treatment to a subject palpably and therefore ludicrously undeserving of it. It differs from poems which are mere parodies on other poems, inasmuch as it burlesques or mocks an entire *class* of poetry; and herein lies its superiority to a mere travesty, such as the *Batrachomyomachia*. As its true predecessors Warton notes the *Rape of the Bucket* (1612) by Alessandro Tassoni, and two other similar Italian works. With Boileau's *Lutrin* (translated into English by Rowe in 1708) the *Rape of the Lock* has in common both nature of subject and method of treatment — a trivial quarrel humorously dignified with epical importance. But while the French poem almost rises to the level of a national satire, the English is rather, to adopt Roscoe's expression, a social 'pleasantry.' The surly cavil of Dennis, that Pope's poem wants a moral and is on that account inferior to the *Lutrin*, scarcely required to be refuted with mock gravity by Dr. Johnson, who declares that 'the freaks, and humours, and spleen, and vanity of women, as they embroil families in discord, and fill houses with disquiet, do more to obstruct the happiness of life in a year than the ambition of the clergy in many centuries.'

Strange to say, the opposite objection has recently been made to a work of which the execution has in general been allowed to possess in a rare degree the double charm which pervades the irony of polite conversation. Mr. Taine would insist that even the *Rape of the Lock* is in its entire scheme nothing more than a practical joke in the fashionable style, and persuade his readers that, like all his English contemporaries, Pope, in representing the life of the world, retained and revealed the contempt which he had for it in his heart. Pope, even here, is according to this consistent critic in reality far from polite, and sins against the good manners of which he affects the varnish. This criticism is perhaps the most striking instance in Mr. Taine's admirable work of his tendency towards straining a special instance in order to make it fit into a general view. It is quite true that the spirit of the age to which Pope belonged was devoid of true delicacy in the appreciation of the nobler relations between the sexes; quite true that Pope individually showed in many of his poems a want of that genuine tenderness which may display itself in satire as well as in erotic verse. But the *Rape*

---

[1] [Mr. Kingsley, in his essay on *Alexander Smith and Alexander Pope*, has pointed out how Pope, in employing the Sylphs as poetic machinery, viewed them, after the precedent of Spenser and Ariosto, solely in their fancied connexion with man; while the relation of such mythological beings to nature (an aspect under which they were equally regarded by the Greeks) was only restored to them in literature by the moderns, Schiller and Goethe and Keats.]

of the Lock being intended as a piece of raillery, can only be condemned if in it raillery passes the bounds of what is pleasing; and though doubtless much might have been put into the poem which is not there, yet what there is in it (if due allowance be made for certain approaches to a coarseness by no means confined to the contemporary literature of any one particular country), is both light and charming; and if a moral be conveyed, it is (except in a single passage towards the beginning of the last Canto) implied with well-bred ease and good humour, and not sourly obtruded upon an unprepared audience.

The *Rape of the Lock* enjoyed the honour of translation by a distinguished French writer. Marmontel's *Boucle de Cheveux enlevée* is upon the whole a spirited and successful effort, not more inaccurate than is usually the case with French translations, and felicitous in some of the more salient passages, as *e.g.* the description of the game at Ombre. But the antithetical brilliancy of Pope's lines, nowhere more observable than in this poem, is all but lost in the easy flow of the French version, which is of course in Alexandrines. If dramatic pieces be left out of the question, the *Rape of the Lock* is probably one of the longest occasional poems in any literature; and yet French literature itself may be challenged to match the sparkling vivacity of its execution no less than the airy grace of its plot and under-plot.]

CANTO I.

WHAT dire offence from am'rous causes springs,
  What mighty contests rise from trivial things,
I sing — This verse to CARYL,[1] Muse! is due:
This, ev'n Belinda may vouchsafe to view:
Slight is the subject, but not so the praise,   5
If She inspire, and He approve my lays.
  Say what strange motive, Goddess! could compel
A well-bred Lord t' assault a gentle Belle?
O say what stranger cause, yet unexplor'd,
Could make a gentle Belle reject a Lord?   10
In tasks so bold, can little men engage,
And in soft bosoms dwells such mighty Rage?
  Sol thro' white curtains shot a tim'rous ray,
And oped those eyes that must eclipse the day:
Now lap-dogs give themselves the rousing shake,   15
And sleepless lovers, just at twelve, awake:
Thrice rung the bell, the slipper knock'd the ground,
And the press'd watch return'd a silver sound.
Belinda still her downy pillow prest,
Her guardian SYLPH prolong'd the balmy rest: 20
'T was He had summon'd to her silent bed
The morning-dream that hover'd o'er her head;
A Youth more glitt'ring than a Birth-night Beau,
(That ev'n in slumber caus'd her cheek to glow)
Seem'd to her ear his winning lips to lay,   25
And thus in whispers said, or seem'd to say.
  "Fairest of mortals, thou distinguish'd care
Of thousand bright Inhabitants of Air!
If e'er one vision touch'd thy infant thought,

---

[1] [John Caryll, a gentleman of an ancient Catholic family in Sussex, and till his death in 1736 a most intimate friend of Pope's. See *Introductory Memoir*.]

Of all the Nurse and all the Priest have taught;   30
Of airy Elves by moonlight shadows seen,
The silver token, and the circled green,
Or virgins visited by Angel-pow'rs,
With golden crowns and wreaths of heav'nly flow'rs;
Hear and believe! thy own importance know,   35
Nor bound thy narrow views to things below,
Some secret truths, from learned pride conceal'd,
To Maids alone and Children are reveal'd:
What tho' no credit doubting Wits may give?
The Fair and Innocent shall still believe.   40
Know, then, unnumber'd Spirits round thee fly,
The light Militia of the lower sky:
These, tho' unseen, are ever on the wing,
Hang o'er the Box, and hover round the Ring.
Think what an equipage thou hast in Air,   45
And view with scorn two Pages and a Chair.
As now your own, our beings were of old,[1]
And once enclos'd in Woman's beauteous mould;
Thence, by a soft transition, we repair
From earthly Vehicles to these of air.   50
Think not, when Woman's transient breath is fled
That all her vanities at once are dead;
Succeeding vanities she still regards,
And tho' she plays no more, o'erlooks the cards.
Her joy in gilded Chariots, when alive,   55
And love of Ombre, after death survive.[2]
For when the Fair in all their pride expire,
To their first Elements their Souls retire:
The Sprites of fiery Termagant in Flame
Mount up, and take a Salamander's name.   60
Soft yielding minds to Water glide away,
And sip, with Nymphs, their elemental Tea.
The graver Prude sinks downward to a Gnome,
In search of mischief still on Earth to roam.
The light Coquettes in Sylphs aloft repair,   65
And sport and flutter in the fields of Air.
"Know further yet; whoever fair and chaste

---

[1] *As now your own, etc.*] He here forsakes the Rosicrucian system; which, in this part, is too extravagant even for poetry; and gives a beautiful fiction of his own, on the Platonic Theology of the continuance of the passions in *another state*, when the mind, before its leaving *this*, has not been purged and purified by philosophy; which furnishes an occasion for much useful satire. *Warburton.*

[2] [Chatto, in his *History of Playing-Cards*, disproves the statement of Barrington, that Ombre was probably introduced by Catherine of Portugal, the queen of Charles II. (since Waller has a poem 'On a card torn at Ombre by the Queen,') by reference to a political pamphlet entitled *The Royal game of Ombre*, published at London in 1660, two years before the Queen's arrival in England. In the reign of Queen Anne, according to Chatto, Ombre was the favourite game of the ladies, as Piquet of the gentlemen. The name of the former game is of course derived from the Spanish word for *a man;* and 'there is reason to believe that it was one of the oldest games at cards played in Europe.']

Rejects mankind, is by some Sylph embrac'd:
For Spirits, freed from mortal laws, with ease
Assume what sexes and what shapes they please.   70
What guards the purity of melting Maids,
In courtly balls, and midnight masquerades,
Safe from the treach'rous friend, the daring spark,
The glance by day, the whisper in the dark,
When kind occasion prompts their warm desires,   75
When music softens, and when dancing fires?
'Tis, but their Sylph, the wise Celestials know,
Tho' Honour is the word with Men below.[1]

"Some nymphs there are, too conscious of their face[2]
For life predestin'd to the Gnomes' embrace.   80
These swell their prospects and exalt their pride,
When offers are disdain'd, and love deny'd:
Then gay Ideas crowd the vacant brain,
While Peers, and Dukes, and all their sweeping train,
And Garters, Stars, and Coronets appear,   85
And in soft sounds, Your Grace salutes their ear.
'Tis these that early taint the female soul,
Instruct the eyes of young Coquettes to roll,
Teach Infant-cheeks a bidden blush to know,
And little hearts to flutter at a Beau.   90

"Oft, when the world imagine women stray,
The Sylphs thro' mystic mazes guide their way,
Thro' all the giddy circle they pursue,
And old impertinence expel by new.
What tender maid but must a victim fall   95
To one man's treat, but for another's ball?
When Florio speaks what virgin could withstand,
If gentle Damon did not squeeze her hand?
With varying vanities, from ev'ry part,
They shift the moving Toyshop of their heart;   100
Where wigs with wigs, with sword-knots sword-knots strive,
Beaux banish beaux, and coaches coaches drive.
This erring mortals Levity may call;
Oh blind to truth! the Sylphs contrive it all.

"Of these am I, who thy protection claim,   105
A watchful sprite, and Ariel is my name.
Late, as I rang'd the crystal wilds of air,
In the clear Mirror[3] of thy ruling Star
I saw, alas! some dread event impend,
Ere to the main this morning sun descend,   110
But heav'n reveals not what, or how, or where:
Warn'd by the Sylph, oh pious maid, beware!

---

[1] *Tho' honour is the word with men below.*] Parody of Homer. *Warburton.*

[2] *too conscious of their face,*] i.e. too sensible of their beauty. *Warburton.*

[3] *In the clear mirror*] The language of the Platonists, the writers of the intelligible world of Spirits, etc. P.

OF THE LOCK.   77

This to disclose is all thy guardian can:
Beware of all, but most beware of Man!"
He said; when Shock,[1] who thought she slept too long, 115
Leap'd up, and wak'd his mistress with his tongue.
'Twas then, Belinda, if report say true,
Thy eyes first open'd on a Billet-doux;
Wounds, Charms, and Ardors were no sooner read,
But all the Vision vanish'd from thy head.   120
And now, unveil'd, the Toilet stands display'd,
Each silver Vase in mystic order laid.
First, rob'd in white, the Nymph intent adores,
With head uncover'd, the Cosmetic pow'rs.[2]
A heav'nly image in the glass appears,   125
To that she bends, to that her eyes she rears;
Th' inferior Priestess,[3] at her altar's side,
Trembling begins the sacred rites of Pride.
Unnumber'd treasures ope at once, and here
The various off'rings of the world appear;   130
From each she nicely culls with curious toil,
And decks the Goddess with the glitt'ring spoil.
This casket India's glowing gems unlocks,
And all Arabia breathes from yonder box.
The Tortoise here and Elephant unite,   135
Transform'd to combs, the speckled, and the white.
Here files of pins extend their shining rows,
Puffs, Powders, Patches, Bibles, Billet-doux.
Now awful Beauty puts on all its arms;
The fair each moment rises in her charms,   140
Repairs her smiles, awakens ev'ry grace,
And calls forth all the wonders of her face;
Sees by degrees a purer blush arise,
And keener lightnings quicken in her eyes.
The busy Sylphs surround their darling care,[4]   145
These set the head, and those divide the hair,
Some fold the sleeve, whilst others plait the gown;
And Betty's prais'd for labours not her own.

---

[1] [Shock = shough (*Macbeth*) i.e. shaggy.]

[2] [Cosmetics formed a separate branch of ancient medicine; and works on the subject were dedicated to Cleopatra and to Plotina the consort of Trajan by their body-physicians. Of Ovid's *Medicamina Faciei* only the first hundred lines remain. See note to chap. 1. of Böttiger's *Sabina*, where the description of the Roman beauty's toilet should be compared with Pope's slighter and graceful touches.]

[3] *Th' inferior Priestess*,] There is a small inaccuracy in these lines. He first makes his heroine the chief priestess, and then the goddess herself. *Warburton*.

[4] *The busy Sylphs, etc.*] Ancient traditions of the Rabbis relate, that several of the fallen angels became amorous of women, and particularize some; among the rest Asael, who lay with Naamah, the wife of Noah, or of Ham; and who, continuing impenitent, still presides over the women's toilets. Bereshi Rabbi in Genes. vi. 2. P.

CANTO II.

Not with more glories, in th' etherial plain,
The Sun first rises o'er the purpled main,
Than, issuing forth, the rival of his beams
Launch'd on the bosom of the silver Thames.
Fair Nymphs, and well-drest Youths around her shone, 5
But ev'ry eye was fix'd on her alone.
On her white breast a sparkling Cross she wore,
Which Jews might kiss, and Infidels adore.
Her lively looks a sprightly mind disclose,
Quick as her eyes, and as unfix'd as those: 10
Favours to none, to all she smiles extends;
Oft she rejects, but never once offends.
Bright as the sun, her eyes the gazers strike,
And, like the sun, they shine on all alike.
Yet graceful ease, and sweetness void of pride, 15
Might hide her faults, if Belles had faults to hide:
If to her share some female errors fall,
Look on her face, and you'll forget 'em all.

  This Nymph, to the destruction of mankind,
Nourish'd two Locks, which graceful hung behind 20
In equal curls, and well conspir'd to deck
With shining ringlets the smooth iv'ry neck.
Love in these labyrinths his slaves detains,
And mighty hearts are held in slender chains.
With hairy springes we the birds betray, 25
Slight lines of hair surprise the finny prey,
Fair tresses man's imperial race ensnare,
And beauty draws us with a single hair.

  Th' advent'rous Baron the bright locks admir'd;
He saw, he wish'd, and to the prize aspir'd. 30
Resolv'd to win, he meditates the way,
By force to ravish, or by fraud betray;
For when success a Lover's toil attends,
Few ask, if fraud or force attain'd his ends.

  For this, ere Phœbus rose, he had implor'd 35
Propitious heav'n, and ev'ry pow'r ador'd,
But chiefly Love — to Love an Altar built,
Of twelve vast French Romances, neatly gilt.
There lay three garters, half a pair of gloves;
And all the trophies of his former loves; 40
With tender Billet-doux he lights the pyre,
And breathes three am'rous sighs to raise the fire.
Then prostrate falls, and begs with ardent eyes
Soon to obtain, and long possess the prize:
The pow'rs gave ear,[1] and granted half his pray'r, 45
The rest, the winds dispers'd in empty air.

[1] Virg. Æn. XI. vv. 794-5. P.

But now secure the painted vessel glides,
The sun-beams trembling on the floating tides:
While melting music steals upon the sky,
And soften'd sounds along the waters die; 50
Smooth flow the waves, the Zephyrs gently play,
Belinda smil'd, and all the world was gay.
All but the Sylph — with careful thoughts opprest,
Th' inpending woe sat heavy on his breast.
He summons strait his Denizens of air; 55
The lucid squadrons round the sails repair:
Soft o'er the shrouds aërial whispers breathe,
That seem'd but Zephyrs to the train beneath.
Some to the sun their insect-wings unfold,
Waft on the breeze, or sink in clouds of gold; 60
Transparent forms, too fine for mortal sight,
Their fluid bodies half dissolv'd in light,
Loose to the wind their airy garments flew,
Thin glitt'ring textures of the filmy dew,
Dipt in the richest tincture of the skies, 65
Where light disports in ever-mingling dyes,
While ev'ry beam new transient colours flings,
Colours that change whene'er they wave their wings.
Amid the circle, on the gilded mast,
Superior by the head, was Ariel plac'd; 70
His purple pinions op'ning to the sun,
He rais'd his azure wand, and thus begun.
"Ye Sylphs and Sylphids, to your chief give ear!
Fays, Fairies, Genii, Elves, and Dæmons, hear![1]
Ye know the spheres and various tasks assign'd 75
By laws eternal to th' aërial kind.
Some in the fields of purest Æther play,
And bask and whiten in the blaze of day.
Some guide the course of wand'ring orbs on high,
Or roll the planets thro' the boundless sky. 80
Some less refin'd, beneath the moon's pale light
Pursue the stars that shoot athwart the night,
Or suck the mists in grosser air below,
Or dip their pinions in the painted bow,
Or brew fierce tempests on the wintry main, 85
Or o'er the glebe distil the kindly rain.
Others on earth o'er human race preside,
Watch all their ways, and all their actions guide:
Of these the chief the care of Nations own,
And guard with Arms divine the British Throne. 90
"Our humbler province is to tend the Fair,
Not a less pleasing, tho' less glorious care;
To save the powder from too rude a gale;
Nor let th' imprison'd essences exhale;

---

[1] [The invocation as in Satan's address to the 'Thrones, Dominations, Princedoms, Virtues, Powers,' in *Paradise Lost*.]

To draw fresh colours from the vernal flow'rs; 95
To steal from rainbows e'er they drop in show'rs
A brighter wash; to curl their waving hairs,
Assist their blushes, and inspire their airs;
Nay oft, in dreams, invention we bestow,
To change a Flounce, or add a Furbelow. 100
  "This day, black Omens threat the brightest Fair,
That e'er deserv'd a watchful spirit's care;
Some dire disaster, or by force, or slight;
But what, or where, the fates have wrapt in night.
Whether the nymph shall break Diana's law, 105
Or some frail China jar receive a flaw;
Or stain her honour or her new brocade;
Forget her pray'rs, or miss a masquerade;
Or lose her heart, or necklace, at a ball;
Or whether Heav'n has doom'd that Shock must fall. 110
Haste, then, ye spirits! to your charge repair:
The flutt'ring fan be Zephyretta's care;
The drops to thee, Brillante, we consign;
And, Momentilla, let the watch be thine;
Do thou, Crispissa, tend her fav'rite Lock; 115
Ariel himself shall be the guard of Shock.
  "To fifty chosen Sylphs, of special note,
We trust th' important charge, the Petticoat:[1]
Oft have we known that seven-fold fence to fail,
Tho' stiff with hoops, and arm'd with ribs of whale; 120
Form a strong line about the silver bound,
And guard the wide circumference around.
  "Whatever spirit, careless of his charge,
His post neglects, or leaves the fair at large,
Shall feel sharp vengeance soon o'ertake his sins, 125
Be stopp'd in vials, or transfix'd with pins;
Or plung'd in lakes of bitter washes lie,
Or wedg'd whole ages in a bodkin's eye:
Gums and Pomatums shall his flight restrain,
While clogg'd he beats his silken wings in vain; 130
Or Alum styptics with contracting pow'r
Shrink his thin essence like a rivel'd flow'r:
Or, as Ixion fix'd, the wretch shall feel
The giddy motion of the whirling Mill,
In fumes of burning Chocolate shall glow, 135
And tremble at the sea that froths below!"
  He spoke; the spirits from the sails descend;
Some, orb in orb, around the nymph extend;
Some thrid the mazy ringlets of her hair;
Some hang upon the pendants of her ear: 140
With beating hearts the dire event they wait,
Anxious, and trembling for the birth of Fate.

[1] It is impossible here not to recollect that matchless piece of raillery and exquisite humour, of Addison, in the 127th *Spectator*, on this important part of female dress. *Warton*.

CANTO III.

CLOSE by those meads, for ever crown'd with flow'rs,
Where Thames with pride surveys his rising tow'rs,
There stands a structure of majestic frame,
Which from the neighb'ring Hampton takes its name.
Here Britain's statesmen oft the fall foredoom   5
Of foreign Tyrants and of Nymphs at home;
Here thou, great ANNA! whom three realms obey,
Dost sometimes counsel take—and sometimes Tea.
  Hither the heroes and the nymphs resort,
To taste awhile the pleasures of a Court;   10
In various talk th' instructive hours they past,
Who gave the ball, or paid the visit last;
One speaks the glory of the British Queen,
And one describes a charming Indian screen;
A third interprets motions, looks, and eyes;   15
At ev'ry word a reputation dies.
Snuff, or the fan, supply each pause of chat,
With singing, laughing, ogling, *and all that*.
  Mean while, declining from the noon of day,
The sun obliquely shoots his burning ray;   20
The hungry Judges soon the sentence sign,
And wretches hang that jury-men may dine;[1]
The merchant from th' Exchange returns in peace,
And the long labours of the Toilet cease.
Belinda now, whom thirst of fame invites,   25
Burns to encounter two advent'rous Knights,
At Ombre singly to decide their doom;
And swells her breast with conquests yet to come.
Straight the three bands prepare in arms to join,
Each band the number of the sacred nine.   30
Soon as she spreads her hand, th' aërial guard
Descend, and sit on each important card:
First Ariel perch'd upon a Matadore,[2]
Then each, according to the rank they bore;
For Sylphs, yet mindful of their ancient race,   35
Are, as when women, wondrous fond of place.
  Behold, four Kings in majesty rever'd,
With hoary whiskers and a forky beard;
And four fair Queens whose hands sustain a flow'r,
Th' expressive emblem of their softer pow'r;   40
Four Knaves in garbs succinct, a trusty band,
Caps on their heads, and halberts in their hand;
And particolour'd troops, a shining train,
Draw forth to combat on the velvet plain.

---

[1] From Congreve. *Warton*.
[2] From the terms used in the game of Ombre —Spadillo, Basto, Matador, Punto, &c.—there can scarcely be a doubt that the other nations of Western Europe derived their knowledge of it from the Spaniards. *Chatto*.

THE RAPE

    The skilful Nymph reviews her force with care: 45
Let Spades be trumps! she said, and trumps they were.
    Now move to war her sable Matadores,[1]
In show like leaders of the swarthy Moors.
Spadillio[2] first, unconquerable Lord!
Led off two captive trumps, and swept the board.   50
As many more Manillio[3] forc'd to yield,
And march'd a victor from the verdant field.
Him Basto[4] follow'd, but his fate more hard
Gain'd but one trump and one Plebeian card.
With his broad sabre next, a chief in years,   55
The hoary Majesty of Spades appears,
Puts forth one manly leg, to sight reveal'd,
The rest, his many-colour'd robe conceal'd.
The rebel Knave, who dares his prince engage,
Proves the just victim of his royal rage.   60
Ev'n mighty Pam, that Kings and Queens o'erthrew[5]
And mow'd down armies in the fights of Lu,[6]
Sad chance of war! now destitute of aid,
Falls undistinguish'd by the victor spade!
    Thus far both armies to Belinda yield;   65
Now to the Baron fate inclines the field.
His warlike Amazon her host invades,
Th' imperial consort of the crown of Spades.
The Club's black Tyrant first her victim dy'd,
Spite of his haughty mien, and barb'rous pride: 70
What boots the regal circle on his head,
His giant limbs, in state unwieldy spread;
That long behind he trails his pompous robe,
And, of all monarch's, only grasps the globe?
    The Baron now his Diamonds pours apace;   75
Th' embroider'd King who shows but half his face,
And his refulgent Queen, with pow'rs combin'd
Of broken troops an easy conquest find.
Clubs, Diamonds, Hearts, in wild disorder seen,
With throngs promiscuous strow the level green.   80
Thus when dispers'd a routed army runs,
Of Asia's troops, and Afric's sable sons,
With like confusion different nations fly,
Of various habit, and of various dye,
The pierc'd battalions dis-united fall,   85
In heaps on heaps; one fate o'erwhelms them all.

---

[1] *Now move to war, etc.*] The whole idea of this description of a game at Ombre, is taken from Vida's description of a game at chess, in his poem intit. *Scacchia Ludus. Warburton.*

[2] [*Spadillio:* the ace of spades, the first trump at Ombre.]

[3] [*Manillio:* the deuce of trumps when trumps are black, the seven when they are red. The second trump at Ombre.]

[4] [*Basto:* the ace of clubs, third trump at Ombre. These three principal trumps are called *Matadores.*]

[5] At certain games the Knave of Clubs is called *Pam. Chatto.*

[6] [*Lu*, the game of Loo, in which *Pam* is the highest card.]

OF THE LOCK.

The Knave of Diamonds tries his wily arts,
And wins (oh shameful chance!) the Queen of Hearts.
At this, the blood the virgin's cheek forsook,
A livid paleness spreads o'er all her look;   90
She sees, and trembles at th' approaching ill,
Just in the jaws of ruin, and Codille.[1]
And now (as oft in some distemper'd State)
On one nice Trick depends the gen'ral fate.
An Ace of Hearts steps forth: The King unseen   95
Lurk'd in her hand, and mourn'd his captive Queen:
He springs to Vengeance with an eager pace,
And falls like thunder on the prostrate Ace.
The nymph exulting fills with shouts the sky;
The walls, the woods, and long canals reply.   100
   Oh thoughtless mortals! ever blind to fate,
Too soon dejected, and too soon elate.
Sudden, these honours shall be snatch'd away,
And curs'd for ever this victorious day.
   For lo! the board with cups and spoons is crown'd,   105
The berries crackle, and the mill turns round;
On shining Altars of Japan they raise
The silver lamp; the fiery spirits blaze:
From silver spouts the grateful liquors glide,
While China's earth receives the smoking tide: 110
At once they gratify their scent and taste,
And frequent cups prolong the rich repast.
Straight hover round the Fair her airy band;
Some, as she sipp'd the fuming liquor fann'd,
Some o'er her lap their careful plumes display'd,   115
Trembling, and conscious of the rich brocade.
Coffee, (which makes the politician wise,
And see thro' all things with his half-shut eyes)[2]
Sent up in vapours to the Baron's brain
New Stratagems, the radiant Lock to gain.   120
Ah cease, rash youth! desist ere 't is too late,
Fear the just Gods, and think of Scylla's Fate![3]
Chang'd to a bird, and sent to flit in air,
She dearly pays for Nisus' injur'd hair!
   But when to mischief mortals bend their will,   125
How soon they find fit instruments of ill!
Just then, Clarissa drew with tempting grace
A two-edg'd weapon from her shining case:
So Ladies in Romance assist their Knight,
Present the spear, and arm him for the fight.   130
He takes the gift with rev'rence, and extends
The little engine on his fingers' ends;

---

[1] [*Codille*, a term in Ombre and Quadrille. When those who defend the pool make more tricks than those who defend the game, they are said to 'win the codille.']

[2] [Pope, like Voltaire, was inordinately addicted to the drinking of coffee.]

[3] *and think of Scylla's fate!*] Vide Ovid. *Metam.* VIII. P.

This just behind Belinda's neck he spread,
As o'er the fragrant steams she bends her head.
Swift to the Lock a thousand Sprites repair, 135
A thousand wings, by turns, blow back the hair;
And thrice they twitch'd the diamond in her ear;
Thrice she look'd back, and thrice the foe drew near.
Just in that instant, anxious Ariel sought
The close recesses of the Virgin's thought; 140
As on the nosegay in her breast reclin'd,
He watch'd th' Ideas rising in her mind,
Sudden he view'd, in spite of all her art,
An earthly Lover lurking at her heart.
Amaz'd, confus'd, he found his pow'r expir'd, 145
Resign'd to fate, and with a sigh retir'd.

    The Peer now spreads the glitt'ring Forfex wide,
T' inclose the Lock; now joins it, to divide.
Ev'n then, before the fatal engine clos'd,
A wretched Sylph too fondly interpos'd; 150
Fate urg'd the shears, and cut the Sylph in twain,
(But airy substance soon unites again)[1]
The meeting points the sacred hair dissever
From the fair head, for ever, and for ever!

    Then flash'd the living lightning from her eyes, 155
And screams of horror rend th' affrighted skies.
Not louder shrieks to pitying heav'n are cast,
When husbands, or when lap-dogs breathe their last;
Or when rich China vessels fall'n from high,
In glitt'ring dust and painted fragments lie! 160

    "Let wreaths of triumph now my temples twine
(The victor cry'd) the glorious Prize is mine!
While fish in streams, or birds delight in air
Or in a coach and six the British Fair,
As long as Atalantis shall be read,[2] 165
Or the small pillow grace a Lady's bed,
While visits shall be paid on solemn days,
When num'rous wax-lights in bright order blaze,
While nymphs take treats, or assignations give,
So long my honour, name, and praise shall live!" 170

    What Time would spare, from Steel receives its date,
And monuments, like men, submit to fate!
Steel could the labour of the Gods destroy,
And strike to dust th' imperial tow'rs of Troy;
Steel could the works of mortal pride confound, 175

---

[1] *But airy substance*] See Milton, lib. vi. of Satan cut asunder by the Angel Michael. P.

[2] *Atalantis*] A famous book written about that time by a woman: full of Court, and Party-scandal; and in a loose effeminacy of style and sentiment, which well suited the debauched taste of the better Vulgar. *Warburton.* [By Mrs. Manley, a lady of doubtful reputation, fo whose play of *Lucius* Prior wrote a most impu dent Epilogue. As a political journalist she co operated with Swift and his Tory friends; an both Swift and Smollett were as novelists unde real obligations to her *New Atalantis.* Sh died in 1724.]

And hew triumphal arches to the ground.
What wonder then, fair nymph! thy hairs should feel,
The conqu'ring force of unresisted steel?

CANTO IV.

BUT anxious cares the pensive nymph oppress'd,
And secret passions labour'd in her breast.
Not youthful kings in battle seiz'd alive,
Not scornful virgins who their charms survive,
Not ardent lovers robb'd of all their bliss,   5
Not ancient ladies when refus'd a kiss,
Not tyrants fierce that unrepenting die,
Not Cynthia when her manteau's pinn'd awry,
E'er felt such rage, resentment, and despair,
As thou, sad Virgin! for thy ravish'd Hair.   10
  For, that sad moment, when the Sylphs withdrew
And Ariel weeping from Belinda flew,
Umbriel, a dusky, melancholy sprite,
As ever sully'd the fair face of light,
Down to the central earth, his proper scene,   15
Repair'd to search the gloomy Cave of Spleen.
  Swift on his sooty pinions flits the Gnome,
And in a vapour reach'd the dismal dome.
No cheerful breeze this sullen region knows,
The dreaded East is all the wind that blows.   20
Here in a grotto, shelter'd close from air,
And screen'd in shades from day's detested glare,
She sighs for ever on her pensive bed,
Pain at her side, and Megrim at her head.[1]
  Two handmaids wait the throne: alike in place,   25
But diff'ring far in figure and in face.
Here stood Ill-nature like an ancient maid,
Her wrinkled form in black and white array'd;
With store of pray'rs, for mornings, nights, and noons,
Her hand is fill'd; her bosom with lampoons.   30
  There Affectation, with a sickly mien,
Shows in her cheek the roses of eighteen,
Practis'd to lisp, and hang the head aside,
Faints into airs, and languishes with pride,
On the rich quilt sinks with becoming woe,   35
Wrapt in a gown, for sickness, and for show.
The fair ones feel such maladies as these,
When each new night-dress gives a new disease.
  A constant Vapour o'er the palace flies;
Strange phantoms rising as the mists arise;   40
Dreadful, as hermit's dreams in haunted shades,
Or bright, as visions of expiring maids.

---

[1] [Megrim (migraine) from ἡμικρανία.]

Now glaring fiends, and snakes on rolling spires,
Pale spectres, gaping tombs, and purple fires:
Now lakes of liquid gold, Elysian scenes,   45
And crystal domes, and angels in machines.
  Unnumber'd throngs on every side are seen,
Of bodies chang'd to various forms by Spleen.
Here living Tea-pots stand, one arm held out,
One bent; the handle this, and that the spout: 50
A Pipkin there, like Homer's Tripod walks;
Here sighs a Jar, and there a Goose-pie talks;[1]
Men prove with child, as pow'rful fancy works,
And maids turn'd bottles, call aloud for corks.
  Safe past the Gnome thro' this fantastic band,   55
A branch of healing Spleenwort in his hand.[2]
Then thus address'd the pow'r: "Hail, wayward Queen!
Who rule the sex to fifty from fifteen:
Parent of vapours and of female wit,
Who give th' hysteric, or poetic fit,   60
On various tempers act by various ways,
Make some take physic, others scribble plays;
Who cause the proud their visits to delay,
And send the godly in a pet to pray.
A nymph there is, that all thy pow'r disdains,   65
And thousands more in equal mirth maintains.
But oh! if e'er thy Gnome could spoil a grace,
Or raise a pimple on a beauteous face,
Like Citron-waters matrons cheeks inflame,[3]
Or change complexions at a losing game;   70
If e'er with airy horns I planted heads,
Or rumpled petticoats, or tumbled beds,
Or caus'd suspicion when no soul was rude,
Or discompos'd the head-dress of a Prude,
Or e'er to costive lap-dog gave disease,   75
Which not the tears of brightest eyes could ease:
Hear me, and touch Belinda with chagrin,
That single act gives half the world the spleen."
  The Goddess with a discontented air
Seems to reject him, tho' she grants his pray'r.   80
A wond'rous Bag with both her hands she binds,
Like that where once Ulysses held the winds;
There she collects the force of female lungs,
Sighs, sobs, and passions, and the war of tongues.
A Vial next she fills with fainting fears,   85
Soft sorrows, melting griefs, and flowing tears.
The Gnome rejoicing bears her gifts away,
Spreads his black wings, and slowly mounts to day.

---

[1] Alludes to a real fact; a lady of distinction imagined herself in this condition. P.

[2] [Spleenwort (*asplenion*), miltwaste. *Johnson.*]

[3] [As to this fashionable indulgence cf. *Moral Ess. Ep.* II. v. 64.]

Sunk in Thalestris' arms the nymph he found,
Her eyes dejected and her hair unbound.
Full o'er their heads the swelling bag he rent,
And all the Furies issu'd at the vent.
Belinda burns with more than mortal ire,
And fierce Thalestris fans the rising fire.
"O wretched maid!" she spread her hands, and cry'd,
(While Hampton's echoes, "Wretched maid!" reply'd)
"Was it for this you took such constant care
The bodkin, comb, and essence to prepare?
For this your locks in paper durance bound,
For this with tort'ring irons wreath'd around?
For this with fillets strain'd your tender head,
And bravely bore the double loads of lead?
Gods! shall the ravisher display your hair,
While the Fops envy, and the Ladies stare!
Honour forbid! at whose unrivall'd shrine
Ease, pleasure, virtue, all our sex resign.
Methinks already I your tears survey,
Already hear the horrid things they say,
Already see you a degraded toast,
And all your honour in a whisper lost!
How shall I, then, your helpless fame defend?
'T will then be infamy to seem your friend!
And shall this prize, th' inestimable prize,
Expos'd thro' crystal to the gazing eyes,
And heighten'd by the diamond's circling rays,
On that rapacious hand for ever blaze?
Sooner shall grass in Hyde-park Circus grow,
And wits take lodgings in the sound of Bow;
Sooner let earth, air, sea, to Chaos fall,
Men, monkeys, lap-dogs, parrots, perish all!"
   She said; then raging to Sir Plume repairs,[1]
And bids her Beau demand the precious hairs:
(Sir Plume of amber snuff-box justly vain,
And the nice conduct of a clouded cane)
With earnest eyes, and round unthinking face,
He first the snuff-box open'd, then the case,
And thus broke out — "My Lord, why, what the devil?
Z—ds! damn the lock! 'fore Gad, you must be civil!
Plague on 't! 't is past a jest — nay prithee, pox!
Give her the hair" — he spoke, and rapp'd his box.
   "It grieves me much" (reply'd the Peer again)
"Who speaks so well should ever speak in vain.

---

[1] *Sir Plume repairs,*] Sir George Brown. He was the only one of the Party who took the thing seriously. He was angry, that the Poet should make him talk nothing but nonsense; and, in truth, one could not well blame him.
   ['If you wanted to have him act so,' Kestner wrote to Goethe concerning his own portraiture as Albert in *Werther*, 'need you have made him such a blockhead?']
Warburton.

But by this Lock, this sacred Lock I swear,
(Which never more shall join its parted hair;
Which never more its honours shall renew, 135
Clipp'd from the lovely head where late it grew)
That while my nostrils draw the vital air,
This hand, which won it, shall for ever wear."
He spoke, and speaking, in proud triumph spread
The long-contended honours of her head. 140

But Umbriel, hateful Gnome! forbears not so;
He breaks the Vial whence the sorrows flow.
Then see! the nymph in beauteous grief appears,
Her eyes half-languishing, half-drown'd in tears;
On her heav'd bosom hung her drooping head, 145
Which, with a sigh, she rais'd; and thus she said.

"For ever curs'd be this detested day,
Which snatch'd my best, my fav'rite curl away!
Happy! ah ten times happy had I been,
If Hampton-Court these eyes had never seen! 150
Yet am not I the first mistaken maid,
By love of Courts to num'rous ills betray'd.
Oh had I rather un-admir'd remain'd
In some lone isle, or distant Northern land;
Where the gilt Chariot never marks the way, 155
Where none learn Ombre, none e'er taste Bohea!
There kept my charms conceal'd from mortal eye,
Like roses, that in deserts bloom and die.
What mov'd my mind with youthful Lords to roam?
Oh had I stay'd, and said my pray'rs at home! 160
'T was this, the morning omens seem'd to tell,
Thrice from my trembling hand the patch-box fell;
The tott'ring China shook without a wind,
Nay, Poll sat mute, and Shock was most unkind!
A Sylph too warn'd me of the threats of fate, 165
In mystic visions, now believ'd too late!
See the poor remnants of these slighted hairs!
My hands shall rend what ev'n thy rapine spares:
These in two sable ringlets taught to break,
Once gave new beauties to the snowy neck; 170
The sister-lock now sits uncouth, alone,
And in its fellow's fate foresees its own;
Uncurl'd it hangs, the fatal shears demands,
And tempts once more thy sacrilegious hands.
Oh hadst thou, cruel! been content to seize 175
Hairs less in sight, or any hairs but these!"

CANTO V.

SHE said: the pitying audience melt in tears.
But Fate and Jove had stopp'd the Baron's ears.
In vain Thalestris with reproach assails,

For who can move when fair Belinda fails?
Not half so fix'd the Trojan could remain,   5
While Anna begg'd and Dido rag'd in vain.[1]
Then grave Clarissa graceful wav'd her fan;
Silence ensu'd, and thus the nymph began.
"Say why are Beauties prais'd and honour'd most,
The wise man's passion, and the vain man's toast?   10
Why deck'd with all that land and sea afford,
Why Angels call'd, and Angel-like ador'd?
Why round our coaches crowd the white-glov'd Beaux,
Why bows the side-box from its inmost rows;
How vain are all these glories, all our pains,   15
Unless good sense preserve what beauty gains:
That men may say, when we the front-box grace:
'Behold the first in virtue as in face!'
Oh! if to dance all night, and dress all day,
Charm'd the small-pox, or chas'd old-age away;   20
Who would not scorn what housewife's cares produce,
Or who would learn one earthly thing of use?
To patch, nay ogle, might become a Saint,
Nor could it sure be such a sin to paint.
But since, alas! frail beauty must decay,   25
Curl'd or uncurl'd, since Locks will turn to grey;
Since painted, or not painted, all shall fade,
And she who scorns a man, must die a maid;
What then remains but well our pow'r to use,
And keep good-humour still whate'er we lose?   30
And trust me, dear! good-humour can prevail,
When airs, and flights, and screams, and scolding fail.
Beauties in vain their pretty eyes may roll;
Charms strike the sight, but merit wins the soul."
So spoke the Dame, but no applause ensu'd;   35
Belinda frown'd, Thalestris call'd her Prude.
"To arms, to arms!" the fierce Virago cries,
And swift as lightning to the combat flies.
All side in parties, and begin th' attack;
Fans clap, silks rustle, and tough whalebones crack;   40
Heroes' and Heroines' shouts confus'dly rise,
And bass, and treble voices strike the skies.
No common weapons in their hands are found,
Like Gods they fight, nor dread a mortal wound.
So when bold Homer makes the Gods engage,[2]   45
And heav'nly breasts with human passions rage;
'Gainst Pallas, Mars; Latona, Hermes arms;
And all Olympus rings with loud alarms:
Jove's thunder roars, heav'n trembles all around,
Blue Neptune storms, the bellowing deeps resound: 50
Earth shakes her nodding tow'rs, the ground gives way,

---

[1] [Virg. Æn. IV. v. 330.]   [2] *So when bold Homer*] Homer, *Il.* xx. P.

And the pale ghosts start at the flash of day!
   Triumphant Umbriel on a sconce's height
Clapp'd his glad wings, and sate to view the fight:
Propp'd on their bodkin spears, the Sprites survey
The growing combat, or assist the fray.
   While thro' the press enrag'd Thalestris flies,
And scatters death around from both her eyes,
A Beau and Witling perish'd in the throng,
One died in metaphor, and one in song.
"O cruel nymph! a living death I bear,"
Cry'd Dapperwit, and sunk beside his chair.
A mournful glance Sir Fopling upwards cast,
"Those eyes are made so killing"— was his last.
Thus on Mæander's flow'ry margin lies
Th' expiring Swan, and as he sings he dies.
   When bold Sir Plume had drawn Clarissa down,
Chloe stepp'd in, and kill'd him with a frown;
She smil'd to see the doughty hero slain,
But, at her smile, the Beau reviv'd again.
   Now Jove suspends his golden scales in air,
Weighs the Men's wits against the Lady's hair;
The doubtful beam long nods from side to side;
At length the wits mount up, the hairs subside.
   See, fierce Belinda on the Baron flies,
With more than usual lightning in her eyes:
Nor fear'd the Chief th' unequal fight to try,
Who sought no more than on his foe to die.
But this bold Lord with manly strength endu'd,
She with one finger and a thumb subdu'd:
Just where the breath of life his nostrils drew,
A charge of Snuff the wily virgin threw;
The Gnomes direct, to ev'ry atom just,
The pungent grains of titillating dust.
Sudden, with starting tears each eye o'erflows,
And the high dome re-echoes to his nose.
   "Now meet thy fate," incens'd Belinda cry'd,
And drew a deadly bodkin from her side.
(The same, his ancient personage to deck,
Her great great grandsire wore about his neck,
In three seal-rings; which after, melted down,
Form'd a vast buckle for his widow's gown:
Her infant grandame's whistle next it grew,
The bells she jingled, and the whistle blew;
Then in a bodkin grac'd her mother's hairs,
Which long she wore, and now Belinda wears.)
   "Boast not my fall" (he cry'd) "insulting foe!
Thou by some other shalt be laid as low,
Nor think, to die dejects my lofty mind:
All that I dread is leaving you behind!
Rather than so, ah let me still survive,

OF THE LOCK.

And burn in Cupid's flames — but burn alive."
"Restore the Lock!" she cries; and all around
"Restore the Lock!" the vaulted roofs rebound.
Not fierce Othello in so loud a strain   105
Roar'd for the handkerchief that caus'd his pain.
But see how oft ambitious aims are cross'd,
And chiefs contend 'till all the prize is lost!
The Lock, obtain'd with guilt, and kept with pain,
In ev'ry place is sought, but sought in vain: 110
With such a prize no mortal must be blest,
So heav'n decrees! with heav'n who can contest?

Some thought it mounted to the Lunar sphere,
Since all things lost on earth are treasur'd there.[1]
There Heros' wits are kept in pond'rous vases,   115
And beaux' in snuff-boxes and tweezer-cases.
There broken vows and death-bed alms are found,
And lovers' hearts with ends of riband bound,
The courtier's promises, and sick man's pray'rs,
The smiles of harlots, and the tears of heirs,   120
Cages for gnats, and chains to yoke a flea,
Dry'd butterflies, and tomes of casuistry.

But trust the Muse — she saw it upward rise,
Tho' mark'd by none but quick, poetic eyes:
(So Rome's great founder to the heav'ns withdrew,   125
To Proculus alone confess'd in view)
A sudden Star, it shot thro' liquid air,
And drew behind a radiant trail of hair.
Not Berenice's Locks first rose so bright,
The heav'ns bespangling with dishevell'd light.   130
The Sylphs behold it kindling as it flies,
And pleas'd pursue its progress thro' the skies.

This the Beau monde shall from the Mall survey,[2]
And hail with music its propitious ray.
This the blest Lover shall for Venus take,   135
And send up vows from Rosamonda's lake.
This Partridge soon shall view in cloudless skies,[3]
When next he looks thro' Galileo's eyes;
And hence th' egregious wizard shall foredoom
The fate of Louis, and the fall of Rome.   140

Then cease, bright Nymph! to mourn thy ravish'd hair,
Which adds new glory to the shining sphere!
Not all the tresses that fair head can boast,
Shall draw such envy as the Lock you lost.

---

[1] *Since all things lost*] Vid. Ariosto. Canto xxxiv. P.

[2] [The evening was the time for walking in the Mall, on the north side of St. James' Park.]

[3] *This Partridge soon*] John Partridge was a ridiculous Star-gazer, who in his Almanacks every year never fail'd to predict the downfall of the Pope, and the King of France, then at war with the English. P. [Partridge was the butt of the entire coterie of Swift's friends, since the publication of Swift's immortal prediction of the prophet's own death, put forth under the name of Bickerstaff in 1707.]

For, after all the murders of your eye,
When after millions slain, yourself shall die:
When those fair suns shall set, as set they must,
And all those tresses shall be laid in dust,
This Lock, the Muse shall consecrate to fame,
And 'midst the stars inscribe Belinda's name.   150

IMITATIONS.

Canto I.

Ver. 54, 55.   'Quæ gratia currum
Armorumque fuit vivis, quæ cura nitentes
Pascere equos, eadem sequitur tellure repostos.'
    Virg. *Æn.* vi. P. [vv. 65-35.]

Ver. 101.
' Jam clypeus clypeis, umbone repellitur umbo,
Ense minax ensis, pede pes et cuspide cuspis,' etc.   *Stat. Warburton.*

Canto II.

Ver. 28. *With a single hair.*] In allusion to those lines of *Hudibras*, applied to the same purpose,
    'And tho' it be a two-foot Trout,
    'T is with a single hair pull'd out.'
            Warburton.

Ver. 45. *The pow'rs gave ear.*] Virg. *Æn.* xi. P. [vv. 794-5.]

Ver. 119.
—' clypei dominus *septemplicis* Ajax.' *Ovid. Warburton.* [*Metam.* lib. xiii. v. 2.]

Ver. 121. *About the silver bound.*] In allusion to the shield of Achilles,
' Thus the broad shield complete the Artist crown'd,
With his last band, and pour'd the Ocean round:
In living *Silver* seem'd the waves to roll,
And beat the Buckler's *verge, and bound the whole.*'   *Warburton.* [*Iliad* bk. xviii.]

Canto III.

Ver. 101.
' Nescia mens hominum fati sortisque futuræ,
Et servare modum, rebus sublata secundis!
Turno tempus erit, magno cum optaverit emptum
Intactum Pallanta: et cum spolia ista diemque
Oderit.' *Virg. Warburton.* [*Æn.* x. 501-5.]

Ver. 163, 170.
' Dum juga montis aper, fluvios dum piscis amabit,
Semper honos, nomenque tuum laudesque manebunt.' *Virg. Warburton.* [*Ecl.* v. 76, 8.]

Ver. 177.
' Ille quoque aversus mons est, etc.
    Quid faciant crines, cum ferro talia cedant?'
        Catull. de com. Berenices.

Canto IV.

Ver. 1. Virg. *Æn.* iv. [v. 1.]
'At regina gravi,' etc. P.

Ver. 51. *Homer's Tripod walks;*] See Hom. *Iliad* xviii. of Vulcan's walking Tripods. *Warburton.*

Ver. 133. *But by this Lock,*] In allusion to Achilles's oath in Homer, *Il.* i. P.

Canto V.

Ver. 35. *So spake the Dame.*] It is a verse frequently repeated in Homer after any speech,
' So spoke — and all the Heroes applauded.' P.

Ver. 53. *Triumphant Umbriel*] Minerva in like manner, during the battle of Ulysses with the Suitors in *Odyss.* perches on a beam of the roof to behold it. P.

Ver. 64. *Those eyes are made so killing.*] The words of a Song in the Opera of *Camilla.* P.

Ver. 65. *Thus on Mæander's flow'ry margin lies*]
' Sic ubi fata vocant, udis abjectus in herbis,
    Ad vada Mæandri concinit albus olor.'
        Ov. *Ep.* P. [*Heroid.* Ep. vii. v. 2.]

Ver. 72. Vid. Homer *Il.* viii and Virg. *Æn.* xii. P.

Ver. 83. *The Gnomes direct,*] These two lines added for the above reason. P.

Ver. 89. *The same, his ancient personage to deck,*] In imitation of the progress of Agamemnon's sceptre in Homer, *Il.* ii. P.

Ver. 128.
' Flammiferumque trahens spatioso limite crinem
Stella micat.'   *Ovid.* P. [*Metam.* lib. xv. vv. 849-50.]

VARIATIONS.

CANTO II.

Ver. 4. *Launch'd on the bosom.*] From hence the poem continues, in the first edition, to v. 46,

The rest the winds dispers'd in empty air;

all after, to the end of this Canto, being additional. P.

CANTO III.

Ver. 24. *And the long labours of the Toilet cease.*] All that follows of the same at *Ombre*, was added since the first Edition, till v. 105,

which connected thus: Sudden the board, etc. P.

Ver. 135-147, 150-3. Added afterwards, P. [And so to the end, wherever the Sylphs are introduced or referred to.]

CANTO V.

Ver. 7. *Then grave Clarissa, etc.*] A new Character introduced in the subsequent Editions, to open more clearly the MORAL of the Poem, in a parody of the speech of Sarpedon to Glaucus in Homer. P.   [*Iliad.* bk. xii.]

ELEGY

TO THE

MEMORY OF AN UNFORTUNATE LADY.[1]

[This Elegy was first published in 1717, but doubtless written earlier. After endless enquiries and conjectures as to the 'Unfortunate Lady' had failed in fixing her identity, it was pointed out that in certain letters of Pope, described by him in the table, of contents as relating to an 'Unfortunate Lady,' we are introduced to a Mrs. W. who had endured a series of hardships and misfortunes. This Mrs. W. has been proved to have been a Mrs. Weston (by birth a Miss Gage, the sister of the first Viscount Gage and of the 'modest Gage' of *Moral Essays*, Ep. III. v. 128), who was soon after her marriage separated from her husband. Her case was warmly taken up by Pope, by whose aid the quarrel was adjusted, though with small thanks to him for interposing. 'Buckingham's lines,' says Carruthers, who discusses the question at length in his *Life of Pope*, Ch. II., 'suggested the outline of the picture, Mrs. Weston's misfortunes and the poet's admiration of her gave it life and warmth, *and imagination did the rest.*' But even if the situation upon which the poem is based were real instead of fictitious, Dr. Johnson's accusation against it as attempting a defence of suicide would remain unwarranted. In execution this elegy ranks with Pope's most consummate efforts, in pathetic power it stands almost alone among his works.]

WHAT beck'ning ghost, along the moon-light shade
Invites my steps, and points to yonder glade?
'T is she! — but why that bleeding bosom gor'd,
Why dimly gleams the visionary sword?

---

[1] See the Duke of Buckingham's verses to a Lady designing to retire into a Monastery compared with Mr. Pope's Letters to several Ladies, p. 206 [86]. She seems to be the same person whose unfortunate death is the subject of this poem. P. If this note was written by Pope (of which we have strong doubts), it must have been written purely for mystification and deception. The Duke's verses were first published in Tonson's *Miscellany* for 1709, when he was in his sixtieth year and married to his third wife! They were, most likely, a much earlier production, and this renders it in the highest degree improbable that the same lady should have also been commemorated by Pope, who was thirty-seven years younger than his friend. *Carruthers.*

Oh ever beauteous, ever friendly! tell,
Is it, in heav'n, a crime to love too well?
To bear too tender, or too firm a heart,
To act a Lover's, or a Roman's part?
Is there no bright reversion in the sky,
For those who greatly think, or bravely die?   10

  Why bade ye else, ye Pow'rs! her soul aspire
Above the vulgar flight of low desire?
Ambition first sprung from your blest abodes;
The glorious fault of Angels and of Gods;
Thence to their images on earth it flows,
And in the breasts of Kings and Heroes glows.
Most souls, 't is true, but peep out once an age,
Dull sullen pris'ners in the body's cage:
Dim lights of life, that burn a length of years
Useless, unseen, as lamps in sepulchres;   20
Like Eastern Kings, a lazy state they keep,
And close confin'd to their own palace, sleep.

  From these perhaps (ere nature bade her die[1])
Fate snatch'd her early to the pitying sky.
As into air the purer spirits flow,
And sep'rate from their kindred dregs below;
So flew the soul to its congenial place,
Nor left one virtue to redeem her Race.

  But thou, false guardian of a charge too good,
Thou, mean deserter of thy brother's blood!   30
See on these ruby lips the trembling breath,
These cheeks now fading at the blast of death:
Cold is that breast which warm'd the world before,
And those love-darting eyes must roll no more.
Thus, if Eternal justice rules the ball,
Thus shall your wives, and thus your children fall;
On all the line a sudden vengeance waits,
And frequent herses shall besiege your gates.
There passengers shall stand, and pointing say,
(While the long fun'rals blacken all the way)   40
"Lo these were they, whose souls the Furies steel'd,
And curs'd with hearts unknowing how to yield."
Thus unlamented pass the proud away,
The gaze of fools, and pageant of a day!
So perish all, whose breast ne'er learn'd to glow
For others good, or melt at others woe.

  What can atone (oh ever-injur'd shade!)
Thy fate unpity'd, and thy rites unpaid?
No friend's complaint, no kind domestic tear
Pleas'd thy pale ghost, or grac'd thy mournful bier.   50
By foreign hands thy dying eyes were clos'd,
By foreign hands thy decent limbs compos'd,

---

[1] [Compare Byron's *Childe Harold*, canto iv. stanza cii.]

By foreign hands thy humble grave adorn'd,
By strangers honour'd, and by strangers mourn'd!
What tho' no friends in sable weeds appear,
Grieve for an hour, perhaps, then mourn a year,
And bear about the mockery of woe
To midnight dances, and the public show?
What tho' no weeping Loves thy ashes grace,
Nor polish'd marble emulate thy face?[1]   60
What tho' no sacred earth allow thee room,
Nor hallow'd dirge be mutter'd o'er thy tomb?
Yet shall thy grave with rising flow'rs be drest,
And the green turf lie lightly on thy breast:
There shall the morn her earliest tears bestow,
There the first roses of the year shall blow;
While Angels with their silver wings o'ershade
The ground, now sacred by thy reliques made.
    So peaceful rests, without a stone, a name,
What once had beauty, titles, wealth, and fame.   70
How lov'd, how honour'd once, avails thee not,
To whom related, or by whom begot;
A heap of dust alone remains of thee,
'T is all thou art, and all the proud shall be!
    Poets themselves must fall, like those they sung,
Deaf the prais'd ear, and mute the tuneful tongue.
Ev'n he, whose soul now melts in mournful lays,
Shall shortly want the gen'rous tear he pays;
Then from his closing eyes thy form shall part,
And the last pang shall tear thee from his heart,   80
Life's idle business at one gasp be o'er,
The Muse forgot, and thou be lov'd no more!

PROLOGUE

TO

MR. ADDISON'S TRAGEDY OF CATO.

[Addison's *Cato* which the author had kept by him in an unfinished state for seven years was produced at Drury Lane on April 14th, 1713; eleven days after the news had reached London of the definitive conclusion of the Peace of Utrecht. The Whigs attempted to identify Cato with the faithful remnant of their own party which still upheld the glories and liberties of the past; while the Tories sagaciously refused to recognise the analogy, and vied with the Whigs in applauding the play, Bolingbroke presenting Booth, who performed Cato, with fifty guineas 'in acknowledgment for defending the cause of liberty so well against a perpetual dictator.' Addison disclaimed all political design, and waived the profits of the performances of the tragedy which continued for a month in London, and then recommenced at Oxford. See Cibber's

---

[1] [It has been fairly asked whether the poet is not in these lines guilty of an anticlimax.]

account in the *Apology*. The epilogue was written by Garth, who dwelt chiefly on those amatory episodes in the play, which Schlegel has so successfully ridiculed. As to the relations between Pope and Addison see *Introductory Memoir*.]

TO wake the soul by tender strokes of art,
    To raise the genius, and to mend the heart;
To make mankind in conscious virtue bold,
Live o'er each scene, and be what they behold:
For this the Tragic Muse first trod the stage,
Commanding tears to stream thro' ev'ry age;
Tyrants no more their savage nature kept,
And foes to virtue wonder'd how they wept.
Our author shuns by vulgar springs to move
The hero's glory, or the virgin's love;   10
In pitying Love, we but our weakness show,
And wild Ambition well deserves its woe.
Here tears shall flow from a more gen'rous cause,
Such Tears as Patriots shed for dying Laws:
He bids your breasts with ancient ardour rise,
And calls forth Roman drops from British eyes.
Virtue confess'd in human shape he draws,
What Plato thought, and godlike Cato was:
No common object to your sight displays,
But what with pleasure Heav'n itself surveys,[1]   20
A brave man struggling in the storms of fate,
And greatly falling, with a falling state.
While Cato gives his little Senate laws,
What bosom beats not in his Country's cause?
Who sees him act, but envies ev'ry deed?
Who hears him groan, and does not wish to bleed?
Ev'n when proud Cæsar 'midst triumphal cars,
The spoils of nations, and the pomp of wars,
Ignobly vain and impotently great,
Show'd Rome her Cato's figure drawn in state;   30
As her dead Father's rev'rend image past,
The pomp was darken'd, and the day o'ercast;
The Triumph ceas'd, tears gush'd from ev'ry eye;
The World's great Victor pass'd unheeded by;
Her last good man dejected Rome ador'd,
And honour'd Cæsar less than Cato's sword.
    Britons, attend: be worth like this approv'd,[2]

---

[1] *But what with pleasure*] This alludes to a famous passage of Seneca, which Mr. Addison afterwards used as a motto to his play, when it was printed. *Warburton*. [It is taken from Sen. *de Divin. Prov.* and runs as follows: 'Ecce spectaculum dignum, ad quod respiciat, intentum operi suo, Deus! Ecce par Deo dignum, vir fortis cum malâ fortunâ compositus! Non video, inquam, quid habeat in terris Jupiter pulchrius, si convertere animum velit, quam ut spectet Catonem, jam paribus non semel fractis, nihilominus inter ruinas publicas erectum.']

[2] *Britons, attend:*] Mr. Pope had written it *arise*, in the spirit of Poetry and Liberty; but Mr. Addison frighten'd at so *daring an expression*, which, he thought, squinted at rebellion, would have it alter'd, in the spirit of Prose and Politics, to *attend*. *Warburton*.

EPILOGUE TO JANE SHORE.

And show, you have the virtue to be mov'd.
With honest scorn the first fam'd Cato view'd
Rome learning arts from Greece, whom she subdu'd; 40
Your scene precariously subsists too long
On French translation, and Italian song.
Dare to have sense yourselves; assert the stage,
Be justly warm'd with your own native rage:
Such Plays alone should win a British ear,
As Cato's self had not disdain'd to hear.[1]

EPILOGUE

TO

MR. ROWE'S[2] JANE SHORE.

Designed for Mrs. Oldfield.

[Rowe's play of *Jane Shore*, which is only partly founded on history, was first acted Feb. 2, 1714, at Drury Lane. The character of Gloucester in this play is taken straight out of Shakspere. Great expectations were formed of the tragedy; and it was acted for nineteen nights. See (Geneste's) *Account of the English Stage*, II. 524. The famous Mrs. Oldfield supported the part of the heroine, but Pope's Epilogue was never spoken.]

PRODIGIOUS this! the Frail-one of our Play
From her own Sex should mercy find to-day!
You might have held the pretty head aside,
Peep'd in your fans, been serious, thus, and cry'd,
The Play may pass — but that strange creature, Shore,
I can't — indeed now — I so hate a whore —
Just as a blockhead rubs his thoughtless skull,
And thanks his stars he was not born a fool;
So from a sister sinner you shall hear,
"How strangely you expose yourself, my dear!" 10
But let me die, all raillery apart,
Our sex are still forgiving at their heart;

---

[1] *As Cato's self, etc.*] This alludes to the famous story of his going into the Theatre, and immediately coming out again, related by Martial. *Warburton*. [Martial. *Lib.* I. *Epigr.* 1.]

[2] [Nicholas Rowe, born in 1673, died in 1718. He was a friend of Addison's; and did good service to the cause of dramatic literature by his edition of Shakspere, accompanied by a biography. In his own plays he adopted blank verse in lieu of the heroic couplet established by Dryden; but has nothing else to approach him to the Elisabethan tragedians. He is perhaps happiest in the delineation of female passion and weakness; but his *Fair Penitent* is a mere adaptation from Massinger.]

And did not wicked custom so contrive,
We 'd be the best good-natur'd things alive.
 There are, 't is true, who tell another tale,
That virtuous ladies envy while they rail;
Such rage without betrays the fire within:
In some close corner of the soul, they sin;
Still hoarding up, most scandalously nice,
Amidst their virtues a reserve of vice.   20
The godly dame, who fleshly failings damns,
Scolds with her maid, or with her chaplain crams.
Would you enjoy soft nights and solid dinners?
Faith, gallants, board with saints, and bed with sinners.
 Well, if our Author in the Wife offends,
He has a Husband that will make amends,
He draws him gentle, tender, and forgiving,
And sure such kind good creatures may be living.
In days of old, they pardon'd breach of vows,
Stern Cato's self was no relentless spouse: 30
Plu-Plutarch, what 's his name that writes his life?
Tells us, that Cato dearly lov'd his Wife:
Yet if a friend, a night or so should need her,
He 'd recommend her as a special breeder.
To lend a wife, few here would scruple make,
But pray, which of you all would take her back!
Tho' with the Stoic Chief our stage may ring,
The Stoic Husband was the glorious thing.
The man had courage, was a sage, 't is true,
And lov'd his country— but what 's that to you?   40
Those strange examples ne'er were made to fit ye
But the kind cuckold might instruct the City:
There, many an honest man may copy Cato,
Who ne'er saw naked sword, or look'd in Plato.
 If, after all, you think it a disgrace,
That Edward's Miss thus perks it in your face;
To see a piece of failing flesh and blood,
In all the rest so impudently good;
Faith, let the modest Matrons of the town
Come here in crowds, and stare the strumpet down.   50

TRANSLATIONS AND IMITATIONS.

ADVERTISEMENT.

THE following Translations were selected from many others done by the Author in his Youth; for the most part indeed but a sort of *Exercises*, while he was improving himself in the Languages, and carried by his early Bent to *Poetry* to perform them rather in Verse than Prose. Mr. *Dryden's Fables* came out about that time, which occasioned the Translations from *Chaucer*. They were first separately printed in Miscellanies by J. Tonson and B. Lintot, and afterwards collected in the Quarto Edition of 1717. The *Imitations of English Authors*, which are added at the end, were done as early, some of them at fourteen or fifteen years old; but having also got into Miscellanies, we have put them here together to complete this Juvenile Volume. P. [It should be observed that, according to Warburton's statement, it was never Pope's intention to include his Juvenile Translations in the edition of his works which he was preparing at the close of his life.]

SAPPHO TO PHAON.

[OVID. *Heroid*. xv.]

<pre>
SAY, lovely youth, that dost my heart command,
  Can Phaon's eyes forget his Sappho's hand?
Must then her name the wretched writer prove,
To thy remembrance lost, as to thy love?
Ask not the cause that I new numbers choose,   5
The Lute neglected, and the Lyric muse;
Love taught my tears in sadder notes to flow,
And tun'd my heart to Elegies of woe.
I burn, I burn, as when thro' ripen'd corn
By driving winds the spreading flames are borne!,   10
Phaon to Ætna's scorching fields retires,
While I consume with more than Ætna's fires!
No more my soul a charm in music finds,
Music has charms alone for peaceful minds.¹
Soft scenes of solitude no more can please,   15
</pre>

¹ [The sense of the Latin is here inappropriately altered, to introduce Congreve's turn of phrase, but the opposite of his sentiment.]

Love enters there, and I'm my own disease.
No more the Lesbian dames my passion move,
Once the dear objects of my guilty love;
All other loves are lost in only thine,
Ah youth ungrateful to a flame like mine!   20
Whom would not all those blooming charms surprize,
Those heav'nly looks, and dear deluding eyes?
The harp and bow would you like Phœbus bear,
A brighter Phœbus Phaon might appear;
Would you with ivy wreath your flowing hair,   25
Not Bacchus' self with Phaon could compare:
Yet Phœbus lov'd, and Bacchus felt the flame,
One Daphne warm'd, and one the Cretan dame,
Nymphs that in verse no more could rival me,
Than ev'n those Gods contend in charms with thee.   30
The Muses teach me all their softest lays,
And the wide world resounds with Sappho's praise,
Tho' great Alcæus more sublimely sings,
And strikes with bolder rage the sounding strings,
No less renown attends the moving lyre,   35
Which Venus tunes, and all her loves inspire;
To me what nature has in charms deny'd,
Is well by wit's more lasting flame supply'd.
Tho' short my stature, yet my name extends
To heav'n itself, and earth's remotest ends.   40
Brown as I am, an Ethiopian dame
Inspir'd young Perseus with a gen'rous flame;
Turtles and doves of diff'ring hues unite,
And glossy jet is pair'd with shining white.
If to no charms thou wilt thy heart resign,   45
But such as merit, such as equal thine,
By none, alas! by none thou canst be mov'd,
Phaon alone by Phaon must be lov'd!
Yet once thy Sappho could thy cares employ,
Once in her arms you center'd all your joy: 50
No time the dear remembrance can remove,
For oh! how vast a memory has love!
My music, then, you could for ever hear,
And all my words were music to your ear;
You stopp'd with kisses my enchanting tongue,   55
And found my kisses sweeter than my song.
In all I pleas'd, but most in what was best;
And the last joy was dearer than the rest.
Then with each word, each glance, each motion fir'd,
You still enjoy'd, and yet you still desir'd,   60
'Till all dissolving in the trance we lay,
And in tumultuous raptures died away.
The fair Sicilians now thy soul inflame;
Why was I born, ye Gods, a Lesbian dame?
But ah beware, Sicilian nymphs! nor boast   65

That wand'ring heart which I so lately lost;
Nor be with all those tempting words abus'd,
Those tempting words were all to Sappho us'd.
And you that rule Sicilia's happy plains,
Have pity, Venus, on your Poet's pains! 70
Shall fortune still in one sad tenor run,
And still increase the woes so soon begun?
Inur'd to sorrow from my tender years,
My parent's ashes drank my early tears:
My brother next, neglecting wealth and fame, 75
Ignobly burn'd in a destructive flame:
An infant daughter late my griefs increas'd,
And all a mother's cares distract my breast.
Alas, what more could fate itself impose,
But thee, the last and greatest of my woes? 80
No more my robes in waving purple flow,
Nor on my hand the sparkling di'monds glow;
No more my locks in ringlets curl'd diffuse
The costly sweetness of Arabian dews,
Nor braids of gold the varied tresses bind, 85
That fly disorder'd with the wanton wind,
For whom should Sappho use such arts as these?
He's gone, whom only she desir'd to please!
Cupid's light darts my tender bosom move,
Still is there cause for Sappho still to love: 90
So from my birth the Sisters[1] fix'd my doom,
And gave to Venus all my life to come;
Or while my Muse in melting notes complains,
My yielding heart keeps measure to my strains.
By charms like thine which all my soul have won, 95
Who might not — ah! who would not be undone?
For those Aurora Cephalus might scorn,
And with fresh blushes paint the conscious morn.
For those might Cynthia lengthen Phaon's sleep,
And bid Endymion nightly tend his sheep. 100
Venus for those had rapt thee to the skies,
But Mars on thee might look with Venus' eyes.
O scarce a youth, yet scarce a tender boy!
O useful time for lovers to employ!
Pride of thy age, and glory of thy race, 105
Come to these arms, and melt in this embrace!
The vows you never will return, receive;
And take at least the love you will not give.
See, while I write, my words are lost in tears;
The less my sense, the more my love appears. 110
Sure 't was not much to bid one kind adieu,
(At least to feign was never hard to you)
Farewell, my Lesbian love, you might have said,

[1] [The Parcæ.]

Or coldly thus, Farewell, oh Lesbian maid!
No tear did you, no parting kiss receive, 115
Nor knew I then how much I was to grieve.
No lover's gift your Sappho could confer,
And wrongs and woes were all you left with her.
No charge I gave you, and no charge could give,
But this, Be mindful of our loves, and live. 120
Now by the Nine, those pow'rs ador'd by me,
And Love, the God that ever waits on thee,
When first I heard (from whom I hardly knew)
That you were fled, and all my joys with you,
Like some sad statue, speechless, pale I stood, 125
Grief chill'd my breast, and stopp'd my freezing blood;
No sigh to rise, no tear had pow'r to flow,
Fix'd in a stupid lethargy of woe:
But when its way th' impetuous passion found,
I rend my tresses, and my breast I wound, 130
I rave, then weep, I curse, and then complain,
Now swell to rage, now melt in tears again.
Not fiercer pangs distract the mournful dame,
Whose first-born infant feeds the fun'ral flame.
My scornful brother with a smile appears, 135
Insults my woes, and triumphs in my tears;
His hated image ever haunts my eyes,
And why this grief? thy daughter lives, he cries.
Stung with my Love, and furious with despair,
All torn my garments, and my bosom bare, 140
My woes, thy crimes, I to the world proclaim;
Such inconsistent things are love and shame!
'T is thou art all my care and my delight,
My daily longing, and my dream by night:
Oh night more pleasing than the brightest day, 145
When fancy gives what absence takes away,
And, dress'd in all its visionary charms,
Restores my fair deserter to my arms!
Then round your neck in wanton wreaths I twine,
Then you, methinks, as fondly circle mine: 150
A thousand tender words I hear and speak;
A thousand melting kisses give, and take:
Then fiercer joys, I blush to mention these,
Yet while I blush, confess how much they please.
But when, with day, the sweet delusions fly, 155
And all things wake to life and joy, but I,
As if once more forsaken, I complain,
And close my eyes to dream of you again:
Then frantic rise, and like some Fury rove
Thro' lonely plains, and thro' the silent grove, 160
As if the silent grove, and lonely plains,
That knew my pleasures, could relieve my pains.
I view the Grotto, once the scene of love,

SAPPHO.
(N. Sichel.)

The rocks around, the hanging roofs above,
That charm'd me more, with native moss o'ergrown, 165
Than Phrygian marble, or the Parian stone.
I find the shades that veil'd our joys before;
But, Phaon gone, those shades delight no more.
Here the press'd herbs with bending tops betray
Where oft entwin'd in am'rous folds we lay; 170
I kiss that earth which once was press'd by you,
And all with tears the with'ring herbs bedew.
For thee the fading trees appear to mourn,
And birds defer their songs till thy return;
Night shades the groves, and all in silence lie, 175
All but the mournful Philomel and I:
With mournful Philomel I join my strain,
Of Tereus she, of Phaon I complain.
  A spring there is, whose silver waters show,
Clear as a glass, the shining sands below: 180
A flow'ry Lotos spreads its arms above,
Shades all the banks, and seems itself a grove;
Eternal greens the mossy margin grace,
Watch'd by the sylvan Genius of the place.
Here as I lay, and swell'd with tears the flood, 185
Before my sight a wat'ry Virgin stood:
She stood and cry'd, "O you that love in vain!
"Fly hence, and seek the fair Leucadian main;
"There stands a rock, from whose impending steep
"Apollo's fane surveys the rolling deep: 190
"There injur'd lovers, leaping from above,
"Their flames extinguish, and forget to love.
"Deucalion once with hopeless fury burn'd,
"In vain he lov'd, relentless Pyrrha scorn'd;
"But when from hence he plung'd into the main, 195
"Deucalion scorn'd, and Pyrrha lov'd in vain.
"Haste, Sappho, haste, from high Leucadia throw
"Thy wretched weight, nor dread the deeps below!"
She spoke, and vanish'd with the voice — I rise,
And silent tears fall trickling from my eyes. 200
I go, ye Nymphs! those rocks and seas to prove;
How much I fear, but ah, how much I love!
I go, ye Nymphs! where furious love inspires;
Let female fears submit to female fires.
To rocks and seas I fly from Phaon's hate, 205
And hope from seas and rocks a milder fate.
Ye gentle gales, beneath my body blow,
And softly lay me on the waves below!
And thou, kind Love, my sinking limbs sustain,
Spread thy soft wings, and waft me o'er the main, 210
Nor let a Lover's death the guiltless flood profane!
On Phœbus' shrine my harp I'll then bestow,
And this Inscription shall be plac'd below.

"Here she who sung, to him that did inspire,
"Sappho to Phœbus consecrates her Lyre;   215
"What suits with Sappho, Phœbus, suits with thee;
"The Gift, the giver, and the God agree."
  But why, alas, relentless youth, ah why
To distant seas must tender Sappho fly?
Thy charms than those may far more pow'rful be,   220
And Phœbus' self is less a God to me.
Ah! cans't thou doom me to the rocks and sea,
O far more faithless and more hard than they?
Ah! canst thou rather see this tender breast
Dash'd on these rocks than to thy bosom prest?   225
This breast which once, in vain! you lik'd so well;
Where the Loves play'd, and where the Muses dwell.
Alas! the Muses now no more inspire,
Untun'd my lute, and silent is my lyre,
My languid numbers have forgot to flow,   230
And fancy sinks beneath a weight of woe.
Ye Lesbian virgins, and ye Lesbian dames,
Themes of my verse, and objects of my flames,
No more your groves with my glad songs shall ring,
No more these hands shall touch the trembling string: 235
My Phaon's fled, and I those arts resign
(Wretch that I am, to call that Phaon mine!)
Return, fair youth, return, and bring along
Joy to my soul, and vigour to my song:
Absent from thee, the Poet's flame expires;   240
But ah! how fiercely burn the Lover's fires!
Gods! can no pray'rs, no sighs, no numbers move
One savage heart, or teach it how to love?
The winds my pray'rs, my sighs, my numbers bear,
The flying winds have lost them all in air!   245
Oh when, alas! shall more auspicious gales
To these fond eyes restore thy welcome sails?
If you return — ah why these long delays?
Poor Sappho dies while careless Phaon stays.
O launch thy bark, nor fear the wat'ry plain;   250
Venus for thee shall smooth her native main.
O launch thy bark, secure of prosp'rous gales;
Cupid for thee shall spread the swelling sails.
I you will fly — (yet ah! what cause can be,
Too cruel youth, that you should fly from me?)   255
If not from Phaon I must hope for ease,
Ah let me seek it from the raging seas:
To raging seas unpity'd I'll remove,
And either cease to live or cease to love!

ELOISA TO ABELARD.

[The deathless story of Abelard and Eloisa is fully given in Papirii Massoni *Annales*, quoted in Rawlinson's edition of their letters. 'Petrus cognomine Abailardus,' after attaining the highest eminence as a teacher of scholasticism in the University of Paris in the second decad of the twelfth century (through the influence of St. Bernard his doctrine of the Trinity was condemned at the Council of Sens in 1140), retired to the Monastery of the Paraclete, of which he was the founder, and died in 1142. Eloisa, first abbess of the Paraclete, died in 1163. Abelard's French love-songs to Eloisa are lost, but their letters have been frequently published. The edition used by Pope was probably that of Rawlinson, completed in the year (1717) in which Pope's Épistle first appeared in Lintot's one-volume collection of his works.—Mr. Hallam charges Pope with injustice to Eloisa in substituting for the real motive of her refusal to marry him (unwillingness to interfere with the prospects of his career) 'an abstract predilection for the name of mistress above that of wife.' A poet however has undoubtedly the right to make such a change. The ordinary objection, that the effect of the whole poem is immoral, is obviously inapplicable to a distinctly dramatic piece. Most readers of this poem will be inclined to consider that its language is appropriate to passion, but not the language of passion itself. From this point of view should be contrasted with it, not Ovid's *Heroides*, of which it is a most felicitous imitation, but such an epistle as that of Julia in the first canto of Byron's *Don Juan*. Yet on forwarding the volume containing *Eloisa to Abelard* to Lady M. W. Montagu at Constantinople, Pope hinted to her that the concluding lines of the poem admitted of a most personal interpretation. This venturesome self-impeachment was very coolly received by his correspondent; nor is the passage in question likely to strike posterity as more dangerously passionate than it seemed to her to be.]

ARGUMENT.

ABELARD and Eloisa flourished in the twelfth Century; they were two of the most distinguished Persons of their age in learning and beauty, but for nothing more famous than for their unfortunate passion. After a long course of calamities, they retired each to a several Convent, and consecrated the remainder of their days to religion. It was many years after this separation, that a letter of Abelard's to a Friend, which contained the history of his misfortune, fell into the hands of Eloisa. This awakening all her Tenderness, occasioned those celebrated letters (out of which the following is partly extracted) which gives so lively a picture of the struggles of grace and nature, virtue and passion. P.

IN these deep solitudes and awful cells,
Where heav'nly-pensive contemplation dwells,
And ever-musing melancholy reigns;
What means this tumult in a Vestal's veins?
Why rove my thoughts beyond this last retreat?   5
Why feels my heart its long-forgotten heat?
Yet, yet I love!—From Abelard it came,
And Eloïsa yet must kiss the name.
  Dear fatal name! rest ever unreveal'd,
Nor pass these lips in holy silence seal'd: 10
Hide it, my heart, within that close disguise,
Where mix'd with God's, his lov'd Idea lies:
O write it not my hand—the name appears
Already written—wash it out, my tears!

In vain lost Eloïsa weeps and prays, 15
Her heart still dictates, and her hand obeys.
　Relentless walls! whose darksome round contains
Repentant sighs, and voluntary pains:
Ye rugged rocks! which holy knees have worn;
Ye grots and caverns shagg'd with horrid thorn! 20
Shrines! where their vigils pale-ey'd virgins keep,
And pitying saints, whose statues learn to weep!
Tho' cold like you, unmov'd and silent grown,
I have not yet forgot myself to stone.[1]
All is not Heav'n's while Abelard has part, 25
Still rebel nature holds out half my heart;
Nor pray'rs nor fasts its stubborn pulse restrain,
Nor tears for ages taught to flow in vain.
　Soon as thy letters trembling I unclose,
That well-known name awakens all my woes. 30
Oh name for ever sad! for ever dear!
Still breath'd in sighs, still usher'd with a tear.
I tremble too, where'er my own I find,
Some dire misfortune follows close behind.
Line after line my gushing eyes o'erflow, 35
Led thro' a sad variety of woe:
Now warm in love, now with'ring in my bloom,
Lost in a convent's solitary gloom!
There stern Religion quench'd th' unwilling flame,
There died the best of passions, Love and Fame. 40
　Yet write, oh write me all, that I may join
Griefs to thy griefs, and echo sighs to thine.
Nor foes nor fortune take this pow'r away;
And is my Abelard less kind than they?
Tears still are mine, and those I need not spare, 45
Love but demands what else were shed in pray'r;
No happier task these faded eyes pursue;
To read and weep is all they now can do.
　Then share thy pain, allow that sad relief;
Ah, more than share it, give me all thy grief. 50
Heav'n first taught letters for some wretch's aid,
Some banish'd lover, or some captive maid;
They live, they speak, they breathe what love inspires,
Warm from the soul, and faithful to its fires,
The virgin's wish without her fears impart, 55
Excuse the blush, and pour out all the heart,
Speed the soft intercourse from soul to soul,
And waft a sigh from Indus to the Pole.
　Thou know'st how guiltless first I met thy flame,
When Love approach'd me under Friendship's name; 60

---

[1] 'Forget thyself to marble,' Milton, *Il Penseroso*. The expression (v. 20) 'caverns shagg'd with horrid thorn,' and the epithets 'pale-ey'd,' 'twilight,' 'low-thoughted care,' and others, are first used in the smaller poems of Milton, which Pope seems to have been just reading. *Warton.*

ELOISA TO ABELARD.

My fancy form'd thee of angelic kind,
Some emanation of th' all-beauteous Mind.
Those smiling eyes, attemp'ring ev'ry ray,
Shone sweetly lambent with celestial day.
Guiltless I gaz'd; heav'n listen'd while you sung; 65
And truths divine came mended from that tongue.
From lips like those what precept fail'd to move?
Too soon they taught me 't was no sin to love:
Back thro' the paths of pleasing sense I ran,
Nor wish'd an Angel whom I lov'd a Man. 70
Dim and remote the joys of saints I see;
Nor envy them that heav'n I lose for thee.
  How oft, when press'd to marriage, have I said,
Curse on all laws but those which love has made?[1]
Love, free as air, at sight of human ties, 75
Spreads his light wings, and in a moment flies.[2]
Let wealth, let honour, wait the wedded dame,
August her deed, and sacred be her fame;
Before true passion all those views remove,
Fame, wealth, and honour! what are you to Love? 80
The jealous God, when we profane his fires,
Those restless passions in revenge inspires,
And bids them make mistaken mortals groan,
Who seek in love for aught but love alone.
Should at my feet the world's great master fall, 85
Himself, his throne, his world, I 'd scorn 'em all:
Not Cæsar's empress would I deign to prove;
No, make me mistress to the man I love;
If there be yet another name more free,
More fond than mistress, make me that to thee! 90
Oh! happy state! when souls each other draw,
When love is liberty, and nature law:
All then is full, possessing, and possess'd,
No craving void left aking in the breast:
Ev'n thought meets thought, ere from the lips it part, 95
And each warm wish springs mutual from the heart.
This sure is bliss (if bliss on earth there be)
And once the lot of Abelard and me.
  Alas, how chang'd! what sudden horrors rise!
A naked Lover bound and bleeding lies! 100
Where, where was Eloïse? her voice, her hand,
Her poniard, had oppos'd the dire command.
Barbarian, stay! that bloody stroke restrain;
The crime was common, common be the pain.
I can no more; by shame, by rage suppress'd, 105

---

[1] 'And own no laws but those which love ordains.' Dryden, *Cinyras and Myrrah*. P.

[2] 'Love will not be confin'd by Maisterie:
When Maisterie comes, the Lord of Love anon
Flutters his wings, and forthwith is he gone.'
Chaucer. P. [*The Frankeleines Tale.*]

Let tears, and burning blushes speak the rest.
  Canst thou forget that sad, that solemn day,
When victims at yon altar's foot we lay?
Canst thou forget what tears that moment fell,
When, warm in youth, I bade the world farewell?   110
As with cold lips I kiss'd the sacred veil,
The shrines all trembled, and the lamps grew pale:
Heav'n scarce believ'd the Conquest it survey'd,
And Saints with wonder heard the vows I made.
Yet then, to those dread altars as I drew,   115
Not on the Cross my eyes were fix'd, but you:
Not grace, or zeal, love only was my call,
And if I lose thy love, I lose my all.
Come! with thy looks, thy words, relieve my woe;[1]
Those still at least are left thee to bestow.   120
Still on that breast enamour'd let me lie,
Still drink delicious poison from thy eye,[2]
Pant on thy lip, and to thy heart be press'd;
Give all thou canst — and let me dream the rest.
Ah no! instruct me other joys to prize,   125
With other beauties charm my partial eyes,
Full in my view set all the bright abode,
And make my soul quit Abelard for God.
  Ah, think at least thy flock deserves thy care,
Plants of thy hand, and children of thy pray'r.   130
From the false world in early youth they fled,
By thee to mountains, wilds, and deserts led.
You rais'd these hallow'd walls;[3] the desert smil'd,
And Paradise was open'd in the Wild.[4]
No weeping orphan saw his father's stores   135
Our shrines irradiate, or emblaze the floors;
No silver saints, by dying misers giv'n,
Here brib'd the rage of ill-requited heav'n:
But such plain roofs as Piety could raise,
And only vocal with the Maker's praise.   140
In these lone walls (their days eternal bound)
These moss-grown domes with spiry turrets crown'd,
Where awful arches make a noon-day night,
And the dim windows shed a solemn light;
Thy eyes diffus'd a reconciling ray,   145
And gleams of glory brighten'd all the day.
But now no face divine contentment wears,
'T is all blank sadness, or continual tears.
See how the force of others' pray'rs I try,
(O pious fraud of am'rous charity!)   150

---

[1] These lines cannot be justified by anything in the letters of Eloisa [where she merely prays Abelard to write to her]. *Roscoe.*

[2] 'Drank dear delicious poison.' Smith's *Phædra and Hippolytus. Carruthers.*

[3] *You rais'd these hallow'd walls;*] He founded the Monastery. P.

[4] 'And Paradise was open'd in his face.' *Dryden. Carruthers.*

But why should I on others' pray'rs depend?
Come thou, my father, brother, husband, friend!
Ah let thy handmaid, sister, daughter move,
And all those tender names in one, thy love!
The darksome pines that o'er yon rocks reclin'd   155
Wave high, and murmur to the hollow wind,
The wand'ring streams that shine between the hills,
The grots that echo to the tinkling rills,
The dying gales that pant upon the trees,
The lakes that quiver to the curling breeze;   160
No more these scenes my meditation aid,
Or lull to rest the visionary maid.
But o'er the twilight groves and dusky caves,
Long-sounding aisles, and intermingled graves,
Black Melancholy sits, and round her throws   165
A death-like silence, and a dead repose:
Her gloomy presence saddens all the scene,
Shades ev'ry flow'r, and darkens ev'ry green,
Deepens the murmur of the falling floods,
And breathes a browner horror on the woods.[1]   170
   Yet here for ever, ever must I stay;
Sad proof how well a lover can obey!
Death, only death, can break the lasting chain:
And here, ev'n then, shall my cold dust remain,
Here all its frailties, all its flames resign,   175
And wait till 't is no sin to mix with thine
   Ah wretch! believ'd the spouse of God in vain,
Confess'd within the slave of love and man.
Assist me, heav'n! but whence arose that pray'r?
Sprung it from piety, or from despair?   180
Ev'n here, where frozen chastity retires,
Love finds an altar for forbidden fires.
I ought to grieve, but cannot what I ought;
I mourn the lover, not lament the fault;
I view my crime, but kindle at the view,   185
Repent old pleasures, and solicit new;
Now turn'd to heav'n, I weep my past offence,
Now think of thee, and curse my innocence.
Of all affliction taught a lover yet,
'T is sure the hardest science to forget!   190
How shall I lose the sin, yet keep the sense,
And love th' offender, yet detest th' offence?
How the dear object from the crime remove,
Or how distinguish penitence from love?
Unequal task! a passion to resign,   195
For hearts so touch'd, so pierc'd, so lost as mine.
Ere such a soul regains its peaceful state,

---

[1] 'Browner horror.' *Dryden*. *Warton*. similar description of Melancholy in Collins's [This passage must have helped to inspire the *Passions*.]

How often must it love, how often hate!
How often hope, despair, resent, regret,
Conceal, disdain, — do all things but forget.
But let heav'n seize it, all at once 't is fir'd:[1]
Not touch'd, but rapt; not waken'd, but inspir'd!
Oh come! oh teach me nature to subdue,
Renounce my love, my life, myself — and you.
Fill my fond heart with God alone, for he
Alone can rival, can succeed to thee.
  How happy is the blameless Vestal's lot!
The world forgetting, by the world forgot:
Eternal sunshine of the spotless mind!
Each pray'r accepted, and each wish resign'd;
Labour and rest, that equal periods keep;
"Obedient slumbers that can wake and weep;"[2]
Desires compos'd, affections ever ev'n;
Tears that delight, and sighs that waft to heav'n.
Grace shines around her with serenest beams,
And whisp'ring Angels prompt her golden dreams.
For her th' unfading rose of Eden blooms,
And wings of Seraphs shed divine perfumes,
For her the Spouse prepares the bridal ring,
For her white virgins Hymenæals sing,
To sounds of heav'nly harps she dies away,
And melts in visions of eternal day.
  Far other dreams my erring soul employ,
Far other raptures, of unholy joy:
When at the close of each sad, sorrowing day,
Fancy restores what vengeance snatch'd away,
Then conscience sleeps, and leaving nature free,
All my loose soul unbounded springs to thee.
Oh curst, dear horrors of all-conscious night;
How glowing guilt exalts the keen delight!
Provoking Dæmons all restraint remove,
And stir within me ev'ry source of love.
I hear thee, view thee, gaze o'er all thy charms,
And round thy phantom glue my clasping arms.
I wake: — no more I hear, no more I view,
The phantom flies me, as unkind as you.
I call aloud; it hears not what I say:
I stretch my empty arms; it glides away.
To dream once more I close my willing eyes;
Ye soft illusions, dear deceits, arise!
Alas, no more! methinks we wand'ring go
Thro' dreary wastes, and weep each other's woe,
Where round some mould'ring tow'r pale ivy creeps,
And low-brow'd rocks hang nodding o'er the deeps.

---

[1] Here is the true doctrine of the Mystics. There are many such strains in Crashaw, particularly in a poem called *The Flaming Heart*, and in the *Seraphical Saint Theresa*. [The same poem.] War[ton.] [shaw.

[2] *Obedient slumbers, etc.*] Taken from Cr[a]

ELOISA TO ABELARD.

Sudden you mount, you beckon from the skies; 245
Clouds interpose, waves roar, and winds arise.
I shriek, start up, the same sad prospect find,
And wake to all the griefs I left behind.[1]
  For thee the fates, severely kind, ordain
A cool suspense from pleasure and from pain; 250
Thy life a long dead calm of fix'd repose;
No pulse that riots, and no blood that glows.
Still as the sea, ere winds were taught to blow,
Or moving spirit bade the waters flow;
Soft as the slumbers of a saint forgiv'n, 255
And mild as op'ning gleams of promis'd heav'n.
  Come, Abelard! for what hast thou to dread?
The torch of Venus burns not for the dead.
Nature stands check'd; Religion disapproves;
Ev'n thou art cold — yet Eloïsa loves. 260
Ah hopeless, lasting flames! like those that burn
To light the dead, and warm th' unfruitful urn.
  What scenes appear where'er I turn my view?
The dear Ideas, where I fly, pursue,
Rise in the grove, before the altar rise, 265
Stain all my soul, and wanton in my eyes.
I waste the Matin lamp in sighs for thee,
Thy image steels between my God and me,
Thy voice I seem in ev'ry hymn to hear,
With ev'ry bead I drop too soft a tear. 270
When from the censer clouds of fragrance roll,
And swelling organs lift the rising soul,
One thought of thee puts all the pomp to flight,
Priests, tapers, temples, swim before my sight:[2]
In seas of flame my plunging soul is drown'd, 275
While Altars blaze, and Angels tremble round.
  While prostrate here in humble grief I lie,
Kind, virtuous drops just gath'ring in my eye,
While praying, trembling, in the dust I roll,
And dawning grace is op'ning on my soul: 280
Come, if thou dar'st, all charming as thou art!
Oppose thyself to heav'n; dispute my heart;
Come, with one glance of those deluding eyes
Blot out each bright Idea of the skies;
Take back that grace, those sorrows, and those tears; 285
Take back my fruitless penitence and pray'rs;
Snatch me, just mounting, from the blest abode;
Assist the fiends, and tear me from my God!
  No, fly me, fly me, far as Pole from Pole;
Rise Alps between us! and whole oceans roll! 290
Ah, come not, write not, think not once of me,

---

[1] [This passage is plagiarised from Davenant.]
[2] 'Priests, tapers, temples, swam before my sight,
   'Altars, and victims.' — Smith's *Phædra and Hippolytus*. *Bowles*.

Nor share one pang of all I felt for thee.
Thy oaths I quit, thy memory resign;
Forget, renounce me, hate whate'er was mine.
Fair eyes, and tempting looks (which yet I view!) 295
Long lov'd, ador'd ideas, all adieu!
Oh Grace serene! oh virtue heav'nly fair!
Divine oblivion of low-thoughted care!
Fresh blooming Hope, gay daughter of the sky!
And Faith, our early immortality! 300
Enter, each mild, each amicable guest;
Receive, and wrap me in eternal rest!
 See in her cell sad Eloïsa spread,
Propt on some tomb, a neighbour of the dead.
In each low wind methinks a Spirit calls, 305
And more than Echoes talk along the walls.
Here, as I watch'd the dying lamps around,
From yonder shrine I heard a hollow sound.
"Come, sister, come! (it said, or seem'd to say)
"Thy place is here, sad sister, come away![1] 310
"Once like thyself, I trembled, wept, and pray'd,
"Love's victim then, tho' now a sainted maid:
"But all is calm in this eternal sleep;
"Here grief forgets to groan, and love to weep,
"Ev'n superstition loses ev'ry fear; 315
"For God, not man, absolves our frailties here."
 I come, I come! prepare your roseate bow'rs,
Celestial palms, and ever-blooming flow'rs.
Thither, where sinners may have rest, I go,
Where flames refin'd in breasts seraphic glow; 320
Thou, Abelard! the last sad office pay,
And smooth my passage to the realms of day;
See my lips tremble, and my eye-balls roll,[2]
Suck my last breath, and catch my flying soul!
Ah no — in sacred vestments may'st thou stand, 325
The hallow'd taper trembling in thy hand,
Present the Cross before my lifted eye,
Teach me at once, and learn of me to die.
Ah then, thy once-loved Eloïsa see!
It will be then no crime to gaze on me. 330
See from my cheek the transient roses fly!
See the last sparkle languish in my eye!
'Till ev'ry motion, pulse, and breath be o'er
And ev'n my Abelard be lov'd no more.
O Death all-eloquent! you only prove 335
What dust we dote on, when 't is man we love.
 Then too, when fate shall thy fair frame destroy,
(That cause of all my guilt, and all my joy)

---

[1] [cf. the second stanza of the *Dying Christian to his Soul*.]
[2] This and the following verse certainly taken from Oldham on the death of Adonis. *Warton* [who enumerates several lines in this epistle taken from various passages of Dryden].

In trance ecstatic may thy pangs be drown'd,[1]
Bright clouds descend, and Angels watch thee round, 340
From op'ning skies may streaming glories shine,
And saints embrace thee with a love like mine.
  May one kind grave unite each hapless name,[2]
And graft my love immortal on thy fame!
Then, ages hence, when all my woes are o'er, 345
When this rebellious heart shall beat no more;
If ever chance two wand'ring lovers' brings
To Paraclete's white walls and silver springs,
O'er the pale marble shall they join their heads,
And drink the falling tears each other sheds; 350
Then sadly say, with mutual pity mov'd,
"Oh may we never love as these have lov'd!"
From the full choir when loud Hosannas rise,
And swell the pomp of dreadful sacrifice,[3]
Amid that scene if some relenting eye 355
Glance on the stone where our cold relics lie,
Devotion's self shall steal a thought from heav'n,
One human tear shall drop and be forgiv'n.
And sure, if fate some future bard shall join
In sad similitude of griefs to mine, 360
Condemn'd whole years in absence to deplore,
And image charms he must behold no more;
Such if there be, who loves so long, so well;
Let him our sad, our tender story tell;
The well-sung woes will sooth my pensive ghost; 365
He best can paint 'em who shall feel 'em most.

THE TEMPLE OF FAME.

(1711)

ADVERTISEMENT.

THE hint of the following piece was taken from Chaucer's *House of Fame*. The design is in a manner entirely altered, the descriptions and most of the particular thoughts my own: yet I could not suffer it to be printed without this acknowledgment. The reader who would compare this with Chaucer, may begin with his third Book of *Fame*, there being nothing in the two first books that answers to their title: wherever any hint is taken from him, the passage itself is set down in the marginal notes. P.

---

[1] These circumstances are conformable to the notions of mystic devotion. The death of St. Jerome is finely and forcibly painted by Domenichino, with such attendant particulars. *Warton.*

[2] *May one kind grave, etc.*] Abelard and Eloïsa were interred in the same grave, or in monuments adjoining, in the Monastery of the Paraclete: he died in the year 1142, she in 1163. [An inscription was placed on their tomb in 1779, which is quoted by Roscoe.]

[3] *dreadful sacrifice,*] The ritual term. *Carruthers.*

THE TEMPLE OF FAME.

[CHAUCER'S *House of Fame* (in which 'booke is shewed how the deedes of all men and women, be they good or bad, are carried by report to posteritie') appears by internal evidence to have been written while he held the office of Comptroller of the Custom of Wool in London, to which he was appointed in 1374. This poem belongs to the second period of his literary career, in which the invention and arrangement of his subjects are already independent of foreign sources. Even Roscoe is unable to trace the *House of Fame* to an Italian original. Pope has both added to Chaucer, and omitted from him; leaving out in particular the bulk of the Second Book, which contains the teachings of the Eagle. The day has happily past when such loose paraphrases are relished; nor will many readers be found to assent to Roscoe's dictum that 'it is almost impossible to distinguish those portions for which Pope is indebted to Chaucer from those of his own invention.' The humorous lines with which Pope accompanied the present of his *Temple of Fame* to a lady will be found among the *Miscellanies*.]

IN that soft season, when descending show'rs [1]
   Call forth the greens, and wake the rising flow'rs;
When op'ning buds salute the welcome day,
And earth relenting feels the genial ray;
As balmy sleep had charm'd my cares to rest,   5
And love itself was banish'd from my breast,
(What time the morn mysterious visions brings,
While purer slumbers spread their golden wings)
A train of phantoms in wild order rose,
And, join'd, this intellectual scene compose.   10
  I stood, methought, betwixt earth, seas, and skies;
The whole creation open to my eyes:
In air self-balanc'd hung the globe below,
Where mountains rise and circling oceans flow;
Here naked rocks, and empty wastes were seen,   15
There tow'ry cities, and the forests green:
Here sailing ships delight the wand'ring eyes:
There trees, and intermingled temples rise;
Now a clear sun the shining scene displays,
The transient landscape now in clouds decays.   20
  O'er the wide Prospect as I gaz'd around,
Sudden I heard a wild promiscuous sound,
Like broken thunders that at distance roar,
Or billows murm'ring on the hollow shore:
Then gazing up, a glorious pile beheld,   25
Whose tow'ring summit ambient clouds conceal'd.
High on a rock of Ice the structure lay,
Steep its ascent, and slipp'ry was the way;
The wond'rous rock like Parian marble shone,
And seem'd, to distant sight, of solid stone.   30
Inscriptions here of various Names I view'd,

---

[1] *In that soft season, etc.*] This Poem is introduced in the manner of the Provençal Poets, whose works were for the most part Visions, or pieces of imagination, and constantly descriptive. From these, Petrarch and Chaucer frequently borrow the idea of their poems. See the *Trionfi* of the former, and the *Dream, Flower and the Leaf*, etc. of the latter. The Author of this therefore chose the same sort of Exordium. P.

The greater part by hostile time subdu'd;
Yet wide was spread their fame in ages past,
And Poets once had promis'd they should last.
Some fresh engrav'd appear'd of Wits renown'd;   35
I look'd again, nor could their trace be found.
Critics I saw, that other names deface,
And fix their own, with labour, in their place:
Their own, like others, soon their place resign'd,
Or disappear'd, and left the first behind.   40
Nor was the work impair'd by storms alone,
But felt th' approaches of too warm a sun;
For Fame, impatient of extremes, decays
Not more by Envy than excess of Praise.
Yet part no injuries of heav'n could feel,   45
Like crystal faithful to the graving steel:
The rock's high summit, in the temple's shade,
Nor heat could melt, nor beating storm invade.
Their names inscrib'd unnumber'd ages past
From time's first birth, with time itself shall last;   50
These ever new, nor subject to decays,
Spread, and grow brighter with the length of days.
　So Zembla's rocks (the beauteous work of frost)
Rise white in air, and glitter o'er the coast;
Pale suns, unfelt, at distance roll away,   55
And on th' impassive ice the light'nings play;
Eternal snows the growing mass supply,
Till the bright mountains prop th' incumbent sky:
As Atlas fix'd, each hoary pile appears,
The gather'd winter of a thousand years.   60
　On this foundation Fame's high temple stands;
Stupendous pile! not rear'd by mortal hands.
Whate'er proud Rome or artful Greece beheld,
Or elder Babylon, its frame excell'd.
Four faces had the dome, and ev'ry face [1]   65
Of various structure, but of equal grace:
Four brazen gates, on columns lifted high,
Salute the diff'rent quarters of the sky.
Here fabled Chiefs in darker ages born,
Or Worthies old, whom arms or arts adorn,   70
Who cities rais'd, or tam'd a monstrous race;
The walls in venerable order grace:
Heroes in animated marble frown,
And Legislators seem to think in stone.
　Westward, a sumptuous frontispiece appear'd,   75
On Doric pillars of white marble rear'd,

---

[1] *Four faces had the dome, etc.*] The Temple is described to be square, the four fronts with open gates facing the different quarters of the world, as an intimation that all nations of the earth may alike be received into it. The western front is of Grecian architecture: the Doric order was peculiarly sacred to Heroes and Worthies. Those whose statues are after mentioned, were the first names of old Greece in arms and arts. P.

Crown'd with an architrave of antique mold,
And sculpture rising on the roughen'd gold.
In shaggy spoils here Theseus was beheld,
And Perseus dreadful with Minerva's shield:
There great Alcides stooping with his toil,[1]
Rests on his club, and holds th' Hesperian spoil.
Here Orpheus sings; trees moving to the sound
Start from their roots, and form a shade around:
Amphion there the loud creating lyre
Strikes, and beholds a sudden Thebes aspire!
Cithæron's echoes answer to his call,
And half the mountain rolls into a wall:
There might you see the length'ning spires ascend,
The domes swell up, the wid'ning arches bend,
The growing tow'rs, like exhalations rise,
And the huge columns heave into the skies.

The Eastern front was glorious to behold,
With di'mond flaming, and Barbaric gold.
There Ninus shone, who spread th' Assyrian fame,
And the great founder of the Persian name:[2]
There in long robes the royal Magi stand,
Grave Zoroaster waves the circling wand,
The sage Chaldæans rob'd in white appear'd,
And Brahmans, deep in desert woods rever'd.
These stopp'd the moon, and call'd th' unbody'd shades
To midnight banquets in the glimm'ring glades;
Made visionary fabrics round them rise,
And airy spectres skim before their eyes;
Of Talismans and Sigils knew the pow'r,
And careful watch'd the Planetary hour.
Superior, and alone, Confucius stood,
Who taught that useful science, to be good.

But on the South, a long majestic race
Of Ægypt's Priests the gilded niches grace,[3]
Who measur'd earth, describ'd the starry spheres,
And trac'd the long records of lunar years.
High on his car Sesostris struck my view,

---

[1] *There great Alcides, etc.*] This figure of Hercules is drawn with an eye to the position of the famous statue of Farnese. P.

[2] *And the great founder of the Persian name:*] Cyrus was the beginning of the Persian, as Ninus was of the Assyrian Monarchy. The Magi and Chaldæans (the chief of whom was Zoroaster) employed their studies upon magic and astrology, which was in a manner almost all the learning of the ancient Asian people. We have scarce any account of a moral philosopher except Confucius, the great lawgiver of the Chinese, who lived about two thousand years ago. P.

[3] *Ægypt's priests, &c.*] The learning of the old Ægyptian Priests consisted for the most part in geometry and astronomy: they also preserved the History of their nation. Their greatest Hero upon record is Sesostris, whose actions and conquests may be seen at large in Diodorus, etc He is said to have caused the Kings he vanquished to draw him in his Chariot. The posture of his statue, in these verses, is correspondent to the description which Herodotus gives of one of them remaining in his own time. P.

THE TEMPLE OF FAME. 117

Whom scepter'd slaves in golden harness drew:
His hands a bow and pointed javelin hold;   115
His giant limbs are arm'd in scales of gold.
Between the statues Obelisks were plac'd
And the learn'd walls with Hieroglyphics grac'd.
Of Gothic structure was the Northern side,[1]
O'erwrought with ornaments of barb'rous pride.   120
There huge Colosses rose, with trophies crown'd,
And Runic characters were grav'd around.
There sate Zamolxis with erected eyes,
And Odin here in mimic trances dies.
There on rude iron columns, smear'd with blood,   125
The horrid forms of Scythian heroes stood,
Druids and Bards (their once loud harps unstrung)[2]
And youths that died to be by Poets sung.
These and a thousand more of doubtful fame,
To whom old fables gave a lasting name,   130
In ranks adorn'd the Temple's outward face;
The wall in lustre and effect like Glass,
Which o'er each object casting various dyes,
Enlarges some, and others multiplies:
Nor void of emblem was the mystic wall,   135
For thus romantic Fame increases all.
   The Temple shakes, the sounding gates unfold,
Wide vaults appear, and roofs of fretted gold:
Rais'd on a thousand pillars, wreath'd around
With laurel-foliage, and with eagles crown'd: 140
Of bright, transparent beryl were the walls,
The friezes gold, and gold the capitals:
As heav'n with stars, the roof with jewels glows,
And ever-living lamps depend in rows.
Full in the passage of each spacious gate,   145
The sage Historians in white garments wait;
Grav'd o'er their seats the form of Time was found,
His scythe revers'd, and both his pinions bound.
Within stood Heroes, who thro' loud alarms
In bloody fields pursu'd renown in arms.   150
High on a throne with trophies charg'd, I view'd
The Youth that all things but himself subdu'd;[3]

---

[1] *Of Gothic structure was the Northern side,*] The Architecture is agreeable to that part of the world. The learning of the northern nations lay more obscure than that of the rest; Zamolxis was the disciple of Pythagoras, who taught the immortality of the soul to the Scythians. Odin, or Woden, was the great Legislator and hero of the Goths. They tell us of him, that being subject to fits, he persuaded his followers, that during those trances he received inspirations, from whence he dictated his laws: he is said to have been the inventor of the Runic characters. P.

[2] *Druids and Bards, etc.*] These were the priests and poets of those people, so celebrated for their savage virtue. Those heroic barbarians accounted it a dishonour to die in their beds, and rushed on to certain death in the prospect of an after-life, and for the glory of a song from their bards in praise of their actions. P.

[3] *The Youth that all things but himself subdu'd;*] Alexander the Great: the Tiara was

His feet on sceptres and tiara's trod,
And his horn'd head bely'd the Libyan God.
There Cæsar, grac'd with both Minerva's, shone; 155
Cæsar, the world's great master, and his own;
Unmov'd, superior still in ev'ry state,
And scarce detested in his Country's fate.
But chief were those, who not for empire fought,
But with their toils their people's safety bought: 160
High o'er the rest Epaminondas stood;
Timoleon, glorious in his brother's blood;[1]
Bold Scipio, saviour of the Roman state;
Great in his triumphs, in retirement great;
And wise Aurelius,[2] in whose well-taught mind 165
With boundless pow'r unbounded virtue join'd,
His own strict judge, and patron of mankind.

Much-suff'ring heroes next their honours claim,
Those of less noisy, and less guilty fame,
Fair Virtue's silent train: supreme of these 170
Here ever shines the godlike Socrates:
He whom ungrateful Athens could expell,[3]
At all times just, but when he sign'd the Shell:
Here his abode the martyr'd Phocion claims,[4]
With Agis, not the last of Spartan names:[5] 175
Unconquered Cato shews the wound he tore,
And Brutus his ill Genius meets no more.[6]

But in the centre of the hallow'd choir,[7]
Six pompous columns o'er the rest aspire;
Around the shrine itself of Fame they stand, 180
Hold the chief honours, and the fane command.
High on the first, the mighty Homer shone;

---

the crown peculiar to the Asian Princes: his desire to be thought the son of Jupiter Ammon, caused him to wear the horns of that God, and to represent the same upon his coins; which was continued by several of his successors. P.

[1] *Timoleon, glorious in his brother's blood;*] Timoleon had saved the life of his brother Timophanes in the battle between the Argives and Corinthians; but afterwards killed him when he affected the tyranny, preferring his duty to his country to all the obligations of blood. P.

[2] [The Roman Emperor Marcus Aurelius, author of the *Meditations* or *Commentaries*.]

[3] *He whom ungrateful Athens, etc.*] Aristides, who for his great integrity was distinguished by the appellation of *the Just*. When his countrymen would have banished him by the Ostracism, where it was the custom for every man to sign the name of the person he voted to exile in an Oyster-shell; a peasant, who could not write, came to Aristides to do it for him, who readily signed his own name. P.

[4] [Phocion, put to death by Polysperchon, B.C. 318, can hardly be described as a martyr to the liberty of Athens, which it had been the business of his life to destroy.]

[5] [Agis, King of Sparta, who endeavoured to restore his state to greatness by a radical agrarian reform, was after a mock trial murdered in prison, B.C. 241.]

[6] ['Thou shalt see me at Philippi.']

[7] *But in the centre of the hallow'd choir*, etc.] In the midst of the temple, nearest the throne of Fame, are placed the greatest names in learning of all antiquity. These are described in such attitudes as express their different characters: the columns on which they are raised are adorned with sculptures, taken from the most striking subjects of their works; which sculpture bears a resemblance, in its manner and character, to the manner and character of their writings. P.

THE TEMPLE OF FAME.

Eternal Adamant compos'd his throne;
Father of verse! in holy fillets drest,
His silver beard wav'd gently o'er his breast;   185
Tho' blind, a boldness in his looks appears;
In years he seem'd, but not impair'd by years.
The wars of Troy were round the Pillar seen:
Here fierce Tydides wounds the Cyprian Queen;
Here Hector glorious from Patroclus' fall,   190
Here dragg'd in triumph round the Trojan wall,
Motion and life did ev'ry part inspire,
Bold was the work, and prov'd the master's fire;
A strong expression most he seem'd t' affect,
And here and there disclos'd a brave neglect.   195
   A golden column next in rank appear'd,
On which a shrine of purest gold was rear'd;
Finish'd the whole, and labour'd ev'ry part,
With patient touches of unweary'd art:
The Mantuan there in sober triumph sate,   200
Compos'd his posture, and his look sedate;
On Homer still he fix'd a rev'rend eye,
Great without pride, in modest majesty.
In living sculpture on the sides were spread
The Latian Wars, and haughty Turnus dead;   205
Eliza stretch'd upon the fun'ral pyre,[1]
Æneas bending with his aged sire:
Troy flam'd in burning gold, and o'er the throne
ARMS AND THE MAN in golden cyphers shone.
   Four swans sustain a car of silver bright,[2]   210
With heads advanc'd, and pinions stretch'd for flight:
Here, like some furious prophet, Pindar rode,
And seem'd to labour with th' inspiring God.
Across the harp a careless hand he flings,
And boldly sinks into the sounding strings.   215
The figur'd games of Greece the column grace,
Neptune and Jove survey the rapid race.
The youths hang o'er their chariots as they run;
The fiery steeds seem starting from the stone;
The champions in distorted postures threat;   220
And all appear'd irregularly great.
   Here happy Horace tun'd th' Ausonian lyre
To sweeter sounds, and temper'd Pindar's fire:
Pleas'd with Alcæus' manly rage t' infuse
The softer spirit of the Sapphic Muse.   225
The polish'd pillar diff'rent sculptures grace;
A work outlasting monumental brass.
Here smiling Loves and Bacchanals appear,

---

[1] [Elissa (Dido.)]
[2] *Four swans sustain, etc.*] Pindar being seated in a chariot, alludes to the chariot-races he celebrated in the Grecian games. The swans are emblems of Poetry, their soaring posture intimates the sublimity and activity of his genius. Neptune presided over the Isthmian, and Jupiter over the Olympian games. P.

The Julian star, and great Augustus here.
The Doves that round the infant poet spread 230
Myrtles and bays, hung hov'ring o'er his head.
    Here in a shrine that cast a dazzling light,
Sate fix'd in thought the mighty Stagirite;
His sacred head a radiant Zodiac crown'd,
And various Animals his sides surround; 235
His piercing eyes, erect, appear to view
Superior worlds, and look all Nature through.
    With equal rays immortal Tully shone,
The Roman Rostra deck'd the Consul's throne:
Gath'ring his flowing robe, he seem'd to stand 240
In act to speak, and graceful stretch'd his hand.
Behind, Rome's Genius waits with Civic crowns,
And the great Father of his country owns.
    These massy columns in a circle rise,
O'er which a pompous dome invades the skies: 245
Scarce to the top I stretch'd my aching sight,
So large it spread, and swell'd to such a height.
Full in the midst proud Fame's imperial seat,
With jewels blaz'd, magnificently great;
The vivid em'ralds there revive the eye, 250
The flaming rubies shew their sanguine dye,
Bright azure rays from lively sapphyrs stream,
And lucid amber casts a golden gleam.
With various-colour'd light the pavement shone,
And all on fire appear'd the glowing throne; 255
The dome's high arch reflects the mingled blaze,
And forms a rainbow of alternate rays.
When on the Goddess first I cast my sight,
Scarce seem'd her stature of a cubit's height;
But swell'd to larger size, the more I gaz'd, 260
Till to the roof her tow'ring front she rais'd.
With her, the Temple ev'ry moment grew,
And ampler Vista's open'd to my view:
Upward the columns shoot, the roofs ascend,
And arches widen, and long aisles extend. 265
Such was her form as ancient bards have told,
Wings raise her arms, and wings her feet infold;
A thousand busy tongues the Goddess bears,
And thousand open eyes, and thousand list'ning ears.
Beneath, in order rang'd, the tuneful Nine 270
(Her virgin handmaids) still attend the shrine:
With eyes on Fame for ever fix'd, they sing;
For Fame they raise the voice, and tune the string;
With time's first birth began the heav'nly lays,
And last, eternal, thro' the length of days. 275
    Around these wonders as I cast a look,
The trumpet sounded, and the temple shook,
And all the nations, summon'd at the call,

From diff'rent quarters fill the crowded hall:
Of various tongues the mingled sounds were heard;   280
In various garbs promiscuous throngs appear'd;
Thick as the bees, that with the spring renew
Their flow'ry toils, and sip the fragrant dew,
When the wing'd colonies first tempt the sky,
O'er dusky fields and shaded waters fly,   285
Or settling, seize the sweets the blossoms yield,
And a low murmur runs along the field.
Millions of suppliant crowds the shrine attend,
And all degrees before the Goddess bend;
The poor, the rich, the valiant, and the sage,   290
And boasting youth, and narrative old-age.[1]
Their pleas were diff'rent, their request the same:
For good and bad alike are fond of Fame.
Some she disgrac'd, and some with honours crown'd;
Unlike successes equal merits found.   295
Thus her blind sister, fickle Fortune, reigns,
And, undiscerning, scatters crowns and chains.
   First at the shrine the Learned world appear,
And to the Goddess thus prefer their pray'r.
"Long have we sought t' instruct and please mankind,   300
With studies pale, with midnight vigils blind;
But thank'd by few, rewarded yet by none,
We here appeal to thy superior throne:
On wit and learning the just prize bestow,
For fame is all we must expect below."   305
   The Goddess heard, and bade the Muses raise
The golden Trumpet of eternal Praise:
From pole to pole the winds diffuse the sound,
That fills the circuit of the world around;
Not all at once, as thunder breaks the cloud;   310
The notes at first were rather sweet than loud:
By just degrees they ev'ry moment rise,
Fill the wide earth, and gain upon the skies.
At ev'ry breath were balmy odours shed,
Which still grew sweeter as they wider spread;   315
Less fragrant scents th' unfolding rose exhales,
Or spices breathing in Arabian gales.
   Next these the good and just, an awful train,
Thus on their knees address the sacred fane.
"Since living virtue is with envy curs'd,   320
And the best men are treated like the worst,
Do thou, just Goddess, call our merits forth,
And give each deed th' exact intrinsic worth."
"Not with bare justice shall your act be crown'd"
(Said Fame) "but high above desert renown'd: 325
Let fuller notes th' applauding world amaze,

---

[1] Dryden uses this adjective in the same sense: 'Age, as Davenant says, is always narrative.' *Richardson.*

And the loud clarion labour in your praise."
  This band dismiss'd, behold another crowd
Preferr'd the same request, and lowly bow'd;
The constant tenour of whose well-spent days   330
No less deserv'd a just return of praise.
But strait the direful Trump of Slander sounds;
Thro' the big dome the doubling thunder bounds;
Loud as the burst of cannon rends the skies,
The dire report thro' ev'ry region flies,   335
In ev'ry ear incessant rumours rung,
And gath'ring scandals grew on ev'ry tongue.
From the black trumpet's rusty concave broke
Sulphureous flames, and clouds of rolling smoke:
The pois'nous vapour blots the purple skies,   340
And withers all before it as it flies.
  A troop came next, who crowns and armour wore,
And proud defiance in their looks they bore:
"For thee" (they cry'd) "amidst alarms and strife,
We sail'd in tempests down the stream of life;   345
For thee whole nations fill'd with flames and blood,
And swam to empire thro' the purple flood.
Those ills we dar'd, thy inspiration own,
What virtue seem'd, was done for thee alone."
"Ambitious fools!" (the Queen reply'd, and frown'd)   350
"Be all your acts in dark oblivion drown'd;
There sleep forgot, with mighty tyrants gone,
Your statues moulder'd, and your names unknown!"
A sudden cloud straight snatch'd them from my sight,
And each majestic phantom sunk in night.   355
  Then came the smallest tribe I yet had seen;
Plain was their dress, and modest was their mien.
"Great idol of mankind! we neither claim
The praise of merit, nor aspire to fame!
But safe in deserts from th' applause of men,   360
Would die unheard of, as we liv'd unseen,
'T is all we beg thee, to conceal from sight
Those acts of goodness, which themselves requite.
O let us still the secret joy partake,
To follow virtue ev'n for virtue's sake."   365
  "And live there men, who slight immortal fame?
Who then with incense shall adore our name?
But mortals! know, 't is still our greatest pride
To blaze those virtues, which the good would hide.
Rise! Muses, rise; add all your tuneful breath,   370
These must not sleep in darkness and in death."
She said: in air the trembling music floats,
And on the winds triumphant swell the notes;
So soft, tho' high, so loud, and yet so clear,
Ev'n list'ning Angels lean'd from heav'n to hear: 375
To farthest shores th' Ambrosial spirit flies,

Sweet to the world, and grateful to the skies.
  Next these a youthful train their vows express'd,
With feathers crown'd, with gay embroid'ry dress'd:
"Hither," they cry'd, "direct your eyes, and see   380
The men of pleasure, dress, and gallantry;
Ours is the place at banquets, balls, and plays,
Sprightly our nights, polite are all our days;
Courts we frequent, where 't is our pleasing care
To pay due visits, and address the fair: 385.
In fact, 't is true, no nymph we could persuade,
But still in fancy vanquish'd ev'ry maid;
Of unknown Duchesses lewd tales we tell,
Yet, would the world believe us, all were well.
The joy let others have, and we the name,   390
And what we want in pleasure, grant in fame."
  The Queen assents, the trumpet rends the skies,
And at each blast a Lady's honour dies.[1]
  Pleas'd with the strange success, vast numbers prest
Around the shrine, and made the same request: 395
"What? you," (she cry'd) "unlearn'd in arts to please,
Slaves to yourselves, and ev'n fatigu'd with ease,
Who lose a length of undeserving days,
Would you usurp the lover's dear-bought praise?
To just contempt, ye vain pretenders, fall,   400
The people's fable, and the scorn of all."
Straight the black clarion sends a horrid sound,
Loud laughs burst out, and bitter scoffs fly round,
Whispers are heard, with taunts reviling loud,
And scornful hisses run thro' all the crowd.   405
  Last, those who boast of mighty mischiefs done,
Enslave their country, or usurp a throne;
Or who their glory's dire foundation lay'd
On Sov'reigns ruin'd, or on friends betray'd;
Calm, thinking villains, whom no faith could fix,   410
Of crooked counsels and dark politics;
Of these a gloomy tribe surround the throne,
And beg to make th' immortal treasons known.
The trumpet roars, long flaky flames expire,
With sparks, that seem'd to set the world on fire.   415
At the dread sound, pale mortals stood aghast,
And startled nature trembled with the blast.
  This having heard and seen, some pow'r unknown
Straight chang'd the scene, and snatch'd me from the throne.
Before my view appear'd a structure fair,   420
Its site uncertain, if in earth or air;
With rapid motion turn'd the mansion round;
With ceaseless noise the ringing walls resound;
Not less in number were the spacious doors,

---

[1] ['At ev'ry word a reputation dies.' *Rape of the Lock*, Canto III. v. 16.]

                Than leaves on trees, or sand upon the shores ;   425
            Which still unfolded stand, by night, by day,
            Pervious to winds, and open ev'ry way.
            As flames by nature to the skies ascend,
            As weighty bodies to the centre tend,
            As to the sea returning rivers roll,   430
            And the touch'd needle trembles to the pole ;
            Hither, as to their proper place, arise
            All various sounds from earth, and seas, and skies,
            Or spoke aloud, or whisper'd in the ear ;
            Nor ever silence, rest, or peace is here.   435
            As on the smooth expanse of crystal lakes
            The sinking stone at first a circle makes :
            The trembling surface by the motion stir'd,
            Spreads in a second circle, then a third ;
            Wide, and more wide, the floating rings advance,   440
            Fill all the wat'ry plain, and to the margin dance :
            Thus ev'ry voice and sound, when first they break,
            On neighb'ring air a soft impression make ;
            Another ambient circle then they move ;
            That, in its turn, impels the next above ;   445
            Thro' undulating air the sounds are sent,
            And spread o'er all the fluid element.[1]
              There various news I heard of love and strife,
            Of peace and war, health, sickness, death, and life,
            Of loss and gain, of famine and of store,   450
            Of storms at sea, and travels on the shore,
            Of prodigies, and portents seen in air,
            Of fires and plagues, and stars with blazing hair,
            Of turns of fortune, changes in the state,
            The falls of fav'rites, projects of the great,   455
            Of old mismanagements, taxations new :
            All neither wholly false, nor wholly true.
              Above, below, without, within, around,
            Confus'd, unnumber'd multitudes are found,
            Who pass, repass, advance, and glide away ;   460
            Hosts rais'd by fear, and phantoms of a day :
            Astrologers, that future fates foreshew,
            Projectors, quacks, and lawyers not a few ;
            And priests, and party-zealots, num'rous bands
            With home-born lies, or tales from foreign lands ;   465
            Each talk'd aloud, or in some secret place,
            And wild impatience star'd in ev'ry face.
            The flying rumours gather'd as they roll'd,
            Scarce any tale was sooner heard than told ;
            And all who told it added something new,   470
            And all who heard it, made enlargements too,
            In ev'ry ear it spread, on ev'ry tongue it grew.

---

[1] [This simile suggested to Pope the famous passage in the *Essay on Man*, Ep. IV. vv. 363–72.]

Thus flying east and west, and north and south,
News travel'd with increase from mouth to mouth.
So from a spark, that kindled first by chance, 475
With gath'ring force the quick'ning flames advance;
Till to the clouds their curling heads aspire,
And tow'rs and temples sink in floods of fire.
　When thus ripe lies are to perfection sprung,
Full grown, and fit to grace a mortal tongue, 480
Thro' thousand vents, impatient, forth they flow,
And rush in millions on the world below.
Fame sits aloft, and points them out their course,
Their date determines, and prescribes their force:
Some to remain, and some to perish soon; 485
Or wane and wax alternate like the moon.
Around, a thousand winged wonders fly,
Borne by the trumpet's blast, and scatter'd thro' the sky.
　There, at one passage, oft you might survey
A lie and truth contending for the way; 490
And long 't was doubtful, both so closely pent,
Which first should issue thro' the narrow vent:
At last agreed, together out they fly,
Inseparable now, the truth and lie;
The strict companions are for ever join'd, 495
And this or that unmix'd, no mortal e'er shall find.
　While thus I stood, intent to see and hear,[1]
One came, methought, and whisper'd in my ear:
"What could thus high thy rash ambition raise?
Art thou, fond youth, a candidate for praise?" 500
　"'T is true," said I, "not void of hopes I came,
For who so fond as youthful bards of Fame?
But few, alas! the casual blessing boast,
So hard to gain, so easy to be lost.
How vain that second life in others breath, 505
Th' estate which wits inherit after death!
Ease, health, and life, for this they must resign,
(Unsure the tenure, but how vast the fine!)
The great man's curse, without the gains, endure,
Be envy'd, wretched, and be flatter'd, poor; 510
All luckless wits their enemies profest,
And all successful, jealous friends at best.
Nor Fame I slight, nor for her favours call;
She comes unlook'd for, if she comes at all.
But if the purchase costs so dear a price, 515
As soothing Folly, or exalting Vice:
Oh! if the Muse must flatter lawless sway,

---

[1] *While thus I stood, &c.*] The hint is taken from a passage in another part of the third book, but here more naturally made the conclusion, with the addition of a *Moral* to the whole. In *Chaucer* he only answers "he came to see the place;" and the book ends abruptly, with his being surprised at the sight of a *Man of great Authority*, and awaking in a fright. P.

And follow still where fortune leads the way;
Or if no basis bear my rising name,
But the fall'n ruin of another's fame; 520
Then teach me, heav'n! to scorn the guilty bays,
Drive from my breast that wretched lust of praise,
Unblemish'd let me live, or die unknown;
Oh grant an honest fame, or grant me none!"

IMITATIONS.

Ver. 11, etc.] These verses are hinted from the following of Chaucer, Book II.:
'Tho beheld I fields and plains,
  Now hills, and now mountains,
  Now valeis, and now forestes,
  And now unneth great bestes,
  Now rivers, now citees,
  Now towns, now great trees,
  Now shippes sayling in the see.' P.

Ver. 27. *High on a rock of Ice, etc.*] Chaucer's third book of *Fame*:
'It stood upon so high a rock,
  Higher standeth none in Spayne —
  What manner stone this rock was,
  For it was like a lymed glass,
  But that it shone full more clere;
  But of what congeled matere
  It was, I niste redily;
  But at the last espied I,
  And found that it was every dele,
  A rock of ise, and not of stele.'

Ver. 31. *Inscriptions here, etc.*]
'Tho saw I all the hill y-grave
  With famous folkes names fele,
  That had been in much wele
  And her fames wide y-blow;
  But well unneth might I know,
  Any letters for to rede
  Ther names by, for out of drede
  They weren almost off-thawen so,
  That of the letters one or two
  Were molte away of every name,
  So unfamous was woxe her fame;
  But men said, what may ever last.' P.

Ver. 41. *Nor was the work impair'd, etc.*]
'Tho gan I in myne harte cast,
  That they were molte away for heate,
  And not away with stormes beate.'

Ver. 45. *Yet part no injuries, etc.*]
'For on that other side I sey
  Of that hill which northward ley,
  How it was written full of names
  Of folke, that had afore great fames,
  Of old time, and yet they were
  As fresh as men had written hem there
  The self day, or that houre
  That I on hem gan to poure:
  But well I wiste what it made;
  It was conserved with the shade
  (All the writing that I sye)
  Of the castle that stoode on high,
  And stood eke in so cold a place,
  That heate might it not deface.' P.

Ver. 132. *The wall in lustre, etc.*]
'It shone lighter than a glass,
  And made well more than it was,
  As kind thing of Fame is.'

Ver. 179. *Six pompous columns, etc.*]
'From the dees many a pillere,
  Of metal that shone not full clere, etc.
  Upon a pillere saw I stonde
  That was of lede and iron fine,
  Him of the sect Saturnine,
  The Ebraicke Josephus the old, etc.
  Upon an iron piller strong,
  That painted was all endlong,
  With tygers blood in every place,
  The Tholosan that hight Stace,
  That bare of Thebes up the name, etc.' P.

Ver. 182.]
'Full wonder hye on a pillere
  Of iron, he the great Omer,
  And with him Dares and Titus, etc.' P.

Ver. 196, etc.]
'There saw I stand on a pillere
  That was of tinned iron cleere,
  The Latin Poet Virgyle,
  That hath bore up of a great while
  The fame of pius Eneas:
  And next him on a pillere was
  Of copper, Venus clerke Ovide,
  That hath sowen wondrous wide

The great God of Love's fame —
Tho saw I on a pillere by
Of iron wrought full sternly,
The great Poet Dan Lucan,
That on his shoulders bore up then
As hye as that I might see,
The fame of Julius and Pompee.
  And next him on a pillere stode
Of sulphur, like as he were wode,
Dan Claudian, sothe for to tell,
That bare up all the fame of hell, etc.' P.

Ver. 224. *Pleas'd with Alcæus' manly rage t' infuse The softer spirit of the Sapphic Muse.*] This expresses the mix'd character of the odes of Horace: the second of these verses alludes to that line of his,
  'Spiritum Graiæ tenuem camœnæ.'
As another which follows, to
  'Exegi monumentum ære perennius.'
The action of the Doves hints at a passage in the fourth ode of his third book,
  'Me fabulosæ Vulture in Appulo
    Altricis extra limen Apuliæ,
    Ludo fatigatumque somno,
      Fronde nova puerum palumbes
  Texêre; mirum quod foret omnibus —
  Ut tuto ab atris corpore viperis
    Dormirem et ursis; ut premerer sacro
      Lauroque collataque myrto,
  Non sine Diis animosus infans.'
Which may be thus englished:
  'While yet a child, I chanc'd to stray,
  And in a desert sleeping lay;
  The savage race withdrew, nor dar'd
  To touch the Muses future bard;
  But Cytherea's gentle dove
  Myrtles and Bays around me spread,
  And crown'd your infant Poet's head,
  Sacred to Music and to Love.' P.

Ver. 259. *Scarce seem'd her stature, etc.*]
  'Methought that she was so lite,
  That the length of a cubite
  Was longer than she seemed be;
  But thus soone in a while she,
  Her selfe tho wonderly straight,
  That with her feet she the earth reight,
  And with head she touchyd heaven — ' P.

Ver. 270. *Beneath, in order rang'd, etc.*]
  'I heard about her throne y-sung
  That all the palays walls rung,
  So sung the mighty Muse, she
  That cleped is Calliope,
  And her seven sisters eke — ' P.

Ver. 276. *Around these wonders, etc.*]
  'I heard a noise approchen blive,
  That far'd as bees done in a hive,
  Against her time of out flying;
  Right such a manere murmuring,
  For all the world it seemed me.
  Tho gan I look about and see
  That there came entring into th' hall,
  A right great company withal;
  And that of sundry regions,
  Of all kind of conditions, — etc.' P.

Ver. 294. *Some she disgrac'd, etc.*]
  'And some of them she granted sone,
  And some she warned well and fair,
  And some she granted the contrair —
  Right as her sister dame Fortune
  Is wont to serve in commune.' P.

Ver. 318. ... *the good and just, etc.*]
  'Tho came the third companye,
  And gan up to the dees to hye,
  And down on knees they fell anone,
  And saiden: We ben everichone
  Folke that han full truely
  Deserved Fame right-fully,
  And prayen you it might be knowe
  Right as it is, and forth blowe.
    I grant, quoth she, for now me list
  That your good works shall be wist.
  And yet ye shall have better loos,
  Right in despite of all your foos,
  Than worthy is, and that anone.
  Let now (quoth she) thy trump gone —
  And certes all the breath that went
  Out of his trump's mouth smel'd
  As men a pot of baume held
  Among a basket full of roses — ' P.

Ver. 328, 338. ... *behold another croud, etc. — From the black trumpet's rusty, etc.*]
  'Therewithal there came anone
  Another huge companye,
  Of good folke —
  What did this Eolus, but he
  Tooke out his trump of brass,
  That fouler than the devil was:
  And gan this trump for to blowe,
  As all the world should overthrowe.
  Throughout every regione
  Went this foul trumpet's soune,
  Swift as a pellet out of a gunne,
  When fire is in the powder runne.
  And such a smoke gan out wende,
  Out of the foul trumpet's ende — etc.' P.

Ver. 356. *Then came the smallest, etc.*]
  'I saw anone the fifth route,
  That to this lady gan loute,
  And downe on knees anone to fall,
  And to her they besoughten all,
  To hiden their good works eke?
  And said, they yeve not a leke
  For no fame ne such renowne;
  For they for contemplacyoune,

And Goddes love had it wrought,
Ne of fame would they ought.
    What, quoth she, and be ye wood?
And ween ye for to do good,
And for to have it of no fame?
Have ye despite to have my name?
Nay ye shall lien everichone:
Blowe thy trump, and that anone
(Quoth she) thou Eolus, I hote,
And ring these folkes workes by rote,
That all the world may of it heare;
And he gan blow their loos so cleare,
In his golden clarioune,
Through the World went the soune,
All so kindly, and eke so soft,
That their fame was blown aloft.' P.

Ver. 378. *Next these a youthful train, etc.*] The Reader might compare these twenty-eight lines following, which contain the same matter, with eighty-four of Chaucer, beginning thus:

'Tho came the sixth companye,
And gan faste to Fame cry, etc.'
being too prolix to be here inserted. P.

Ver. 406. *Last, those who boast of mighty, etc.*]

'Tho came another companye,
That had y-done the treachery, etc.' P.

Ver. 418. *This having heard and seen, etc.*] The Scene here changes from the temple of Fame to that of Rumour, which is almost entirely Chaucer's. The particulars follow.

'Tho saw I stonde in a valey,
Under the castle fast by
A house, that Domus Dedali
That Labyrinthus cleped is,
Nas made so wonderly, I wis,
Ne half so queintly y-wrought;
And evermo as swift as thought,
This queint house about went
That never more is still stent—
And eke this house hath of entrees
As many as leaves are on trees,
In summer, when they ben grene;
And in the roof yet men may sene
A thousand hoels and well mo,
To letten the soune out go;
And by day in every tide
Ben all the doors open wide,
And by night each one unshet;
No porter is there one to let,
No manner tydings in to pace:
Ne never rest is in that place.' P.

Ver. 428. *As flames by nature to the, etc.*] This thought is transferred hither out of the third book of *Fame*, where it takes up no less than one hundred and twenty verses, beginning thus,

'Geffray, thou wottest well this, etc.' P.

Ver. 448. *There various news I heard, etc.*]
'Of werres, of peace, of marriages,
Of rest, of labour, of voyages,
Of abode, of dethe, and of life,
Of love and hate, accord and strife,
Of loss, of lore, and of winnings,
Of hele, of sickness, and lessings,
Of divers transmutations
Of estates and eke of regions,
Of truste, of drede, of jealousy,
Of wit, of winning, and of folly,
Of good, or bad government,
Of fire, and of divers accident.' P.

Ver. 458. *Above, below, without, within, etc.*]

'But such a grete Congregation
Of folke as I saw roame about,
Some within, and some without,
Was never seen, ne shall be eft—
    And every wight that I saw there
Rowned everich in others ear.
A new tyding privily,
Or else he told it openly
Right thus, and said, Knowst not thou
That is betide to night now?
No, quoth he, tell me what?
And then he told him this and that, etc.]
———— Thus north and south
Went every tyding fro mouth to mouth,
And that encreasing evermo,
As fire is wont to quicken and go
From a sparkle sprong amiss,
Till all the citee brent up is.' P.

Ver. 489. *There, at one passage, etc.*]
'And sometime I saw there at once,
A lesing and a sad sooth saw
That gonnen at adventure draw
Out of a window forth to pace—
And no man, be he ever so wrothe,
Shall have one of these two, but bothe, etc.'
                                              P.

JANUARY AND MAY:

OR

THE MERCHANT'S TALE.

FROM CHAUCER.

THIS Translation was done at sixteen or seventeen years of Age. P. [It appeared, with the *Pastorals*, in *Tonson's Miscellany* in 1709. Tyrwhitt doubts whether the source of the story, although its scene is laid in Italy, is Italian; and traces the adventure of the Pear-tree to Adolphus' Latin Fables (1315). The machinery of the Fairies, he thinks, was probably added by Chaucer himself. It is not impossible that it may have suggested that of the Sylphs in the *Rape of the Lock*.]

THERE liv'd in Lombardy, as authors write,
In days of old, a wise and worthy knight;
Of gentle manners, as of gen'rous race,
Blest with much sense, more riches, and some grace,
Yet led astray by Venus' soft delights,   5
He scarce could rule some idle appetites:
For long ago, let Priests say what they cou'd,
Weak sinful laymen were but flesh and blood.
 But in due time, when sixty years were o'er,
He vow'd to lead this vicious life no more;   10
Whether pure holiness inspir'd his mind,
Or dotage turn'd his brain, is hard to find;
But his high courage prick'd him forth to wed,
And try the pleasures of a lawful bed.
This was his nightly dream, his daily care,   15
And to the heav'nly pow'rs his constant pray'r,
Once, ere he died, to taste the blissful life
Of a kind husband, and a loving wife.
 These thoughts he fortify'd with reasons still,
(For none want reasons to confirm their will.)   20
Grave authors say, and witty poets sing,
That honest wedlock is a glorious thing:
But depth of judgment most in him appears,
Who wisely weds in his maturer years.
Then let him choose a damsel young and fair,   25
To bless his age, and bring a worthy heir;
To sooth his cares, and, free from noise and strife,
'Conduct him gently to the verge of life.
Let sinful batchelors their woes deplore,
Full well they merit all they feel, and more: 30
Unaw'd by precepts, human or divine,
Like birds and beasts, promiscuously they join:

K

Nor know to make the present blessing last,
To hope the future, or esteem the past:
But vainly boast the joys they never try'd, 35
And find divulg'd the secrets they would hide.
The marry'd man may bear his yoke with ease,
Secure at once himself and heav'n to please;
And pass his inoffensive hours away,
In bliss all night, and innocence all day: 40
Tho' fortune change, his constant spouse remains,
Augments his joys, or mitigates his pains.
    But what so pure, which envious tongues will spare?
Some wicked wits have libell'd all the fair.
With matchless impudence they style a wife 45
The dear-bought curse, and lawful plague of life;
A bosom-serpent, a domestic evil,
A night-invasion and a mid-day-devil.
Let not the wife these sland'rous words regard,
But curse the bones of ev'ry lying bard. 50
All other goods by fortune's hand are giv'n,
A wife is the peculiar gift of heav'n:
Vain fortune's favours, never at a stay,
Like empty shadows, pass, and glide away;
One solid comfort, our eternal wife, 55
Abundantly supplies us all our life:
This blessing lasts, (if those who try, say true)
As long as heart can wish — and longer too.
    Our grandsire Adam, ere of Eve possess'd,
Alone, and ev'n in Paradise unbless'd, 60
With mournful looks the blissful scenes survey'd,
And wander'd in the solitary shade:
The Maker saw, took pity, and bestow'd
Woman, the last, the best reserv'd of God.
    A Wife! ah gentle deities, can he 65
That has a wife, e'er feel adversity?
Would men but follow what the sex advise,
All things would prosper, all the world grow wise.
'T was by Rebecca's aid that Jacob won
His father's blessing from an elder son: 70
Abusive Nabal ow'd his forfeit life
To the wise conduct of a prudent wife:
Heroic Judith, as old Hebrews show,
Preserv'd the Jews, and slew th' Assyrian foe:
At Hester's suit, the persecuting sword 75
Was sheath'd, and Israel liv'd to bless the Lord.
    These weighty motives, January the sage
Maturely ponder'd in his riper age;
And charm'd with virtuous joys, and sober life,
Would try that christian comfort, call'd a wife. 80
His friends were summon'd on a point so nice,
To pass their Judgment, and to give advice;

JANUARY AND MAY.

But fix'd before, and well resolv'd was he;
(As men that ask advice are wont to be).
"My friends," he cry'd (and cast a mournful look   85
Around the room, and sigh'd before he spoke:)
"Beneath the weight of threescore years I bend,
And, worn with cares, am hast'ning to my end;
How I have liv'd, alas! you know too well,
In worldly follies, which I blush to tell;   90
But gracious heav'n has oped my eyes at last,
With due regret I view my vices past,
And, as the precept of the Church decrees,
Will take a wife, and live in holy ease.
But since by counsel all things should be done,   95
And many heads are wiser still than one;
Choose you for me, who best shall be content
When my desire's approv'd by your consent.
  "One caution yet is needful to be told,
To guide your choice; this wife must not be old: 100
There goes a saying, and 't was shrewdly said,
Old fish at table, but young flesh in bed.
My soul abhors the tasteless, dry embrace
Of a stale virgin with a winter face:
In that cold season Love but treats his guest   105
With bean-straw, and tough forage at the best.
No crafty widows shall approach my bed;
Those are too wise for bachelors to wed;
As subtle clerks by many schools are made,
Twice-marry'd dames are mistresses o' th' trade: 110
But young and tender virgins, rul'd with ease,
We form like wax, and mould them as we please.
  "Conceive me, Sirs, nor take my sense amiss;
'T is what concerns my soul's eternal bliss;
Since if I found no pleasure in my spouse,   115
As flesh is frail, and who (God help me) knows?
Then should I live in lewd adultery,
And sink downright to Satan when I die.
Or were I curs'd with an unfruitful bed,
The righteous end were lost, for which I wed;   120
To raise up seed to bless the pow'rs above,
And not for pleasure only, or for love.
Think not I dote; 't is time to take a wife,
When vig'rous blood forbids a chaster life:
Those that are blest with store of grace divine,   125
May live like saints, by heav'n's consent, and mine.
  "And since I speak of wedlock, let me say,
(As, thank my stars, in modest truth I may)
My limbs are active, still I 'm sound at heart,
And a new vigour springs in ev'ry part.   130
Think not my virtue lost, tho' time has shed
These rev'rend honours on my hoary head;

Thus trees are crown'd with blossoms white as snow,
The vital sap then rising from below:
Old as I am, my lusty limbs appear 135
Like winter greens, that flourish all the year.
Now, Sirs, you know to what I stand inclin'd,
Let ev'ry friend with freedom speak his mind."

He said; the rest in diff'rent parts divide;
The knotty point was urg'd on either side: 140
Marriage, the theme on which they all declaim'd,
Some prais'd with wit, and some with reason blam'd.
Till, what with proofs, objections, and replies,
Each wond'rous positive, and wond'rous wise,
There fell between his brothers a debate, 145
Placebo this was call'd, and Justin that.

First to the Knight Placebo thus begun,
(Mild were his looks, and pleasing was his tone)
"Such prudence, Sir, in all your words appears,
As plainly proves, experience dwells with years! 150
Yet you pursue sage Solomon's advice,
To work by counsel when affairs are nice:
But, with the wiseman's leave, I must protest,
So may my soul arrive at ease and rest
As still I hold your own advice the best. 155

"Sir, I have liv'd a Courtier all my days,
And study'd men, their manners, and their ways;
And have observ'd this useful maxim still,
To let my betters always have their will.
Nay, if my lord affirm'd that black was white, 160
My word was this, Your honour's in the right.
Th' assuming Wit, who deems himself so wise,
As his mistaken patron to advise,
Let him not dare to vent his dang'rous thought,
A noble fool was never in a fault. 165
This, Sir, affects not you, whose ev'ry word
Is weigh'd with judgment, and befits a Lord:
Your will is mine; and is (I will maintain)
Pleasing to God, and should be so to Man;
At least, your courage all the world must praise, 170
Who dare to wed in your declining days.
Indulge the vigour of your mounting blood,
And let grey fools be indolently good,
Who, past all pleasure, damn the joys of sense,
With rev'rend dulness and grave impotence." 175

Justin, who silent sate, and heard the man,
Thus, with a Philosophic frown, began.

"A heathen author, of the first degree,
(Who, tho' not Faith, had Sense as well as we)
Bids us be certain our concerns to trust 180
To those of gen'rous principles, and just.
The venture's greater, I'll presume to say,

JANUARY AND MAY.

To give your person, than your goods away:
And therefore, Sir, as you regard your rest,
First learn your Lady's qualities at least: 185
Whether she 's chaste or rampant, proud or civil;
Meek as a saint, or haughty as the devil;
Whether an easy, fond, familiar, fool,
Or such a wit as no man e'er can rule?
'T is true, perfection none must hope to find 190
In all this world, much less in woman-kind;
But if her virtues prove the larger share,
Bless the kind fates, and think your fortune rare.
Ah, gentle Sir, take warning of a friend,
Who knows too well the state you thus commend; 195
And spite of all his praises must declare,
All he can find is bondage, cost, and care.
Heav'n knows, I shed full many a private tear,
And sigh in silence, lest the world should hear:
While all my friends applaud my blissful life, 200
And swear no mortal 's happier in a wife;
Demure and chaste as any vestal Nun,
The meekest creature that beholds the sun!
But, by th' immortal pow'rs, I feel the pain,
And he that smarts has reason to complain. 205
Do what you list, for me; you must be sage,
And cautious sure; for wisdom is in Age:
But at these years, to venture on the fair!
By him, who made the ocean, earth, and air,
To please a wife, when her occasions call, 210
Would busy the most vig'rous of us all.
And trust me, Sir, the chastest you can choose
Will ask observance, and exact her dues.
If what I speak my noble Lord offend,
My tedious sermon here is at an end." 215
"'T is well, 't is wondrous well," the Knight replies,
"Most worthy kinsman, faith you're mighty wise!
We, Sirs, are fools; and must resign the cause
To heath'nish authors, proverbs, and old saws."
He spoke with scorn, and turn'd another way:— 220
"What does my friend, my dear Placebo say?"
"I say," quoth he, "by heav'n the man 's to blame,
To slander wives, and wedlock's holy name."
At this the council rose, without delay;
Each, in his own opinion, went his way; 225
With full consent, that, all disputes appeas'd,
The knight should marry, when and where he pleas'd.
  Who now but January exults with joy?
The charms of wedlock all his soul employ:
Each nymph by turns his wav'ring mind possest, 230
And reign'd the short-liv'd tyrant of his breast;
While fancy pictur'd ev'ry lively part,

And each bright image wander'd o'er his heart.
Thus, in some public Forum fix'd on high,
A Mirror shows the figures moving by; 235
Still one by one, in swift succession, pass
The gliding shadows o'er the polish'd glass.
This Lady's charms the nicest could not blame,
But vile suspicions had aspers'd her fame;
That was with sense, but not with virtue, blest; 240
And one had grace, that wanted all the rest.
Thus doubting long what nymph he should obey,
He fix'd at last upon the youthful May.
Her faults he knew not, Love is always blind,
But ev'ry charm revolv'd within his mind: 245
Her tender age, her form divinely fair,
Her easy motion, her attractive air,
Her sweet behaviour, her enchanting face,
Her moving softness, and majestic grace.

  Much in his prudence did our Knight rejoice, 250
And thought no mortal could dispute his choice:
Once more in haste he summon'd ev'ry friend,
And told them all, their pains were at an end.
"Heav'n, that" (said he) "inspir'd me first to wed,
Provides a consort worthy of my bed: 255
Let none oppose th' election, since on this
Depends my quiet, and my future bliss.

  " A dame there is, the darling of my eyes,
Young, beauteous, artless, innocent, and wise;
Chaste, tho' not rich; and tho' not nobly born, 260
Of honest parents, and may serve my turn.
Her will I wed, if gracious heav'n so please;
To pass my age in sanctity and ease:
And thank the pow'rs, I may possess alone
The lovely prize, and share my bliss with none! 265
If you, my friends, this virgin can procure,
My joys are full, my happiness is sure.

  "One only doubt remains: Full oft I 've heard,
By casuists grave, and deep divines averr'd;
That 't is too much for human race to know 270
The bliss of heav'n above, and earth below.
Now should the nuptial pleasures prove so great,
To match the blessings of the future state,
Those endless joys were ill exchang'd for these;
Then clear this doubt, and set my mind at ease." 275

  This Justin heard, nor could his spleen control,
Touch'd to the quick, and tickled at the soul.
"Sir Knight," he cry'd, "if this be all you dread,
Heav'n put it past your doubt, whene'er you wed;
And to my fervent pray'rs so far consent, 280
That ere the rites are o'er, you may repent!
Good heav'n, no doubt, the nuptial state approves,

JANUARY AND MAY.

Since it chastises still what best it loves.
"Then be not, Sir, abandon'd to despair;
Seek, and perhaps you 'll find among the fair,   285
One, that may do your business to a hair;
Not ev'n in wish, your happiness delay,
But prove the scourge to lash you on your way:
Then to the skies your mounting soul shall go,
Swift as an arrow soaring from the bow!   290
Provided still, you moderate your joy,
Nor in your pleasures all your might employ,
Let reason's rule your strong desires abate,
Nor please too lavishly your gentle mate.
Old wives there are, of judgment most acute,   295
Who solve these questions beyond all dispute;
Consult with those, and be of better cheer;
Marry, do penance, and dismiss your fear."
   So said, they rose, nor more the work delay'd;
The match was offer'd, the proposals made.   300
The parents, you may think, would soon comply;
The Old have int'rest ever in their eye.
Nor was it hard to move the Lady's mind;
When Fortune favours, still the Fair are kind.
   I pass each previous settlement and deed,   305
Too long for me to write, or you to read;
Nor will with quaint impertinence display
The pomp, the pageantry, the proud array.
The time approach'd, to Church the parties went,
At once with carnal and devout intent: 310
Forth came the Priest, and bade th' obedient wife
Like Sarah or Rebecca lead her life:
Then pray'd the pow'rs the fruitful bed to bless,
And made all sure enough with holiness.
   And now the palace-gates are open'd wide,   315
The guests appear in order, side by side,
And plac'd in state, the bridegroom and the bride.
The breathing flute's soft notes are heard around,
And the shrill trumpets mix their silver sound;
The vaulted roofs with echoing music ring,   320
These touch the vocal stops, and those the trembling string.
Not thus Amphion tun'd the warbling lyre,
Nor Joab the sounding clarion could inspire,
Nor fierce Theodamas, whose sprightly strain
Could swell the soul to rage, and fire the martial train.[1]   325
   Bacchus himself, the nuptial feast to grace,
(So Poets sing) was present on the place:
And lovely Venus, Goddess of delight,
Shook high her flaming torch in open sight:

[1] [Tyrwhitt suspects that Chaucer had met with the name of Theodamas, who occurs again as a famous trumpeter in the *House of Fame*, but is otherwise unknown, in some Romantic History of Thebes.]

And danc'd around, and smil'd on ev'ry Knight: 330
Pleas'd her best servant would his courage try,
No less in wedlock, than in liberty.
Full many an age old Hymen had not spy'd
So kind a bridegroom, or so bright a bride.
Ye bards! renown'd among the tuneful throng 335
For gentle lays, and joyous nuptial song;
Think not your softest numbers can display
The matchless glories of this blissful day:
The joys are such, as far transcend your rage,
When tender youth has wedded stooping age. 340

The beauteous dame sate smiling at the board,
And darted am'rous glances at her Lord.
Not Hester's self, whose charms the Hebrews sing,
E'er look'd so lovely on her Persian King:
Bright as the rising sun, in summer's day, 345
And fresh and blooming as the month of May!
The joyful Knight survey'd her by his side,
Nor envy'd Paris with the Spartan bride.
Still as his mind revolv'd with vast delight
Th' entrancing raptures of th' approaching night, 350
Restless he sate, invoking ev'ry pow'r
To speed his bliss, and haste the happy hour.
Mean time the vig'rous dancers beat the ground,
And songs were sung, and flowing bowls went round.
With od'rous spices they perfum'd the place, 355
And mirth and pleasure shone in ev'ry face.

Damian alone, of all the menial train,
Sad in the midst of triumphs, sigh'd for pain;
Damian alone, the Knight's obsequious squire,
Consum'd at heart, and fed a secret fire. 360
His lovely mistress all his soul possess'd,
He look'd, he languish'd, and could take no rest:
His task perform'd, he sadly went his way,
Fell on his bed, and loath'd the light of day.
There let him lie; till his relenting dame 365
Weep in her turn, and waste in equal flame.

The weary sun, as learned Poets write,
Forsook th' Horizon, and roll'd down the light;
While glitt'ring stars his absent beams supply,
And night's dark mantle overspread the sky. 370
Then rose the guests; and as the time requir'd,
Each paid his thanks, and decently retir'd.

The foe once gone, our Knight prepar'd t' undress,
So keen he was, and eager to possess:
But first thought fit th' assistance to receive, 375
Which grave Physicians scruple not to give;
Satyrion near, with hot Eringo's stood,[1]

---

[1] Sea-holly. *Johnson.*

Cantharides, to fire the lazy blood,
Whose use old Bards describe in luscious rhymes,[1]
And Critics learn'd explain to modern times.   380
  By this the sheets were spread, the bride undress'd,
The room was sprinkled, and the bed was bless'd.
What next ensu'd beseems not me to say;
'T is sung, he labour'd till the dawning day,
Then briskly sprung from bed, with heart so light, ⎫ 385
As all were nothing he had done by night;   ⎬
And sipp'd his cordial as he sate upright.   ⎭
He kiss'd his balmy spouse with wanton play,
And feebly sung a lusty roundelay:
Then on the couch his weary limbs he cast;   390
For ev'ry labour must have rest at last.
  But anxious cares the pensive Squire oppress'd,
Sleep fled his eyes, and peace forsook his breast;
The raging flames that in his bosom dwell,
He wanted art to hide, and means to tell.   395
Yet hoping time th' occasion might betray,
Compos'd a sonnet to the lovely May;
Which writ and folded with the nicest art,
He wrapp'd in silk, and laid upon his heart.
  When now the fourth revolving day was run,   400
('T was June, and Cancer had receiv'd the Sun)
Forth from her chamber came the beauteous bride;
The good old knight mov'd slowly by her side.
High mass was sung; they feasted in the hall;
The servants round stood ready at their call.   405
The Squire alone was absent from the board,
And much his sickness griev'd his worthy lord,
Who pray'd his spouse, attended with her train,
To visit Damian, and divert his pain.
Th' obliging dames obey'd with one consent;   410
They left the hall, and to his lodging went.
The female tribe surround him as he lay,
And close beside him sat the gentle May:
Where, as she try'd his pulse, he softly drew
A heaving sigh, and cast a mournful view!   415
Then gave his bill,[2] and brib'd the pow'rs divine,
With secret vows to favour his design.
  Who studies now but discontented May?
On her soft couch uneasily she lay:
The lumpish husband snor'd away the night,   420
Till coughs awak'd him near the morning light.
What then he did, I'll not presume to tell,
Nor if she thought herself in heav'n or hell:
Honest and dull in nuptial bed they lay,
Till the bell toll'd, and all arose to pray.   425

---

[1] [Ovid, in his *Remedia Amoris*.]   [2] [i.e. gave her what he had written.]

Were it by forceful destiny decreed,
Or did from chance, or nature's pow'r proceed;
Or that some star, with aspect kind to love,
Shed its selectest influence from above;
Whatever was the cause, the tender dame   430
Felt the first motions of an infant flame;
Receiv'd th' impressions of the love-sick Squire,
And wasted in the soft infectious fire.
Ye fair, draw near, let May's example move
Your gentle minds to pity those who love!   435
Had some fierce tyrant in her stead been found,
The poor adorer sure had hang'd, or drown'd:
But she, your sex's mirror, free from pride,
Was much too meek to prove a homicide.
 But to my tale: Some sages have defin'd   440
Pleasure the sov'reign bliss of humankind:
Our Knight (who study'd much, we may suppose)
Deriv'd his high philosophy from those;
For, like a Prince, he bore the vast expence
Of lavish pomp, and proud magnificence: 445
His house was stately, his retinue gay,
Large was his train, and gorgeous his array.
His spacious garden made to yield to none,
Was compass'd round with walls of solid stone;
Priapus could not half describe the grace   450
(Tho' God of gardens) of this charming place:
A place to tire the rambling wits of France
In long descriptions, and exceed Romance;
Enough to shame the gentlest bard that sings
Of painted meadows, and of purling springs.   455
 Full in the centre of the flow'ry ground,
A crystal fountain spread its streams around,
The fruitful banks with verdant laurels crown'd:
About this spring (if ancient fame say true)
The dapper Elves their moon-light sports pursue: 460
Their pygmy king,[1] and little fairy queen,
In circling dances gamboll'd on the green,
While tuneful sprites a merry concert made,
And airy music warbled thro' the shade.
 Hither the noble knight would oft repair,   465
(His scene of pleasure, and peculiar care)
For this he held it dear, and always bore
The silver key that lock'd the garden door.
To this sweet place in summer's sultry heat,
He us'd from noise and bus'ness to retreat;   470
And here in dalliance spend the live-long day,
Solus cum sola, with his sprightly May.

---

[1] *Their pygmy king.*] Pope has here shewn his judgment in adopting the lighter 'fairy race' of Shakespear and Milton. Chaucer has 'Kyng Pluto, and his Queene Proserpina.' *Bowles.*

JANUARY AND MAY.

For whate'er work was undischarg'd a-bed,
The duteous knight in this fair garden sped.
  But ah! what mortal lives of bliss secure,   475
How short a space our worldly joys endure?
O Fortune, fair, like all thy treach'rous kind,
But faithless still, and wav'ring as the wind!
O painted monster, form'd mankind to cheat,
With pleasing poison, and with soft deceit!   480
This rich, this am'rous, venerable knight,
Amidst his ease, his solace, and delight,
Struck blind by thee, resigns his days to grief,
And calls on death, the wretch's last relief.
  The rage of jealousy then seiz'd his mind,   485
For much he fear'd the faith of woman-kind.
His wife not suffer'd from his side to stray,
Was captive kept, he watch'd her night and day,
Abridg'd her pleasures and confin'd her sway.
Full oft in tears did hapless May complain,   490
And sigh'd full oft; but sigh'd and wept in vain;
She look'd on Damian with a lover's eye;
For oh, 't was fixt; she must possess or die!
Nor less impatience vex'd her am'rous Squire,
Wild with delay, and burning with desire.   495
Watch'd as she was, yet could he not refrain,
By secret writing to disclose his pain:
The dame by signs reveal'd her kind intent,
Till both were conscious what each other meant.
  Ah, gentle knight, what would thy eyes avail,   500
Tho' they could see as far as ships can sail?
'T is better, sure, when blind, deceiv'd to be,
Than be deluded when a man can see!
  Argus himself, so cautious and so wise,
Was over-watch'd, for all his hundred eyes: 505
So many an honest husband may, 't is known
Who, wisely, never thinks the case his own.
  The dame at last, by diligence and care,
Procur'd the key her knight was wont to bear;
She took the wards in wax before the fire,   510
And gave th' impression to the trusty Squire.
By means of this, some wonder shall appear,
Which, in due place and season, you may hear.
  Well sung sweet Ovid, in the days of yore,
What sleight is that, which love will not explore?   515
And Pyramus and Thisbe plainly show
The feats true lovers, when they list, can do:
Tho' watch'd and captive, yet in spite of all,
They found the art of kissing thro' a wall.
  But now no longer from our tale to stray;   520
It happ'd that once upon a summer's day,
Our rev'rend Knight was urg'd to am'rous play:

He rais'd his spouse ere Matin-bell was rung,
And thus his morning canticle he sung.
"Awake, my love, disclose thy radiant eyes;   525
Arise, my wife, my beauteous lady, rise!
Hear how the doves with pensive notes complain,
And in soft murmurs tell the trees their pain:
The winter's past; the clouds and tempest fly;
The sun adorns the fields, and brightens all the sky.   530
Fair without spot, whose ev'ry charming part
My bosom wounds, and captivates my heart;
Come, and in mutual pleasures let's engage,
Joy of my life, and comfort of my age."
This heard, to Damian straight a sign she made,   535
To haste before; the gentle Squire obey'd:
Secret, and undescry'd he took his way,
And ambush'd close behind an arbour lay.
It was not long ere January came,
And hand in hand with him his lovely dame;   540
Blind as he was, not doubting all was sure,
He turn'd the key, and made the gate secure.
"Here let us walk," he said, "observ'd by none,
Conscious of pleasures to the world unknown:
So may my soul have joy, as thou, my wife,   545
Art far the dearest solace of my life;
And rather would I choose, by heav'n above,
To die this instant, than to lose thy love.
Reflect what truth was in my passion shewn,
When unendow'd, I took thee for my own,   550
And sought no treasure but thy heart alone.
Old as I am, and now depriv'd of sight,
Whilst thou art faithful to thy own true Knight,
Nor age, nor blindness rob me of delight.
Each other loss with patience I can bear,   555
The loss of thee is what I only fear.
"Consider then, my lady and my wife,
The solid comforts of a virtuous life.
As first, the love of Christ himself you gain;
Next, your own honour undefil'd maintain;   560
And lastly, that which sure your mind must move,
My whole estate shall gratify your love:
Make your own terms, and ere to-morrow's sun
Displays his light, by heav'n it shall be done.
I seal the contract with a holy kiss,   565
And will perform, by this — my dear, and this —
Have comfort, spouse, nor think thy Lord unkind;
'Tis love, not jealousy, that fires my mind.
For when thy charms my sober thoughts engage,
And join'd to them my own unequal age,   570
From thy dear side I have no pow'r to part,
Such secret transports warm my melting heart.

JANUARY AND MAY.

For who that once possess those heav'nly charms,
Could live one moment absent from thy arms?"
    He ceas'd, and May with modest grace reply'd;   575
(Weak was her voice, as while she spoke she cry'd:)
"Heav'n knows" (with that a tender sigh she drew)
"I have a soul to save as well as you:
And, what no less you to my charge commend,
My dearest honour, will to death defend.   580
To you in holy Church I gave my hand,
And join'd my heart in wedlock's sacred band:
Yet after this, if you distrust my care,
Then hear, my Lord, and witness what I swear:
    "First may the yawning earth her bosom rend,   585
And let me hence to hell alive descend;
Or die the death I dread no less than hell,
Sew'd in a sack, and plung'd into a well:
Ere I my fame by one lewd act disgrace,
Or once renounce the honour of my race.   590
For know, Sir Knight, of gentle blood I came,
I loathe a whore, and startle at the name.
But jealous men on their own crimes reflect,
And learn from thence their ladies to suspect:
Else why these needless cautions, Sir, to me?   595
These doubts and fears of female constancy!
This chime still rings in ev'ry lady's ear,
The only strain a wife must hope to hear."
    Thus while she spoke a sidelong glance she cast,
Where Damian kneeling, worshipp'd as she past.   600
She saw him watch the motions of her eye,
And singled out a pear-tree planted nigh:
'T was charg'd with fruit that made a goodly show,
And hung with dangling pears was ev'ry bough.
Thither th' obsequious Squire address'd his pace,   605
And climbing, in the summit took his place;
The Knight and Lady walk'd beneath in view,
Where let us leave them, and our tale pursue.
    'T was now the season when the glorious sun
His heav'nly progress thro' the Twins had run;   610
And Jove, exalted, his mild influence yields,
To glad the glebe, and paint the flow'ry fields:
Clear was the day, and Phœbus rising bright,
Had streak'd the azure firmament with light;
He pierc'd the glitt'ring clouds with golden streams,   615
And warm'd the womb of earth with genial beams.
    It so befel, in that fair morning-tide,
The Fairies sported on the garden side,
And in their midst their Monarch and his bride.
So featly tripp'd the light-foot ladies round,   620
The knights so nimbly o'er the green sword bound,
That scarce they bent the flow'rs, or touch'd the ground.

The dances ended, all the fairy train
For pinks and daisies search'd the flow'ry plain;
While on a bank reclin'd of rising green, 625
Thus, with a frown, the King bespoke his Queen.
  "'T is too apparent, argue what you can,
The treachery you women use to man:
A thousand authors have this truth made out,
And sad experience leaves no room for doubt. 630
  "Heav'n rest thy spirit, noble Solomon,
A wiser monarch never saw the sun:
All wealth, all honours, the supreme degree
Of earthly bliss, was well bestow'd on thee!
For sagely hast thou said: Of all mankind, 635
One only just, and righteous, hope to find:
But should'st thou search the spacious world around,
Yet one good woman is not to be found.
  "Thus says the King who knew your wickedness;
The son of Sirach testifies no less. 640
So may some wildfire on your bodies fall,
Or some devouring plague consume you all;
As well you view the lecher in the tree,
And well this honourable Knight you see:
But since he 's blind and old (a helpless case) 645
His Squire shall cuckold him before your face.
  "Now by my own dread majesty I swear,
And by this awful sceptre which I bear,
No impious wretch shall 'scape unpunish'd long,
That in my presence offers such a wrong. 650
I will this instant undeceive the Knight,
And, in the very act restore his sight:
And set the strumpet here in open view,
A warning to these Ladies, and to you,
And all the faithless sex, for ever to be true." 655
  "And will you so," reply'd the Queen, "indeed?
Now, by mother's soul it is decreed,
She shall not want an answer at her need.
For her, and for her daughters, I 'll engage,
And all the sex in each succeeding age; 660
Art shall be theirs to varnish an offence,
And fortify their crimes with confidence.
Nay, were they taken in a strict embrace,
Seen with both eyes, and pinion'd on the place;
All they shall need is to protest and swear, 665
Breathe a soft sigh, and drop a tender tear;
Till their wise husbands, gull'd by arts like these,
Grow gentle, tractable, and tame as geese.
  "What tho' this sland'rous Jew, this Solomon,
Call'd women fools, and knew full many a one; 670
The wiser wits of later times declare,
How constant, chaste, and virtuous women are:

JANUARY AND MAY.

Witness the martyrs, who resign'd their breath,
Serene in torments, unconcern'd in death;
And witness next what Roman Authors tell, 675
How Arria, Portia, and Lucretia fell.
"But since the sacred leaves to all are free,
And men interpret texts, why should not we?
By this no more was meant, than to have shown,
That sov'reign goodness dwells in him alone 680
Who only Is, and is but only One.
But grant the worst; shall women then be weigh'd
By ev'ry word that Solomon has said?
What tho' this King (as ancient story boasts)
Built a fair temple to the Lord of hosts; 685
He ceas'd at last his Maker to adore,
And did as much for Idol gods, or more.
Beware what lavish praises you confer
On a rank lecher and idolater;
Whose reign indulgent God, says holy writ, 690
Did but for David's righteous sake permit;
David, the monarch after heav'n's own mind,
Who lov'd our sex, and honour'd all our kind.
 "Well, I 'm a Woman, and as such must speak;
Silence would swell me, and my heart would break. 695
Know then, I scorn your dull authorities,
Your idle wits, and all their learned lies.
By heav'n, those authors are our sex's foes,
Whom, in our right, I must and will oppose."
 "Nay," (quoth the King), "dear Madam, be not wroth: 700
I yield it up; but since I gave my oath,
That this much-injur'd Knight again should see;
It must be done — I am a King," said he,
"And one, whose faith has ever sacred been."
 "And so has mine" (she said) — "I am a Queen: 705
Her answer she shall have, I undertake;
And thus an end of all dispute I make.
Try when you list; and you shall find, my Lord,
It is not in our sex to break our word."
 We leave them here in this heroic strain, 710
And to the Knight our story turns again;
Who in the garden, with his lovely May,
Sung merrier than the Cuckoo or the Jay:
This was his song; "Oh kind and constant be,
Constant and kind I'll ever prove to thee." 715
 Thus singing as he went, at last he drew
By easy steps, to where the Pear-tree grew:
The longing dame look'd up, and spy'd her Love
Full fairly perch'd among the boughs above.
She stopp'd, and sighing: "Oh good Gods," she cry'd, 720
"What pangs, what sudden shoots distend my side?
O for that tempting fruit, so fresh, so green;

Help, for the love of heav'n's immortal Queen!
Help, dearest lord, and save at once the life
Of thy poor infant, and thy longing wife!"   725
　Sore sigh'd the Knight to hear his Lady's cry,
But could not climb, and had no servant nigh:
Old as he was, and void of eye-sight too,
What could, alas, a helpless husband do?
"And must I languish then," she said, "and die,   730
Yet view the lovely fruit before my eye?
At least, kind Sir, for charity's sweet sake,
Vouchsafe the trunk between your arms to take;
Then from your back I might ascend the tree;
Do you but stoop, and leave the rest to me."   735
　"With all my soul," he thus reply'd again,
"I 'd spend my dearest blood to ease thy pain."
With that, his back against the trunk he bent,
She seiz'd a twig, and up the tree she went.
　Now prove your patience, gentle Ladies all!   740
Nor let on me your heavy anger fall:
'T is truth I tell, tho' not in phrase refin'd;
Tho' blunt my tale, yet honest is my mind.
What feats the lady in the tree might do,
I pass, as gambols never known to you;   745
But sure it was a merrier fit, she swore,
Than in her life she ever felt before.
　In that nice moment, lo! the wond'ring knight
Look'd out, and stood restor'd to sudden sight.
Straight on the tree his eager eyes he bent,   750
As one whose thoughts were on his spouse intent;
But when he saw his bosom-wife so dress'd,
His rage was such as cannot be express'd:
Not frantic mothers when their infants die,
With louder clamours rend the vaulted sky: 755
He cry'd, he roar'd, he storm'd, he tore his hair;
"Death! hell! and furies! what dost thou do there?"
　"What ails my lord?" the trembling dame reply'd;
"I thought your patience had been better try'd:
Is this your love, ungrateful and unkind,   760
This my reward for having cur'd the blind?
Why was I taught to make my husband see,
By struggling with a Man upon a Tree?
Did I for this the pow'r of magic prove?
Unhappy wife, whose crime was too much love!"   765
　"If this be struggling, by this holy light,
'T is struggling with a vengeance," (quoth the Knight),
"So heav'n preserve the sight it has restor'd,
As with these eyes I plainly saw thee whor'd;
Whor'd by my slave—perfidious wretch! may hell   770
As surely seize thee, as I saw too well."
　"Guard me, good angels!" cry'd the gentle May,

"Pray heav'n, this magic work the proper way!
Alas, my love! 't is certain, could you see,
You ne'er had us'd these killing words to me;   775
So help me, fates, as 't is no perfect sight,
But some faint glimm'ring of a doubtful light."
  "What I have said" (quoth he); "I must maintain,
For, by th' immortal pow'rs it *seem'd* too plain — "
  "By all those pow'rs, some frenzy seiz'd your mind,"   780
(Reply'd the dame,) "are these the thanks I find?
Wretch that I am, that e'er I was so kind!"
She said; a rising sigh express'd her woe,
The ready tears apace began to flow,
And as they fell she wip'd from either eye   785
The drops (for women, when they list, can cry).
  The Knight was touch'd; and in his looks appear'd
Signs of remorse, while thus his spouse he cheer'd.
"Madam, 't is past, and my short anger o'er;
Come down, and vex your tender heart no more: 790
Excuse me, dear, if aught amiss was said,
For, on my soul, amends shall soon be made:
Let my repentance your forgiveness draw,
By heav'n, I swore but what I *thought* I saw."
  "Ah my lov'd lord! 't was much unkind (she cry'd)   795
On bare suspicion thus to treat your bride.
But till your sight 's establish'd, for a while,
Imperfect objects may your sense beguile.
Thus when from sleep we first our eyes display,
The balls are wounded with the piercing ray,   800
And dusky vapours rise, and intercept the day
So just recov'ring from the shades of night,
Your swimming eyes are drunk with sudden light,
Strange phantoms dance around, and skim before your sight:
  "Then, Sir, be cautious, nor too rashly deem;   805
Heav'n knows how seldom things are what they seem!
Consult your reason, and you soon shall find
'T was you were jealous, not your wife unkind:
Jove ne'er spoke oracle more true than this,
None judge so wrong as those who think amiss."   810
  With that she leap'd into her Lord's embrace,
With well-dissembled virtue in her face.
He hugg'd her close, and kiss'd her o'er and o'er,
Disturb'd with doubts and jealousies no more:
Both, pleas'd and bless'd, renew'd their mutual vows,   815
A fruitful wife, and a believing spouse.
  Thus ends our tale, whose moral next to make,
Let all wise husbands hence example take;
And pray, to crown the pleasure of their lives,
To be so well deluded by their wives.   820

THE WIFE OF BATH.

FROM CHAUCER.

IN 1714, Pope's *Wife of Bath*, with two translations from the *Odyssey* (the arrival of Ulysses in Ithaca and the Garden of Alcinous) were published [by Tonson] in a volume of miscellanies, edited by Steele. To this miscellany, Hughes, the author of the *Siege of Damascus*, &c., sent several pieces, but finding, before publication, that Pope's *Wife of Bath* and some other pieces, which were inconsistent with his ideas of decency and decorum, had been admitted, he immediately withdrew most of his own, and allowed only two small poems, and those without his name, to appear. *Carruthers*. The greatest part of the *Wife of Bath's* Prologue must have been of Chaucer's own invention, though one may plainly see that he had been reading the popular invectives against marriage, and women in general; such as the *Roman de la Rose, Valerius ad Rufinum de non ducendâ uxore*, and particularly *Hieronymus contra Jovinianum. Tyrwhitt*. [The *Wife of Bath's Tale*, to which this is the Prologue, was modernised by Dryden. Happily the latter did not, like Pope, confine himself to the reproduction of Chaucer's humorous, and, to modern taste, indecorous pieces.]

BEHOLD the woes of matrimonial life,
And hear with rev'rence an experienc'd wife!
To dear-bought wisdom give the credit due,
And think, for once, a woman tells you true.
In all these trials I have borne a part, 5
I was myself the scourge that caus'd the smart;
For, since fifteen, in triumph have I led
Five captive husbands from the church to bed.

    Christ saw a wedding once, the scripture says,
And saw but one, 't is thought, in all his days; 10
Whence some infer, whose conscience is too nice,
No pious Christian ought to marry twice.

    But let them read, and solve me, if they can,
The words address'd to the Samaritan:
Five times in lawful wedlock was she join'd; 15
And sure the certain stint was ne'er defin'd.

    Increase and multiply, was heav'n's command,
And that 's a text I clearly understand.
This too, "Let men their sires and mothers leave,
And to their dearer wives for ever cleave." 20
More wives than one by Solomon were try'd,
Or else the wisest of mankind 's belied.
I 've had myself full many a merry fit;
And trust in heav'n I may have many yet.
For when my transitory spouse, unkind, 25
Shall die, and leave his woeful wife behind,
I 'll take the next good Christian I can find.

    Paul, knowing one could never serve our turn,
Declar'd 't was better far to wed than burn.
There 's danger in assembling fire and tow; 30
I grant 'em that, and what it means you know.
The same Apostle too has elsewhere own'd,

THE WIFE OF BATH.

No precept for Virginity he found:
'T is but a counsel—and we women still
Take which we like, the counsel, or our will. 35
 I envy not their bliss, if he or she
Think fit to live in perfect chastity;
Pure let them be, and free from taint of vice;
I, for a few slight spots, am not so nice.
Heav'n calls us diff'rent ways, on these bestows 40
One proper gift, another grants to those:
Not ev'ry man 's oblig'd to sell his store,
And give up all his substance to the poor;
Such as are perfect, may, I can't deny;
But, by your leave, Divines, so am not I. 45
 Full many a Saint, since first the world began,
Liv'd an unspotted maid, in spite of man:
Let such (a God's name) with fine wheat be fed,
And let us honest wives eat barley bread.
For me, I 'll keep the post assign'd by heav'n, 50
And use the copious talent it has giv'n:
Let my good spouse pay tribute, do me right,
And keep an equal reck'ning ev'ry night:
His proper body is not his, but mine;
For so said Paul, and Paul 's a sound divine. 55
 Know then, of those five husbands I have had,
Three were just tolerable, two were bad.
The three were old, but rich and fond beside,
And toil'd most piteously to please their bride:
But since their wealth (the best they had) was mine, 60
The rest, without much loss, I could resign.
Sure to be lov'd, I took no pains to please.
Yet had more Pleasure far than they had Ease.
 Presents flow'd in apace: with show'rs of gold,
They made their court, like Jupiter of old. 65
If I but smil'd, a sudden youth they found,
And a new palsy seiz'd them when I frown'd.
 Ye sov'reign wives! give ear and understand,
Thus shall ye speak, and exercise command.
For never was it giv'n to mortal man, 70
To lie so boldly as we women can:
Forswear the fact, tho' seen with both his eyes,
And call your maids to witness how he lies.
"Hark, old Sir Paul!" ('t was thus I us'd to say)
"Whence is our neighbour's wife so rich and gay?" 75
Treated, caress'd, where'er she 's pleased to roam—
I sit in tatters, and immur'd at home.
Why to her house dost thou so oft repair?
Art thou so am'rous? and is she so fair?
If I but see a cousin or a friend, 80
Lord! how you swell and rage like any fiend!
But you reel home, a drunken beastly bear,

Then preach till midnight in your easy chair;
Cry, wives are false, and ev'ry woman evil,
And give up all that 's female to the devil. 85
    "If poor (you say) she drains her husband's purse
If rich, she keeps her priest, or something worse;
If highly born, intolerably vain,
Vapours and pride by turns possess her brain,
Now gayly mad, now sourly splenetic, 90
Freakish when well, and fretful when she 's sick.
If fair, then chaste she cannot long abide,
By pressing youth attack'd on ev'ry side:
If foul, her wealth the lusty lover lures,
Or else her wit some fool-gallant procures, 95
Or else she dances with becoming grace,
Or shape excuses the defects of face.
There swims no goose so grey, but soon or late,
She finds some honest gander for her mate.
    "Horses (thou say'st) and asses, men may try, 100
And ring suspected vessels ere they buy:
But wives, a random choice, untry'd they take,
They dream in courtship, but in wedlock wake:
Then, nor till then, the veil 's remov'd away,
And all the woman glares in open day. 105
    "You tell me, to preserve your wife's good grace,
Your eyes must always languish on my face,
Your tongue with constant flatt'ries feed my ear,
And tag each sentence with, My life! my dear!
If by strange chance a modest blush be rais'd, 110
Be sure my fine complexion must be prais'd.
My garments always must be new and gay,
And feasts still kept upon my wedding-day.
Then must my nurse be pleas'd, and fav'rite maid;
And endless treats, and endless visits paid, 115
To a long train of kindred, friends, allies;
All this thou say'st, and all thou say'st are lies.
    "On Jenkin too you cast a squinting eye:
What! can your prentice raise your jealousy?
Fresh are his ruddy cheeks, his forehead fair, 120
And like the burnish'd gold his curling hair.
But clear thy wrinkled brow, and quit thy sorrow,
I 'd scorn your prentice, should you die to-morrow.
    "Why are thy chests all lock'd? on what design?
Are not thy worldly goods and treasure mine? 125
Sir, I 'm no fool: nor shall you, by St. John,
Have goods and body to yourself alone.
One you shall quit, in spite of both your eyes—
I heed not, I, the bolts, the locks, the spies.
If you had wit, you 'd say, 'Go where you will, 130
Dear spouse, I credit not the tales they tell:
Take all the freedoms of a married life;

THE WIFE OF BATH.

I know thee for a virtuous, faithful wife.'
"Lord! when you have enough, what need you care
How merrily soever others fare?
Tho' all the day I give and take delight,
Doubt not, sufficient will be left at night.
'T is but a just and rational desire,
To light a taper at a neighbour's fire.
"There's danger too, you think, in rich array,
And none can long be modest that are gay:
The Cat, if you but singe her tabby skin,
The chimney keeps, and sits content within;
But once grown sleek, will from her corner run,
Sport with her tail, and wanton in the sun;
She licks her fair round face, and frisks abroad,
To show her fur, and to be catterwaw'd."
Lo thus, my friends, I wrought to my desires
These three right ancient venerable sires.
I told 'em, Thus you say, and thus you do,
And told 'em false, but Jenkin swore 't was true.
I, like a dog, could bite as well as whine,
And first complain'd, whene'er the guilt was mine.
I tax'd them oft with wenching and amours,
When their weak legs scarce dragg'd 'em out of doors;
And swore the rambles that I took by night,
Were all to spy what damsels they bedight.
That colour brought me many hours of mirth;
For all this wit is giv'n us from our birth.
Heav'n gave to woman the peculiar grace
To spin, to weep, and cully human race.
By this nice conduct, and this prudent course,
By murm'ring, wheedling, stratagem, and force,
I still prevail'd, and would be in the right,
Or curtain-lectures made a restless night.
If once my husband's arm was o'er my side,
What! so familiar with your spouse? I cry'd:
I levied first a tax upon his need;
Then let him — 't was a nicety indeed!
Let all mankind this certain maxim hold,
Marry who will, our sex is to be sold.
With empty hands no tassels [1] you can lure,
But fulsome love for gain we can endure;
For gold we love the impotent and old,
And heave, and pant, and kiss, and cling, for gold.
Yet with embraces, curses oft I mixt,
Then kiss'd again, and chid and rail'd betwixt.
Well, I may make my will in peace, and die.
For not one word in man's arrears am I.
To drop a dear dispute I was unable,

---

[1] *Tassel*, another form of tiercel; the male hawk.]

Ev'n tho' the Pope himself had sat at table.
But when my point was gain'd, then thus I spoke,
" Billy, my dear, how sheepishly you look?
" Approach, my spouse, and let me kiss thy cheek;
" Thou should'st be always thus, resign'd and meek!   185
" Of Job's great patience since so oft you preach,
" Well should you practise, who so well can teach.
" 'T is difficult to do, I must allow,
" But I, my dearest, will instruct you how.
"Great is the blessing of a prudent wife,   190
" Who puts a period to domestic strife.
" One of us two must rule, and one obey;
" And since in man right reason bears the sway,
" Let that frail thing, weak woman, have her way.
" The wives of all my family have rul'd   195
" Their tender husbands, and their passions cool'd.
" Fie, 't is unmanly thus to sigh and groan;
" What! would you have me to yourself alone?
" Why take me, Love! take all and every part!
" Here 's your revenge! you love it at your heart   200
" Would I vouchsafe to sell what nature gave,
" You little think what custom I could have.
" But see! I 'm all your own — nay hold — for shame!
" What means my dear — indeed — you are to blame."
  Thus with my first three Lords I past my life;   205
A very woman, and a very wife.
What sums from these old spouses I could raise,
Procur'd young husbands in my riper days.
Tho' past my bloom, nor yet decay'd was I,
Wanton and wild, and chatter'd like a pye.   210
In country dances still I bore the bell,
And sung as sweet as ev'ning Philomel.
To clear my quail-pipe, and refresh my soul,
Full oft I drain'd the spicy nut-brown bowl;
Rich luscious wines, that youthful blood improve,   215
And warm the swelling veins to feats of love:
For 't is as sure, as cold engenders hail,
A liqu'rish mouth must have a lech'rous tail;
Wine lets no lover unrewarded go,
As all true gamesters by experience know.   220
  But oh, good Gods! whene'er a thought I cast
On all the joys of youth and beauty past,
To find in pleasures I have had my part,
Still warms me to the bottom of my heart.
This wicked world was once my dear delight;   225
Now all my conquests, all my charms, good night!
The flour consum'd, the best that now I can,
Is e'en to make my market of the bran.
  My fourth dear spouse was not exceeding true;
He kept, 't was thought, a private miss or two: 230

THE WIFE OF BATH.

But all that score I paid — as how? you'll say,
Not with my body in a filthy way:
But I so dress'd and danc'd, and drank, and din'd,
And view'd a friend, with eyes so very kind,
As stung his heart, and made his marrow fry, 235
With burning rage and frantic jealousy.
His soul, I hope, enjoys eternal glory,
For here on earth I was his purgatory.
Oft, when his shoe the most severely wrung,
He put on careless airs, and sat and sung. 240
How sore I gall'd him, only heav'n could know,
And he that felt, and I that caus'd the woe.
He died, when last from pilgrimage I came,
With other gossips, from Jerusalem;
And now lies buried underneath a Rood, 245
Fair to be seen, and rear'd of honest wood.
A tomb indeed with fewer sculptures grac'd,
Than that Mausolus' pious widow plac'd,
Or where inshrin'd the great Darius lay;
But cost on graves is merely thrown away. 250
The pit fill'd up, with turf we cover'd o'er;
So bless the good man's soul, I say no more.
  Now for my fifth lov'd Lord, the last and best;
(Kind heav'n afford him everlasting rest)
Full hearty was his love, and I can shew, 255
The tokens on my ribs in black and blue;
Yet, with a knack, my heart he could have won,
While yet the smart was shooting in the bone.
How quaint an appetite in women reigns!
Free gifts we scorn, and love what costs us pains: 260
Let men avoid us, and on them we leap;
A glutted market makes provision cheap.
  In pure good will I took this jovial spark,
Of Oxford he, a most egregious clerk.
He boarded with a widow in the town, 265
A trusty gossip, one dame Alison.
Full well the secrets of my soul she knew,
Better than e'er our parish Priest could do.
To her I told whatever could befall:
Had but my husband piss'd against a wall, 270
Or done a thing that might have cost his life,
She — and my niece — and one more worthy wife,
Had known it all: what most he would conceal,
To these I made no scruple to reveal.
Oft has he blush'd from ear to ear for shame, 275
That e'er he told a secret to his dame.
It so befel, in holy time of Lent,
That oft a day I to this gossip went;
(My husband, thank my stars, was out of town)
From house to house we rambled up and down, 280

This clerk, myself, and my good neighbour Alse,
To see, be seen, to tell, and gather tales.
Visits to ev'ry Church we daily paid,
And march'd in ev'ry holy Masquerade,
The Stations duly, and the Vigils kept;   285
Not much we fasted, but scarce ever slept.
At Sermons too I shone in scarlet gay,
The wasting moth ne'er spoil'd my best array;
The cause was this, I wore it ev'ry day.
'T was when fresh May her early blossoms yields,   290
This Clerk and I were walking in the fields.
We grew so intimate I can't tell how,
I pawn'd my honour and engag'd my vow,
If e'er I laid my husband in his urn,
That he, and only he, should serve my turn.   295
We straight struck hands, the bargain was agreed;
I still have shifts against a time of need:
The mouse that always trusts to one poor hole,
Can never be a mouse of any soul.

I vow'd, I scarce could sleep since first I knew him   300
And durst be sworn he had bewitch'd me to him;
If e'er I slept, I dream'd of him alone,
And dreams foretell, as learned men have shown:
All this I said; but dreams, sirs, I had none:
I follow'd but my crafty Crony's lore,   305
Who bid me tell this lie — and twenty more.

Thus day by day, and month by month we past;
It pleas'd the Lord to take my spouse at last.
I tore my gown, I soil'd my locks with dust,
And beat my breasts, as wretched widows — must.   310
Before my face my handkerchief I spread,
To hide the flood of tears I did not shed.
The good man's coffin to the Church was borne;
Around, the neighbours, and my clerk too, mourn.
But as he march'd, good Gods! he show'd a pair   315
Of legs and feet, so clean, so strong, so fair!
Of twenty winters age he seem'd to be;
I (to say truth) was twenty more than he;
But vig'rous still, a lively buxom dame;
And had a wond'rous gift to quench a flame.   320
A Conj'rer once, that deeply could divine,
Assur'd me, Mars in Taurus was my sign.
As the stars order'd, such my life has been:
Alas, alas, that ever love was sin!
Fair Venus gave me fire, and sprightly grace,   325
And Mars assurance, and a dauntless face.
By virtue of this pow'rful constellation,
I follow'd always my own inclination.

But to my tale: A month scarce pass'd away,
With dance and song we kept the nuptial day.   330

THE WIFE OF BATH.

All I possess'd I gave to his command,
My goods and chattels, money, house, and land:
But oft repented, and repent it still;
He prov'd a rebel to my sovereign will:
Nay once by heav'n he struck me on the face; 335
Hear but the fact, and judge yourselves the case.
   Stubborn as any Lioness was I;
And knew full well to raise my voice on high;
As true a rambler as I was before,
And would be so in spite of all he swore. 340
He against this right sagely would advise,
And old examples set before my eyes,
Tell how the Roman matrons led their life,
Of Gracchus' mother and Duilius' wife;
And chose the sermon, as beseem'd his wit, 345
With some grave sentence out of holy writ.
Oft would he say, who builds his house on sands,
Pricks his blind horse across the fallow lands,
Or lets his wife abroad with pilgrims roam,
Deserves a fool's-cap and long ears at home. 350
All this avail'd not; for whoe'er he be
That tells my faults, I hate him mortally:
And so do numbers more, I'll boldly say,
Men, women, clergy, regular, and lay.
   My spouse, (who was, you know, to learning bred) 355
A certain treatise oft at ev'ning read,
Where divers Authors (whom the dev'l confound
For all their lies) were in one volume bound.
Valerius, whole; and of St. Jerome, part;
Chrysippus and Tertullian, Ovid's Art, 360
Solomon's proverbs, Eloïsa's loves;
And many more than sure the Church approves.
More legends were there here of wicked wives,
Than good in all the Bible and Saints-lives.
Who drew the Lion vanquish'd? 'T was a Man. 365
But could we women write as scholars can,
Men should stand mark'd with far more wickedness,
Than all the sons of Adam could redress.
Love seldom haunts the breast where Learning lies,
And Venus sets ere Mercury can rise. 370
Those play the scholars who can't play the men,
And use that weapon which they have, their pen;
When old, and past the relish of delight,
Then down they sit, and in their dotage write,
That not one woman keeps her marriage-vow. 375
(This by the way, but to my purpose now.)
   It chanc'd my husband, on a winter's night,
Read in this book, aloud, with strange delight,
How the first female (as the Scriptures show)
Brought her own spouse and all his race to woe. 380

How Samson fell; and he whom Dejanire
Wrapp'd in th' envenom'd shirt, and set on fire.
How curs'd Eryphile her lord betray'd,
And the dire ambush Clytæmnestra laid.
But what most pleas'd him was the Cretan dame, 385
And husband-bull — oh monstrous! fie for shame!
 He had by heart, the whole detail of woe
Xanthippe made her good man undergo;
How oft she scolded in a day, he knew,
How many piss-pots on the sage she threw; 390
Who took it patiently, and wip'd his head;
"Rain follows thunder," that was all he said.
 He read, how Arius to his friend complain'd,
A fatal Tree was growing in his land,
On which three wives successively had twin'd 395
A sliding noose; and waver'd in the wind.
"Where grows this plant" (reply'd the friend) "oh where?
For better fruit did never orchard bear.
Give me some slip of this most blissful tree,
And in my garden planted shall it be." 400
 Then how two wives their lord's destruction prove
Thro' hatred one, and one thro' too much love;
That for her husband mix'd a pois'nous draught,
And this for lust an am'rous philtre bought:
The nimble juice soon seiz'd his giddy head, 405
Frantic at night, and in the morning dead.
 How some with swords their sleeping lords have slain,
And some have hammer'd nails into their brain,
And some have drench'd them with a deadly potion;
All this he read, and read with great devotion. 410
 Long time I heard, and swell'd and blush'd, and frown'd
But when no end of these vile tales I found,
When still he read, and laugh'd, and read again,
And half the night was thus consum'd in vain;
Provok'd to vengeance, three large leaves I tore 415
And with one buffet fell'd him on the floor.
With that my husband in a fury rose,
And down he settled me with hearty blows.
I groan'd, and lay extended on my side;
"Oh! thou hast slain me for my wealth" (I cry'd) 420
"Yet I forgive thee — take my last embrace —"
He wept, kind soul! and stoop'd to kiss my face;
I took him such a box as turn'd him blue,
Then sigh'd and cry'd, "Adieu, my dear, adieu!"
 But after many a hearty struggle past, 425
I condescended to be pleas'd at last.
Soon as he said, "My mistress and my wife,
Do what you list, the term of all your life:"
I took to heart the merits of the cause,
And stood content to rule by wholesome laws; 430

THEBAIS OF STATIUS, BOOK I.

Receiv'd the reins of absolute command, }
With all the government of house and land, }
And empire o'er his tongue, and o'er his hand. }
As for the volume that revil'd the dames,
'T was torn to fragments, and condemn'd to flames. 435
Now heav'n on all my husbands gone bestow
Pleasures above, for tortures felt below:
The rest they wish'd for, grant them in the grave,
And bless those souls my conduct help'd to save.

———o·o·❋·o·o———

THE FIRST BOOK

OF

STATIUS HIS THEBAIS.

[TRANSLATED IN THE YEAR 1703.]

[The First Book of the *Thebais* of Statius was published in 1712, in *Lintot's Miscellany*. Pope had tried his hand at translating part of *Statius* before he was twelve years of age; and his efforts were revised by his early friend Henry Cromwell, so mysteriously described by Gay in *Alexander Pope his safe return from Troy* as 'honest hatless Cromwell, with red breeches.' — P. Papinius Statius, born at Naples about 50 A.D., was the most popular poet of the Flavian epoch, and besides his epics, the *Thebais* (in 12 books) and the *Achilleis* (in 2), wrote the *Sylvæ* (5 books of occasional pieces). Of his *Thebais*, said to have been founded on the Greek poem by Antimachus, a criticism will be found in Merivale's *Romans under the Empire*, chap. LXIV., where it is designated as perhaps the most perfect in form and arrangement of ancient epics, but confused in its general effect from want of breadth and largeness of treatment.]

ARGUMENT.

ŒDIPUS King of Thebes having by mistake slain his father Laius, and marry'd his mother Jocasta, put out his own eyes, and resign'd the realm to his sons Eteocles and Polynices. Being neglected by them, he makes his prayer to the fury Tisiphone, to sow debate betwixt the brothers. They agree at last to reign singly, each a year by turns, and the first lot is obtain'd by Eteocles. Jupiter, in a council of the Gods, declares his resolution of punishing the Thebans, and Argives also by means of a marriage betwixt Polynices and one of the daughters of Adrastus King of Argos. Juno opposes, but to no effect; and Mercury is sent on a message to the shades, to the ghost of Laius, who is to appear to Eteocles, and provoke him to break the agreement. Polynices in the mean time departs from Thebes by night, is overtaken by a storm, and arrives at Argos; where he meets with Tydeus, who had fled from Calydon, having kill'd his brother. Adrastus entertains them, having receiv'd an oracle from Apollo that his daughter should be marry'd to a Boar and a Lion, which he understands to be meant of these strangers by whom the hides of these beasts were worn, and who arriv'd at the time when he kept an annual feast in honour of that God. The rise of this solemnity he relates to his guests, the loves of Phœbus and Psamathe, and the story of Chorœbus. He enquires, and is made acquainted with that descent and quality: The sacrifice is renew'd, and the book concludes with a Hymn to Apollo.

The Translator hopes he needs not apologize for his Choice of this piece, which was made almost in his Childhood. But finding the Version better than he expected, he gave it some Correction a few years afterwards. P.

FRATERNAL Rage the guilty Thebes alarms,
Th' alternate reign destroy'd by impious arms
Demand our song; a sacred fury fires
My ravish'd breast, and all the Muse inspires.
O goddess! say, shall I deduce my rhymes 5
From the dire nation in its early times,
Europa's rape, Agenor's stern decree,
And Cadmus searching round the spacious sea?
How with the serpent's teeth he sow'd the soil,
And reap'd an iron harvest of his toil; 10
Or how from joining stones the city sprung,
While to his harp divine Amphion sung?
Or shall I Juno's hate to Thebes resound,
Whose fatal rage th' unhappy Monarch found?
The sire against the son his arrows drew, 15
O'er the wide fields the furious mother flew,
And while her arms a second hope contain,
Sprung from the rocks, and plung'd into the main.
  But waive whate'er to Cadmus may belong,
And fix, O Muse! the barrier of thy song 20
At Œdipus — from his disasters trace
The long confusions of his guilty race:
Nor yet attempt to stretch thy bolder wing,
And mighty Cæsar's[1] conquering eagles sing;
How twice he tam'd proud Ister's rapid flood, 25
While Dacian mountains stream'd with barbarous blood;
Twice taught the Rhine beneath his laws to roll,
And stretch'd his empire to the frozen pole;
Oh, long before, with early valour strove
In youthful arms t' assert the cause of Jove. 30
And thou, great heir of all thy father's fame,
Increase of glory to the Latian name!
Oh bless thy Rome with an eternal reign,
Nor let desiring worlds entreat in vain.
What tho' the stars contract their heav'nly space, 35
And crowd their shining ranks to yield thee place;
Though all the skies, ambitious of thy sway,
Conspire to court thee from our world away;
Tho' Phœbus longs to mix his rays with thine,
And in thy glories more serenely shine; 40
Tho' Jove himself no less content would be
To part his throne, and share his heav'n with thee;
Yet stay, great Cæsar! and vouchsafe to reign
O'er the wide earth, and o'er the wat'ry main;
Resign to Jove his empire of the skies, 45
And people heav'n with Roman deities.
  The time will come when a diviner flame[2]

---

[1] [The Emperor Domitian seems to have assumed the title of *Dacicus* in virtue of victories in which he had no personal share.]

[2] [As to the ascription of the divine character to Domitian, insinuated by both Statius and Martial, see Merivale, *u.s.* chapter LXII. He

Shall warm my breast to sing of Cæsar's fame:[1]
Meanwhile permit that my precluding Muse
In Theban wars an humbler theme may choose: 50
Of furious hate surviving death she sings,
A fatal throne to two contending kings,
And fun'ral flames that, parting wide in air,
Express the discord of the souls they bear:
Of towns dispeopled, and the wand'ring ghosts 55
Of kings unburied in the wasted coasts:
When Dirce's fountain blush'd with Grecian blood,
And Thetis, near Ismenos' swelling flood,
With dread beheld the rolling surges sweep
In heaps his slaughter'd sons into the deep. 60
  What Hero, Clio! wilt thou first relate?
The rage of Tydeus, or the Prophet's[2] fate?
Or how, with hills of slain on every side,
Hippomedon repell'd the hostile tide?
Or how the youth, with ev'ry grace adorn'd,[3] 65
Untimely fell, to be for ever mourn'd?
Then to fierce Capaneus thy verse extend,
And sing with horror his prodigious end.
  Now wretched Œdipus, depriv'd of sight,
Led a long death in everlasting night; 70
But while he dwells where not a cheerful ray
Can pierce the darkness, and abhors the day;
The clear reflecting mind presents his sin
In frightful views, and makes it day within;
Returning thoughts in endless circles roll, 75
And thousand furies haunt his guilty soul:
The wretch then lifted to th' unpitying skies
Those empty orbs from whence he tore his eyes,
Whose wounds, yet fresh, with bloody hands he strook,
While from his breast these dreadful accents broke. 80
  "Ye gods! that o'er the gloomy regions reign,
Where guilty spirits feel eternal pain;
Thou, sable Styx! whose livid streams are roll'd
Through dreary coasts, which I tho' blind behold;
Tisiphone! that oft has heard my prayer, 85
Assist, if Œdipus deserve thy care.
If you receive me from Jocasta's womb,
And nurs'd the hope of mischiefs yet to come;
If, leaving Polybus, I took my way
To Cirrha's temple, on that fatal day 90
When by the son the trembling father died,
Where the three roads the Phocian fields divide;
If I the Sphinx's riddles durst explain,
Taught by thyself to win the promis'd reign;

was actually addressed in a public document as *dominus et deus*, and victims were slaughtered before his statues.]

[1] [This pious intention Statius appears to have left unfulfilled.] [2] [Amphiaraus.]
[3] *Or how the Youth*] Parthenopæus. P.

If wretched I, by baleful Furies led,   95
With monstrous mixture stain'd my mother's bed;
For hell and thee begot an impious brood,
And with full lust those horrid joys renew'd;
Then, self-condemn'd, to shades of endless night,
Forc'd from these orbs the bleeding balls of sight;   100
Oh hear! and aid the vengeance I require,
If worthy thee, and what thou might'st inspire.
My sons their old, unhappy sire despise,
Spoil'd of his kingdom, and depriv'd of eyes;
Guideless I wander, unregarded mourn,   105
While these exalt their sceptres o'er my urn;
These sons, ye Gods! who with flagitious pride
Insult my darkness and my groans deride.
Art thou a father, unregarding Jove!
And sleeps thy thunder in the realms above?   110
Thou fury! then some lasting curse entail,
Which o'er their children's children shall prevail;
Place on their heads that crown distain'd[1] with gore,
Which these dire hands from my slain father tore;
Go! and a parent's heavy curses bear;   115
Break all the bonds of nature, and prepare
Their kindred souls to mutual hate and war.
Give them to dare, what I might wish to see,
Blind as I am, some glorious villany!
Soon shalt thou find, if thou but arm their hands,   120
Their ready guilt preventing thy commands:
Couldst thou some great proportion'd mischief frame,
They 'd prove the father from whose loins they came."

  The Fury heard, while on Cocytus' brink
Her snakes, untied, sulphureous waters drink;   125
But at the summons roll'd her eyes around,
And snatch'd the starting serpents from the ground.
Not half so swiftly shoots along in air,
The gliding lightning, or descending star.
Thro' crowds of airy shades she wing'd her flight,   130
And dark dominions of the silent night;
Swift as she pass'd, the flitting ghosts withdrew,
And the pale spectres trembled at her view:
To th' iron gates of Tænarus she flies,
There spreads her dusky pinions to the skies,   135
The day beheld, and sick'ning at the sight,
Veil'd her fair glories in the shades of night.
Affrighted Atlas, on the distant shore,
Trembled, and shook the heav'ns and gods he bore.
Now from beneath Malea's airy height   140
Aloft she sprung, and steer'd to Thebes her flight;
With eager speed the well-known journey took,

---

[1] [*Distain'd*, i.e. stain'd.]

THEBAIS OF STATIUS, BOOK I.

Nor here regrets the hell she late forsook.
A hundred snakes her gloomy visage shade,
A hundred serpents guard her horrid head, 145
In her sunk eye-balls dreadful meteors glow:
Such rays from Phœbe's bloody circle flow,
When lab'ring with strong charms, she shoots from high
A fiery gleam, and reddens all the sky.
Blood stain'd her cheeks, and from her mouth there came 150
Blue steaming poisons, and a length of flame.
From ev'ry blast of her contagious breath,
Famine and drought proceed, and plagues, and death.
A robe obscene was o'er her shoulders thrown,
A dress by Fates and Furies worn alone. 155
She toss'd her meagre arms; her better hand [1]
In waving circles whirl'd a fun'ral brand:
A serpent from her left was seen to rear
His flaming crest, and lash the yielding air.

But when the Fury took her stand on high, 160
Where vast Cithæron's top salutes the sky,
A hiss from all the snaky tire went round:
The dreadful signal all the rocks rebound,
And thro' the Achaian cities send the sound.
Oete, with high Parnassus, heard the voice; 165
Eurotas' banks remurmur'd to the noise;
Again Leucothoë shook at these alarms,
And press'd Palæmon closer in her arms.
Headlong from thence the glowing Fury springs,
And o'er the Theban palace spreads her wings, 170
Once more invades the guilty dome, and shrouds
Its bright pavilions in a veil of clouds.
Straight with the rage of all their race possess'd,
Stung to the soul, the brothers start from rest,
And all their Furies wake within their breast. 175
Their tortur'd minds repining Envy tears,
And Hate, engender'd by suspicious fears;
And sacred Thirst of sway; and all the ties
Of Nature broke; and royal Perjuries;
And impotent Desire to reign alone, 180
That scorns the dull reversion of a throne;
Each would the sweets of sov'reign rule devour,
While Discord waits upon divided pow'r.

As stubborn steers by brawny ploughmen broke,
And join'd reluctant to the galling yoke, 185
Alike disdain with servile necks to bear
Th' unwonted weight, or drag the crooked share,
But rend the reins, and bound a diff'rent way,
And all the furrows in confusion lay:
Such was the discord of the royal pair, 190

[1] [i.e. her right hand — But Statius merely has *hæc ... hæc manus.*]

Whom fury drove precipitate to war.
In vain the chiefs contriv'd a specious way,
To govern Thebes by their alternate sway:
Unjust decree! while this enjoys the state,
That mourns in exile his unequal fate, 195
And the short monarch of a hasty year
Foresees with anguish his returning heir.
Thus did the league their impious arms restrain,
But scarce subsisted to the second reign.
 Yet then, no proud aspiring piles were rais'd, 200
No fretted roofs with polish'd metals blaz'd;
No labour'd columns in long order plac'd,
No Grecian stone the pompous arches grac'd;
No nightly bands in glitt'ring armour wait
Before the sleepless Tyrant's guarded gate; 205
No chargers then were wrought in burnish'd gold,
Nor silver vases took the forming mould;
Nor gems on bowls emboss'd were seen to shine,
Blaze on the brims, and sparkle in the wine—
Say, wretched rivals! what provokes your rage? 210
Say, to what end your impious arms engage?
Not all bright Phœbus views in early morn,
Or when his ev'ning beams the west adorn,
When the south glows with his meridian ray,
And the cold north receives a fainter day; 215
For crimes like these, not all those realms suffice,
Were all those realms the guilty victor's prize!
 But fortune now (the lots of empire thrown)
Decrees to proud Eteocles the crown:
What joys, oh Tyrant! swell'd thy soul that day, 220
When all were slaves thou could'st around survey,
Pleas'd to behold unbounded pow'r thy own,
And singly fill a fear'd and envy'd throne!
 But the vile Vulgar, ever discontent,
Their growing fears in secret murmurs vent; 225
Still prone to change, tho' still the slaves of state,
And sure the monarch whom they have, to hate;
New lords they madly make, then tamely bear,
And softly curse the Tyrants whom they fear.
And one of those who groan beneath the sway 230
Of Kings impos'd and grudgingly obey,
(Whom envy to the great, and vulgar spite
With scandal arm'd, th' ignoble mind's delight,)
Exclaim'd—"O Thebes! for these what fates remain,
What woes attend this inauspicious reign? 235
Must we, alas! our doubtful necks prepare,
Each haughty master's yoke by turns to bear,
And still to change whom chang'd we still must fear?
These now control a wretched people's fate,
These can divide, and these reverse the state; 240

Ev'n Fortune rules no more : — O servile land,
Where exil'd tyrants still by turns command!
Thou sire of Gods and men, imperial Jove!
Is this th' eternal doom decreed above?
On thy own offspring hast thou fix'd this fate,   245
From the first birth of our unhappy state;
When banish'd Cadmus, wand'ring o'er the main,
For lost Europa search'd the world in vain,
And fated in Bœotian fields to found
A rising empire on a foreign ground,   250
First rais'd our walls on that ill-omen'd plain,
Where earth-born brothers were by brothers slain?
What lofty looks th' unrivall'd monarch bears!
How all the tyrant in his face appears!
What sullen fury clouds his scornful brow!   255
Gods! how his eyes with threat'ning ardour glow!
Can this imperious lord forget to reign,
Quit all his state, descend, and serve again?
Yet, who, before, more popularly bow'd,
Who more propitious to the suppliant crowd?   260
Patient of right, familiar in the throne?
What wonder then? he was not then alone.
Oh wretched we, a vile, submissive train,
Fortune's tame fools, and slaves in ev'ry reign!
    As when two winds with rival force contend,   265
This way and that, the wav'ring sails they bend,
While freezing Boreas, and black Eurus blow,
Now here, now there, the reeling vessel throw:
Thus on each side, alas! our tott'ring state
Feels all the fury of resistless fate,   270
And doubtful still, and still distracted stands,
While that Prince threatens, and while this commands.
    And now th' almighty Father of the Gods
Convenes a council in the blest abodes:
Far in the bright recesses of the skies,   275
High o'er the rolling heav'ns, a mansion lies,
Whence, far below, the Gods at once survey
The realms of rising and declining day,
And all th' extended space of earth, and air, and sea.
Full in the midst, and on the starry Throne,   280
The Majesty of heav'n superior shone;
Serene he look'd, and gave an awful nod,
And all the trembling spheres confess'd the God.
At Jove's assent, the deities around
In solemn state the consistory crown'd.   285
Next a long order of inferior pow'rs
Ascend from hills, and plains, and shady bow'rs
Those from whose urns the rolling rivers flow,
And those that give the wand'ring winds to blow:
Here all their rage, and ev'n their murmurs cease,   290

And sacred silence reigns, and universal peace.
A shining synod of majestic Gods
Gilds with new lustre the divine abodes;
Heav'n seems improv'd with a superior ray,
And the bright arch reflects a double day.   295
The Monarch then his solemn silence broke,
The still creation listen'd while he spoke,
Each sacred accent bears eternal weight,
And each irrevocable word is Fate.

"How long shall man the wrath of heav'n defy,   300
And force unwilling vengeance from the sky!
Oh race confed'rate into crimes, that prove
Triumphant o'er th' eluded rage of Jove!
This weary'd arm can scarce the bolt sustain,
And unregarded thunder rolls in vain: 305
Th' o'erlabour'd Cyclop from his task retires;
Th' Æolian forge exhausted of its fires.
For this, I suffer'd Phœbus' steeds to stray,
And the mad ruler to misguide the day.
When the wide earth to heaps of ashes turn'd   310
And heav'n itself the wand'ring chariot burn'd.
For this, my brother of the wat'ry reign
Releas'd th' impetuous sluices of the main:
But flames consum'd, and billows rag'd in vain.
Two races now, ally'd to Jove, offend;   315
To punish these, see Jove himself descend.
The Theban Kings their line from Cadmus trace,
From godlike Perseus those of Argive race.
Unhappy Cadmus' fate who does not know?
And the long series of succeeding woe: 320
How oft the Furies, from the deeps of night,
Arose, and mix'd with men in mortal fight:
Th' exulting mother, stain'd with filial blood;
The savage hunter and the haunted wood:
The direful banquet why should I proclaim,   325
And crimes that grieve the trembling Gods to name?
Ere I recount the sins of these profane,
The sun would sink into the western main,
And rising gild the radiant east again.
Have we not seen (the blood of Laius shed)   330
The murd'ring son ascend his parent's bed,
Thro' violated nature force his way,
And stain the sacred womb where once he lay?
Yet now in darkness and despair he groans,
And for the crimes of guilty fate atones;   335
His sons with scorn their eyeless father view,
Insult his wounds, and make them bleed anew.
Thy curse, oh Œdipus, just heav'n alarms,
And sets th' avenging thunderer in arms.
I from the root thy guilty race will tear,   340

And give the nations to the waste of war.
Adrastus soon, with Gods averse, shall join,
In dire alliance with the Theban line;
Hence strife shall rise, and mortal war succeed;
The guilty realms of Tantalus shall bleed;   345
Fix'd is their doom; this all-rememb'ring breast
Yet harbours vengeance for the tyrant's feast."
He said; and thus the Queen of heav'n return'd;
(With sudden Grief her lab'ring bosom burn'd);
"Must I, whose cares Phoroneus' tow'rs defend,   350
Must I, oh Jove, in bloody wars contend?
Thou know'st those regions my protection claim,
Glorious in arms, in riches, and in fame:
Tho' there the fair Ægyptian heifer fed,
And there deluded Argus slept, and bled;   355
Tho' there the brazen tow'r was storm'd of old,
When Jove descended in almighty gold,
Yet I can pardon those obscurer rapes,
Those bashful crimes disguis'd in borrow'd shapes;
But Thebes, where shining in celestial charms   360
Thou cam'st triumphant to a mortal's arms,
When all my glories o'er her limbs were spread,
And blazing light'nings danc'd around her bed;
Curs'd Thebes the vengeance it deserves, may prove
Ah why should Argos feel the rage of Jove?   365
Yet since thou wilt thy sister-queen control,
Since still the lust of discord fires thy soul,
Go, rase my Samos, let Mycenæ fall,
And level with the dust the Spartan wall;
No more let mortals Juno's pow'r invoke,   370
Her fanes no more with eastern incense smoke,
Nor victims sink beneath the sacred stroke;
But to your Isis all my rites transfer,
Let altars blaze and temples smoke for her;
For her, thro' Ægypt's fruitful clime renown'd,   375
Let weeping Nilus hear the timbrel sound.
But if thou must reform the stubborn times,
Avenging on the sons the fathers'[1] crimes,
And from the long records of distant age
Derive incitements to renew thy rage;   380
Say, from what period then has Jove design'd
To date his vengeance, to what bounds confin'd?
Begin from thence, where first Alpheus hides
His wand'ring stream, and thro' the briny tides
Unmix'd to his Sicilian river glides.   385
Thy own Arcadians there the thunder claim,
Whose impious rites disgrace thy mighty name;
Who raise thy temples where the chariot stood

---

[1] Not 'father's,' as in Warburton and subsequent editions; 'auctorum crimina' in the original.]

Of fierce Oenomäus, defil'd with blood;
Where once his steeds their savage banquet found, 390
And human bones yet whiten all the ground.
Say, can those honours please: and can'st thou love
Presumptuous Crete that boasts the tomb of Jove?
And shall not Tantalus's kingdoms share
Thy wife and sister's tutelary care? 395
Reverse, O Jove, thy too severe decree,
Nor doom to war a race deriv'd from thee;
On impious realms and barb'rous Kings impose
Thy plagues, and curse 'em with such Sons as those." [1]
  Thus, in reproach and pray'r, the Queen express'd 400
The rage and grief contending in her breast;
Unmov'd remain'd the ruler of the sky,
And from his throne return'd this stern reply.
" 'T was thus I deem'd thy haughty soul would bear
The dire, tho' just, revenge which I prepare 405
Against a nation, thy peculiar care:
No less Dione might for Thebes contend,
Nor Bacchus less his native town defend,
Yet these in silence see the fates fulfil
Their work, and rev'rence our superior will. 410
For by the black infernal Styx I swear,
(That dreadful oath which binds the Thunderer)
'T is fix'd; th' irrevocable doom of Jove;
No force can bend me, no persuasion move.
Haste then, Cyllenius, thro' the liquid air; 415
Go mount the winds, and to the shades repair;
Bid hell's black monarch my commands obey,
And give up Laius to the realms of day,
Whose ghost yet shiv'ring on Cocytus' sand,
Expects its passage to the further strand: 420
Let the pale sire revisit Thebes, and bear
These pleasing orders to the tyrant's ear;
That, from his exil'd brother, swell'd with pride
Of foreign forces, and his Argive bride,
Almighty Jove commands him to detain 425
The promis'd empire, and alternate reign:
Be this the cause of more than mortal hate:
The rest, succeeding times shall ripen into Fate."
  The God obeys, and to his feet applies
Those golden wings that cut the yielding skies; 430
His ample hat his beamy locks o'erspread,
And veil'd the starry glories of his head!
He seiz'd the wand that causes sleep to fly,
Or in soft slumbers seals the wakeful eye;
That drives the dead to dark Tartarean coasts, 435
Or back to life compels the wand'ring ghosts.

[1] Eteocles and Polynices. P.

Thus, thro' the parting clouds, the son of May
Wings on the whistling winds his rapid way;
Now smoothly steers thro' air his equal flight,
Now springs aloft, and tow'rs th' ethereal height; 440
Then wheeling down the steep of heav'n he flies,
And draws a radiant circle o'er the skies.
  Meantime the banish'd Polynices roves
(His Thebes abandon'd) thro' th' Aonian groves,
While future realms his wand'ring thoughts delight, 445
His daily vision and his dream by night;
Forbidden Thebes appears before his eye,
From whence he sees his absent brother fly,
With transport views the airy rule his own,
And swells on an imaginary throne, 450
Fain would he cast a tedious age away,
And live out all in one triumphant day.
He chides the lazy progress of the sun,
And bids the year with swifter motion run.
With anxious hopes his craving mind is tost, 455
And all his joys in length of wishes lost.
  The hero then resolves his course to bend
Where ancient Danaus' fruitful fields extend,
And fam'd Mycenæ's lofty tow'rs ascend,
(Where late the sun did Atreus' crimes detest, 460
And disappear'd in horror of the feast).
·And now by chance, by fate, or furies led,
From Bacchus' consecrated caves he fled,
Where the shrill cries of frantic matrons sound,
And Pentheus' blood enrich'd the rising ground. 465
Then sees Cithæron tow'ring o'er the plain,
And thence declining gently to the main.
Next to the bounds of Nisus' realm repairs,
Where treach'rous Scylla cuts the purple hairs:
The hanging cliffs of Scyron's rock explores,[2] 470
And hears the murmurs of the diff'rent shores:
Passes the strait that parts the foaming seas,
And stately Corinth's pleasing site surveys.
  'T was now the time when Phœbus yields to night
And rising Cynthia sheds her silver light, 475
Wide o'er the world in solemn pomp she drew
Her airy chariot hung with pearly dew;
All birds and beast lie hush'd; sleep steals away
The wild desires of men, and toils of day,
And brings, descending thro' the silent air, 480
A sweet forgetfulness of human care.
Yet no red clouds, with golden borders gay,
Promise the skies the bright return of day;

[1] [Megara. See Ov. *Metam.* VIII. vv. 6 *ff.*]
[2] [Pope evidently confounds the island of Scyros in the Ægean with the rocks between Megaris and Attica infested by the robber Sciron whom Theseus slew. See Ov. *Metam*, VII. v. 444.]

No faint reflections of the distant light
Streak with long gleams the scatt'ring shades of night;   485
From the damp earth impervious vapours rise,
Increase the darkness and involve the skies.
At once the rushing winds with roaring sound
Burst from th' Æolian caves, and rend the ground,
With equal rage their airy quarrel try,   490
And win by turns the kingdom of the sky:
But with a thicker night black Auster shrouds
The heav'ns, and drives on heaps the rolling clouds,
From whose dark womb a rattling tempest pours,
Which the cold north congeals to haily show'rs.   495
From pole to pole the thunder roars aloud,
And broken lightnings flash from ev'ry cloud.
Now smokes with show'rs the misty mountain-ground
And floated fields lie undistinguish'd round.
Th' Inachian streams with headlong fury run,   500
And Erasinus rolls a deluge on:
The foaming Lerna swells above its bounds,
And spreads its ancient poisons o'er the grounds:
Where late was dust, now rapid torrents play,
Rush thro' the mounds, and bear the dams away;   505
Old limbs of trees from crackling forests torn,
Are whirl'd in air, and on the winds are borne,
The storm the dark Lycæan groves display'd,
And first to light expos'd the sacred shade.
Th' intrepid Theban hears the bursting sky,   510
Sees yawning rocks in massy fragments fly,
And views astonish'd, from the hills afar,
The floods descending, and the wat'ry war,
That, driv'n by storms and pouring o'er the plain,
Swept herds, and hinds, and houses to the main.   515
Thro' the brown horrors of the night he fled,
Nor knows, amaz'd, what doubtful path to tread,
His brother's image to his mind appears,
Inflames his heart with rage, and wings his feet with fears.
  So fares a sailor on the stormy main,   520
When clouds conceal Boötes' golden wain,
When not a star its friendly lustre keeps,
Nor trembling Cynthia glimmers on the deeps;
He dreads the rocks, and shoals, and seas, and skies,
While thunder roars, and lightning round him flies.   525
  Thus strove the chief, on ev'ry side distress'd,
Thus still his courage, with his toils increas'd;
With his broad shield oppos'd, he forc'd his way
Thro' thickest woods, and rous'd the beasts of prey.
Till he beheld, where from Larissa's height   530
The shelving walls reflect a glancing light:
Thither with haste the Theban hero flies;
On this side Lerna's pois'nous water lies,

On that Prosymna's grove and temple rise:
He pass'd the gates which then unguarded lay,   535
And to the regal palace bent his way;
On the cold marble, spent with toil, he lies,
And waits till pleasing slumbers seal his eyes.
  Adrastus here his happy people sways,
Blest with calm peace in his declining days,   540
By both his parents of descent divine,
Great Jove and Phœbus grac'd his noble line:
Heav'n had not crown'd his wishes with a son,
But two fair daughters heir'd his state and throne.
To him Apollo (wond'rous to relate!   545
But who can pierce into the depths of fate?)
Had sung — "Expect thy sons on Argos' shore,
A yellow lion and a bristly boar."
This long revolv'd in his paternal breast,
Sate heavy on his heart, and broke his rest;   550
This, great Amphiaraus, lay hid from thee,
Tho' skill'd in fate, and dark futurity.
The father's care and prophet's art were vain,
For thus did the predicting God ordain.
  Lo hapless Tydeus, whose ill-fated hand   555
Had slain his brother, leaves his native land,
And seiz'd with horror in the shades of night,
Thro' the thick deserts headlong urg'd his flight:
Now by the fury of the tempest driv'n,
He seeks a shelter from th' inclement heav'n,   560
'Till led by fate, the Theban's steps he treads,
And to fair Argos' open court succeeds.
  When thus the chiefs from diff'rent lands resort
T' Adrastus' realms, and hospitable court;
The King surveys his guests with curious eyes,   565
And views their arms and habit with surprise.
A lion's yellow skin the Theban wears,
Horrid his mane, and rough with curling hairs;
Such once employ'd Alcides' youthful toils,
Ere yet adorn'd with Nemea's dreadful spoils.   570
A boar's stiff hide, of Calydonian breed,
Oenides' manly shoulders overspread.
Oblique his tusks, erect his bristles stood,
Alive, the pride and terror of the wood.
  Struck with the sight, and fix'd in deep amaze,   575
The King th' accomplish'd Oracle surveys,
Reveres Apollo's vocal caves, and owns
The guiding Godhead, and his future sons.
O'er all his bosom secret transports reign,
And a glad horror shoots thro' ev'ry vein.   580
To heav'n he lifts his hands, erects his sight,
And thus invokes the silent Queen of night.
  "Goddess of shades, beneath whose gloomy reign

Yon' spangled arch glows with the starry train:
You who the cares of heav'n and earth allay, } 585
'Till nature quicken'd by th' inspiring ray
Wakes to new vigour with the rising day.
Oh thou who freest me from my doubtful state,
Long lost and wilder'd in the maze of Fate!
Be present still, oh Goddess! in our aid; 590
Proceed, and firm [1] those omens thou hast made.
We to thy name our annual rites will pay,
And on thy altars sacrifices lay;
The sable flock shall fall beneath the stroke,
And fill thy temples with a grateful smoke. 595
Hail, faithful Tripos! hail, ye dark abodes
Of awful Phœbus! I confess the Gods!"
 Thus, seiz'd with sacred fear, the monarch pray'd;
Then to his inner court the guests convey'd;
Where yet thin fumes from dying sparks arise, } 600
And dust yet white upon each altar lies,
The relics of a former sacrifice.
The King once more the solemn rites requires,
And bids renew the feasts, and wake the fires.
His train obey, while all the courts around 605
With noisy care and various tumult sound.
Embroider'd purple clothes the golden beds;
This slave the floor, and that the table spreads;
A third dispels the darkness of the night,
And fills depending lamps with beams of light; 610
Here loaves in canisters are pil'd on high,
And there in flames, the slaughter'd victims fry.
Sublime in regal state Adrastus shone,
Stretch'd on rich carpets on his iv'ry throne;
A lofty couch receives each princely guest; 615
Around, at awful distance, wait the rest.
 And now the king, his royal feast to grace,
Acestis calls, the guardian of his race,
Who first their youth in arts of virtue train'd,
And their ripe years in modest grace maintain'd. 620
Then softly whisper'd in her faithful ear,
And bade his daughters at the rites appear.
When from the close apartments of the night,
The royal Nymphs approach divinely bright;
Such was Diana's, such Minerva's face; 625
Nor shine their beauties with superior grace,
But that in these a milder charm endears,
And less of terror in their looks appears,
As on the heroes first they cast their eyes,
O'er their fair cheeks the glowing blushes rise, 630
Their downcast looks a decent shame confess'd,

---

[1] [firm, i.e. confirm, accomplish.]

Then on their father's rev'rend features rest.
　The banquet done, the monarch gives the sign
To fill the goblet high with sparkling wine,
Which Danaus us'd in secret rites of old, 635
With sculpture grac'd, and rough with rising gold.
Here to the clouds victorious Perseus flies,
Medusa seems to move her languid eyes,
And ev'n in gold, turns paler as she dies.
There from the chase Jove's tow'ring eagle bears 640
On golden wings, the Phrygian to the stars:
Still as he rises in th' etherial height,
His native mountains lessen to his sight;
While all his sad companions upward gaze,
Fix'd on the glorious scene in wild amaze; 645
And the swift hounds, affrighted as he flies,
Run to the shade, and bark against the skies.
　This golden bowl with gen'rous juice was crown'd,
The first libations sprinkled on the ground,
By turns on each celestial pow'r they call; 650
With Phœbus' name resounds the vaulted hall.
The courtly train, the strangers, and the rest,
Crown'd with chaste laurel, and with garlands dress'd,
While with rich gums the fuming altars blaze,
Salute the God in num'rous [1] hymns of praise. 655
　Then thus the King: "Perhaps, my noble guests,
These honour'd altars, and these annual feasts
To bright Apollo's awful name design'd,
Unknown, with wonder may perplex your mind.
Great was the cause; our old solemnities 660
From no blind zeal or fond tradition rise;
But sav'd from death, our Argives yearly pay
These grateful honours to the God of Day.
　"When by a thousand darts the Python slain
With orbs unroll'd lay cov'ring all the plain, 665
(Transfix'd as o'er Castalia's streams he hung,
And suck'd new poisons with his triple tongue)
To Argos' realms the victor god resorts,
And enters old Crotopus' humble courts.
This rural prince one only daughter blest, 670
That all the charms of blooming youth possess'd;
Fair was her face, and spotless was her mind,
Where filial love with virgin sweetness join'd.
Happy! and happy still she might have prov'd,
Were she less beautiful, or less belov'd! 675
But Phœbus lov'd, and on the flow'ry side
Of Nemea's stream, the yielding fair enjoy'd:
Now, ere ten moons their orb with light adorn,
Th' illustrious offspring of the God was born,

---

[1] [num'rous, i.e. harmonious.]

THEBAIS OF STATIUS, BOOK I.

The Nymph, her father's anger to evade, 680
Retires from Argos to the sylvan shade;
To woods and wilds the pleasing burden bears,
And trusts her infant to a shepherd's cares.
"How mean a fate, unhappy child! is thine!
Ah how unworthy those of race divine! 685
On flow'ry herbs in some green covert laid,
His bed the ground, his canopy the shade,
He mixes with the bleating lambs his cries,
While the rude swain his rural music tries,
To call soft slumbers on his infant eyes. 690
Yet ev'n in those obscure abodes to live,
Was more, alas! than cruel fate would give,
For on the grassy verdure as he lay,
And breath'd the freshness of the early day,
Devouring dogs the helpless infant tore, 695
Fed on his trembling limbs, and lapp'd the gore.
Th' astonish'd mother, when the rumour came,
Forgets her father, and neglects her fame,
With loud complaints she fills the yielding air,
And beats her breast, and rends her flowing hair; 700
Then wild with anguish to her sire she flies:
Demands the sentence, and contented dies.

" But touch'd with sorrow for the dead too late,
The raging God prepares t' avenge her fate.
He sends a monster, horrible and fell, 705
Begot by furies in the depths of hell,
The pest a virgin's face and bosom bears;
High on a crown a rising snake appears,
Guards her black front, and hisses in her hairs:
About the realm she walks her dreadful round, 710
When night with sable wings o'erspreads the ground,
Devours young babes before their parents' eyes,
And feeds and thrives on public miseries.

" But gen'rous rage the bold Chorœbus warms,
Chorœbus, fam'd for virtue, as for arms; 715
Some few like him, inspir'd with martial flame,
Thought a short life well lost for endless fame.
These, where two ways in equal parts divide,
The direful monster from afar descry'd;
Two bleeding babes depending at her side; 720
Whose panting vitals, warm with life, she draws,
And in their hearts embrues her cruel claws.
The youths surround her with extended spears;
But brave Chorœbus in the front appears,
Deep in her breast he plung'd his shining sword, 725
And hell's dire monster back to hell restor'd.
Th' Inachians view the slain with vast surprise,
Her twisting volumes and her rolling eyes,
Her spotted breast, and gaping womb embru'd

THEBAIS OF STATIUS, BOOK I.

With livid poison, and our children's blood. 730
The crowd in stupid wonder fix'd appear,
Pale ev'n in joy, nor yet forget to fear.
Some with vast beams the squalid corpse engage,
And weary all the wild efforts of rage.
The birds obscene, that nightly flock'd to taste, 735
With hollow screeches fled the dire repast;
And rav'nous dogs, allur'd by scented blood,
And starving wolves, ran howling to the wood.
  " But fir'd with rage, from cleft Parnassus' brow
Avenging Phœbus bent his deadly bow, 740
And hissing flew the feather'd fates below;
A night of sultry clouds involv'd around
The tow'rs, the fields and the devoted ground:
And now a thousand lives together fled,
Death with his scythe cut off the fatal thread, 745
And a whole province in his triumph led.
  " But Phœbus, ask'd why noxious fires appear,
And raging Sirius blasts the sickly year;
Demands their lives by whom his monster fell,
And dooms a dreadful sacrifice to hell. 750
  " Bless'd be thy dust, and let eternal fame
Attend thy Manes, and preserve thy name;
Undaunted hero! who divinely brave,
In such a cause disdain'd thy life to save;
But view'd the shrine with a superior look, 755
And its upbraided Godhead thus bespoke.
  " ' With piety, the soul's securest guard,
And conscious virtue, still its own reward,
Willing I come, unknowing how to fear;
Nor shalt thou, Phœbus, find a suppliant here. 760
Thy monster's death to me was ow'd alone,
And 't is a deed too glorious to disown.
Behold him here, for whom, so many days,
Impervious clouds conceal'd thy sullen rays;
For whom, as Man no longer claim'd thy care, 765
Such numbers fell by pestilential air!
But if th' abandon'd race of human kind
From Gods above no more compassion find;
If such inclemency in heav'n can dwell,
Yet why must unoffending Argos feel 770
The vengeance due to this unlucky steel?
On me, on me, let all thy fury fall,
Nor err from me, since I deserve it all:
Unless our desert cities please thy sight,
Or fun'ral flames reflect a grateful light. 775
Discharge thy shafts, this ready bosom rend,
And to the shades a ghost triumphant send;
But for my Country let my fate atone,
Be mine the vengeance, as the crime my own.'

"Merit distress'd, impartial heav'n relieves : 780
Unwelcome life relenting Phœbus gives ;
For not the vengeful pow'r, that glow'd with rage
With such amazing virtue durst engage.
The clouds dispers'd, Apollo's wrath expir'd,
And from the wond'ring God th' unwilling youth retir'd. 785
Thence we these altars in his temple raise,
And offer annual honours, feasts, and praise ;
These solemn feasts propitious Phœbus please :
These honours, still renew'd, his ancient wrath appease.
"But say, illustrious guest" (adjoin'd the King) 790
"What name you bear, from what high race you spring?
The noble Tydeus stands confess'd, and known
Our neighbour Prince, and heir of Calydon.
Relate your fortunes, while the friendly night
And silent hours to various talk invite." 795
The Theban bends on earth his gloomy eyes,
Confus'd, and sadly thus at length replies :
"Before these altars how shall I proclaim
(Oh gen'rous prince) my nation or my name,
Or thro' what veins our ancient blood has roll'd? 800
Let the sad tale for ever rest untold!
Yet if propitious to a wretch unknown,
You seek to share in sorrows not your own ;
Know then from Cadmus I derive my race,
Jocasta's son, and Thebes my native place." 805
To whom the King (who felt his gen'rous breast
Touch'd with concern for his unhappy guest)
Replies — "Ah why forbears the son to name
His wretched father known too well by fame?
Fame, that delights around the world to stray, 810
Scorns not to take our Argos in her way,
E'en those who dwell where suns at distance roll,
In northern wilds, and freeze beneath the pole ;
And those who tread the burning Libyan lands,
The faithless Syrtes and the moving sands ; 815
Who view the western sea's extremest bounds,
Or drink of Ganges in their eastern grounds ;
All these the woes of Œdipus have known,
Your fates, your furies, and your haunted town.
If on the sons the parents' crimes descend, 820
What Prince from those his lineage can defend?
Be this thy comfort, that 't is thine t' efface ⎫
With virtuous acts thy ancestor's disgrace, ⎬
And be thyself the honour of thy race. ⎭
But see! the stars begin to steal away, 825
And shine more faintly at approaching day ;
Now pour the wine ; and in your tuneful lays
Once more resound the great Apollo's praise."
"Oh father Phœbus! whether Lycia's coast

And snowy mountains thy bright presence boast; 830
Whether to sweet Castalia thou repair,
And bathe in silver dews thy yellow hair;
Or pleas'd to find fair Delos float no more,
Delight in Cynthus, and the shady shore;
Or choose thy seat in Ilion's proud abodes, 835
The shining structures rais'd by lab'ring Gods,
By thee the bow and mortal shafts are borne;
Eternal charms thy blooming youth adorn:
Skill'd in the laws of secret fate above,
And the dark counsels of almighty Jove, 840
'T is thine the seeds of future war to know,
The change of Sceptres, and impending woe;
When direful meteors spread thro' glowing air
Long trails of light, and shake their blazing hair.
Thy rage the Phrygian felt, who durst aspire 845
T' excel the music of thy heav'nly lyre;
Thy shafts aveng'd lewd Tityus' guilty flame,
Th' immortal victim of thy mother's fame;
Thy hand slew Python, and the dame who lost
Her num'rous offspring for a fatal boast. 850
In Phlegyas' doom thy just revenge appears,
Condemn'd to furies and eternal fears;
He views his food, but dreads, with lifted eye,
The mould'ring rock that trembles from on high.
"Propitious hear our pray'r, O Pow'r divine! 855
And on thy hospitable Argos shine,
Whether the style of Titan please thee more,
Whose purple rays th' Achæmenes [1] adore;
Or great Osiris, who first taught the swain
In Pharian fields to sow the golden grain; 860
Or Mitra, to whose beams the Persian bows,
And pays, in hollow rocks, his awful vows;
Mitra, whose head the blaze of light adorns,[2]
Who grasps the struggling heifer's lunar horns."

THE FABLE OF DRYOPE.

FROM THE NINTH BOOK OF OVID'S METAMORPHOSES. [vv. 324-393.]

UPON occasion of the death of Hercules, his mother Alcmena recounts her misfortunes to Iole, who answers with a relation of those of her own family, in particular the Transformation of her sister Dryope, which is the subject of the ensuing Fable. P.

---

[1] Achæmenes. [Pope means 'Achæmenids,' or descendants of Achæmenes, the grandfather of Cyrus; *i.e.* the Persians.]

[2] [These foreign worships were fully naturalised at Rome about the time when the Thebais was written.]

FABLE OF DRYOPE.

SHE said,[1] and for her lost Galanthis sighs,
When the fair Consort of her son replies.
"Since you a servant's ravish'd form bemoan,
And kindly sigh for sorrows not your own;
Let me (if tears and grief permit) relate
A nearer woe, a sister's stranger fate.
No Nymph of all Œchalia could compare
For beauteous form with Dryope the fair,
Her tender mother's only hope and pride,
(Myself the offspring of a second bride)
This Nymph compress'd by him who rules the day,
Whom Delphi and the Delian isle obey,
Andræmon lov'd; and, bless'd in all those charms
That pleas'd a God, succeeded to her arms.

"A lake there was, with shelving banks around,
Whose verdant summit fragrant myrtles crown'd.
These shades, unknowing of the fates, she sought,
And to the Naiads flow'ry garlands brought;
Her smiling babe (a pleasing charge) she prest
Within her arms, and nourish'd at her breast.
Not distant far, a wat'ry Lotos grows,
The spring was new, and all the verdant boughs
Adorn'd with blossoms promis'd fruits that vie
In glowing colours with the Tyrian dye:
Of these she cropp'd to please her infant son,
And I myself the same rash act had done:
But lo! I saw, (as near her side I stood)
The violated blossoms drop with blood;
Upon the tree I cast a frightful look;
The trembling tree with sudden horror shook.
Lotis the nymph (if rural tales be true)
As from Priapus' lawless lust she flew,
Forsook her form; and fixing here became
A flow'ry plant, which still preserves her name.

"This change unknown, astonish'd at the sight
My trembling sister strove to urge her flight,
And first the pardon of the nymphs implor'd,
And those offended sylvan powers ador'd:
But when she backward would have fled, she found
Her stiff'ning feet were rooted in the ground:
In vain to free her fasten'd feet she strove,
And as she struggles, only moves above;
She feels th' encroaching bark around her grow
By quick degrees, and cover all below:
Surpris'd at this, her trembling hand she heaves
To rend her hair; her hand is fill'd with leaves:
Where late was hair, the shooting leaves are seen
To rise, and shade her with a sudden green.

---

[1] Alcmena. Galanthis, one of her female servants, had been turned into a weasel. Io, "fair consort" of her grandson, Hyllus.

FABLE OF DRYOPE.

The child Amphissus, to her bosom prest,
Perceiv'd a colder and a harder breast,   50
And found the springs, that ne'er till then deny'd
Their milky moisture, on a sudden dry'd.
I saw, unhappy! what I now relate,
And stood the helpless witness of thy fate,
Embrac'd thy boughs, thy rising bark delay'd,   55
There wish'd to grow, and mingle shade with shade.
 "Behold Andræmon and th' unhappy sire
Appear, and for their Dryope enquire;
A springing tree for Dryope they find,
And print warm kisses on the panting rind.   60
Prostrate, with tears their kindred plant bedew,
And close embrace as to the roots they grew,
The face was all that now remain'd of thee,
No more a woman, nor yet quite a tree;
Thy branches hung with humid pearls appear,   65
From ev'ry leaf distils a trickling tear,
And straight a voice, while yet a voice remains,
Thus thro' the trembling boughs in sighs complains.
 "'If to the wretched any faith be giv'n,
I swear by all th' unpitying pow'rs of heav'n,   70
No wilful crime this heavy vengeance bred;
In mutual innocence our lives we led:
If this be false, let these new greens decay,
Let sounding axes lop my limbs away,
And crackling flames on all my honours prey.   75
But from my branching arms this infant bear,
Let some kind nurse supply a mother's care:
And to his mother let him oft be led,
Sport in her shades, and in her shades be fed;
Teach him, when first his infant voice shall frame   80
Imperfect words, and lisp his mother's name,
To hail this tree; and say with weeping eyes,
Within this plant my hapless parent lies:
And when in youth he seeks the shady woods,
Oh, let him fly the crystal lakes and floods,   85
Nor touch the fatal flow'rs; but, warn'd by me,
Believe a Goddess shrin'd in ev'ry tree.
My sire, my sister, and my spouse farewell!
If in your breasts or love, or pity dwell,
Protect your plant, nor let my branches feel   90
The browsing cattle or the piercing steel.
Farewell! and since I cannot bend to join
My lips to yours, advance at least to mine.
My son, thy mother's parting kiss receive,
While yet thy mother has a kiss to give.   95
I can no more; the creeping rind invades
My closing lips, and hides my head in shades:
Remove your hands, the bark shall soon suffice

Without their aid to seal these dying eyes.'
"She ceas'd at once to speak, and ceas'd to be; 100
And all the nymph was lost within the tree;
Yet latent life thro' her new branches reign'd,
And long the plant a human heat retain'd."

———oo;o;oo———

VERTUMNUS AND POMONA.

From the Fourteenth Book of Ovid's Metamorphoses.

[vv. 623-771. First published in 1712, in Lintot's Miscellany.]

<pre>
THE fair Pomona flourish'd in his reign;[1]
  Of all the Virgins of the sylvan train,
None taught the trees a nobler race to bear,
Or more improv'd the vegetable care.
To her the shady grove, the flow'ry field,   5
The streams and fountains, no delights could yield;
'T was all her joy the ripening fruits to tend,
And see the boughs with happy burthens bend.
The hook she bore instead of Cynthia's spear,
To lop the growth of the luxuriant year,   10
To decent form the lawless shoots to bring,
And teach th' obedient branches where to spring.
Now the cleft rind inserted graffs receives,
And yields an offspring more than nature gives;
Now sliding streams the thirsty plants renew,   15
And feed their fibres with reviving dew.
  These cares alone her virgin breast employ,
Averse from Venus and the nuptial joy.
Her private orchards, wall'd on ev'ry side,
To lawless sylvans all access deny'd.   20
How oft the Satyrs and the wanton Fawns,
Who haunt the forests, or frequent the lawns,
The God whose ensign scares the birds of prey,[2]
And old Silenus, youthful in decay,
Employ'd their wiles, and unavailing care,   25
To pass the fences, and surprise the fair.
Like these, Vertumnus own'd his faithful flame,
Like these, rejected by the scornful dame.
To gain her sight a thousand forms he wears,
And first a reaper from the field appears,   30
Sweating he walks, while loads of golden grain
O'ercharge the shoulders of the seeming swain.
Oft o'er his back a crooked scythe is laid,
</pre>

---

[1] [In the reign of Proca (or Procus) one of the ancient Kings of Latium residing at Alba enumerated by Ovid.]   [2] [Priapus.]

VERTUMNUS AND POMONA.

And wreathes of hay his sun-burnt temples shade:
Oft in his harden'd hand a goad he bears, 35
Like one who late unyok'd the sweating steers.
Sometimes his pruning-hook corrects the vines,
And the loose stragglers to their ranks confines.
Now gath'ring what the bounteous year allows,
He pulls ripe apples from the bending boughs. 40
A soldier now, he with his sword appears;
A fisher next, his trembling angle bears;
Each shape he varies, and each art he tries,
On her bright charms to feast his longing eyes.
   A female form at last Vertumnus wears, 45
With all the marks of rev'rend age appears,
His temples thinly spread with silver hairs;
Propp'd on his staff, and stooping as he goes,
A painted mitre shades his furrow'd brows.
The God in this decrepit form array'd, 50
The gardens enter'd, and the fruit survey'd,
And "Happy you!" (he thus address'd the maid)
"Whose charms as far all other nymphs out-shine,
As other gardens are excell'd by thine!"
Then kiss'd the fair; (his kisses warmer grow 55
Than such as women on their sex bestow.)
Then plac'd beside her on the flow'ry ground,
Beheld the trees with autumn's bounty crown'd.
An Elm was near, to whose embraces led,
The curling vine her swelling clusters spread: 60
He view'd her twining branches with delight,
And prais'd the beauty of the pleasing sight.
"Yet this tall elm, but for his vine" (he said)
"Had stood neglected, and a barren shade;
And this fair vine, but that her arms surround 65
Her marry'd elm, had crept along the ground.
Ah beauteous maid, let this example move
Your mind, averse from all the joys of love.
Deign to be lov'd, and ev'ry heart subdue!
What nymph could e'er attract such crowds as you? 70
Not she whose beauty urg'd the Centaurs' arms,
Ulysses' Queen, nor Helen's fatal charms.
Ev'n now, when silent scorn is all they gain,
A thousand court you, tho' they court in vain,
A thousand sylvans, demigods, and gods, 75
That haunt our mountains and our Alban woods.
But if you'll prosper, mark what I advise,
Whom age, and long experience render wise,
And one whose tender care is far above
All that these lovers ever felt of love, 80
(Far more than e'er can by yourself be guess'd)
Fix on Vertumnus, and reject the rest.
For his firm faith I dare engage my own;

N

Scarce to himself, himself is better known.
To distant lands Vertumnus never roves; 85
Like you contented with his native groves;
Nor at first sight, like most, admires the fair;
For you he lives; and you alone shall share
His last affection, as his early care.
Besides, he's lovely far above the rest, 90
With youth immortal, and with beauty blest.
Add, that he varies ev'ry shape with ease,
And tries all forms that may Pomona please.
But what should most excite a mutual flame,
Your rural cares, and pleasures are the same: 95
To him your orchard's early fruits are due,
(A pleasing off'ring when 't is made by you)
He values these; but yet (alas!) complains,
That still the best and dearest gift remains.
Not the fair fruit that on yon' branches glows 100
With that ripe red th' autumnal sun bestows;
Nor tasteful herbs that in these gardens rise,
Which the kind soil with milky sap supplies;
You, only you, can move the God's desire:
Oh crown so constant and so pure a fire! 105
Let soft compassion touch your gentle mind;
Think, 't is Vertumnus begs you to be kind!
So may no frost, when early buds appear,
Destroy the promise of the youthful year;
Nor winds, when first your florid orchard blows, 110
Shake the light blossoms from their blasted boughs!"
   This when the various God had urg'd in vain,
He straight assum'd his native form again;
Such, and so bright an aspect now he bears,
As when thro' clouds th' emerging sun appears, 115
And thence exerting his refulgent ray,
Dispels the darkness, and reveals the day.
Force he prepar'd but check'd the rash design;
For when, appearing in a form divine,
The Nymph surveys him, and beholds the grace 120
Of charming features, and a youthful face,
In her soft breast consenting passions move,
And the warm maid confess'd a mutual love.

IMITATIONS OF ENGLISH POETS.

DONE BY THE AUTHOR IN HIS YOUTH.

[These Imitations, of which the precise date is unknown, besides proving the imitative powers of Pope as a boy show him to have been even at that period of his life the most facile of versifiers. There is considerable humour, and unfortunately not a little pruriency, in some of these productions. The imitation of Spenser, while hitting a blot of which it would be difficult to deny the presence in some passages of the noblest of English poets, is in spirit unworthy of even the most juvenile parodist. Thomson who in his *Castle of Indolence* considered that 'the obsolete words, and a simplicity of diction in some of the lines, which borders on the ludicrous, were necessary to make the imitation more perfect,' can hardly be said either to have honoured Spenser's poetic name, or raised his own by that elaborate attempt at a reverential burlesque. Waller was one of the poets who exercised the greatest influence upon Pope's versification; yet the imitations are hardly successful, except as to the treatment of the subject in the lines *on a Fan*. *The Garden* (Cowley) is a feeble attempt to reproduce the play of fancy, admirable even in its extravagance, of the most magnificent among the poets of the English Fantastic School. *Weeping* is perhaps slightly more successful in this direction. In the remaining Imitations Pope found both fairer and easier game. Rochester's triplets *on Nothing* are happily parodied in those *on Silence*, so far as in the first part of the former they anticipated the meaningless sonorousness of reflexions equal in value to the famous

'Nought is everything, and everything is nought'—

but they miss the touch of genuine wit which redeems Rochester's lines towards the close. Dorset's queer mixture of French frivolity and Dutch coarseness is fairly reproduced in *Artemisia* and *Phryne*; though an imitation at least equally amusing exists from the hand of Fenton, who among the styles of other poets was so successful in appropriating that of Pope himself. The *Happy Life of a Country Parson* is in Swift's best vein, and might be easily mistaken for some of the Dean's own verse, differing from prose solely by the quality of being the best and easiest English verse ever written.]

I.

CHAUCER.[1]

WOMEN ben full of Ragerie,
 Yet swinken not sans secresie.
Thilke Moral shall ye understond,
From Schoole-boy's Tale of fayre Irelond:
Which to the Fennes hath him betake,   5
To filch the gray Ducke fro the Lake.
Right then, there passen by the Way
His Aunt, and eke her Daughters tway.
Ducke in his Trowses hath he hent,
Not to be spid of Ladies gent.   10
" But ho! our Nephew," (crieth one)

[1] [Geoffry Chaucer, born in 1328 died in 1400. The above imitates the style of some of the *Canterbury Tales*, of which however none is in the metre adopted by Pope, which is that of Chaucer's earlier poems, the *Romaunt of the Rose* and the *House of Fame*.]

"Ho!" quoth another, " Cozen John;"
And stoppen, and lough, and callen out,—
This sely Clerk full low doth lout:
They asken that, and talken this, 15
"Lo here is Coz, and here is Miss."
But, as he glozeth with Speeches soote,
The Ducke sore tickleth his Erse-roote:
Fore-piece and buttons all-to-brest,
Forth thrust a white neck, and red crest. 20
"Te-he," cry'd Ladies; Clerke nought spake:
Miss star'd: and gray Ducke crieth Quake.
"O Moder, Moder," (quoth the daughter)
"Be thilke same thing Maids longer a'ter?
Bette is to pyne on coals and chalke, 25
Then trust on Mon, whose yerde can talke."

II.

SPENSER.[1]

I.

IN ev'ry Town, where Thamis rolls his Tyde,
  A narrow pass there is, with Houses low;
Where ever and anon, the Stream is ey'd,
And many a Boat soft sliding to and fro.
There oft are heard the notes of Infant Woe, 5
The short thick Sob, loud Scream, and shriller Squall:
How can ye, Mothers, vex your Children so?
Some play, some eat, some cack against the wall,
And as they crouchen low, for bread and butter call.

II.

And on the broken pavement, here and there, 10
Doth many a stinking sprat and herring lie;
A brandy and tobacco shop is near,
And hens, and dogs, and hogs are feeding by;
And here a sailor's jacket hangs to dry.
At ev'ry door are sun-burnt matrons seen, 15
Mending old nets to catch the scaly fry;
Now singing shrill, and scolding eft between;
Scolds answer foul-mouth'd scolds; bad neighbourhood I ween.

III.

The snappish cur, (the passengers' annoy)
Close at my heel with yelping treble flies; 20

---

[1] [Edmund Spenser, born in 1553, died in 1599. His *Faerie Queene*, of which Pope has ventured to parody some of the inferior passages was published in instalments from the year 1590.

EDMUND SPENSER.

IMITATIONS OF ENGLISH POETS.

The whimp'ring girl, and hoarser-screaming boy,
Join to the yelping treble shrilling cries;
The scolding Quean to louder notes doth rise,
And her full pipes those shrilling cries confound;
To her full pipes the grunting hog replies; 25
The grunting hogs alarm the neighbours round,
And curs, girls, boys, and scolds, in the deep bass are drown'd.

IV.

Hard by a Sty, beneath a roof of thatch,
Dwelt Obloquy, who in her early days
Baskets of fish at Billingsgate did watch, 30
Cod, whiting, oyster, mackrel, sprat, or plaice:
There learn'd she speech from tongues that never cease.
Slander beside her, like a Mag-pie, chatters,
With Envy, (spitting Cat) dread foe to peace;
Like a curs'd Cur, Malice before her clatters, 35
And vexing ev'ry wight, tears clothes and all to tatters.

V.

Her dugs were mark'd by ev'ry Collier's hand,
Her mouth was black as bull-dogs at the stall:
She scratched, bit, and spar'd ne lace ne band,
And bitch and rogue her answer was to all; 40
Nay, e'en the parts of shame by name would call:
Yea, when she passed by or lane or nook,
Would greet the man who turn'd him to the Wall,
And by his hand obscene the porter took,
Nor ever did askance like modest Virgin look. 45

VI.

Such place hath Deptford, navy-building town,
Woolwich and Wapping smelling strong of pitch;
Such Lambeth, envy of each band and gown,
And Twick'nam such, which fairer scenes enrich,
Grots, statues, urns, and Jo—n's [1] Dog and Bitch, 50
Ne village is without, on either side,
All up the silver Thames, or all adown;
Ne Richmond's self, from whose tall front are ey'd
Vales, spires, meandring streams, and Windsor's tow'ry pride.

---

[1] Old Mr. Johnston, the retired Scotch Secretary of State, who lived at Twickenham. *Carruthers.*

III.

WALLER.[1]

OF A LADY SINGING TO HER LUTE.

FAIR Charmer, cease, nor make your voice's prize,
  A heart resign'd, the conquest of your eyes:
Well might, alas! that threat'ned[2] vessel fail,
Which winds and light'ning both at once assail.
We were too blest with these enchanting lays, 5
Which must be heav'nly when an Angel plays:
But killing charms your lover's death contrive,
Lest heav'nly music should be heard alive.
Orpheus could charm the trees, but thus a tree,
Taught by your hand, can charm no less than he: 10
A poet made the silent wood pursue,
This vocal wood had drawn the Poet too.

ON A FAN OF THE AUTHOR'S DESIGN, IN WHICH WAS PAINTED THE STORY OF CEPHALUS AND PROCRIS, WITH THE MOTTO, AURA VENI.

"COME gentle Air!" th' Æolian shepherd said,
  While Procris panted in the secret shade:
"Come, gentle Air," the fairer Delia cries,
While at her feet her swain expiring lies.
Lo the glad gales o'er all her beauties stray, 5
Breathe on her lips, and in her bosom play!
In Delia's hand this toy is fatal found,
Nor could that fabled dart more surely wound:
Both gifts destructive to the givers prove;
Alike both lovers fall by those they love. 10
Yet guiltless too this bright destroyer lives,
At random wounds, nor knows the wound she gives:
She views the story with attentive eyes,
And pities Procris, while her lover dies.

IV.

COWLEY.[3]

THE GARDEN.

FAIN would my Muse the flow'ry Treasures sing,
  And humble glories of the youthful Spring;
Where opening Roses breathing sweets diffuse,

---

[1] [Edmund Waller, born in 1605, died in 1687. He has written innumerable pieces, in which the complimentary element overpowers the erotic, and which may have suggested these imitative attempts.]

[2] [I prefer placing the apostrophe as above, since Waller was in the habit of sounding the *e* in the pret. and part. ending.]

[3] [Abraham Cowley was born in 1618 and lived till 1667. His *Pindaric Odes* constitute

And soft Carnations show'r their balmy dews;
Where Lilies smile in virgin robes of white, 5
The thin Undress of superficial Light,
And vary'd Tulips show so dazzling gay,
Blushing in bright diversities of day.
Each painted flow'ret in the lake below
Surveys its beauties, whence its beauties grow; 10
And pale Narcissus on the bank, in vain
Transformed, gazes on himself again.
Here aged trees Cathedral Walks compose,
And mount the Hill in venerable rows:
There the green Infants in their beds are laid, 15
The Garden's Hope and its expected shade.
Here Orange-trees with blooms and pendants shine,
And vernal honours to their autumn join;
Exceed their promise in the ripen'd store,
Yet in the rising blossom promise more. 20
There in bright drops the crystal Fountains play,
By Laurels shielded from the piercing day;
Where Daphne, now a tree as once a maid,
Still from Apollo vindicates her shade,
Still turns her Beauties from th' invading beam, 25
Nor seeks in vain for succour to the Stream.
The stream at once preserves her virgin leaves,
At once a shelter from her boughs receives,
Where Summer's beauty midst of Winter stays,
And Winter's Coolness spite of Summer's rays. 30

WEEPING.

WHILE Celia's Tears make sorrow bright,
　　Proud Grief sits swelling in her eyes;
The Sun, next those the fairest light,
　　Thus from the Ocean first did rise:
And thus thro' Mists we see the Sun, 5
Which else we durst not gaze upon.

These silver drops, like morning dew,
　　Foretell the fervour of the day:
So from one Cloud soft show'rs we view,
　　And blasting lightnings burst away. 10
The Stars that fall from Celia's eye
Declare our Doom in drawing nigh.

his chief title to poetic fame; but his love of Botany to which *The Garden* alludes, is specially exemplified in his Latin poem, in six books, of Plants. The conceits in the second of these parodies fall short of Cowley's ordinary manner in variety and vigour, as well as in extravagance.]

The Baby in that sunny Sphere
  So like a Phaëthon appears,
That heav'n, the threaten'd World to spare,   15
  Thought fit to drown him in her tears:
Else might th' ambitious Nymph aspire,
To set, like him, Heav'n too on fire.

V.

E. OF ROCHESTER.[1]

ON SILENCE.

I.

SILENCE! coeval with Eternity;
  Thou wert, ere Nature's-self began to be,
'T was one vast Nothing, all, and all slept fast in thee.

II.

Thine was the sway, ere heav'n was form'd, or earth,
Ere fruitful Thought conceiv'd creation's birth,   5
Or midwife Word gave aid, and spoke the infant forth.

III.

Then various elements, against thee join'd,
  In one more various animal combin'd,
And fram'd the clam'rous race of busy Human-kind.

IV.

The tongue mov'd gently first, and speech was low,   10
'Till wrangling Science taught it noise and show,
And wicked Wit arose, thy most abusive foe.

V.

But rebel Wit deserts thee oft' in vain;
  Lost in the maze of words he turns again,
And seeks a surer state, and courts thy gentle reign.   15

---

[1] [John Wilmot Earl of Rochester, born at Ditchley near Woodstock in Oxfordshire, in 1647, came to court in his eighteenth year, and was soon admitted into the closest familiarity with the Merry Monarch. He behaved gallantly during a naval campaign in which he took part in 1665, and after his return to court became a kind of coarse Alcibiades of his age. His poems have little wit and much effrontery — perhaps the best specimen of either quality will be found in his impudent *Trial of the Poets for the Bays*, imitated from Boileau. The verses *on Nothing*, parodied by Pope, are said to have been due in part to George Villiers Duke of Buckingham. See Horace Walpole's account of Rochester's writings, prefixed to the narrative in which bishop Burnet unctuously recounts his conversion of so unpromising a subject on the eve of death (1680).]

VI.

Afflicted Sense thou kindly dost set free,
Oppress'd with argumental tyranny,
And routed Reason finds a safe retreat in thee.

VII.

With thee in private modest Dulness lies,
And in thy bosom lurks in Thought's disguise;　　20
Thou varnisher of Fools, and cheat of all the Wise!

VIII.

Yet thy indulgence is by both confest:
Folly by thee lies sleeping in the breast,
And 't is in thee at last that Wisdom seeks for rest.

IX.

Silence the knave's repute, the whore's good name,　　25
The only honour of the wishing dame;
Thy very want of tongue makes thee a kind of Fame.

X.

But could'st thou seize some tongues that now are free,
How Church and State should be oblig'd to thee!
At Senate, and at Bar, how welcome would'st thou be!　　30

XI.

Yet speech ev'n there, submissively withdraws,
From rights of subjects, and the poor man's cause:
Then pompous Silence reigns, and still the noisy Laws.

XII.

Past services of friends, good deeds of foes,
What Fav'rites gain, and what the Nation owes,　　35
Fly the forgetful world, and in thy arms repose.

XIII.

The country wit, religion of the town,
The courtier's learning, policy o' th' gown.
Are best by thee express'd; and shine in thee alone.

XIV.

The parson's cant, the lawyer's sophistry,　　40
Lord's quibble, critic's jest; all end in thee,
All rest in peace at last, and sleep eternally.

VI.

E. OF DORSET.[1]

ARTEMISIA.

THO' Artemisia talks, by fits,
   Of councils, classics, fathers, wits;
     Reads Malbranche, Boyle, and Locke:
Yet in some things methinks she fails,
'T were well if she would pare her nails,   5
     And wear a cleaner smock.

Haughty and huge as High-Dutch bride,
Such nastiness, and so much pride
     Are oddly join'd by fate:
On her large squab you find her spread,   10
Like a fat corpse upon a bed,
     That lies and stinks in state.

She wears no colours (sign of grace)
On any part except her face;
     All white and black beside: 15
Dauntless her look, her gesture proud,
Her voice theatrically loud,
     And masculine her stride.

So have I seen, in black and white
A prating thing, a Magpye hight,   20
     Majestically stalk;
A stately, worthless animal,
That plies the tongue, and wags the tail,
     All flutter, pride, and talk.

PHRYNE.

PHRYNE had talents for mankind,
   Open she was, and unconfin'd,
     Like some free port of trade:
Merchants unloaded here their freight,
And Agents from each foreign state,   5
     Here first their entry made.

Her learning and good breeding such,
Whether th' Italian or the Dutch,
     Spaniards or French came to her:

---

[1] [Charles Sackville Earl of Dorset was born in 1637, a lineal descendant of the illustrious author of the *Mirror for Magistrates* and *Gorboduc*. He took part in the Dutch war under the Duke of York, and before the engagement which ended in the blowing up of the Dutch admiral Opdam's vessel, composed his famous ballad *To all you Ladies now at land*. He afterwards became a favourite courtier of King William III. and died in 1706. See *Epitaph*, No. 1. *infra*.]

To all obliging she'd appear: 10
'T was *Si Signior*, 't was *Yaw Mynheer*,
    'T was *S'il vous plaist, Monsieur*.

Obscure by birth, renown'd by crimes,
Still changing names, religions, climes,
    At length she turns a Bride: 15
In di'monds, pearls, and rich brocades,
She shines the first of batter'd jades,
    And flutters in her pride.

So have I known those Insects fair
(Which curious Germans hold so rare) 20
    Still vary shapes and dyes;
Still gain new Titles with new forms;
First grubs obscene, then wriggling worms,
    Then painted butterflies.

VII.

DR. SWIFT.

THE HAPPY LIFE OF A COUNTRY PARSON.

PARSON, these things in thy possessing
Are better than the Bishop's blessing.
A Wife that makes conserves; a Steed
That carries double when there's need:
October store, and best Virginia, 5
Tithe-Pig, and mortuary Guinea:
Gazettes sent gratis down, and frank'd,
For which thy Patron's weekly thank'd:
A large Concordance, bound long since:
Sermons to Charles the First, when Prince; 10
A Chronicle of ancient standing;
A Chrysostom to smooth thy band in.
The Polyglot — three parts, — my text,
Howbeit, — likewise — now to my next.
Lo here the Septuagint, — and Paul, 15
To sum the whole, — the close of all.
  He that has these, may pass his life,
Drink with the 'Squire, and kiss his wife;
On Sundays preach, and eat his fill;
And fast on Fridays — if he will; 20
Toast Church and Queen, explain the News,
Talk with Church-Wardens about Pews,
Pray heartily for some new Gift,
And shake his head at Doctor S—t.

MORAL ESSAYS.

[It may be well to preface such introductory remarks as appear called for by the series of poems comprehended by Warburton under the general title of *Moral Essays*, by a statement of the chronological order in which they were originally given to the world. It will thus be seen at a glance, that their present arrangement was due solely to the editorial ingenuity of Pope's friend and commentator, to whose suggestions, as he informs us, the poet readily agreed.

The 5th Epistle of the *Moral Essays* (to Addison) was written in 1715, and first published, with the lines on Craggs added, in Tickell's edition of Addison's Works in 1720. The 4th Epistle of the *Moral Essays* (to the Earl of Burlington) was published in 1731, under the title *Of Taste*, subsequently altered to *Of False Taste*, and ultimately to *Of the Use of Riches*. The 3rd Epistle (*Of the Use of Riches*, to Lord Bathurst) followed in 1732. In the same year appeared the first two Epistles of the *Essay on Man*, the third succeeding in 1733. In this year also came out the Epistle *On the Knowledge and Characters of Men*, addressed to Lord Cobham, now the first of the *Moral Essays*. The 4th Epistle of the *Essay on Man* was published in 1734, when the whole *Essay on Man* was also brought out in its present form. The Epistle (now the 2nd of the *Moral Essays*) to a Lady, *On the Characters of Women*, appeared in 1735; and finally the *Universal Prayer*, which now appropriately follows the *Essay on Man*, was not published till the year 1738. Pope died before the entire series had been published in its present order in the complete edition of his works.

From Pope's own statement with regard to the design of his work, repeated in various passages of his correspondence, it is certain that what he actually wrote only formed part of a great scheme which he had long carried about either on paper, or in his mind; but which he never accomplished in its fulness. So much it is impossible to doubt, without in the least degree falling in with the belief that the system as developed at length by Warburton, who in his *Commentary*, became a kind of moral sponsor to the *Essay on Man*, was ever clearly in Pope's head. Warburton states that the *Essay* was intended to have been comprised in four books: the first (which we have in the four Epistles bearing the general title) treating of man in the abstract and considering him under all his relations; the second taking up the subject of Ep. I. and II. of the first, and treating of man in his intellectual capacity at large (of this a part might be found in Bk. IV. of the *Dunciad*); the third resuming the subject of Ep. III. of the first, and discussing Man in his social, political and religious capacity (which Pope afterwards thought might best be done in the form of an Epic poem); the fourth pursuing the subject of Ep. IV. of the first, and treating of practical morality. Of this fourth and last book, he continues, the epistles, bearing the title of *Moral Essays*, were detached portions, the two first (on the Characters of Men and Women) forming its introductory part.

In any case, therefore, and even supposing the above scheme to have been Pope's own, the four Epistles which bear the title of the *Essay on Man* claim to be regarded as complete in themselves. The system which the *Essay on Man* (to restrict the application of that title in the remainder of these remarks to those four Epistles) developes, or purports to develope, was explained at great length in Warburton's *Commentary*. Pope's own words (in a letter to Warburton of April 11, 1739) are sufficient to shew the relation between the work and the exegesis: 'You have made my system as clear as I ought to have done and could not. It is indeed the same system as mine, but illustrated with a ray of your own, as they say our natural body is still the same when glorified. I am sure I like it better than I did before, and so will every man else. I know I meant just what you explain, but I did not explain my meaning so well as you. You understand me as well as I do myself, but you express me better than I could express myself. Pray accept the sincerest acknowledgments.' It therefore becomes necessary to enquire in the first place, what is the system which the *Essay on Man* actually places before us; and secondly, from what sources the poet derived the philosophy which he has endeavoured to express. The following brief summary, founded chiefly on Aikin's Introduction, may supply an answer to the former question.

The *first* Epistle is especially occupied with Man, with respect to the place which he holds in the system of the Universe; and the principal topic is the refutation of all objections against the wisdom and benevolence of the Providence which placed man here, objections derived from the weakness and imperfection of his nature. The first principle of philosophical enquiry is reasoning from what we know to what we do not know. But if we are to inform ourselves as to man's place in the universe, we are hampered by our ignorance of the latter itself, of which we know only a small part, viz. our own earth. Observation, however, teaches that the Universe contains a scale of beings, rising in due gradation one above the other, and each endowed with the faculties necessary for its station. Those, who in their imperfect knowledge are fain to interfere with that scale, presumptuously demand to re-settle the Order of Heaven. It is this Pride which surveys the system of the Universe solely from its own point of view, assuming everything to exist for the benefit of the individual as he conceives it. Man cannot read the riddles of Providence; he must therefore accept the double truth that the Universe and all its several parts constitute a divine and perfect Order, but that this order is not visible or recognisable in its perfection to imperfect man. The *second* Epistle proceeds to lead up to the special truth illustrating the general truth enunciated by its predecessor, viz. that even in the passions and imperfections of man, the ends of Providence and its scheme of universal good are fulfilled. (It is this special part of the scheme of the Universe which man is qualified to study; God he may not scan.) In human nature, two principles contend for mastery: self-love, which stimulates, and reason, which restrains. In both, although to us the one appears evil and the other good, the scheme of Creation is working out its beneficent ends. The *third* Epistle once more resumes the general proposition of which the *second* presented us with a special application, and insists that the end of divine government is the production of general good, although by means of which we are not always able to distinguish the correlation. The main argument of this Epistle tends to illustrate this, by proving that in the divine scheme self-love and social work to the same end. The *fourth* Epistle offers, so to speak, the practical application of the fundamental idea of the entire Essay. The scheme of the Universe being perfect, is of course designed for the happiness of all; all happiness therefore is general, and all particular happiness depends on general. It is therefore necessary, in order to estimate the happiness of the individual at its true value, to estimate it, not according as it is felt by the individual, but as it finds its place in the general system. All men are equally happy who recognise the Order which assigns to them their place; and God has given to all that happiness which springs from taking the right means towards attaining to it. Thus the poem at its close recurs to its fundamental idea of the benevolent system of the Universe, in which every virtue, as well as every passion, has its object and end.

If the above fairly represent the outline of the argument of this celebrated essay, it will be sufficient to add only a very few words, in order to shew where it halts. The optimistic conclusion of the *first* Epistle cannot be said to be logically drawn from its premises. The presumptuousness of attempting to judge the system of the Universe from the peculiar point of view of Man, is incontestably demonstrated; but the perfection of the entire system is merely generalised out of a few phenomena, which man may misjudge as utterly as, according to the poet, he misjudges extraordinary occurrences which seem evils to him. And from an ethical point of view, the result, if logically followed out, is pure fatalism; and man, as completely as every other organic part of creation, reduced to a puppet. To avert this conclusion, Pope in the *Universal Prayer* addresses Providence as binding nature, i. e. the rest of nature, fast in fate, but leaving the human will free! With regard to the application of the general proposition to the special case of human nature in the *second* Epistle, it is obvious that the distinction drawn between self-love and reason, is wholly illogical; inasmuch as reason, being a power of the mind, may be employed by self-love for its own purposes, so that, as has been well pointed out, it depends upon the use of reason, not upon the direction given to self-love, what tendency the moral being of man will assume. The *third* Epistle, resuming the argument of the first, lands us in the same result. The theory that self-love and social are the same, amounts to nothing short of this: that civilisation is only the product of man's instinct of self-defence and self-advancement, that the institutions of society are merely means adopted for satisfying in the most convenient manner the necessities of the individual; and that men are therefore, like Mandeville's bees, only being guided by another power to co-operate in a system of which they unconsciously form part. This view, which since Pope's day has reappeared in many forms, may be true or false; it is certain that it is not the view which Pope designed to enforce.

The truth is, that Pope endeavoured to develope a moral system which (whether perfect or imperfect in itself) was at all events imperfectly understood by him. The *Essay on Man*, even if the anecdote be untrustworthy according to which its scheme was originally drawn up in writing by Bolingbroke, was undoubtedly due, if not to the suggestion, at all events to the influence and conversation, of that nobleman upon Pope's receptive mind. The philosophic *stamina* of the Essay, to use Johnson's expression, belonged to Bolingbroke; and it was only with regard to the execution that the latter could have expressed to Swift (letter of November 19, 1729) that the work, 'in Pope's hands, would be an original.' Bolingbroke's most recent biographer, Mr. Macknight, has therefore not said too much when he avers: 'There is no doubt whatever, but that Pope received from Bolingbroke the leading principles of his *Essay on Man*. Pope, indeed, acknowledges his obligations in the fullest sense at the beginning of the first, and the end of the fourth Book; and, notwithstanding Warburton's defence, the *Essay on Man* and the principles of Bolingbroke must be considered one and the same, though they are less openly expressed in the poem, and disguised with poetical ornament. It is impossible to find in any couplet any acknowledgment of revealed religion; but, on the contrary, all that admiration of nature, of looking upward through nature to nature's God, which was Bolingbroke's main tenet. . . . The tendency' [of the leading sentiments of the *Essay*], 'so far as they have a tendency, is undoubtedly to that blind fatalism and naturalism, which Bolingbroke called pure theism. His condemnation of metaphysics really meant everything that is called theology.'

Even, therefore, if Pope (as had been concluded from certain passages which prove him to have been acquainted with parts at least of these works) had read the *Theodicée* of Leibnitz, whose optimism is that of the first Epistle, Archbishop King's *Origin of Evil*, and other metaphysical treatises, it is in the Essay of Bolingbroke that the germ of Pope's argument is to be found. These Essays (which their author had not the courage to publish before his death) attempt to apply the inductive method to that part of philosophy which concerns the relations between God and man; and, assuming that all human knowledge is derived through the medium of the senses, to shew that it is only from a study of the works of God that a knowledge of his character is attainable by us. This is, in one word, the *natural theology* of Bolingbroke, which regards all other theology not only as superfluous, but as futile and vain.

Pope, as Bolingbroke on one occasion roundly said of him, though in a different connexion, was 'a very great wit, and a very indifferent philosopher.' The consequence is, that although as the development of a doubtful system by one who imperfectly understood it, the *Essay on Man* is without permanent value as a philosophical treatise, it has many unquestionable merits of its own. Beattie (see Forbes's *Life of B.* vol. I. p. 120) appears to characterise it very justly in describing 'its sentiments' as 'noble and affecting'; 'its images and allusions' as 'apposite, beautiful and new'; its wit as 'transcendently excellent'; but the 'scientific part' as 'very exceptionable.' If the *Essay on Man* were shivered into fragments, it would not lose its value; for it is precisely its details which constitute its moral so well as literary beauties. Nowhere has Pope so abundantly displayed his incomparable talent of elevating truisms into proverbs, in his mastery over language and poetic form. It is particularly in the fourth Epistle, where the poet undertakes to prove the incontestable truth that all men may be happy, if they will take the right road to happiness, that he is thoroughly in his element;

and demonstrates so palpable a truism by a brilliant series of arguments and illustrations which beguile the reader into a belief that he needed to be convinced.

The *Moral Essays*, which at Warburton's suggestion were pressed into the service of the general scheme, appear to explain themselves. The idea of the Master-Passion, which swallows all the rest (*Essay on Man*, II. 131), if carried to its logical consequences, results, as Johnson points out, in a kind of moral predestination; if taken *cum grano*, is sufficiently trite and commonplace. As illustrated by the first and second of these Epistles, it resembles that which suggested the title and subject of Young's *Universal Passion*. Young, however, treats the Love of Fame as the Universal Passion in either sex. The third and fourth are on a subject familiar to all satirists, ancient and modern: the fifth is only perforce included in the series, although it may, in the place which it occupies, be regarded as a kind of corollary to the fourth, as Warburton desired.]

AN ESSAY ON MAN.

TO

H. ST. JOHN LORD BOLINGBROKE.[1]

THE DESIGN.

HAVING proposed to write some pieces on Human Life and Manners, such as (to use my Lord Bacon's expression [2]) *come home to Men's Business and Bosoms*, I thought it more satisfactory to begin with considering *Man* in the abstract, his *Nature* and his

[1] [Henry St. John, afterwards Viscount Bolingbroke, was born about the year 1678. Educated at Eton and Christ Church, he commenced a life of dissipation in the metropolis towards the close of the century, manifesting however literary tastes by poetical productions, which neither Swift nor Pope could ever bring themselves to praise. In 1701 he took his seat in Parliament, as member for the family borough of Wootton Bassett, which he afterwards exchanged for the family county of Wilts. In politics, he at once became a Tory of the Tories, and a High Churchman of the High Churchmen; soon raising himself by the fire of his oratory, the bitterness of his sarcasm, and the cruel unscrupulousness of his invective, to a distinguished position. Such different judges as Pitt and Brougham agree in concluding him to have been one of the most consummate orators of any age. In 1704 he became Secretary-at-war in the so-called Compromise ministry, and followed Harley out of office in 1708. Though he had, according to his avowal, done for ever with politics and ambition, he returned into office as Secretary of State, when the famous intrigue of 1710 brought the Tories into power. It was this ministry which resolved upon the termination of the war with France; and the famous *Examiner* contained no bitterer and more effective onslaughts upon Marlborough, than those written by his former protégé St. John. He was at this time on intimate terms with Prior and Swift, with whom he founded the Brothers' Club; but at the same time this literary minister was one of the most determined enemies of the freedom of the press, and the author of the Stamp Act, from which, in the end, as might have been expected, the Tory publications suffered more than the Whig. In 1712, he was created Viscount Bolingbroke and Baron St. John; and his rivalry with Harley (now Earl of Oxford) was fast rising into open enmity. They held out together

[2] [See Bacon's *Dedication* of his Essays *to the Duke of* Buckingham.]

FRONTISPIECE TO THE ESSAY ON MAN.
(Designed by Pope to represent the vanity of human glory.)

ESSAY ON MAN.

State; since, to prove any moral duty, to enforce any moral precept, or to examine the perfection or imperfection of any creature whatsoever, it is necessary first to know what *condition* and *relation* it is placed in, and what is the proper *end* and *purpose* of its *being.*

The science of Human Nature is, like all other sciences, reduced to a *few clear points :* There are not *many certain truths* in this world. It is therefore in the Anatomy of the mind as in that of the Body; more good will accrue to mankind by attending to the large, open, and perceptible parts, than by studying too much such finer nerves and vessels, the conformations and uses of which will for ever escape our observation. The *disputes* are all upon these last, and, I will venture to say, they have less sharpened the *wits* than the *hearts* of men against each other, and have diminished the practice, more than advanced the theory of Morality. If I could flatter myself that this Essay has any merit, it is in steering betwixt the extremes of doctrines seemingly opposite, in passing over terms utterly unintelligible, and in forming a *temperate* yet not *inconsistent*, and a *short* yet not *imperfect* system of Ethics.

This I might have done in prose, but I chose verse, and even rhyme, for two reasons. The one will appear obvious; that principles, maxims, or precepts so written, both strike the reader more strongly at first, and are more easily retained by him afterwards: The other may seem odd, but is true, I found I could express them more *shortly* this way than in prose itself; and nothing is more certain, than that much of the *force* as well as *grace* of arguments or instructions, depends on their *conciseness.* I was unable to treat this part of my subject more in *detail*, without becoming dry and tedious; or more *poetically*, without sacrificing perspicuity to ornament, without wandring from the precision, or breaking the chain of reasoning: If any man can unite all these without diminution of any of them, I freely confess he will compass a thing above my capacity.

What is now published, is only to be considered as a *general Map* of MAN, marking out no more than the *greater parts*, their *extent*, their *limits*, and their *connection*, and

long enough to ensure the conclusion of the peace of Utrecht in 1713, to further which Bolingbroke had in 1712 visited Paris, when he was reported to have had an interview with the Pretender. At all events, it is certain that with the latter Bolingbroke was, from 1713, engaged in secret intrigues: and had involved himself so deeply, that after the death of Queen Anne, a prosecution threatened him, from which he saved himself by flight to Paris, in March 1715. In his absence he was attainted of treason, and his name erased from the roll of peers. Before the attainder, he had accepted at the hands of the Pretender the seals of the Secretary of State. The death of Louis XIV. in September put an end to the Pretender's chances, and the rising in Scotland with which the year closed, was undertaken against the express opinion of Bolingbroke. Scotch, Irish, Jesuit and female intrigues caused him to be rejected by the Pretender; and he remained a total exile from politics till 1725. In his retirement at La Source near Orleans, he composed his affected *Reflexions on Exile*, and his celebrated *Letter to Sir William Windham* (not published till 1753), the latter an elaborate vindication of his political conduct. He also occupied himself with the philosophical studies which resulted in the Essays published after his death by Mallet. In 1723, he obtained a pardon, but not a reversal of his attainder; in 1725, on his return to Eng-

land, he recovered his property and was thus, to use his own expression, 'two-thirds restored.' During the years from 1725 to 1735, he resided at Dawley near Uxbridge, in the immediate neighbourhood of Twickenham, the abode of his friend and admirer Pope. In the year 1727 he again commenced political writing, with the hope of overthrowing the influence of Walpole. But the death of George I. failing to overthrow that minister, Bolingbroke continued his hopeless attacks, in the vain hope of influencing the mind of the heir to the throne of George II., Frederick prince of Wales. His letters *on the Spirit of Patriotism* and *the Idea of a Patriot King* were political bids concealed under the pretence of a philosophy above parties. In 1744, after his father's death, he settled down for the remainder of his life in his ancestral home at Battersea, where he died in 1751, confident that posterity would do justice to his memory when acquainted with the fulness of his genius from his posthumous writings. Patriotism and philosophy were ideas with which he had been wont to make free throughout his life; selfishness, which is consonant with neither, was the motive of all his actions and the spirit which dictated all his works. The national instinct was sure enough to recognise his philosophy as dangerous, and his patriotism as rotten.]

leaving the particular to be more fully delineated in the charts which are to follow. Consequently, these Epistles in their progress (if I have health and leisure to make any progress) will be less dry, and more susceptible of poetical ornament. I am here only opening the *fountains*, and clearing the passage. To deduce the *rivers*, to follow them in their course, and to observe their effects, may be a task more agreeable. P.

ARGUMENT OF EPISTLE I.

Of the Nature and State of Man, with respect to the UNIVERSE.

Of Man in the abstract. I. *That we can judge only with regard to our own system, being ignorant of the relations of systems and things,* v. 17, &c. II. *That Man is not to be deemed imperfect, but a Being suited to his place and rank in the creation, agreeable to the general Order of things, and conformable to Ends and Relations to him unknown,* v. 35, &c. III. *That it is partly upon his ignorance of future events, and partly upon the hope of a future state, that all his happiness in the present depends,* v. 77, &c. IV. *The pride of aiming at more knowledge, and pretending to more Perfection, the cause of Man's error and misery. The impiety of putting himself in the place of God, and judging of the fitness or unfitness, perfection or imperfection, justice or injustice of his dispensations,* v. 109, &c. V. *The absurdity of conceiving himself the final cause of the creation, or expecting that perfection in the moral world, which is not in the natural,* v. 131, &c. VI. *The unreasonableness of his complaints against Providence, while on the one hand he demands the Perfections of the Angels, and on the other the bodily qualifications of the Brutes; though, to possess any of the sensitive faculties in a higher degree, would render him miserable,* v. 173, &c. VII. *That throughout the whole visible world, an universal order and gradation in the sensual and mental faculties is observed, which causes a subordination of creature to creature, and of all creatures to Man. The gradations of sense, instinct, thought, reflection, reason; that Reason alone countervails all the other faculties,* v. 207. VIII. *How much further this order and subordination of living creatures may extend, above and below us; were any part of which broken, not that part only, but the whole connected creation must be destroyed,* v. 233. IX. *The extravagance, madness, and pride of such a desire,* v. 250. X. *The consequence of all, the absolute submission due to Providence, both as to our present and future state,* v. 281, &c. *to the end.*

EPISTLE I.

AWAKE, my ST. JOHN! leave all meaner things
To low ambition, and the pride of Kings.
Let us (since Life can little more supply
Than just to look about us and to die)
Expatiate free o'er all this scene of Man;   5
A mighty maze! but not without a plan; [1]
A Wild, where weeds and flow'rs promiscuous shoot;
Or Garden, tempting with forbidden fruit.
Together let us beat this ample field,
Try what the open, what the covert yield;   10
The latent tracts, the giddy heights, explore
Of all who blindly creep, or sightless soar;
Eye Nature's walks, shoot Folly as it flies, [2]

---

[1] [This line originally read thus: 'A mighty maze *of walks without a plan.*' The emendation was not superfluous, since, as Dr. Johnson remarks, 'if there were no plan, it was in vain to describe or to trace the maze.']

[2] Dryden, *Absalom and Achitophel*, part II.: 'and shoots their treasons as they fly.' *Wakefield.*

And catch the Manners living as they rise;
Laugh where we must, be candid where we can;   15
But vindicate the ways of God to Man.¹
　I. Say first, of God above, or Man below,
What can we reason, but from what we know?
Of Man, what see we but his station here,
From which to reason, or to which refer?   20
Thro' worlds unnumber'd tho' the God be known,
'T is ours to trace him only in our own.
He, who thro' vast immensity can pierce,
See worlds on worlds compose one universe,
Observe how system into system runs,   25
What other planets circle other suns,
What vary'd Being peoples ev'ry star,
May tell why Heav'n has made us as we are.
But of this frame the bearings, and the ties,
The strong connexions, nice dependencies,   30
Gradations just, has thy pervading soul
Look'd thro'? or can a part contain the whole?²
　Is the great chain, that draws all to agree,
And drawn supports, upheld by God, or thee?
　II. Presumptuous Man! the reason wouldst thou find,   35
Why form'd so weak, so little, and so blind?
First, if thou canst, the harder reason guess,
Why form'd no weaker, blinder, and no less?
Ask of thy mother earth, why oaks are made
Taller or stronger than the weeds they shade?   40
Or ask of yonder argent fields above,
Why JOVE's satellites³ are less than JOVE?
　Of Systems possible, if 't is confest
That Wisdom infinite must form the best,
Where all must full or not coherent be,⁴   45
And all that rises, rise in due degree;
Then, in the scale of reas'ning life, 't is plain,
There must be, somewhere, such a rank as Man:
And all the question (wrangle e'er so long)
Is only this, if God has plac'd him wrong?   50
　Respecting Man, whatever wrong we call,
May, must be right, as relative to all.
In human works, tho' labour'd on with pain,⁵
A thousand movements scarce one purpose gain;

---

¹ Milton's phrase, judiciously altered, who says JUSTIFY *the ways of God to Man.* Milton was addressing himself to *believers*, . . . Pope . . . to *unbelievers* . . .; he, therefore, more fitly employs the word *vindicate*, which conveys the idea of a confutation attended with punishment. *Warburton.*

[There is no question of punishment, only of a decisive and final confutation.]

² [*Warton* quotes the Platonic, ' The part is created for the sake of the whole, and not the whole for the sake of the part.']

³ [*Satellites* is here a tetrasyllable, as in the original Latin.]

⁴ [i.e. where there can be no gap, unless there is to be a want of cohesion.]

⁵ Verbatim from Bolingbroke, *Fragments* 43 and 63. *Warton.*

In God's, one single can its end produce; 55
Yet serves to second too some other use.
So Man, who here seems principal alone,
Perhaps acts second to some sphere unknown,
Touches some wheel, or verges to some goal;
'T is but a part we see, and not a whole. 60
    When the proud steed shall know why Man restrains
His fiery course, or drives him o'er the plains:
When the dull Ox, why now he breaks the clod,
Is now a victim, and now Ægypt's God:[1]
Then shall Man's pride and dulness comprehend 65
His actions', passions', being's, use and end;
Why doing, suff'ring, check'd, impell'd; and why
This hour a slave, the next a deity.
    Then say not Man's imperfect, Heav'n in fault;
Say rather, Man's as perfect as he ought: 70
His knowledge measur'd to his state and place;
His time a moment, and a point his space.
If to be perfect in a certain sphere,
What matter, soon or late, or here or there?
The blest to day is as completely so, 75
As who began a thousand years ago.
    III.   Heav'n from all creatures hides the book of Fate,
All but the page prescrib'd, their present state:
From brutes what men, from men what spirits know:
Or who could suffer Being here below? 80
The lamb thy riot dooms to bleed to-day,
Had he thy Reason, would he skip and play?
Pleas'd to the last, he crops the flow'ry food,
And licks the hand just rais'd to shed his blood.
Oh blindness to the future! kindly giv'n, 85
That each may fill the circle mark'd by Heav'n:
Who sees with equal eye, as God of all,
A hero perish, or a sparrow fall,[2]
Atoms or systems into ruin hurl'd,
And now a bubble burst, and now a world. 90
    Hope humbly then; with trembling pinions soar;
Wait the great teacher Death; and God adore.
What future bliss, he gives not thee to know,
But gives that Hope to be thy blessing now.
Hope springs eternal in the human breast: 95
Man never Is, but always To be blest:[3]
The soul, uneasy and confin'd from home,
Rests and expatiates in a life to come.
    Lo, the poor Indian! whose untutor'd mind

---

[1] [Apis.]
[2] After v. 88 in the MS.
'No great, no little; 't is as much decreed
   That Virgil's Gnat should die as Cæsar
bleed.' *Warburton.* [Vergil's gnat is the *Culex*, the hero of the poem formerly ascribed to Vergil.]
[3] [Johnson's strange commentary on this passage has only a biographical value. See Boswell *ad ann.* 1775.]

ESSAY ON MAN. 197

Sees God in clouds, or hears him in the wind: 100
His soul, proud Science never taught to stray
Far as the solar walk, or milky way;
Yet simple Nature to his hope has giv'n,
Behind the cloud-topt hill, an humbler heav'n;
Some safer world in depth of woods embrac'd, 105
Some happier island in the watry waste,
Where slaves once more their native land behold,
No fiends torment, no Christians thirst for gold.[1]
To Be, contents his natural desire,
He asks no Angel's wing, no Seraph's fire; 110
But thinks, admitted to that equal sky,
His faithful dog shall bear him company.
 IV. Go, wiser thou! and, in thy scale of sense,
Weigh thy Opinion against Providence;
Call imperfection what thou fancy'st such, 115
Say, here he gives too little, there too much:
Destroy all Creatures for thy sport or gust,
Yet cry, If Man's unhappy, God's unjust;
If Man alone engross not Heav'n's high care,
Alone made perfect here, immortal there: 120
Snatch from his hand the balance and the rod,
Re-judge his justice, be the GOD of GOD.
In Pride, in reas'ning Pride, our error lies;
All quit their sphere, and rush into the skies.
Pride still is aiming at the blest abodes, 125
Men would be Angels, Angels would be Gods.
Aspiring to be Gods, if Angels fell,
Aspiring to be Angels, Men rebel:
And who but wishes to invert the laws
Of ORDER, sins against th' Eternal Cause. 130
 V. Ask for what end the heav'nly bodies shine,
Earth for whose use? Pride answers, "'T is for mine:
For me kind Nature wakes her genial Pow'r,
Suckles each herb, and spreads out ev'ry flow'r;
Annual for me, the grape, the rose renew 135
The juice nectareous, and the balmy dew;
For me, the mine a thousand treasures brings;
For me, health gushes from a thousand springs;
Seas roll to waft me, suns to light me rise;
My foot-stool earth, my canopy the skies."[2] 140
But errs not Nature from this gracious end,[3]

---

[1] After v. 108 in the first Ed.
'But does he say the maker is not good,
Till he's exalted to what state he wou'd:
Himself alone high Heav'n's peculiar care,
Alone made happy when he will, and where?'
       Warburton.
[2] Warburton compares *Ep.* III. v. 27.
[3] Bayle was the person who, by stating the difficulties concerning the Origin of Evil, in his *Dictionary*, 1695, with much acuteness and ability, revived the Manichean controversy that had been long dormant. He was soon answered by Le Clerc in his *Parrhasiana*, and by many articles in his *Bibliothèques*. But by no writer was Bayle so powerfully attacked, as by the excellent Archbishop King, in his Treatise *De*

From burning suns when livid deaths descend,
When earthquakes swallow, or when tempests sweep
Towns to one grave, whole nations to the deep?[1]
"No, ('t is reply'd) the first Almighty Cause   145
Acts not by partial, but by gen'ral laws;
Th' exceptions few; some change since all began:
And what created perfect?"—Why then Man?
If the great end be human Happiness,
Then Nature deviates; and can Man do less?[2]   150
As much that end a constant course requires
Of show'rs and sun-shine, as of Man's desires;
As much eternal springs and cloudless skies,
As Men for ever temp'rate, calm, and wise.
If plagues or earthquakes break not Heav'n's design,   155
Why then a Borgia, or a Catiline?
Who knows but he, whose hand the lightning forms,
Who heaves old Ocean, and who wings the storms;
Pours fierce Ambition in a Cæsar's mind,
Or turns young Ammon loose to scourge mankind?[3]   160
From pride, from pride, our very reas'ning springs;
Account for moral, as for nat'ral things:
Why charge we Heav'n in those, in these acquit?
In both, to reason right is to submit.

   Better for Us, perhaps, it might appear,   165
Were there all harmony, all virtue here;
That never air or ocean felt the wind;
That never passion discompos'd the mind.
But ALL subsists by elemental strife;[4]
And Passions are the elements of Life.   170
The gen'ral ORDER, since the whole began,
Is kept in Nature, and is kept in Man.
  VI. What would this Man? Now upward will he soar,

Origine Mali, 1702.... Lord Shaftesbury... in 1709, wrote the famous Dialogue, entitled *The Moralists*, as a direct confutation of the opinions of Bayle.... In 1710, Leibnitz wrote his famous *Theodicée*.... In 1720, Dr. John Clarke published his *Enquiry into the Cause and Origin of Evil*, a work full of sound reasoning; but almost every argument on this most difficult of all subjects had been urged many years before any of the above-named treatises appeared, viz. 1678, by that truly great scholar and divine, Cudworth, in that inestimable treasury of learning and philosophy, his *Intellectual System of the Universe*, to which so many authors have been indebted, without owning their obligations. *Warton.*

[1] [Such doubts arose in the mind of Goethe, *in his sixth year*, at the very time when they were being agitated by Voltaire, on the occasion of the great earthquake at Lisbon. See Lewes *Life of Goethe*, Bk. I, chap. 3.]

[2] Ver. 150. *Then Nature deviates, &c.* "While comets move in very eccentric orbs, in all manner of positions, blind fate could never make all the planets move one and the same way in orbs concentric; some inconsiderable irregularities excepted, which may have risen from mutual actions of comets and planets upon one another, and which will be apt to increase 'till this system wants a reformation." *Sir Isaac Newton's Optics, Quest. ult. Warburton.*

[3] [Alexander the Great, who was saluted as of divine origin by the priests of the Libyan Zeus Ammon; cf. *Temple of Fame*, v. 154.]

[4] *But all subsists, &c.*] See this subject extended in Ep. ii. from v. 90 to 112, 155, &c *Warburton.*

ESSAY ON MAN.

And little less than Angel,[1] would be more;
Now looking downwards, just as griev'd appears   175
To want the strength of bulls, the fur of bears.
Made for his use all creatures if he call,
Say what their use, had he the pow'rs of all?
Nature to these, without profusion, kind,
The proper organs, proper pow'rs assign'd;   180
Each seeming want compensated of course,
Here with degrees of swiftness, there of force;[2]
All in exact proportion to the state;
Nothing to add, and nothing to abate.
Each beast, each insect, happy in its own: 185
Is Heav'n unkind to Man, and Man alone?
Shall he alone, whom rational we call,
Be pleas'd with nothing, if not bless'd with all?
  The bliss of Man (could Pride that blessing find)
Is not to act or think beyond mankind;   190
No pow'rs of body or of soul to share,
But what his nature and his state can bear.
Why has not Man a microscopic eye?[3]
For this plain reason, Man is not a Fly.
Say what the use, were finer optics giv'n,   195
T' inspect a mite, not comprehend the heav'n?
Or touch, if tremblingly alive all o'er,
To smart and agonize at every pore?
Or quick effluvia darting thro' the brain,
Die of a rose in aromatic pain?   200
If nature thunder'd in his op'ning ears,
And stunn'd him with the music of the spheres,[4]
How would he wish that Heav'n had left him still
The whisp'ring Zephyr, and the purling rill?
Who finds not Providence all good and wise,   205
Alike in what it gives, and what denies?
  VII. Far as Creation's ample range extends,
The scale of sensual, mental pow'rs ascends:
Mark how it mounts, to Man's imperial race,
From the green myriads in the peopled grass: 210
What modes of sight betwixt each wide extreme,
The mole's dim curtain, and the lynx's beam:

---

[1] *And little less than Angel, &c.*] Thou hast made him a little lower than the Angels, and hast crowned him with glory and honour. Psalm viii. 9. *Warburton*.

[2] *Here with degrees of swiftness, &c.*] It is a certain axiom in the anatomy of creatures, that in proportion as they are formed for strength, their swiftness is lessened; or as they are formed for swiftness, their strength is abated. P.

[3] That particular expression, *microscopic eye*, and the whole reasoning of this astonishing piece of poetry, is taken from Locke's *Essay on the Human Understanding*, Bk. II. chap. 3, sec. 12. *Wakefield*.

[4] *stunn'd him with the music of the spheres,*] This instance is poetical and even sublime, but misplaced. He is arguing philosophically in a case that required him to employ the *real* objects of sense only: And what is worse, he speaks of this as a *real* object. *Warburton*.

Of smell, the headlong lioness between,[1]
And hound sagacious on the tainted green:
Of hearing, from the life that fills the Flood,   215
To that which warbles thro' the vernal wood:
The spider's touch, how exquisitely fine!
Feels at each thread, and lives along the line:
In the nice bee, what sense so subtly true
From pois'nous herbs extracts the healing dew?   220
How Instinct varies in the grov'ling swine,
Compar'd, half-reas'ning elephant, with thine!
'Twixt that, and Reason, what a nice barrier,[2]
For ever sep'rate, yet for ever near!
Remembrance and Reflection how ally'd;   225
What thin partitions Sense from Thought divide:[3]
And Middle natures, how they long to join,
Yet never pass th' insuperable line!
Without this just gradation, could they be
Subjected, these to those, or all to thee?   230
The pow'rs of all subdu'd by thee alone,
Is not thy Reason all these pow'rs in one?
   VIII. See, thro' this air, this ocean, and this earth,
All matter quick, and bursting into birth.
Above, how high, progressive life may go!   235
Around, how wide! how deep extend below!
Vast chain of Being! which from God began,
Natures ethereal, human, angel, man,[4]
Beast, bird, fish, insect, what no eye can see,
No glass can reach; from Infinite to thee,   240
From thee to Nothing. — On superior pow'rs[5]
Were we to press, inferior might on ours:
Or in the full creation leave a void,
Where, one step broken, the great scale's destroy'd:
From Nature's chain whatever link you strike,[6]   245
Tenth or ten thousandth, breaks the chain alike.

---

[1] *the headlong lioness*] The manner of the Lions hunting their prey in the deserts of Africa is this: At their first going out in the night-time they set up a loud roar, and then listen to the noise made by the beasts in their flight, pursuing them by the ear, and not by the nostril. It is probable the story of the jackal's hunting for the lion, was occasioned by observation of this defect of scent in that terrible animal. P.

[2] [Dissyllable.]

[3] *What thin partitions, &c.*] So *thin*, that the Atheistic philosophers, as Protagoras, held that *thought was only sense;* and from thence concluded, that *every imagination or opinion of every man was true*. *Warburton*. [Hence his formula that 'Man is the measure of all things.' The phraseology of these lines is of course taken from Dryden's Absalom and Achitophel.]

[4] Ver. 238, Ed. 1,
'Ethereal essence, spirit, substance, man.'
                 Warburton.

[5] Warton compares:
     'Has any seen
The mighty chain of beings, lessening down
From infinite Perfection, to the brink
Of dreary Nothing, desolate abyss!
From which astonished Thought recoiling turns?'
   Thomson [Seasons, Summer].
[The whole of this passage was added by Thomson in the second edition of his poem.]

[6] Almost the words of Marcus Aurelius, l. v. c. 8; as also v. 265 from the same. *Warton.*

ESSAY ON MAN.

And, if each system in gradation roll
Alike essential to th' amazing Whole,
The least confusion but in one, not all
That system only, but the Whole must fall.   250
Let Earth unbalanc'd from her orbit fly,
Planets and Suns run lawless thro' the sky;
Let ruling angels from their spheres be hurl'd,[1]
Being on Being wreck'd, and world on world;
Heav'n's whole foundations to their centre nod,   255
And Nature tremble to the throne of God.
All this dread ORDER break — for whom? for thee?
Vile worm! — Oh Madness! Pride! Impiety!
   IX. What if the foot, ordain'd the dust to tread,[2]
Or hand, to toil, aspir'd to be the head?   260
What if the head, the eye, or ear repin'd
To serve mere engines to the ruling Mind?
Just as absurd for any part to claim
To be another, in this gen'ral frame:
Just as absurd, to mourn the tasks or pains,[3]   265
The great directing MIND of ALL ordains.
   All are but parts of one stupendous whole,
Whose body Nature is, and God the soul;[4]
That, chang'd thro' all, and yet in all the same;
Great in the earth, as in th' ethereal frame;   270
Warms in the sun, refreshes in the breeze,
Glows in the stars, and blossoms in the trees,
Lives thro' all life, extends thro' all extent,
Spreads undivided, operates unspent;
Breathes in our soul, informs our mortal part,   275
As full, as perfect, in a hair as heart:
As full, as perfect, in vile Man that mourns,
As the rapt Seraph that adores and burns :[5]
To him no high, no low, no great, no small;
He fills, he bounds, connects, and equals all.   280
   X. Cease then, nor ORDER Imperfection name:
Our proper bliss depends on what we blame.[6]
Know thy own point: This kind, this due degree

---

[1] *Let ruling angels &c.*] The poet, throughout this poem, with great art uses an advantage, which his employing a *Platonic* principle for the foundation of his Essay had afforded him; and that is the expressing himself (as here) in Platonic notions; which, luckily for his purpose, are highly poetical, at the same time that they add a grace to the uniformity of his reasoning. *Warburton.*

[2] *What if the foot, &c.*] This fine illustration in defence of the *System of Nature*, is taken from St. *Paul*, who employed it to defend the *System of Grace* [1 Cor. xii. 15-21].

[3] *Just as absurd, &c.*] See the Prosecution and application of this in Ep. iv. P.

[4] [Warburton has a long and ingenious note on this passage, intended to vindicate Pope from the charge of having given vent to a pantheistical and 'Spinozist' conception, by adducing other passages from the Essay in which a personal God is acknowledged.]

[5] *As the rapt Seraph, &c.*] Alluding to the name *Seraphim,* signifying *burners.* *Warburton.*

[6] After v. 282, in the MS.
'Reason, to think of God when she pretends,
Begins a Censor, an Adorer ends.' *Warburton.*

Of blindness, weakness, Heav'n bestows on thee.
Submit.— In this, or any other sphere, 285
Secure to be as blest as thou canst bear:
Safe in the hand of one disposing Pow'r,
Or in the natal, or the mortal hour.[1]
All Nature is but Art, unknown to thee;
All Chance, Direction, which thou canst not see; 290
All Discord, Harmony not understood;
All partial Evil, universal Good:
And, spite of Pride, in erring Reason's spite,
One truth is clear, WHATEVER IS, IS RIGHT.[2]

ARGUMENT OF EPISTLE II.

Of the Nature and State of Man with respect to Himself, as an Individual.

I. THE *business of Man not to pry into* God, *but to study* himself. *His* Middle Nature; *his Powers and Frailties*, v. 1 to 19. *The Limits of his* Capacity, v. 19, &c. II. *The two Principles of Man*, Self-love *and* Reason, *both necessary*, v. 53, &c. Self-love *the stronger, and why*, v. 67, &c. *Their end the same*, v. 81, &c. III. *The* PASSIONS, *and their use*, v. 93 to 130. *The* predominant Passion, *and its force*, v. 132 to 160. *Its Necessity, in directing Men to different purposes*, v. 165, &c. *Its providential Use, in fixing our Principle, and ascertaining our Virtue*, v. 177. IV. Virtue *and* Vice *joined in our* mixed Nature; *the limits near, yet the things* separate *and* evident: *What is the Office of* Reason, v. 202 to 216. V. *How odious* Vice *in itself, and how we deceive ourselves into it*, v. 217. VI. *That, however, the* Ends *of* Providence *and* general Good *are answered in our Passions and Imperfections*, v. 238, &c. *How usefully these are distributed to all* Orders of Men, v. 241. *How useful they are to* Society, v. 251. *And to the* Individuals, v. 263. *In every* state, *and every* age *of life*, v. 273, &c.

EPISTLE II.

I. KNOW then thyself, presume not God to scan;
The proper study of Mankind is Man.[3]
Plac'd on this isthmus of a middle state,
A Being darkly wise, and rudely great:
With too much knowledge for the Sceptic side,[4] 5
With too much weakness for the Stoic's pride,

---

[1] [What Bolingbroke says in the fine passage quoted by Warton (with the pious wish 'Si sic omnia dixisset') was more briefly, but as finely expressed by the child Goethe (v. *ante*): 'God knows very well that an immortal soul can receive no injury from a mortal accident.']

[2] [Warburton thus explains the conclusion deduced from the argument of the Epistle: *That Nature being neither a blind chain of Causes and Effects, nor yet the fortuitous result of wandering atoms, but the wonderful Art and Direction of an all-wise, all-good, and free Being;* WHATEVER IS, IS RIGHT, *with regard to the Disposition of God, and its ultimate Tendency;* which once granted, all complaints against Providence are at an end.]

[3] Ver. 2, Ed. 1.
'The only science of Mankind is Man.'
Warburton.

[4] [*Sceptics* was one of the names assumed by the followers of Pyrrhon, who 'always considered and never discovered;' whose philosophy therefore was negative; while the *Stoics* proclaimed the doctrine that the true end of life and the real happiness of man consist in the performance of duty and the pursuit of virtue.]

ESSAY ON MAN.

He hangs between; in doubt to act, or rest;
In doubt to deem himself a God, or Beast;
In doubt his Mind or Body to prefer;
Born but to die, and reas'ning but to err;   10
Alike in ignorance, his reason such,
Whether he thinks too little, or too much:
Chaos of Thought and Passion, all confus'd;
Still by himself abus'd, or disabus'd;
Created half to rise, and half to fall;   15
Great lord of all things, yet a prey to all;
Sole judge of Truth, in endless Error hurl'd:[1]
The glory, jest, and riddle of the world!
  Go, wond'rous creature! mount where Science guides,
Go, measure earth, weigh air, and state the tides;   20
Instruct the planets in what orbs to run,
Correct old Time, and regulate the Sun;[2]
Go, soar with Plato to th' empyreal sphere,
To the first good, first perfect, and first fair;
Or tread the mazy round his follow'rs trod,   25
And quitting sense call imitating God;
As Eastern priests in giddy circles run,[3]
And turn their heads to imitate the Sun.
Go, teach Eternal Wisdom how to rule —
Then drop into thyself, and be a fool![4]   30
  Superior beings, when of late they saw
A mortal Man unfold all Nature's law,
Admir'd such wisdom in an earthly shape,
And shew'd a NEWTON as we shew an Ape.[5]
  Could he, whose rules the rapid Comet bind,   35
Describe or fix one movement of his Mind?
Who saw its fires here rise, and there descend,
Explain his own beginning, or his end?
Alas what wonder! Man's superior part
Uncheck'd may rise, and climb from art to art;   40

---

[1] *in endless Error hurl'd.*] To *hurl* signifies, not simply to *cast*, but to *cast backward and forward*, and is taken from the rural game called *hurling*. Warburton. [Scoticè: curling.]

[2] *Correct old Time,*] This alludes to Sir Isaac Newton's Grecian Chronology, which he reformed on those two sublime conceptions, the difference between the reigns of kings, and the generations of men; and the position of the colures of the equinoxes and solstices at the time of the Argonautic expedition. *Warburton.*

[3] [*Eastern priests,* as e.g. the priests of the Sun-God Baal.]

[4] *Go, teach Eternal Wisdom &c.*] These two lines are a conclusion from all that had been said from v. 18. *Warburton.*

[5] *as we shew an Ape.*] Evidently borrowed from the following passage in the *Zodiac* of Palingenius, and not, as hath been suggested by Dr. Hurd, from Plato. Pope was a reader and publisher [he published a selection in 1740, founded on an earlier anthology of 1684] of the modern poets of Italy who wrote in Latin. The words are —
'Simia Cœlicolum risusque jocusque Deorum est
Tunc Homo, cum temere ingenio confidit, et audet
Abdita Naturæ scrutari arcanaque Divum.'
Warton. This is however an entirely different sense from that in which Pope has used the similitude: in the one case the superior beings *admire the wisdom,* in the other, they laugh at the folly. *Roscoe.*

ESSAY ON MAN.

But when his own great work is but begun,
What Reason weaves, by Passion is undone.
    Trace Science then, with Modesty thy guide;
First strip off all her equipage of Pride;
Deduct what is but Vanity, or Dress,   45
Or Learning's Luxury, or Idleness;[1]
Or tricks to shew the stretch of human brain,[2]
Mere curious pleasure, or ingenious pain;
Expunge the whole, or lop th' excrescent parts
Of all our Vices have created Arts;[3]   50
Then see how little the remaining sum,
Which serv'd the past, and must the times to come!
    II. Two Principles in human nature reign;
Self-love, to urge, and Reason, to restrain;
Nor this a good, nor that a bad we call,   55
Each works its end, to move or govern all:
And to their proper operation still,
Ascribe all Good; to their improper, Ill.
    Self-love, the spring of motion, acts[4] the soul;
Reason's comparing balance rules the whole.   60
Man, but for that, no action could attend,
And but for this, were active to no end:
Fix'd like a plant on his peculiar spot,
To draw nutrition, propagate, and rot;
Or, meteor-like, flame lawless thro' the void,   65
Destroying others, by himself destroy'd.
    Most strength the moving principle requires;
Active its task, it prompts, impels, inspires.
Sedate and quiet the comparing lies,
Form'd but to check, delib'rate, and advise.   70
Self-love still stronger, as its objects nigh;
Reason 's at distance, and in prospect lie:[5]
That sees immediate good by present sense;
Reason, the future and the consequence.[6]
Thicker than arguments, temptations throng,   75
At best more watchful this, but that more strong.
The action of the stronger to suspend,
Reason still use, to Reason still attend.
Attention, habit and experience gains;

---

[1] [i.e. what is done by Learning after a fashion intended to make a show or to save trouble. Learning's Luxury and Idleness both resort to that profuse abuse of words which Mephistopheles recommends to the Scholar in *Faust*.]

[2] ['*Tours de force*.']

[3] [i.e. expunge all this (the equipage of Pride), or lop the excrescent parts *which* have created arts (τέχναι) out of all our vices. The reference is obviously to such arts or sciences as gastronomy, which seek to gratify the carnal demands of human nature.]

[4] *acts* for *actuates*. Bowles. [The verb is used in the same sense by South.]

[5] [A false concord; unless, which seems improbable, Pope originally wrote *Reasons* plur.]

[6] *Reason, the future and the consequence.*] *i.e.* By *experience* Reason collects the *future;* and by *argumentation*, the *consequence*. Warburton. From Bacon: 'The *Affections* carry even an appetite to good, as *Reason* doth. The difference is, that the Affection beholdeth *merely* the *present;* Reason beholdeth the *future* and *sum* of time.' Bowles.

ESSAY ON MAN. 205

Each strengthens Reason, and Self-love restrains. 80
Let subtle schoolmen teach these friends to fight,[1]
More studious to divide than to unite;
And Grace and Virtue, Sense and Reason split,
With all the rash dexterity of wit.
Wits, just like Fools, at war about a name, 85
Have full as oft no meaning, or the same.[2]
Self-love and Reason to one end aspire,
Pain their aversion, Pleasure their desire;
But greedy That, its object would devour,
This taste the honey, and not wound the flow'r; 90
Pleasure, or wrong or rightly understood,
Our greatest evil, or our greatest good.
  III. Modes of Self-love the Passions we may call;
'T is real good, or seeming, moves them all:
But since not ev'ry good we can divide, 95
And Reason bids us for our own provide;
Passions, tho' selfish, if their means be fair,
List[3] under Reason, and deserve her care;
Those, that imparted, court a nobler aim,
Exalt their kind, and take some Virtue's name. 100
  In lazy Apathy let Stoics boast
Their Virtue fix'd; 't is fix'd as in a frost;[4]
Contracted all, retiring to the breast;
But strength of mind is Exercise, not Rest:
The rising tempest puts in act the soul, 105
Parts it may ravage, but preserves the whole.
On life's vast ocean diversely we sail,
Reason the card,[5] but Passion is the gale;[6]

---

[1] *Let subtle schoolmen &c.*] From this description of Self-love and Reason it follows, as the poet observes (from v. 80 to 93), that both conspire to one end, namely, human happiness, though they be not equally expert in the choice of the means; the difference being this, that the first hastily seizes every thing which hath the appearance of good; the other weighs and examines whether it *be indeed* what it appears.

This shews, as he next observes, the folly of the schoolmen, who consider them as two opposite principles, the one good and the other evil. The observation is seasonable and judicious; for this dangerous school-opinion gives great support to the Manichean or Zoroastrian error, the confutation of which was one of the author's chief ends in writing. For if there be *two principles* in Man, a *good* and *bad*, it is natural to think him the joint product of the two Manichean deities (the first of which contributed to his *Reason*, the other to his *Passions*) rather than the creature of one Individual Cause. This was Plutarch's notion, and, as we may see in him, of the more ancient Manicheans. *Warburton.*

[2] After v. 86, in the MS.
'Of good and evil Gods what frighted Fools,
Of good and evil Reason puzzled Schools,
Deceiv'd, deceiving, taught —.' *Warburton.*

[3] [*List*, i.e. enlist or range themselves.]

[4] [Warton, in an admirable note, points out the injustice of 'the universal censure that has been passed upon the Stoics, as if they constantly and strenuously inculcated a total insensibility with respect to passion, to which these lines of Pope allude; when it is certain the Stoics meant only a freedom from strong perturbation, from irrational and excessive agitations of the soul; and no more.]

[5] [*The card*, i.e. the compass.] This passage is exactly copied from Fontenelle, tom. 1. p. 109. *Warton.*

[6] After ver. 108, in the MS.
'A tedious Voyage! where how useless lies
The compass, if no pow'rful gusts arise?'
Warburton.

Nor God alone in the still calm we find,
He mounts the storm, and walks upon the wind.   110
    Passions, like Elements, tho' born to fight,
Yet, mix'd and soften'd, in his work unite:[1]
These 't is enough to temper and employ;
But what composes Man, can Man destroy?
Suffice that Reason keep to Nature's road,   115
Subject, compound them, follow her and God.
Love, Hope, and Joy, fair Pleasure's smiling train,
Hate, Fear, and Grief, the family of Pain,
These mix'd with art, and to due bounds confin'd,
Make and maintain the balance of the mind: 120
The lights and shades, whose well accorded strife
Gives all the strength and colour of our life.
    Pleasures are ever in our hands or eyes;
And when in act they cease, in prospect rise:
Present to grasp, and future still to find,   125
The whole employ of body and of mind.
All spread their charms, but charm not all alike;
On diff'rent senses diff'rent objects strike;
Hence diff'rent Passions more or less inflame,
As strong or weak, the organs of the frame;   130
And hence one MASTER PASSION in the breast,
Like Aaron's serpent, swallows up the rest.[2]
    As Man, perhaps, the moment of his breath,[3]
Receives the lurking principle of death;
The young disease, that must subdue at length,   135
Grows with his growth, and strengthens with his strength:
So, cast and mingled with his very frame,
The Mind's disease, its RULING PASSION came;
Each vital humour which should feed the whole,
Soon flows to this, in body and in soul: 140
Whatever warms the heart, or fills the head,
As the mind opens, and its functions spread,
Imagination plies her dang'rous art,
And pours it all upon the peccant part.
    Nature its mother, Habit is its nurse;   145
Wit, Spirit, Faculties, but make it worse;
Reason itself but gives it edge and pow'r;[4]
As Heav'n's blest beam turns vinegar more sour.

---

[1] After ver. 112, in the MS.
'The soft reward the virtuous, or invite;
The fierce, the vicious punish or affright.'
                    Warburton.

[2] [The theory that every man has one *master passion* which at length absorbs all the rest,] the poet illustrates at large in his epistle to Lord Cobham. Here (from v. 126 to 149) he gives us the cause of it. *Warburton.*

[3] *As Man, perhaps, &c.*] Antipater Sidonius Poëta omnibus annis uno die natali tantum corripiebatur febre, et eo consumptus est satis longa senecta. Plin. l. vii. N. H. This *Antipater* was in the times of Crassus, and is celebrated for the quickness of his Parts by Cicero [*de Orat.* III. 50]. *Warburton.*

[4] Warburton quotes in illustration the character of Cotta in the Epistle (III.) *of the use of Riches* (vv. 177 ff.).

We, wretched subjects, tho' to lawful sway,
In this weak queen some fav'rite still obey: 150
Ah! if she lend not arms, as well as rules,
What can she more than tell us we are fools?
Teach us to mourn our Nature, not to mend,
A sharp accuser, but a helpless friend!
Or from a judge turn pleader, to persuade 155
The choice we make, or justify it made;
Proud of an easy conquest all along,
She but removes weak passions for the strong:
So, when small humours gather to a gout,
The doctor fancies he has driv'n them out. 160
    Yes, Nature's road must ever be preferr'd;
Reason is here no guide, but still a guard:
'T is hers to rectify, not overthrow,
And treat this passion more as friend than foe:
A mightier Pow'r the strong direction sends, 165
And sev'ral Men impels to sev'ral ends:
Like varying winds, by other passions tost,
This drives them constant to a certain coast.
Let pow'r or knowledge, gold or glory, please,
Or (oft more strong than all) the love of ease; 170
Thro' life 't is follow'd, ev'n at life's expense;
The merchant's toil, the sage's indolence,
The monk's humility, the hero's pride,
All, all alike, find Reason on their side.
    Th' Eternal Art educing good from ill, 175
Grafts on this Passion our best principle:
'T is thus the Mercury of Man is fix'd,
Strong grows the Virtue with his nature mix'd;
The dross cements what else were too refin'd,
And in one int'rest body acts with mind. 180
    As fruits, ungrateful to the planter's care,
On savage stocks inserted, learn to bear;
The surest Virtues thus from Passions shoot,
Wild Nature's vigour working at the root.
What crops of wit and honesty appear 185
From spleen, from obstinacy, hate, or fear!
See anger, zeal and fortitude supply;
Ev'n av'rice, prudence; sloth, philosophy;
Lust, thro' some certain strainers well refin'd,
Is gentle love, and charms all womankind; 190
Envy, to which th' ignoble mind 's a slave,
Is emulation in the learn'd or brave;
Nor Virtue, male or female, can we name,
But what will grow on Pride, or grow on Shame.[1]

---

[1] After v. 194, in the MS.
'How oft, with Passion, Virtue points her Charms!
Then shines the Hero, then the Patriot warms.
Peleus' great Son, or Brutus, who had known,
Had Lucrece been a Whore, or Helen none?
But Virtues opposite to make agree,
That, Reason! is thy task; and worthy Thee,

Thus Nature gives us (let it check our pride) 195
The virtue nearest to our vice ally'd:
Reason the bias turns to good from ill,
And Nero reigns a Titus, if he will.
The fiery soul abhorr'd in Catiline,
In Decius charms, in Curtius is divine:[1] 200
The same ambition can destroy or save,
And makes a patriot as it makes a knave.
  This light and darkness in our chaos join'd,
What shall divide? The God within the mind:
  Extremes in Nature equal ends produce, 205
In Man they join to some mysterious use;
Tho' each by turns the other's bound invade,
As, in some well-wrought picture, light and shade,
And oft so mix, the diff'rence is too nice
Where ends the Virtue, or begins the Vice. 210
  Fools! who from hence into the notion fall,
That Vice or Virtue there is none at all.
If white and black blend, soften, and unite
A thousand ways, is there no black or white?
Ask your own heart, and nothing is so plain; 215
'T is to mistake them costs the time and pain.
  Vice is a monster of so frightful mien,
As, to be hated, needs but to be seen;
Yet seen too oft, familiar with her face,
We first endure, then pity, then embrace. 220
But where th' Extreme of Vice, was ne'er agreed:
Ask where 's the North? at York, 't is on the Tweed;
In Scotland, at the Orcades; and there,
At Greenland, Zembla, or the Lord knows where.
No creature owns it in the first degree, 225
But thinks his neighbour further gone than he;[2]
Ev'n those who dwell beneath its very zone,
Or never feel the rage, or never own;
What happier natures shrink at with affright,
The hard inhabitant contends is right. 230
  Virtuous and vicious ev'ry Man must be,
Few in th' extreme, but all in the degree;
The rogue and fool by fits is fair and wise;

Hard task, cries Bibulus, and reason weak.
— Make it a point, dear Marquess! or a pique.
Once, for a whim, persuade yourself to pay
A debt to reason, like a debt at play.
For right or wrong have mortals suffer'd more
B— for his Prince, or * * for his Whore?
Whose self-denials nature most controul?
His, who would save a Sixpence or his Soul?
Web for his health, a Chartreux for his Sin,
Contend they not which soonest shall grow thin.
What, we resolve, we can: but here 's the fault,
We ne'er resolve to do the thing we ought.'

[1] [The famous heroes of the battle of Vesuvius, and the Curtian Gulf.]
[2] After v. 226, in the MS.
'The Col'nel swears the Agent is a dog,
The Scriv'ner vows th' Attorney is a rogue.
Against the Thief th' Attorney loud inveighs,
For whose ten pound the County twenty pays.
The Thief damns Judges, and the Knaves of State;
And dying, mourns small Villains hang'd by great.'

And ev'n the best, by fits, what they despise.
'T is but by parts we follow good or ill; 235
For, Vice or Virtue, Self directs it still;
Each individual seeks a sev'ral goal;
But HEAV'N'S great view is One, and that the Whole.
That counter-works each folly and caprice;
That disappoints th' effect of ev'ry vice; 240
That, happy frailties to all ranks apply'd,
Shame to the virgin, to the matron pride,
Fear to the statesman, rashness to the chief,
To kings presumption, and to crowds belief:
That, Virtue's ends from Vanity can raise, 245
Which seeks no int'rest, no reward but praise;
And build on wants, and on defects of mind,
The joy, the peace, the glory of Mankind.
   Heav'n forming each on other to depend,
A master, or a servant, or a friend, 250
Bids each on other for assistance call,
Till one Man's weakness grows the strength of all.
Wants, frailties, passions, closer still ally
The common int'rest, or endear the tie.
To these we owe true friendship, love sincere, 255
Each home-felt joy that life inherits here;
Yet from the same we learn, in its decline,
Those joys, those loves, those int'rests to resign;
Taught half by Reason, half by mere decay,
To welcome death, and calmly pass away. 260
   Whate'er the Passion, knowledge, fame, or pelf,
Not one will change his neighbour with himself.
The learn'd is happy nature to explore,
The fool is happy that he knows no more;
The rich is happy in the plenty giv'n, 265
The poor contents him with the care of Heav'n.
See the blind beggar dance, the cripple sing,
The sot a hero, lunatic a king;
The starving chemist in his golden views
Supremely blest, the poet in his Muse.[1] 270
   See some strange comfort ev'ry state attend,[2]
And Pride bestow'd on all, a common friend;
See some fit Passion ev'ry age supply,

---

[1] *the poet in his Muse.*] The author having said, that no one would change his profession or views for those of another, intended to carry his observation still further, and shew that Men were unwilling to exchange their own acquirements even for those of the same kind, confessedly larger, and infinitely more eminent, in another. To this end he wrote,

'What partly pleases, totally will shock:
  I question much, if *Toland* would be *Locke:*'

but wanting another proper instance of this truth when he published his last Edition of the Essay, he reserved the lines above for some following one. *Warburton.*

[2] [Warton quotes Gray's beautiful lines:

'Still where rosy Pleasure leads
  See a kindred grief pursue;
  Behind the steps that Misery treads
  Approaching Comfort view, &c.;

and the same thought is felicitously expanded in Akenside's *Pleasures of the Imagination* (Bk. II. 'Ask the faithful youth,' &c.).]

Hope travels thro', nor quits us when we die.
  Behold the child, by Nature's kindly law,   275
Pleas'd with a rattle, tickled with a straw:
Some livelier play-thing gives his youth delight,
A little louder, but as empty quite:
Scarfs, garters, gold, amuse his riper stage,
And beads and pray'r-books are the toys of age: 280
Pleas'd with this bauble still, as that before;
'Till tir'd he sleeps, and Life's poor play is o'er.
  Mean-while Opinion gilds with varying rays
Those painted clouds that beautify our days;
Each want of happiness by hope supply'd,   285
And each vacuity of sense by Pride:
These build as fast as knowledge can destroy;
In Folly's cup still laughs the bubble, joy;
One prospect lost, another still we gain;
And not a vanity is giv'n in vain;   290
Ev'n mean Self-love becomes, by force divine,
The scale to measure others' wants by thine.
See! and confess, one comfort still must rise,
'T is this, Tho' Man's a fool, yet God is WISE.

ARGUMENT OF EPISTLE III.

Of the Nature and State of Man with respect to Society.

I. *The whole Universe one system of Society,* v. 7, &c. *Nothing made wholly for itself, nor yet wholly for another,* v. 27. *The happiness of Animals mutual,* v. 49. II. Reason *or* Instinct *operate alike to the good of each Individual,* v. 79. Reason *or* Instinct *operate also to Society, in all animals,* v. 109. III. *How far Society carried by Instinct,* v. 115. *How much farther by Reason,* v. 128. IV. *Of that which is called the* State of Nature, v. 144. *Reason instructed by Instinct in the invention of* Arts, v. 166, *and in the Forms of* Society, v. 176. V. *Origin of Political Societies,* v. 196. *Origin of Monarchy,* v. 207. *Patriarchal government,* v. 212. VI. *Origin of true Religion and Government, from the same principle, of Love,* v. 231, &c. *Origin of Superstition and Tyranny, from the same principle, of Fear,* v. 237, &c. *The Influence of Self-love operating to the* social *and* public *Good,* v. 266. *Restoration of true Religion and Government on their first principle,* v. 285. *Mixt Government,* v. 288. *Various Forms of each, and the true end of all,* v. 300, &c.

EPISTLE III.

I.   HERE then we rest: "The Universal Cause[1]
      Acts to one end, but acts by various laws."
In all the madness of superfluous health,
The trim of pride, the impudence of wealth,
Let this great truth be present night and day;   5
But most be present, if we preach or pray.
  Look round our World; behold the chain of Love

---

[1] In several Edit. 4to. — 'Learn, Dulness, learn! "The Universal Cause,"' &c. *Warburton.*

Combining all below and all above.
See plastic Nature working to this end,
The single atoms each to other tend, 10
Attract, attracted to, the next in place
Form'd and impell'd its neighbour to embrace.
See Matter next, with various life endu'd,
Press to one centre still, the gen'ral Good.
See dying vegetables life sustain, 15
See life dissolving vegetate again:
All forms that perish other forms supply,
(By turns we catch the vital breath, and die,)
Like bubbles on the sea of Matter born,
They rise, they break, and to that sea return. 20
Nothing is foreign: Parts relate to whole;
One all-extending, all-preserving Soul [1]
Connects each being, greatest with the least; [2]
Made Beast in aid of Man, and Man of Beast;
All serv'd, all serving: nothing stands alone; 25
The chain holds on, and where it ends, unknown.
　　Has God, thou fool! work'd solely for thy good,
Thy joy, thy pastime, thy attire, thy food?
Who for thy table feeds the wanton fawn,
For him as kindly spread the flow'ry lawn: 30
Is it for thee the lark ascends and sings?
Joy tunes his voice, joy elevates his wings.
Is it for thee the linnet pours his throat?
Loves of his own and raptures swell the note.
The bounding steed you pompously bestride, 35
Shares with his lord the pleasure and the pride.
Is thine alone the seed that strews the plain?
The birds of heav'n shall vindicate their grain.
Thine the full harvest of the golden year?
Part pays, and justly, the deserving steer: 40
The hog, that ploughs not nor obeys thy call,
Lives on the labours of this lord of all.
　　Know, Nature's children all divide her care;
The fur that warms a monarch, warm'd a bear.
While Man exclaims, " See all things for my use !" 45
" See man for mine !" replies a pamper'd goose: [3]

---

[1] *One all-extending, all-preserving Soul*] Which, in the language of Sir Isaac Newton, is *Deus omnipræsens est, non per virtutem solam, sed etiam per substantiam: nam virtus sine substantia subsistere non potest.* Newt. Princ. Schol. gan. sub fin. *Warburton.*

[2] *greatest with the least;*] As acting more strongly and immediately in beasts, whose instinct is plainly an external reason; which made an old school-man say, with great elegance, *Deus est anima brutorum. Warburton.*
[Bowles cites Vergil's

'Spiritus intus alit, totamque infusa per artus
Mens agitat molem et magno se corpore miscet.'
Æn. VI. 726-7.]

[3] Taken from Peter Charron [the author of the book *de la Sagesse*, into which he admitted, with modifications, many thoughts from his friend Montaigne's famous *Essais*]. *Warton.*
After v. 46, in the former Editions,
'What care to tend, to lodge, to cram, to treat
　him!
All this he knew; but not that 't was to eat
　him.

And just as short of reason he must fall,
Who thinks all made for one, not one for all.
　Grant that the pow'rful still the weak controul;
Be Man the Wit and Tyrant of the whole:[1]　　　　50
Nature that Tyrant checks; he only knows,
And helps, another creature's wants and woes.
Say, will the falcon, stooping from above,
Smit with her varying plumage, spare the dove?
Admires the jay the insect's gilded wings?　　　　55
Or hears the hawk when Philomela sings?
Man cares for all: to birds he gives his woods,
To beasts his pastures, and to fish his floods;
For some his Int'rest prompts him to provide,
For more his pleasure, yet for more his pride:　　60
All feed on one vain Patron, and enjoy
Th' extensive blessing of his luxury.
That very life his learned hunger craves,
He saves from famine, from the savage saves;
Nay, feasts the animal he dooms his feast,　　　65
And, 'till he ends the being, makes it blest;
Which sees no more the stroke, or feels the pain,
Than favour'd Man by touch ethereal slain.[2]
The creature had his feast of life before;
Thou too must perish, when thy feast is o'er!　　70
　To each unthinking being Heav'n, a friend,
Gives not the useless knowledge of its end:[3]
To Man imparts it; but with such a view
As, while he dreads it, makes him hope it too:
The hour conceal'd, and so remote the fear,　　75
Death still draws nearer, never seeming near.
Great standing miracle! that Heav'n assign'd
Its only thinking thing this turn of mind.
　II. Whether with Reason, or with Instinct blest,
Know, all enjoy that pow'r which suits them best;　80
To bliss alike by that direction tend,
And find the means proportion'd to their end.
Say, where full Instinct is th' unerring guide,
What Pope or Council can they need beside?
Reason, however able, cool at best,　　　　　　85
Cares not for service, or but serves when prest,
Stays 'till we call, and then not often near;
But honest Instinct comes a volunteer,

As far as Goose could judge, he reason'd right;
But as to Man, mistook the matter quite.'
　　　　　　　　　　　　Warburton.

[1] [i.e. grant that man's intellect rules all creation.]

[2] *Than favour'd Man &c.*] Several of the ancients, and many of the Orientals since, esteemed those who were struck by lightning as sacred persons, and the particular favourites of Heaven. P. The expression, 'by touch ethereal slain,' is from Milton. *Warton.* [*Samson Agonistes*, 549.]

[3] [This passage finely turns the common contrast between man and beast, which is drawn in Charron, *de la Sagesse*, Liv. I. chap. 8.]

Sure never to o'er-shoot, but just to hit;
While still too wide or short is human Wit; 90
Sure by quick Nature happiness to gain,
Which heavier Reason labours at in vain,
This too serves always, Reason never long;
One must go right, the other may go wrong.
See then the acting and comparing pow'rs 95
One in their nature, which are two in ours;
And Reason raise o'er Instinct as you can,
In this 't is God directs, in that 't is Man.
  Who taught the nations of the field and flood
To shun their poison, and to choose their food? 100
Prescient, the tides or tempests to withstand,
Build on the wave, or arch beneath the sand?
Who made the spider parallels design,
Sure as Demoivre,[1] without rule or line?
Who did the stork, Columbus-like, explore 105
Heav'ns not his own, and worlds unknown before?
Who calls the council, states the certain day,
Who forms the phalanx, and who points the way?
  III. God in the nature of each being founds
Its proper bliss, and sets its proper bounds: 110
But as he fram'd a Whole, the Whole to bless,
On mutual Wants built mutual Happiness:
So from the first, eternal ORDER ran,
And creature link'd to creature, man to man.
Whate'er of life all-quick'ning æther keeps, 115
Or breathes thro' air, or shoots beneath the deeps,
Or pours profuse on earth, one nature feeds
The vital flame, and swells the genial seeds.
Not Man alone, but all that roam the wood,
Or wing the sky, or roll along the flood, 120
Each loves itself, but not itself alone,
Each sex desires alike, 'till two are one.
Nor ends the pleasure with the fierce embrace;
They love themselves, a third time, in their race.
Thus beast and bird their common charge attend, 125
The mothers nurse it, and the sires defend;
The young dismiss'd to wander earth or air,
There stops the Instinct, and there ends the care;
The link dissolves, each seeks a fresh embrace,
Another love succeeds, another race. 130
A longer care Man's helpless kind demands;
That longer care contracts more lasting bands:
Reflection, Reason, still the ties improve,
At once extend the int'rest, and the love;
With choice we fix, with sympathy we burn; 135

---

[1] [*Demoivre*. This famous mathematician was born at Virty in Champagne in 1667. The allusion in the text is to his fame in trigonometry.]

Each Virtue in each Passion takes its turn;
And still new needs, new helps, new habits rise,
That graft benevolence on charities.
Still as one brood, and as another rose,
These nat'ral love maintain'd, habitual those: 140
The last, scarce ripen'd into perfect Man,
Saw helpless him from whom their life began:
Mem'ry and fore-cast just returns engage,
That pointed back to youth, this on to age;
While pleasure, gratitude, and hope, combin'd,   145
Still spread the int'rest, and preserv'd the kind.
   IV. Nor think, in NATURE'S STATE they blindly trod;
The state of Nature was the reign of God:
Self-love and Social at her birth began,
Union the bond of all things, and of Man.   150
Pride then was not; nor Arts, that Pride to aid;
Man walk'd with beast, joint tenant of the shade;[1]
The same his table, and the same his bed;
No murder cloth'd him, and no murder fed.
In the same temple, the resounding wood,   155
All vocal beings hymn'd their equal God:
The shrine with gore unstain'd, with gold undrest,
Unbrib'd, unbloody, stood the blameless priest:
Heav'n's attribute was Universal Care,
And Man's prerogative to rule, but spare.   160
Ah! how unlike the man of times to come!
Of half that live the butcher and the tomb;[2]
Who, foe to Nature, hears the gen'ral groan,
Murders their species, and betrays his own.
But just disease to luxury succeeds,   165
And ev'ry death its own avenger breeds;
The Fury-passions from that blood began,
And turn'd on Man a fiercer savage, Man.
   See him from Nature rising slow to Art!
To copy Instinct then was Reason's part;   170
Thus then to Man the voice of Nature spake —
"Go, from the Creatures thy instructions take:
Learn from the birds[3] what food the thickets yield;
Learn from the beasts the physic of the field;[4]

---

[1] *Man walk'd with beast, joint tenant of the shade;*] The poet still takes his imagery from Platonic ideas, for the reason given above. Plato had said from old tradition, that, during the Golden age, and under the reign of Saturn, the primitive language then in use was common to man and beasts. Moral philosophers took this in the popular sense, and so invented those fables which give speech to the whole brute-creation. The naturalists understood the tradition to signify, that, in the first ages, Men used inarticulate sounds like beasts to express their wants and sensations; and that it was by slow degrees they came to the use of speech. This opinion was afterwards held by Lucretius, Diodorus Sic. and Gregory of Nyss. *Warburton.*

[2] [Thomson's diatribe in the *Seasons*, against the barbarous practice of eating animal food, will be remembered; as well as the circumstance that he draws the line at fish.]

[3] *Learn from the birds, &c.*] Taken, but finely improved, from Bacon's *Advancement of Learning* [Bk. II.]. *Warton.*

[4] *Learn from the beasts, &c.*] See Pliny's

ESSAY ON MAN.   215

Thy arts of building from the bee receive;   175
Learn of the mole to plough, the worm to weave;
Learn of the little Nautilus to sail,[1]
Spread the thin oar, and catch the driving gale.
Here too all forms of social union find,
And hence let Reason, late, instruct Mankind: 180
Here subterranean works and cities see;
There towns aerial on the waving tree.
Learn each small People's genius, policies,
The Ant's republic, and the realm of Bees;
How those in common all their wealth bestow,   185
And Anarchy without confusion know;
And these for ever, tho' a Monarch reign,
Their sep'rate cells and properties maintain.
Mark what unvary'd laws preserve each state,
Laws wise as Nature, and as fix'd as Fate.   190
In vain thy Reason finer webs shall draw,
Entangle Justice in her net of Law,
And right, too rigid, harden into wrong;
Still for the strong too weak, the weak too strong.
Yet go! and thus o'er all the creatures sway,   195
Thus let the wiser make the rest obey;
And, for those Arts mere Instinct could afford,
Be crown'd as Monarchs, or as Gods ador'd."
   V. Great Nature spoke; observant Men obey'd;
Cities were built, Societies were made: 200
Here rose one little state; another near
Grew by like means, and join'd, thro' love or fear.
Did here the trees with ruddier burdens bend,
And there the streams in purer rills descend?
What War could ravish, Commerce could bestow,   205
And he return'd a friend, who came a foe.
Converse and Love mankind might strongly draw,
When Love was Liberty, and Nature Law.
Thus States were form'd; the name of King unknown,
'Till common int'rest plac'd the sway in one.   210
'T was VIRTUE ONLY [2] (or in arts or arms,
Diffusing blessings, or averting harms)
The same which in a Sire the Sons obey'd,
A Prince the Father of a People made.

Nat. Hist. L. VIII. c. 27, where several instances are given of Animals discovering the medicinal efficacy of herbs, by their own use of them; pointing out to some operations in the art of healing, by their own practice. *Warburton.*

[1] *Learn of the little Nautilus*] Oppian. *Halieut.* Lib. I. describes this fish in the following manner: " They swim on the surface of the sea, on the back of their shells, which exactly resemble the hulk of a ship; they raise two feet like masts, and extend a membrane between, which serves as a sail; the other two feet they employ as oars at the side. They are usually seen in the Mediterranean." P.

[2] *'T was Virtue only, &c.*] Our author hath good authority for his account of the origin of kingship. Aristotle assures us of this truth, that it was Virtue only, or in arts or arms. [*Polit.* V. 10. 3.] *Warburton.*

VI. 'Till then, by Nature crown'd, each Patriarch sate, 215
King, priest, and parent of his growing state;
On him, their second Providence, they hung,
Their law his eye, their oracle his tongue.
He from the wond'ring furrow call'd the food,
Taught to command the fire, control the flood, 220
Draw forth the monsters of th' abyss profound,
Or fetch th' aerial eagle to the ground.
'Till drooping, sick'ning, dying they began
Whom they rever'd as God to mourn as Man:
Then, looking up from sire to sire, explor'd 225
One great first Father, and that first ador'd.
Or plain tradition that this All begun,
Convey'd unbroken faith from sire to son;
The worker from the work distinct was known,
And simple Reason never sought but one: 230
Ere Wit oblique had broke that steady light,[1]
Man, like his Maker, saw that all was right;
To Virtue, in the paths of Pleasure, trod,
And own'd a Father when he own'd a God.
LOVE all the faith, and all th' allegiance then; 235
For Nature knew no right divine in Men,
No ill could fear in God; and understood
A sov'reign being but a sov'reign good.
True faith, true policy, united ran,
This was but love of God, and this of Man. 240
  Who first taught souls enslav'd, and realms undone,
Th' enormous faith [2] of many made for one;
That proud exception to all Nature's laws,
T' invert the world, and counter-work its Cause?
Force first made Conquest, and that conquest, Law; 245
'Till Superstition taught the tyrant awe,
Then shar'd the Tyranny, then lent it aid,
And Gods of Conqu'rors, Slaves of Subjects made:
She 'midst the lightning's blaze, and thunder's sound,
When rock'd the mountains, and when groan'd the ground, 250
She taught the weak to bend, the proud to pray,
To Pow'r unseen, and mightier far than they:
She, from the rending earth and bursting skies,
Saw Gods descend, and fiends infernal rise:
Here fix'd the dreadful, there the blest abodes; 255

---

[1] *Ere Wit oblique &c.*] A beautiful allusion to the effects of the prismatic glass on the rays of light. *Warburton.* [' For however men may amuse themselves, and admire, or almost adore the mind, it is certain that, like an irregular glass, it alters the rays of things by its figure and different intersections.' Bacon, *Inst. Magn.* There is a similar passage in the *Advancement of Learning,* Bk. II.]

[2] *Th' enormous faith &c.*] In this Aristotle placeth the difference between a King and a Tyrant, that the first supposeth himself made for the People; the other, that the People are made for him. Pol. Lib. v. cap. 10. *Warburton.* [i.e. the unnatural doctrine that many are made for one — ' the mania of the Cæsars,' as it has been finely called.]

Fear made her Devils, and weak Hope her Gods;
Gods partial, changeful, passionate, unjust,
Whose attributes were Rage, Revenge, or Lust;
Such as the souls of cowards might conceive,
And, form'd like tyrants, tyrants would believe.   260
Zeal then, not charity, became the guide;
And hell was built on spite, and heav'n on pride,
Then sacred seem'd th' ethereal vault no more;
Altars grew marble then, and reek'd with gore:
Then first the Flamen tasted living food;[1]   265
Next his grim idol smear'd with human blood;[2]
With Heav'n's own thunders shook the world below,
And play'd the God an engine on his foe.
So drives Self-love, thro' just and thro' unjust,
To one Man's pow'r, ambition, lucre, lust: 270
The same Self-love, in all, becomes the cause
Of what restrains him, Government and Laws.
For, what one likes if others like as well,
What serves one will, when many wills rebel?
How shall he keep, what, sleeping or awake,   275
A weaker may surprise, a stronger take?
His safety must his liberty restrain:
All join to guard what each desires to gain.
Forc'd into virtue thus by Self-defence,
Ev'n Kings learn'd justice and benevolence: 280
Self-love forsook the path it first pursu'd,
And found the private in the public good.
'T was then, the studious head or gen'rous mind,
Follow'r of God or friend of human-kind,
Poet or Patriot, rose but to restore   285
The Faith and Moral Nature gave before;
Re-lum'd her ancient light, not kindled new;
If not God's image, yet his shadow drew:
Taught Pow'r's due use to People and to Kings,
Taught not to slack, nor strain its tender strings,   290
The less, or greater, set so justly true,
That touching one must strike the other too;
'Till jarring int'rests, of themselves create
Th' according music of a well-mix'd State.[3]
Such is the World's great harmony, that springs   295

---

[1] [*living*, i.e. animal. By employing the term *flamen*, Pope does not appear to refer specially to the priests and sacrifices of the Roman cultus, though among the latter it is certain that human sacrifices were up to a late period included.]

[2] Warton quotes from Milton [*Paradise Lost*, Bk. I. v. 392 foll.]:
'First Moloch, horrid king, *besmear'd with blood*
Of human sacrifice and parents' tears,
Tho' for the noise of drums and timbrels loud,
Their children's cries unheard that pass'd thro' fire
To his *grim idol.*'
[The passage is parodied in the *Dunciad*, Bk. IV. v. 142.]

[3] ' Quæ harmonia a musicis dicitur in cantu, ea est in civitate concordia.' Cicero, *de Republ. Warton.*

From Order, Union, full Consent of things:
Where small and great, where weak and mighty, made
To serve, not suffer, strengthen, not invade;
More pow'rful each as needful to the rest,
And, in proportion as it blesses, blest; 300
Draw to one point, and to one centre bring
Beast, Man, or Angel, Servant, Lord, or King.

For Forms of Government let fools contest;
Whate'er is best administer'd is best:
For Modes of Faith let graceless zealots fight; 305
His can't be wrong whose life is in the right:[1]
In Faith and Hope the world will disagree,
But all Mankind's concern is Charity:
All must be false that thwart this One great End;
And all of God, that bless Mankind or mend. 310

Man, like the gen'rous vine, supported lives;
The strength he gains is from th' embrace he gives.
On their own Axis as the Planets run,
Yet make at once their circle round the Sun;[2]
So two consistent motions act[3] the Soul; 315
And one regards Itself, and one the Whole.

Thus God and Nature link'd the gen'ral frame,
And bade Self-love and Social be the same.

ARGUMENT OF EPISTLE IV.

Of the Nature and State of Man with respect to HAPPINESS.

I. *FALSE Notions of Happiness, Philosophical and Popular, answered from* v. 19 *to* 77. II. *It is the End of all Men, and attainable by all,* v. 30. *God intends Happiness to be equal; and to be so, it must be social, since all particular happiness depends on general, and since he governs by* general, *not particular Laws,* v. 37. *As it is necessary for* Order, *and the peace and welfare of* Society, *that* external goods *should be* unequal, *Happiness is not made to consist in these,* v. 51. *But, notwithstanding that inequality, the balance of Happiness among Mankind is kept even by Providence, by the two Passions of* Hope *and* Fear, v. 70. III. *What the Happiness of* Individuals *is, as far as is consistent with the constitution of this world; and that the* good Man *has here the advantage,* v. 77. *The error of imputing to* Virtue *what are only the calamities of* Nature, *or of* Fortune, v. 94. IV. *The folly of expecting that God should alter his general Laws in favour of particulars,* v. 121. V. *That we are not judges who are good; but that, whoever they are, they must be happiest,* v. 133, &c. VI. *That* external goods *are not the proper rewards, but often inconsistent with, or destructive of Virtue,* v. 165. *That even these can make no Man happy without Virtue: Instanced in* Riches, v. 183. Honours, v. 191. Nobility, v. 203. Greatness, v. 215. Fame, v. 235. Superior Talents, v. 257, &c. *With pictures of human Infelicity in Men possessed of them all,* v. 267, &c. VII. *That* Virtue *only constitutes a Happiness, whose object is* universal, *and whose prospect* eternal, v. 307, &c. *That the* perfection *of* Virtue *and* Happiness *consists in a* conformity *to the* ORDER *of* PROVIDENCE *here, and a* Resignation *to it here and hereafter,* v. 326, &c.

---

[1] ['His faith perhaps, in some nice tenets might
Be wrong; his life, I'm sure, was in the right.'
Cowley, *on the Death of Mr. Crashaw.*

Warton thinks that Cowley may have himself taken the hint from a Latin distich by Lord Herbert of Cherbury.]

[2] [*at once,* i.e. at one and the same time.]

[3] [*act.* See above, Ep. II. line 59.]

ESSAY ON MAN. 219

EPISTLE IV.

OH HAPPINESS! our being's end and aim![1]
  Good, Pleasure, Ease, Content! whate'er thy name:
That something still which prompts th' eternal sigh,
For which we bear to live, or dare to die,
Which still so near us, yet beyond us lies, 5
O'er-look'd, seen double,[2] by the fool, and wise.
Plant of celestial seed! if dropt below,
Say, in what mortal soil thou deign'st to grow?
Fair op'ning to some Court's propitious shine,[3]
Or deep with di'monds in the flaming mine? 10
Twin'd with the wreaths Parnassian laurels yield,
Or reap'd in iron harvests of the field?
Where grows? — where grows it not? If vain our toil,
We ought to blame the culture, not the soil:
Fix'd to no spot is Happiness sincere,[4] 15
'Tis nowhere to be found, or ev'rywhere;
'Tis never to be bought, but always free,
And fled from monarchs, ST. JOHN! dwells with thee.
  Ask of the Learn'd the way? The Learn'd are blind;
This bids to serve, and that to shun mankind; 20
Some place the bliss in action,[5] some in ease,
Those call it Pleasure, and Contentment these;
Some sunk to Beasts, find pleasure end in pain;
Some swell'd to Gods, confess ev'n Virtue vain;
Or indolent, to each extreme they fall, 25
To trust in ev'ry thing, or doubt of all.
  Who thus define it, say they more or less
Than this, that Happiness is Happiness?
Take Nature's path, and mad Opinion's leave;

---

[1] *Oh Happiness! &c.*] in the MS. thus,
'Oh happiness! to which we all aspire,
Wing'd with strong hope, and borne by full desire;
That ease, for which in want, in wealth we sigh;
That ease, for which we labour and we die.'
Warburton [The same editor points out how the lines afterwards substituted for these successfully imitate the classical mode of invoking a Deity by his several names and places of abode, as in the Homeric Hymns (or in several Odes of Horace). Eudaimonia, Harmonia, Hygieia, Paidia, Pandaisia and others were often represented by the Greeks as daughters, or as handmaids, of Aphrodite.]

[2] *O'erlook'd, seen double,*] O'erlook'd by those who place Happiness in any thing exclusive of Virtue; *seen double* by those who admit any thing else to have a share with Virtue in procuring Happiness; these being the two general mistakes that this epistle is employed in confuting. *Warburton.*

[3] [*shine,* a substantive; so used in Spenser *F. Q.* Bk. I. Canto x. st. 67; and in the Prayer-book Psalms, xcvii. 4: 'his lightnings gave shine into the world.']

[4] [*sincere,* i.e. pure, unalloyed.]

[5] *Some place the bliss in action, — Some sunk to Beasts, &c.*] 1. Those who place Happiness, or the *summum bonum*, in Pleasure, such as the Cyrenaic sect. 2. Those who place it in a certain tranquillity or calmness of Mind, such as the Democritic sect. 3. The Epicurean. 4. The Stoic. 5. The Protagorean, which held that Man was *the measure of all things;* for that all things which appear to him *are,* and those things which appear not to any Man *are not;* so that every imagination or opinion of every man was true. 6. The Sceptic. *Warburton.*

All states can reach it, and all heads conceive; 30
Obvious her goods, in no extreme they dwell;
There needs but thinking right, and meaning well;
And mourn our various portions as we please,
Equal is Common Sense, and Common Ease.
    Remember, Man, "the Universal Cause 35
Acts not by partial, but by gen'ral laws;"
And makes what Happiness we justly call
Subsist not in the good of one, but all.
There 's not a blessing Individuals find,
But some way leans and hearkens to the kind: 40
No Bandit fierce, no Tyrant mad with pride,
No cavern'd Hermit, rests self-satisfy'd:
Who most to shun or hate Mankind pretend,
Seek an admirer, or would fix a friend:
Abstract what others feel, what others think, 45
All pleasures sicken, and all glories sink:
Each has his share; and who would more obtain,
Shall find, the pleasure pays not half the pain.
    ORDER is Heav'n's first law; and this confest,
Some are, and must be, greater than the rest,[1] 50
More rich, more wise; but who infers from hence
That such are happier, shocks all common sense.[2]
Heav'n to Mankind impartial we confess,
If all are equal in their Happiness:
But mutual wants this Happiness increase; 55
All Nature's diff'rence keeps all Nature's peace.
Condition, circumstance is not the thing;
Bliss is the same in subject or in king,
In who obtain defence, or who defend,
In him who is, or him who finds a friend: 60
Heav'n breathes thro' ev'ry member of the whole
One common blessing, as one common soul.
But Fortune's gifts if each alike possest,
And each were equal, must not all contest?
If then to all Men Happiness was meant, 65
God in Externals could not place Content.
    Fortune her gifts may variously dispose,
And these be happy call'd, unhappy those;
But Heav'n's just balance equal will appear,
While those are plac'd in Hope, and these in Fear: 70
Nor present good or ill, the joy or curse,
But future views of better, or of worse.

---

[1] Warton aptly refers to passages distinguishing between the true and false doctrines of Equality in Montesquieu (*Esprit des Lois*, VIII. 3) and Voltaire (*Esprit des Nations*, c. 67).

[2] After v. 52, in the MS.
'Say not, "Heav'n's here profuse, there poorly saves,
And for one Monarch makes a thousand slaves."
You 'll find, when Causes and their Ends are known,
'T was for the thousand Heav'n has made that one.'

TURENNE.
From a print in the National Library.

ESSAY ON MAN.

Oh sons of earth! attempt ye still to rise,
By mountains pil'd on mountains, to the skies?[1]
Heav'n still with laughter the vain toil surveys, 75
And buries madmen in the heaps they raise.
Know, all the good that individuals find,
Or God and Nature meant to mere Mankind,
Reason's whole pleasure, all the joys of Sense,
Lie in three words, Health, Peace, and Competence.[2] 80
But Health consists with Temperance alone;
And Peace, oh Virtue! Peace is all thy own.
The good or bad the gifts of Fortune gain;
But these less taste them, as they worse obtain.
Say, in pursuit of profit or delight, 85
Who risk the most, that take wrong means, or right?
Of Vice or Virtue, whether blest or curst,
Which meets contempt, or which compassion first?
Count all th' advantage prosp'rous Vice attains,
'T is but what Virtue flies from and disdains: 90
And grant the bad what happiness they would,
One they must want, which is, to pass for good.[3]
Oh blind to Truth, and God's whole scheme below,
Who fancy Bliss to Vice, to Virtue Woe![4]
Who sees and follows that great scheme the best, 95
Best knows the blessing, and will most be blest.
But fools the Good alone unhappy call,
For ills or accidents that chance to all.
See FALKLAND[5] dies, the virtuous and the just![5]
See god-like TURENNE prostrate on the dust![6] 100
See SIDNEY bleeds amid the martial strife![7]

[1] [Alluding to the Titans' attempt to scale Olympus.]
[2] [The πλουθυγίεια of Aristophanes.]
[3] After v. 92, in the MS.
'Let sober Moralists correct their speech,
No bad man's happy: he is great or rich.'
                                    Warburton.
[4] [i.e. that Bliss accompanies Vice, and Woe Virtue.]
[5] [Lucius Cary Lord Falkland, who after taking part in the opposition against the oppressive measures of Charles I. and the policy of Strafford, seceded with Hyde and others from the popular party at the time of the Grand Remonstrance, was appointed Secretary of State, and fell, fighting under the Royal Standard, in the battle of Newbury, Sept. 20, 1643. It is of him that Clarendon, in one of the most eloquent passages of his History, speaks as of that 'incomparable young man who in the brief span of life allotted to him' (for he fell in his 34th year) 'had so much dispatched the business of life, that the oldest rarely attain to that immense knowledge, and the youngest enter not the world with more innocence.' Waller, the most fastidious of English poets, would have gladly welcomed Falkland among their sacred order:
'Ah, noble friend! with what impatience all
That know thy worth, and know how prodigal
Of thy great soul thou art (longing to twist
Bays with that ivy which so early kissed
Thy youthful temples), with what horror we
Think of the blind events of war and thee!']

[6] [Henry, Vicomte de Turenne, Marshal of France, after commanding the French armies in the latter part of the Thirty Years' War, raised his military fame to the highest pitch, without preserving it intact from the blot of barbarous conduct, in the Alsatian and Palatinate campaigns developed out of the peace of Westphalia. He was struck dead by a cannon-ball at Salzbach in Baden in 1675; and was buried among the Kings of France at St. Denis.]

[7] Sir Philip Sidney, the author of the *Arcadia*, who was wounded to the death in the glorious but useless cavalry charge at Zutphen in 1586.]

Was this their Virtue, or Contempt of Life?
Say, was it Virtue, more tho' Heav'n ne'er gave,
Lamented DIGBY!¹ sunk thee to the grave?
Tell me, if Virtue made the Son expire, 105
Why, full of days and honour, lives the Sire?
Why drew Marseille's good bishop purer breath,²
When Nature sicken'd, and each gale was death?³
Or why so long (in life if long can be)
Lent Heav'n a parent to the poor and me?⁴ 110
    What makes all physical or moral ill?
There deviates Nature, and here wanders Will.
God sends not ill; if rightly understood,
Or partial Ill is universal Good,
Or Change admits, or Nature lets it fall; 115
Short, and but rare, till Man improv'd it all.⁵
We just as wisely might of Heav'n complain
That righteous Abel was destroy'd by Cain,
As that the virtuous son is ill at ease
When his lewd father gave the dire disease. 120
Think we, like some weak Prince, th' Eternal Cause
Prone for his fav'rites to reverse his laws?
    Shall burning Ætna,⁶ if a sage requires,
Forget to thunder, and recall her fires?
On air or sea new motions be imprest, 125
Oh blameless Bethel!⁷ to relieve thy breast?
When the loose mountain trembles from on high,
Shall gravitation cease, if you go by?
Or some old temple, nodding to its fall,

---

¹ [The Hon. Robert Digby, third son of Lord Digby, who died in 1724. See *Epitaph* VII. and Note.]

² *Marseille's good bishop.*] M. de Belsance was made bishop of Marseilles in 1709. In the plague of that city, in the year 1720, he distinguished himself by his zeal and activity, being the pastor, the physician, and the magistrate of his flock, whilst that horrid calamity prevailed. [After receiving extraordinary distinctions in recognition of his services both from the Pope and King Louis XV.] He died in the year 1755.
    Warton.

[' I believe your prayers will do me more good than those of all the Prelates in both kingdoms, or any Prelates in Europe except the Bishop of Marseilles.' Swift to Pope, May 12, 1735.]

³ Warton refers to Dryden's *Miscellanies*, v. 6.]

⁴ The mother of the author, a person of great piety and charity, died the year this poem was finished, viz. 1733. *Warburton.* [For Pope's relations to his mother, see *Introductory Memoir.*]

⁵ After v. 116, in the MS.
'Of ev'ry evil, since the world began,
The real source is not in God, but man.'
    Warburton.

⁶ *Shall burning Ætna, &c.*] Alluding to the fate of those two great Naturalists, Empedocles and Pliny, who both perished by too near an approach to Ætna and Vesuvius, while they were exploring the cause of their eruptions.
    Warburton.

⁷ Pope seems to hint at this passage in a letter written to Mr. Bethel, soon after the death of his mother: 'I have now too much melancholy leisure, and no other care but to finish my *Essay on Man.* There will be in it but one line that will offend you (I fear), and yet I will not alter it or omit it, unless you come to town and prevent it. It is all a poor Poet can do, to bear testimony to the virtue he cannot reach.' *Ruffhead.* [Mr. Hugh Bethell, a Yorkshire gentleman and one of Pope's intimate friends, to whom the *Imitation of the Second Satire of the Second Book of Horace* is addressed. See note to this *Imit.*]

ESSAY ON MAN.

For Chartres' head reserve the hanging wall?[1] 130
But still this world (so fitted for the knave)
Contents us not. A better shall we have?
A kingdom of the Just then let it be:
But first consider how those Just agree.
The good must merit God's peculiar care; 135
But who, but God, can tell us who they are?
One thinks on Calvin Heav'n's own spirit fell;
Another deems him instrument of hell;
If Calvin feel Heav'n's blessing, or its rod,
This cries there is, and that, there is no God. 140
What shocks one part will edify the rest,
Nor with one system can they all be blest.
The very best will variously incline,
And what rewards your Virtue, punish mine.
WHATEVER IS, IS RIGHT. — This world, 't is true, 145
Was made for Cæsar — but for Titus too:
And which more blest? who chain'd his country, say,
Or he whose Virtue sigh'd to lose a day?[2]
" But sometimes Virtue starves, while Vice is fed."
What then? Is the reward of Virtue bread? 150
That, Vice may merit, 't is the price of toil;
The knave deserves it, when he tills the soil,
The knave deserves it, when he tempts the main,
Where Folly fights for kings, or dives for gain.
The good man may be weak, be indolent; 155
Nor is his claim to plenty, but content.
But grant him Riches, your demand is o'er?
"No — shall the good want Health, the good want Pow'r?"
Add Health, and Pow'r, and ev'ry earthly thing,
"Why bounded Pow'r? why private? why no king?" 160
Nay, why external for internal giv'n?
Why is not Man a God, and Earth a Heav'n?
Who ask and reason thus, will scarce conceive
God gives enough, while he has more to give:
Immense the pow'r, immense were the demand; 165
Say, at what part of nature will they stand?
What nothing earthly gives, or can destroy,
The soul's calm sunshine, and the heart-felt joy,
Is Virtue's prize: A better would you fix?
Then give humility a coach and six, 170
Justice a Conq'ror's sword, or Truth a gown,
Or Public Spirit its great cure, a Crown.
Weak, foolish man! will Heav'n reward us there
With the same trash mad mortals wish for here?

---

[1] Eusebius is weak enough to relate, from the testimonies of Irenæus and Polycarp, that the roof of the building under which Cerinthus the heretic was bathing, providentially fell down and crushed him to death. Lib. III. cap. 29.

Warton. [For Pope's own sketch of the character of Chartres, see his note to *Moral Essays*, III. 20.]

[2] [Sueton. *Titus*, c. 8.]

The Boy and Man an individual makes,[1]　　　175
Yet sigh'st thou now for apples and for cakes?
Go, like the Indian,[2] in another life
Expect thy dog, thy bottle, and thy wife:
As well as dream such trifles are assign'd,
As toys and empires, for a god-like mind.　　　180
Rewards, that either would to Virtue bring
No joy, or be destructive of the thing:
How oft by these at sixty are undone
The Virtues of a saint at twenty-one!
To whom can Riches give Repute, or Trust,　　　185
Content, or Pleasure, but the Good and Just?
Judges and Senates have been bought for gold,
Esteem and Love were never to be sold.
Oh fool! to think God hates the worthy mind,
The lover and the love of human-kind,　　　190
Whose life is healthful, and whose conscience clear,
Because he wants a thousand pounds a year.

　　Honour and shame from no Condition rise;
Act well your part, there all the honour lies.
Fortune in Men has some small diff'rence made,　　　195
One flaunts in rags, one flutters in brocade;
The cobbler apron'd, and the parson gown'd,
The friar hooded, and the monarch crown'd.
"What differ more (you cry) than crown and cowl?"
I'll tell you, friend! a wise man and a Fool.　　　200
You'll find, if once the monarch acts the monk,
Or, cobbler-like, the parson will be drunk,
Worth makes the man, and want of it, the fellow;
The rest is all but leather or prunella.[3]

　　Stuck o'er with titles and hung round with strings,　　　205
That thou may'st be by kings, or whores of kings.[4]
Boast the pure blood of an illustrious race,
In quiet flow from Lucrece to Lucrece:[5]
But by your fathers' worth if yours you rate,
Count me those only who were good and great.　　　210
Go! if your ancient, but ignoble blood
Has crept thro' scoundrels ever since the flood,
Go! and pretend your family is young;
Nor own your fathers have been fools so long.
What can ennoble sots, or slaves, or cowards?　　　215
Alas! not all the blood of all the HOWARDS.

　　Look next on Greatness; say where Greatness lies?
"Where, but among the Heroes and the wise?"

---

[1] [*The Boy and Man*, i.e. the conjunction of boy and man; hence the verb is properly in the singular.]

[2] *Go, like the Indian, &c.*] Alluding to the example of the Indian in Epist. I. v. 99. *Warburton.*

[3] [*prunella;* because clergymen's gowns were often made of this kind of stuff.]

[4] [*That* is here the demonstrative.]

[5] These two lines are taken from Boileau (*Sat.* v. vv. 85-6.) *Warton.* [Hence the French pronunciation of the name *Lucrece.*]

ESSAY ON MAN.

Heroes are much the same, the point 's agreed,
From Macedonia's madman to the Swede;[1]   220
The whole strange purpose of their lives, to find
Or make, an enemy of all mankind!
Not one looks backward, onward still he goes,
Yet ne'er looks forward farther than his nose.
No less alike the Politic and Wise;   225
All sly slow things, with circumspective eyes:
Men in their loose unguarded hours they take,
Not that themselves are wise, but others weak.
But grant that those can conquer, these can cheat;
'T is phrase absurd to call a Villain Great: 230
Who wickedly is wise, or madly brave,
Is but the more a fool, the more a knave.
Who noble ends by noble means obtains,
Or failing, smiles in exile or in chains,
Like good Aurelius[2] let him reign, or bleed   235
Like Socrates,[3] that Man is great indeed.
What 's Fame? a fancy'd life in others' breath,
A thing beyond us, ev'n before our death.
Just what you hear, you have, and what's unknown
The same (my Lord) if Tully's, or your own.   240
All that we feel of it begins and ends
In the small circle of our foes or friends;
To all beside as much an empty shade
An Eugene living,[4] as a Cæsar dead;
Alike or when, or where, they shone, or shine,   245
Or on the Rubicon, or on the Rhine.
A Wit 's a feather, and a Chief a rod;[5]
An honest Man 's the noblest work of God.[6]

---

[1] [It is of course only a shallow misconception of a great historical character which can view Alexander the Great as a madman, or (see *ante*, Ep. I. v. 160) as the scourge of mankind. He was 'great,' says Thirlwall, 'not merely in the vast compass, and the persevering ardour, of his ambition: nor in the qualities by which he was enabled to gratify it, and to crowd so many memorable actions within so short a period: but in the course which his ambition took, in the collateral aims which ennobled and purified it, so that it almost grew into one with the highest of which man is capable, the desire of knowledge, and the love of good. In a word, great as one of the benefactors of his kind.' Warton justly observes that 'Charles XII. deserved not to be joined with him: Charles XII. tore out the leaf in which Boileau had censured Alexander.' Charles XII. was with admirable tact substituted by Johnson in his *Vanity of Human Wishes* for Juvenal's Hannibal to 'point the moral' of the vanity of ambition. Voltaire's *Histoire de Charles XII.* had appeared in 1730.]

[2] [Marcus Aurelius Antoninus reigned from 161 to 180 A.D. Whatever may have been the errors of judgment into which he was led by the 'unsuspecting goodness of his heart' (Gibbon), his character remains one of the purest and noblest in the history of the Empire of which he witnessed the first Decline. A comparison, says Merivale, 'might be drawn with unusual precision between the wise, the virtuous, the much-suffering Aurelius, and our own great and good King Alfred.']

[3] Considering the manner in which Socrates was put to death, the word 'bleed' seems to be improperly used. *Warton.*

[4] [Prince Eugene of Savoy, the commander of the Imperial armies in the war of the Spanish Succession, and the joint hero with Marlborough of Blenheim and Malplaquet.]

[5] [i.e. a mere scourge, as was said of Attila.]

[6] *noble*, for *noblest*, in Warburton's edition,

Fame but from death a villain's name can save,
As Justice tears his body from the grave;   250
When what t' oblivion better were resign'd,
Is hung on high, to poison half mankind.
All fame is foreign, but of true desert;
Plays round the head, but comes not to the heart:
One self-approving hour whole years out-weighs   255
Of stupid starers, and of loud huzzas;
And more true joy Marcellus exil'd feels,[1]
Than Cæsar with a senate at his heels.

In Parts superior what advantage lies?
Tell (for You can) what is it to be wise?   260
'T is but to know how little can be known;
To see all others' faults, and feel our own:
Condemn'd in bus'ness or in arts to drudge,
Without a second, or without a judge:
Truths would you teach, or save a sinking land   265
All fear, none aid you, and few understand.
Painful pre-eminence! yourself to view
Above life's weakness, and its comforts too.

Bring then these blessings to a strict account;
Make fair deductions; see to what they mount: 270
How much of other each is sure to cost;
How each for other oft is wholly lost;
How inconsistent greater goods with these;
How sometimes life is risk'd, and always ease:
Think, and if still the things thy envy call,[2]   275
Say, would'st thou be the Man to whom they fall?
To sigh for ribbands if thou art so silly,
Mark how they grace Lord Umbra,[3] or Sir Billy:
Is yellow dirt the passion of thy life?

---

is obviously a misprint. Mr. Darley, in his Introduction to the works of Beaumont and Fletcher, points out that Fletcher, in his poem of *An Honest Man's Fortune*, gave the same criterion of human perfection:

'Man is his own star; and that soul that can
Be honest, is the only perfect man.'

'If,' adds Mr. Darley, 'Pope stole this aphorism, he should have improved it, for it is false, and degrading to man, derogatory to God. An honest man is no more the noblest work of God than an honest *book* is the noblest of a writer; an honest *able* book is nobler than a dull book be it ever so honest. . . . Fletcher came nearer the truth elsewhere (in the *Triumph of Love*, Sc. 2): "An honest *able* man 's a prince's mate."']

[1] [M. Marcellus, one of the most determined opponents of Julius Cæsar, had fled to Mitylene after the battle of Pharsalus; and as he dared not himself solicit pardon, it was asked of the Dictator by his friends, Cicero making in his behalf an oration conceived in a very different spirit from that which Pope attributes to the orator's client. Its genuineness has however been doubted. Marcellus was assassinated at Athens on his way home.] By Marcellus, Pope was said to mean the Duke of Ormond. *Warton.* [The Duke of Ormond, as commander of the English forces in Flanders, refused to act on the offensive against the enemy with Prince Eugene, and drew off with 20,000 men from the allied army. In 1715 he disappointed the hopes of the Jacobites by his precipitate flight to France; was attainted; and after Bolingbroke's dismissal became Secretary of State to the Pretender, whose cause his rash counsels helped finally to ruin.]

[2] [*call*, i.e. demand. So again, *infra*, v. 285.]

[3] [*Lord Umbra, or Sir Billy*, see *Ep. to Arbuthnot*, v. 280 and Note.]

Look but on Gripus or on Gripus' wife :[1]   280
If Parts allure thee, think how Bacon shin'd,
The wisest, brightest, meanest of mankind :[2]
Or ravish'd with the whistling of a Name,[3]
See Cromwell, damn'd to everlasting fame!
If all, united, thy ambition call,   285
From ancient story learn to scorn them all.
There, in the rich, the honour'd, fam'd, and great,
See the false scale of Happiness complete!
In hearts of Kings, or arms of Queens who lay,
How happy! those to ruin, these betray.   290
Mark by what wretched steps their glory grows,
From dirt and sea-weed as proud Venice rose ;[4]
In each how guilt and greatness equal ran,
And all that rais'd the Hero, sunk the Man :
Now Europe's laurels on their brows behold,   295
But stain'd with blood, or ill exchang'd for gold :
Then see them broke with toils, or sunk in ease,
Or infamous for plunder'd provinces.[5]
Oh wealth ill-fated! which no act of fame
E'er taught to shine, or sanctify'd from shame!   300
What greater bliss attends their close of life?
Some greedy minion, or imperious wife.
The trophy'd arches, story'd halls invade
And haunt their slumbers in the pompous shade.
Alas! not dazzled with their noon-tide ray,   305
Compute the morn and ev'ning to the day ;
The whole amount of that enormous fame,
A Tale, that blends their glory with their shame!
  Know then this truth (enough for Man to know)
" Virtue alone is Happiness below."   310
The only point where human bliss stands still,
And tastes the good without the fall[6] to ill ;
Where only Merit constant pay receives,
Is blest in what it takes, and what it gives ;

[1] [The name *Gripus* translates that of *Harpagon*, the hero of Molière's *Avare*. Gripe is a character in Vanbrugh's *Confederacy*, whose wife spends his money.]

[2] That part of Macaulay's brilliant essay on Bacon, which may be described as a paraphrase of the above famous line, has been criticised by many writers, by none more keenly than by Kuno Fischer (whose book has been translated into English by Mr. Oxenford) with the object of showing the fallacy involved in the antithesis.]

[3] From Cowley, in his imitation of Virgil;
' Charm'd with the foolish whistlings of a name.'
                                    Warton.

[4] [The city of Venice was built in 809 on the island of the Rialto, in the midst of the marshes called *Lagune*, where the inhabitants of the great cities of Venetia had taken refuge from the Huns three centuries and a half before that date.]

[5] In the MSS. it was thus:
  —' or sunk in years,
  Lost in unmeaning, unrepenting tears.'
Meaning the great Duke of Marlborough, who sunk in the latter part of his life into a state of perfect childhood and dotage. *Warton*. [The personal allusion is clear from the references to the ' wealth ill-fated ' and the ' imperious wife.' See note to *Moral Essays*, Ep. II. v. 115. This passage probably contains the gist of the character of the Duke of Marlborough suppressed by Pope. As to the cause of this suppression see *Introductory Memoir*.]

[6] [*without the fall*, i.e. without inclining.]

The joy unequall'd, if its end it gain, 315
And if it lose, attended with no pain:[1]
Without satiety, tho' e'er so bless'd,
And but more relish'd as the more distress'd:
The broadest mirth unfeeling Folly wears,
Less pleasing far than Virtue's very tears: 320
Good, from each object, from each place acquir'd,
For ever exercis'd, yet never tir'd;
Never elated, while one man 's oppress'd;
Never dejected, while another 's bless'd;
And where no wants, no wishes can remain, 325
Since but to wish more Virtue, is to gain.

See the sole bliss Heav'n could on all bestow!
Which who but feels can taste, but thinks can know:
Yet poor with fortune, and with learning blind,
The bad must miss; the good, untaught, will find; 330
Slave to no sect, who takes no private road,
But looks thro' Nature up to Nature's God;[2]
Pursues that Chain which links th' immense design,
Joins heav'n and earth, and mortal and divine;
Sees, that no Being any bliss can know, 335
But touches some above, and some below;
Learns, from this union of the rising Whole,
The first, last purpose of the human soul;
And knows, where Faith, Law, Morals, all began,
All end, in LOVE OF GOD, and LOVE OF MAN. 340

For him alone, Hope leads from goal to goal,
And opens still, and opens on his soul;[3]
'Till lengthen'd on to Faith, and unconfin'd,
It pours the bliss that fills up all the mind.
He sees, why Nature plants in Man alone 345
Hope of known bliss, and Faith in bliss unknown:
(Nature, whose dictates to no other kind
Are giv'n in vain, but what they seek they find;)
Wise in her present; she connects in this
His greatest Virtue with his greatest Bliss; 350
At once his own bright prospect to be blest,
And strongest motive to assist the rest.

Self-love thus push'd to social, to divine,
Gives thee to make thy neighbour's blessing thine.
Is this too little for the boundless heart? 355

---

[1] After v. 316 in the MS.
' Ev'n while it seems unequal to dispose,
And checquers all the good Man's joys with woes,
'T is but to teach him to support each state,
With patience this, with moderation that;
And raise his base on that one solid joy,
Which conscience gives, and nothing can destroy.'
Warburton.

[2] Verbatim from Bolingbroke's Letters to Pope. *Warton.*

[3] [Warburton compares Plato *de Republ.* 1. c. 5, in which a beautiful passage is quoted from Pindar (*Fragm.* 130; and Euripides, *Herc. Fur.* vv. 105-6). The sublimation of Hope into Faith, of which Pope speaks, constitutes the climax of Campbell's noble poem.]

ESSAY ON MAN.

Extend it, let thy enemies have part:
Grasp the whole worlds of Reason, Life, and Sense,
In one close system of Benevolence:
Happier as kinder, in whate'er degree,
And height of Bliss but height of Charity.   360
  God loves from Whole to Parts: but human soul
Must rise from Individual to the Whole.
Self-love but serves the virtuous mind to wake,
As the small pebble stirs the peaceful lake;
The centre mov'd, a circle straight succeeds,   365
Another still, and still another spreads;[1]
Friend, parent, neighbour, first it will embrace;
His country next; and next all human race;
Wide and more wide, th' o'erflowings of the mind
Take ev'ry creature in, of ev'ry kind;   370
Earth smiles around, with boundless bounty blest,
And Heav'n beholds its image in his breast.
  Come then, my Friend! my Genius! come along;
Oh master of the poet, and the song!
And while the Muse now stoops, or now ascends,   375
To Man's low passions, or their glorious ends,
Teach me, like thee, in various nature wise,
To fall with dignity, with temper rise;
Form'd by thy converse, happily to steer
From grave to gay, from lively to severe;   380
Correct with spirit, eloquent with ease,
Intent to reason, or polite to please.
Oh! while along the stream of Time thy name
Expanded flies, and gathers all its fame,
Say, shall my little bark attendant sail,   385
Pursue the triumph, and partake the gale?
When statesmen, heroes, kings, in dust repose,
Whose sons shall blush their fathers were thy foes,
Shall then this verse to future age pretend
Thou wert my guide, philosopher, and friend?   390
That urg'd by thee, I turn'd the tuneful art
From sounds to things, from fancy to the heart;
For Wit's false mirror held up Nature's light;
Shew'd erring Pride, WHATEVER IS, IS RIGHT;
That REASON, PASSION, answer one great aim;   395
That true SELF-LOVE and SOCIAL are the same;
That VIRTUE only makes our Bliss below;
And all our Knowledge is, OURSELVES TO KNOW.[2]

---

[1] Pope took the simile of the Lake from Chaucer, whose *House of Fame* he had imitated. (Book II. vv. 280 ff.) *Bowles.*

[2] *That Virtue only, &c.*] In the MS. thus,
  'That just to find a God is all we can
  And all the Study of Mankind is Man.'
                                        Warburton.

THE UNIVERSAL PRAYER.[1]

DEO OPT. MAX.

[The Universal Prayer, put forth in 1738, may be fairly ascribed to Pope's desire to avail himself of the Commentary of Warburton, which had been designed to show that the system developed in the *Essay on Man* recognises freewill and does *not* logically tend to the establishment of fatalism. It can hardly be called a Paraphrase of the Lord's Prayer, which it only follows at the commencement, and in the last four stanzas. Warton states that the prayer was by 'many orthodox persons' called the Deist's Prayer, and that on account of translating it a French advocate, Le Franc de Pompignan, incurred a reprimand from the Chancellor Aguesseau.]

FATHER of All! in ev'ry Age,
   In ev'ry Clime ador'd,
By Saint, by Savage, and by Sage,
   Jehovah, Jove, or Lord!

Thou Great First Cause, least understood: 5
   Who all my Sense confin'd
To know but this, that Thou art Good,
   And that myself am blind;

Yet gave me, in this dark Estate,
   To see the Good from Ill;   10
And binding Nature fast in Fate,
   Left free the Human Will.[2]

What Conscience dictates to be done,
   Or warns me not to do,
This, teach me more than Hell to shun,   15
   That, more than Heav'n pursue.

---

[1] *Universal Prayer.*] Concerning this poem, it may be proper to observe, that some passages, in the preceding *Essay*, having been unjustly suspected of a tendency towards Fate and *Naturalism*, the author composed this Prayer as the sum of all, to shew that his system was founded in *free-will*, and terminated in piety; That the First Cause was as well the Lord and Governor of the Universe as the Creator of it; and that, by submission to his will (the great Principle inforced throughout the *Essay*) was not meant the suffering ourselves to be carried along with a blind determination; but a religious acquiescence, and confidence full of *Hope* and Immortality. To give all this the greater weight and reality, the poet chose for his model the LORD'S PRAYER, which of all others, best deserves the title prefixed to this Paraphrase. *Warburton.*

[2] Originally Pope had written another stanza immediately after this:
  'Can sins of moments claim the rod
    Of everlasting fires?
  And that offend great Nature's God
    Which Nature's self inspires?'
               Warton.
[This 'licentious stanza' was, according to Mrs. Piozzi, discovered by a curious clergyman (whose name seems to have been Dr. Lort) and the idea was traced by Johnson to Guarini's *Pastor Fido.*]

What Blessings thy free Bounty gives,
  Let me not cast away;
For God is pay'd when Man receives,
  T' enjoy is to obey.   20

Yet not to Earth's contracted Span
  Thy Goodness let me bound,
Or think Thee Lord alone of Man,
  When thousand Worlds are round:

Let not this weak, unknowing hand   25
  Presume thy bolts to throw,
And deal damnation round the land,
  On each I judge thy Foe.

If I am right, thy grace impart,
  Still in the right to stay;   30
If I am wrong, oh teach my heart
  To find that better way.

Save me alike from foolish Pride,
  Or impious Discontent,
At aught thy Wisdom has deny'd,   35
  Or aught thy Goodness lent.

Teach me to feel another's Woe,
  To hide the Fault I see;
That Mercy I to others show,
  That Mercy show to me.   40

Mean tho' I am, not wholly so,
  Since quick'ned by thy Breath;
Oh lead me wheresoe'er I go,
  Thro' this day's Life or Death.

This day, be Bread and Peace my Lot: 45
  All else beneath the Sun,
Thou know'st if best bestow'd or not;
  And let Thy Will be done.

To thee, whose Temple is all Space,
  Whose Altar Earth, Sea, Skies,   50
One Chorus let all Being raise,
  All Nature's Incense rise!

MORAL ESSAYS,

IN FOUR EPISTLES TO SEVERAL PERSONS.

> Est brevitate opus, ut currat sententia, neu se
> Impediat verbis lassis onerantibus aures:
> Et sermone opus est modo tristi, sæpe jocoso,
> Defendente vicem modo Rhetoris atque Poetæ,
> Interdum urbani, parcentis viribus, atque
> Extenuantis eas consultò. — Hor. [*Sat*. 1. x. 17-22.]

EPISTLE I.

To Sir Richard Temple, Lord Cobham.[1]

ARGUMENT.

Of the Knowledge and Characters of MEN.

I. *THAT it is not sufficient for this knowledge to consider Man in the* Abstract: Books *will not serve the purpose, nor yet our own* Experience *singly*, v. 1. *General maxims, unless they be formed upon* both, *will be but notional*, v. 10. *Some Peculiarity in every man, characteristic to himself, yet varying from himself,* v. 15. *Difficulties arising from our own Passions, Fancies, Faculties,* &c. v. 31. *The shortness of Life, to observe in, and the uncertainty of the* Principles of action *in men, to observe by,* v. 37, &c. *Our own Principle of action often hid from ourselves*, v. 41. *Some few Characters plain, but in general confounded, dissembled, or inconsistent,* v. 51. *The same man utterly different in different places and seasons,* v. 71. *Unimaginable weaknesses in the greatest,* v. 70, &c. *Nothing constant and certain but God and* Nature, v. 95. *No judging of the Motives from the actions; the same actions proceeding from contrary Motives, and the same Motives influencing contrary actions,* v. 100. II. *Yet to form* Characters, *we can only take the* strongest actions *of a man's life, and try to make them agree: The utter uncertainty of this, from* Nature *itself, and from* Policy, v. 120. Characters *given according to the* rank *of men of the world,* v. 135. *And some reason for it,* v. 140. Education *alters the* Nature, *or at least* Character *of many,* v. 149. Actions, Passions, Opinions, Manners, Humours, *or* Principles *all subject to change. No judging by* Nature, *from* v. 158 to 178. III. *It only remains to find (if we can) his* RULING PASSION: *That will certainly influence all the rest, and can reconcile the seeming or real inconsistency of all his actions,* v. 175. *Instanced in the extraordinary character of* Clodio, v. 179. *A caution against* mistaking second qualities *for* first, *which will destroy all possibility of the knowledge of mankind,* v. 210. *Examples of the strength of the* Ruling Passion, *and its continuation to the last breath,* v. 222, &c.

---

[1] [Sir Richard Temple, created Viscount Cobham by George I. in 1718, and made a Field Marshal in 1742, was on intimate terms with Pope during the latter part of the Poet's life. Pope speaks, in his last letter to Swift, of 'generally rambling in the summer for a month to Lord Cobham's, the Bath, or elsewhere.' (The beauties of Lord Cobham's seat at Stowe are enthusiastically described in the 4th of these Epistles, v. 70 and foll.) Lord Cobham, writing to Pope from Stowe Nov. 1, 1733, gracefully says that 'though he has not modesty enough to be pleased with the extraordinary compliment paid him, he has wit enough to know how little he deserves it;' and after declaring the Epistle to be 'the clearest and cleanest of all' Pope has written, recommends a judicious alteration of a passage which might have militated against the applicability of one of these epithets.]

MORAL ESSAYS. 233

YES, you despise the man to Books confin'd,
Who from his study rails at human kind;
Tho' what he learns he speaks, and may advance
Some gen'ral maxims, or be right by chance.
The coxcomb bird, so talkative and grave,[1] 5
That from his cage cries Cuckold, Whore, and Knave,
Tho' many a passenger he rightly call,
You hold him no Philosopher at all.
　　And yet the fate of all extremes is such,
Men may be read as well as Books, too much.[2] 10
To observations which ourselves we make,
We grow more partial for th' Observer's sake;
To written Wisdom, as another's, less:
Maxims are drawn from Notions, these from Guess.
There 's some Peculiar in each leaf and grain, 15
Some unmark'd fibre, or some varying vein:
Shall only Man be taken in the gross?
Grant but as many sorts of Mind as Moss.
　　That each from other differs, first confess;
Next, that he varies from himself no less: 20
Add Nature's, Custom's, Reason's, Passion's strife,
And all Opinion's colours cast on life.
　　Our depths who fathoms, or our shallows finds,
Quick whirls, and shifting eddies, of our minds?
On human actions reason tho' you can, 25
It may be Reason, but it is not Man:
His Principle of action once explore,
That instant 't is his Principle no more.
Like following life thro' creatures you dissect,
You lose it in the moment you detect. 30
　　Yet more; the diff'rence is as great between
The optics seeing, as the object seen.
All Manners take a tincture from our own;
Or come discolour'd thro' our Passions shown.
Or Fancy's beam enlarges, multiplies, 35
Contracts, inverts, and gives ten thousand dyes.
　　Nor will Life's stream for Observation stay
It hurries all too fast to mark their way:
In vain sedate reflections we would make,
When half our knowledge we must snatch, not take 40
Oft, in the Passions' wild rotation tost,
Our spring of action to ourselves is lost:
Tir'd, not determin'd, to the last we yield,

---

[1] *The coxcomb bird, &c.*] A fine turn'd allusion to what Philostratus said of Euxenus, the Tutor of Apollonius, that he could only repeat some sentences of Pythagoras, like those *coxcomb birds*, who were taught their εὖ πράττε and their Ζεὺς ἵλεως, but knew not what they signified. *Warburton*.

[2] 'Say what they will of the great Book of the World, we must read others to know how to read that.' Mad. de Sévigné to M. Rabutin. *Warton*. [Warburton thinks that the passage in the text covertly refers to the *Maxims* of Rochefoucault.]

And what comes then is master of the field.
As the last image of that troubled heap, 45
When Sense subsides, and Fancy sports in sleep,
(Tho' past the recollection of the thought,)
Becomes the stuff of which our dream is wrought:
Something as dim to our internal view,
Is thus, perhaps, the cause of most we do. 50
 True, some are open, and to all men known;
Others so very close, they 're hid from none;
(So Darkness strikes the sense no less than Light)
Thus gracious CHANDOS[1] is belov'd at sight;
And ev'ry child hates Shylock, tho' his soul
Still sits at squat, and peeps not from its hole.
At half mankind when gen'rous Manly raves,[2]
All know 't is Virtue, for he thinks them knaves:
When universal homage Umbra pays,[3]
All see 't is Vice, and itch of vulgar praise. 60
When Flatt'ry glares, all hate it in a Queen,[4]
While one there is who charms us with his Spleen.[5]
 But these plain Characters we rarely find;
Tho' strong the bent, yet quick the turns of mind:
Or puzzling Contraries confound the whole; 65
Or Affectations quite reverse the soul.
The Dull, flat Falsehood serves for policy;
And in the Cunning, Truth itself 's a lie:
Unthought-of Frailties cheat us in the Wise;
The Fool lies hid in inconsistencies. 70
 See the same man, in vigour, in the gout;
Alone, in company; in place, or out;
Early at Bus'ness, and at Hazard late;
Mad at a Fox-chase, wise at a Debate;
Drunk at a Borough, civil at a Ball; 75
Friendly at Hackney, faithless at Whitehall.

---

[1] [James Brydges, first Duke of Chandos, for whose splendid hospitality and supposed personal munificence to Pope the latter was accused of having made a base return by satirising the decorations and furniture of the Duke's house at Canons in the Epistle *on Taste*, subsequently entitled *of False Taste*, and finally incorporated with the Moral Essays as the fourth of the series, under the same title as the third, *of the Use of Riches*. See Ep. IV. lines 97 and foll. Pope denied the pecuniary obligation, and defended himself against the charge of his having alluded to the Duke's house. The Duke accepted the explanation; and the line in the text is due to Pope's recognition of the urbanity displayed by his noble acquaintance. See also Pope's note to *Ep.* III. on p. 220. B. was Paymaster of the Forces under Godolphin; and when, in 1711, the public accounts of the latter were examined by Harley's friends and 35 millions found not passed, about 14 of these belonged to the Paymaster's department. He was successfully defended by St. John.]

[2] [Manly is the hero of Wycherley's *Plain Dealer*, a coarse caricature of the *Misanthrope* of Molière. The play and character were so popular, that the author himself was commonly known by the flattering title of Manly Wycherley.]

[3] [Umbra is Bubb Doddington. See *Epistle to Arbuthnot*, v. 280.]

[4] [Supposed to refer to Queen Caroline, the wife of George II., who was also the subject of Swift's irony.]

[5] Closely copied from Boileau:

'Un esprit né plait par son chagrin même.'

It is a compliment to Swift. *Warton.*

MORAL ESSAYS. 235

Catius[1] is ever moral, ever grave,
Thinks who endures a knave, is next a knave,
Save just at dinner — then, prefers, no doubt,
A Rogue with Ven'son to a Saint without.   80
Who would not praise Patritio's high desert,[2]
His hand unstain'd, his uncorrupted heart,
His comprehensive head! all Int'rests weigh'd,
All Europe sav'd, yet Britain not betray'd.
He thanks you not, his pride is in Piquet,   85
New-market-fame, and judgment at a Bet.[3]
What made (say Montagne, or more sage Charron![4])
Otho a warrior,[5] Cromwell a buffoon?
A perjur'd Prince a leaden Saint revere,[6]
A godless Regent tremble at a Star?[7]   90
The throne a Bigot keep, a Genius quit,[8]
Faithless thro' Piety, and dup'd thro' Wit?
Europe a Woman, Child, or Dotard rule,
And just her wisest monarch made a fool?[9]
Know, GOD and NATURE only are the same: 95
In Man, the judgment shoots at flying game,
A bird of passage! gone as soon as found,
Now in the Moon perhaps, now under ground.

In vain the Sage, with retrospective eye,
Would from th' apparent What conclude the Why,   100
Infer the Motive from the Deed, and shew,
That what we chanc'd was what we meant to do.
Behold! If Fortune or a Mistress frowns,
Some plunge in bus'ness, others shave their crowns:
To ease the Soul of one oppressive weight,   105

---

[1] Charles Dartineuf. *Carruthers.* [See *Imitations of Horace*, Bk. II. Ep. II. v. 87, note.]

[2] Lord G—n. *Warburton.* [Lord Godolphin, appointed Lord Treasurer at the accession of Queen Anne, a Whig and the patron of Addison. 'Most of the time which he could save from public business was spent in racing, cardplaying, and cock-fighting.' *Macaulay.*]

[3] After v. 86 in the former Editions,
'Triumphant leaders, at an army's head,
Hemm'd round with glories, pilfer cloth or bread;
As meanly plunder as they bravely fought,
Now save a People, and now save a groat.'
[Alluding to the Duke of Marlborough.]

[4] [See note to *Essay on Man*, Ep. III. v. 46, p. 209.]

[5] [The Roman Emperor Otho, the effeminate associate of Nero's debauches, for a time displayed a manful spirit against Vitellius.]

[6] *A perjur'd Prince*] Louis XI. of France, wore in his Hat a leaden image of the Virgin Mary, which when he swore by, he feared to break his oath. P.

[7] *A godless Regent tremble at a Star?*] Philip Duke of Orleans, Regent of France in the minority of Louis XV., superstitious in judicial astrology, tho' an unbeliever in all religion. *Warburton.*

[8] *The throne a Bigot keep, a Genius quit,*] Philip V. of Spain, who, after renouncing the throne for Religion, resumed it to gratify his Queen; and Victor Amadeus II. King of Sardinia, who resigned the Crown, and trying to reassume it, was imprisoned till his death. P.

[9] [The reference appears to be to the succession of Tsarinas in Russia, and to the protracted reign of Louis XIV., and the minority of his successor, in France. If her wisest monarch signify Louis XIV., the agent who subjected him to the process referred to might possibly be Mme. de Maintenon; but it is impossible to find chapter and verse for such vague allusions as those in the text.]

This quits an Empire, that embroils a State:
The same adust complexion has impell'd
Charles to the Convent, Philip to the Field.[1]
  Not always Actions shew the man: we find
Who does a kindness, is not therefore kind;   110
Perhaps Prosperity becalm'd his breast,
Perhaps the Wind just shifted from the east:
Not therefore humble he who seeks retreat,
Pride guides his steps, and bids him shun the great:
Who combats bravely is not therefore brave,   115
He dreads a death-bed like the meanest slave
Who reasons wisely is not therefore wise,
His pride in Reas'ning, not in Acting lies.
  But grant that Actions best discover man;
Take the most strong, and sort them as you can.   120
The few that glare each character must mark,
You balance not the many in the dark.
What will you do with such as disagree?
Suppress them, or miscall them Policy?
Must then at once (the character to save)   125
The plain rough Hero turn a crafty Knave?
Alas! in truth the man but chang'd his mind,
Perhaps was sick, in love, or had not din'd.
Ask why from Britain Cæsar would retreat?
Cæsar himself might whisper he was beat.   130
Why risk the world's great empire for a Punk?[2]
Cæsar perhaps might answer he was drunk.
But, sage historians! 't is your task to prove
One action Conduct; one, heroic Love.
  'T is from high Life high Characters are drawn;   135
A Saint in Crape[3] is twice a Saint in Lawn;
A Judge is just, a Chanc'llor juster still;
A Gownman, learn'd; a Bishop, what you will;
Wise, if a Minister; but, if a King,
More wise, more learn'd, more just, more ev'rything.[4] 140
Court-virtues bear, like Gems, the highest rate,
Born where Heav'n's influence scarce can penetrate
In life's low vale, the soil the Virtues like,
They please as beauties, here as wonders strike.
Tho' the same Sun with all-diffusive rays   145
Blush in the Rose, and in the Di'mond blaze,
We prize the stronger effort of his pow'r,

---

[1] [The complexion of Charles V. has been attributed by modern historians to an imperfect and over-tried digestion; but he was certainly 'impelled to the field' more frequently than his son Philip II.]

[2] [Cleopatra. It need hardly be added that this view of Cæsar's conduct in Egypt is fallacious.]

[3] [i.e. in the gown of an ordinary clergyman.]

[4] [The merits of great and small are judged in the inverse ratio of that applied to their foibles, according to the familiar passage in *Measure for Measure*, Act II. Sc. 2: 'What in the captain's,' &c.]

And justly set the Gem above the Flow'r.
'T is Education forms the common mind,
Just as the Twig is bent, the Tree 's inclin'd. 150
Boastful and rough, your first Son is a Squire;
The next a Tradesman, meek, and much a liar;
Tom struts a Soldier, open, bold, and brave;
Will sneaks a Scriv'ner, an exceeding knave:
Is he a Churchman? then he 's fond of pow'r: 155
A Quaker? sly: A Presbyterian? sour:
A smart Free-thinker? all things in an hour.
   Ask men's Opinions: Scoto¹ now shall tell
How Trade increases, and the world goes well;
Strike off his Pension, by the setting sun, 160
And Britain, if not Europe, is undone.
   That gay Free-thinker, a fine talker once,
What turns him now a stupid silent dunce?
Some God, or Spirit he has lately found:
Or chanc'd to meet a Minister that frown'd. 165
   Judge we by Nature? Habit can efface,
Int'rest o'ercome, or Policy take place:
By Actions? those Uncertainty divides:
By Passions? these Dissimulation hides:
Opinions? they still take a wider range: 170
Find, if you can, in what you cannot change.
   Manners with Fortunes, Humours turn with Climes,
Tenets with Books, and Principles with Times.

   Search then the RULING PASSION:² there, alone,
The Wild are constant, and the Cunning known; 175
The Fool consistent, and the False sincere;
Priests, Princes, Women, no dissemblers here.
This clue once found, unravels all the rest,
The prospect clears, and Wharton stands confest.³
Wharton, the scorn and wonder of our days, 180
Whose ruling Passion was the Lust of Praise:
Born with whate'er could win it from the Wise,
Women and Fools must like him or he dies:
Tho' wond'ring Senates hung on all he spoke,
The Club must hail him master of the joke. 185
Shall parts so various aim at nothing new?
He 'll shine a Tully and a Wilmot too.⁴

---

¹ In the first edition: 'J—n now shall tell;' meaning perhaps Johnston, the Scottish Secretary ... a neighbour of Pope's at Twickenham. *Carruthers*.

² *Search then the Ruling Passion:*] See Essay on Man, Ep. II. v. 133. & seq. *Warburton*.

³ [Philip Duke of Wharton, the notorious son of an only less notorious father (Addison's patron), after a life of mad dissipation and adventure, died in the year 1731 in a Spanish convent in the habit of the monks who had given him a last refuge. His career is described in Vol. II. of Lord Stanhope's *Hist. of Engl.*]

⁴ John Wilmot, E. of Rochester, famous for his Wit and Extravagancies in the time of Charles the Second. P. [See note p. 184.]

Then turns repentant, and his God adores
With the same spirit that he drinks and whores;[1]
Enough if all around him but admire, 190
And now the Punk applaud, and now the Friar.
Thus with each gift of nature and of art,
And wanting nothing but an honest heart;
Grown all to all, from no one vice exempt;
And most contemptible, to shun contempt: 195
His Passion still, to covet gen'ral praise,
His Life, to forfeit it a thousand ways;
A constant Bounty which no friend has made;
An angel Tongue, which no man can persuade;
A Fool with more of Wit than half mankind, 200
Too rash for Thought, for Action too refin'd:
A Tyrant to the wife his heart approves;
A Rebel to the very king he loves;
He dies, sad outcast of each church and state,
And, harder still! flagitious, yet not great. 205
Ask you why Wharton broke thro' ev'ry rule?
'T was all for fear the Knaves should call him Fool.[2]
　　Nature well known, no prodigies remain,[3]
Comets are regular, and Wharton plain.
　　Yet, in this search, the wisest may mistake, 210
If second qualities for first they take.
When Catiline by rapine swell'd his store;
When Cæsar made a noble dame[4] a whore;
In this the Lust, in that the Avarice
Were means, not ends; Ambition was the vice. 215
That very Cæsar, born in Scipio's days,
Had aim'd, like him, by Chastity at praise.[5]
Lucullus, when Frugality could charm,
Had roasted turnips in the Sabine farm.[6]
　　In vain th' observer eyes the builder's toil, 220
But quite mistakes the scaffold for the pile.
In this one Passion man can strength enjoy,
As Fits give vigour, just when they destroy.
Time, that on all things lays his lenient hand,
Yet tames not this; it sticks to our last sand. 225
Consistent in our follies and our sins,
Here honest Nature ends as she begins.

---

[1] *With the same* spirit] *Spirit*, for principle, not passion. *Warburton*.

[2] [Goethe makes Werther as the supposed author of the *Letters from Switzerland* express a similar idea: 'one would always rather appear vicious than ridiculous to anyone else.']

[3] In the former Editions, v. 208.

'Nature well known, no *Miracles* remain.'
Alter'd as above, for very obvious reasons.
　　　　　　　　Warburton.

[4] [Servilia, the sister of Cato and the mother of Brutus. According to Sueton. *Julius*, c. 51.]

[5] [Alluding to the famous story of Scipio the elder and Sophonisba.]

[6] [L. Licinius Lucullus, who after his Eastern campaigns introduced many luxuries into Roman life.]

MORAL ESSAYS.

Old Politicians chew on wisdom past,
And totter on in bus'ness to the last;
As weak, as earnest; and as gravely out,   230
As sober Lanesb'row [1] dancing in the gout.
Behold a rev'rend sire, whom want of grace
Has made the father of a nameless race,
Shov'd from the wall perhaps, or rudely press'd
By his own son, that passes by unbless'd: 235
Still to his wench he crawls on knocking knees,
And envies ev'ry sparrow that he sees.
A salmon's belly, Helluo,[2] was thy fate;
The doctor call'd, declares all help too late:
"Mercy!" cries Helluo, "mercy on my soul!"   240
"Is there no hope? — Alas! — then bring the jowl."[3]
The frugal Crone, whom praying priests attend,
Still tries to save the hallow'd taper's end,
Collects her breath, as ebbing life retires,
For one puff more, and in that puff expires.[4]   245
"Odious! in woollen! 't would a Saint provoke,"
(Were the last words that poor Narcissa spoke) [5]
"No, let a charming Chintz, and Brussels lace
Wrap my cold limbs, and shade my lifeless face:
One would not, sure, be frightful when one's dead —   250
And — Betty — give this Cheek a little Red."[6]
The Courtier smooth, who forty years had shin'd
An humble servant to all human kind,
Just brought out this, when scarce his tongue could stir,
"If — where I'm going — I could serve you, Sir?"   255

---

[1] *Lanesb'row.*] An ancient Nobleman, who continued this practice long after his legs were disabled by the gout. Upon the death of Prince George of Denmark, he demanded an audience of the Queen, to advise her to preserve her health and dispel her grief from *Dancing*. P. [Viscount Lanesborough died at Dublin in 1736. He is often alluded to as the dancing peer in Irish pasquinades of the day. *Carruthers.*]

[2] [A Latin word signifying a glutton.]

[3] Warton traces this story to Athenæus, Bk. VIII., where it is told of the poet Philoxenus; but thinks Pope derived it from La Fontaine.]

[4] A fact told him by Lady Bolingbroke, of an old Countess at Paris. *Warburton.* [It is rather an odd circumstance that, although the professed subject of this Epistle is 'the Characters of *Men*,' Pope has taken two of the examples to illustrate his theory from *Women*, the 'frugal crone' and 'poor Narcissa,' and yet he says, in the next Epistle, on Women,

'In Men, we various Ruling Passions find;
In Women, *two* almost divide the kind,
The Love of Pleasure, and the Love of Sway.'

Neither of these Passions belonged to the Women, whose examples he has introduced to illustrate the Character and Ruling Passion of Men. *Bowles.*]

[5] — *the last words that poor Narcissa spoke*)] This story, as well as the others, is founded on fact, tho' the author had the goodness not to mention the names. Several attribute this in particular to a very celebrated Actress, who, in detestation of the thought of being buried in woollen, gave these her last orders with her dying breath. P. [According to Warton the actress in question was the famous Mrs. Oldfield, and Betty, her friend and confidante, Mrs. Saunders.]

[6] [No reader of Dickens will fail to remember the last words of Cleopatra in *Dombey and Son*, just as the next illustration but one will remind many of Tennyson's *Northern Farmer*. Euclio's very words are said by Warton to have been used by Sir William Bateman on his deathbed. But Wakefield states Euclio to have been designed for Sir Charles Duncombe of Helmsley; which is probable from *Imit. of Horace*, Sat. II. v. 183.]

"I give and I devise (old Euclio said,
And sigh'd) my lands and tenements to Ned."
"Your money, Sir;" "My money, Sir, what all?
Why, — if I must — (then wept) I give it Paul."
"The Manor, Sir?" — "The Manor! hold," he cry'd,   260
"Not that, — I cannot part with that" — and died.
  And you! brave COBHAM, to the latest breath
Shall feel your ruling passion strong in death:
Such in those moments as in all the past,
"Oh, save my Country, Heav'n!" shall be your last.[1]   265

EPISTLE II.[2]

TO A LADY.[3]

Of the Characters of WOMEN.

NOTHING so true as what you once let fall,
  "Most Women have no Characters at all."
Matter too soft a lasting mark to bear,
And best distinguish'd by black, brown, or fair.
  How many pictures of one Nymph we view,   5
All how unlike each other, all how true!
Arcadia's Countess,[4] here, in ermin'd pride,
Is, there, Pastora by a fountain side.
Here Fannia, leering on her own good man,
And there, a naked Leda with a Swan.   10
Let then the Fair one beautifully cry,
In Magdalen's loose hair, and lifted eye,
Or drest in smiles of sweet Cecilia shine,[5]

---

[1] Whatever were the precise last words of William Pitt, this was the spirit which dictated them. Compare the *Epitaph* (XIII.) *on Atterbury*.]

[2] [Of this Epistle, which was published in 1735, parts had been long before written and even printed. As originally published, it wanted the portraits of Philomede, Chloe and Atossa. According to Warburton's statement, Pope communicated the character of Atossa to the Duchess of Marlborough as intended for the Duchess of Buckingham; according to Walpole he repeated the experiment vice versa. Immediately on the death of Pope, the Duchess of Marlborough applied to one of his executors, Lord Marchmont, with the view of ascertaining whether the poet had left behind him any satire on the Duke or himself. Marchmont consulted Bolingbroke; and it was found that in the edition of the *Moral Essays* prepared for the press by Pope just before his death, and printed off ready for publication, the character of Atossa was inserted. If Lord Marchmont made the statement attributed to him by the editor of his papers (Rose), Pope had received from the Duchess £1000, the acceptance of which implied forbearance towards the house of Marlborough. If this be so, it is probable that the motive which prompted Pope to the acceptance of this 'favour' was the desire to settle Martha Blount in independent circumstances for life. See the account of this transaction in Carruthers' *Life of Pope*, pp. 392-6. On the general subject of the Epistle, compare the 6th Satire of Juvenal, the 10th Satire of Boileau, and Young's two Satires *On Women*.]

[3] [Generally supposed to be Martha Blount, concerning whom see *Introductory Memoir*, p. xxx.]

[4] [The *Arcadia* of Sir Philip Sidney was inscribed to his sister, the Countess of Pembroke.]

[5] *Arcadia's Countess, — Pastora by a foun-*

ST. CECILIA.
(Carlo Dolci.)

MORAL ESSAYS.

With simp'ring Angels, Palms, and Harps divine;
Whether the Charmer sinner it, or saint it,   15
If Folly grow romantic, I must paint it.
   Come then, the colors and the ground prepare!
Dip in the Rainbow, trick her off in Air;
Choose a firm Cloud, before it fall, and in it
Catch, ere she change, the Cynthia of this minute.[1]   20
   Rufa, whose eye quick-glancing o'er the Park,[2]
Attracts each light gay meteor of a Spark,
Agrees as ill with Rufa studying Locke,[3]
As Sappho's di'monds with her dirty smock;[4]
Or Sappho at her toilet's greasy task,   25
With Sappho fragrant at an ev'ning Masque:
So morning Insects that in muck begun,
Shine, buzz, and fly-blow in the setting-sun.
   How soft is Silia! fearful to offend;[5]
The Frail one's advocate, the Weak one's friend: 30
To her, Calista prov'd her conduct nice;
And good Simplicius asks of her advice.
Sudden, she storms! she raves! You tip the wink,
But spare your censure; Silia does not drink.
All eyes may see from what the change arose,   35
All eyes may see — a Pimple on her nose.
   Papillia, wedded to her am'rous spark,[5]
Sighs for the shades — "How charming is a Park!"
A Park is purchas'd, but the Fair he sees
All bath'd in tears — "Oh odious, odious Trees!"   40
   Ladies, like variegated Tulips, show;
'T is to their Changes half their charms we owe;

---

tain — Leda with a swan — Magdalen — Cecilia —] Attitudes in which several ladies affected to be drawn, and sometimes one lady in them all. The poet's politeness and complaisance to the sex is observable in this instance, amongst others, that, where, as in the *Characters of Men* he has sometimes made use of real names, in the *Characters of Women* always fictitious. P. [The reader must remember the portraits by Kneller and his contemporaries to appreciate the aptness of the illustration.]

[1] *Catch, ere she change, the Cynthia of this minute.*] Alluding to the precept of Fresnoy:
   '*formæ veneres captando fugaces.*'
                                   Warburton.

[2] Instances of contrarieties, given even from such Characters as are most strongly mark'd and seemingly therefore most consistent; as I.: In the *Affected*, v. 21, &c., P.

[3] [Warburton compares the first stanza of Pope's first *Imitation of Dorset.* See p. 183. The person referred to is supposed to be Queen-Caroline; but this seems unlikely, as the Queen appears, v. 181.]

[4] [*Sappho* is Lady Mary Wortley Montagu, as to whose relations with Pope see *Introductory Memoir*, p. xxxi, where the different passages in which she is attacked by him are enumerated. He had first addressed her as Sappho in some panegyrical lines written in 1722, and afterwards transferred to Martha Blount. Lady Mary Pierrepoint was born at Thoresby in Notts. about 1690; in 1712 married Edward Wortley Montagu, whom she accompanied to Constantinople on his appointment to that embassy in 1716. Shortly after her return in 1718 she fixed her summer residence at Twickenham. In the year 1739 declining health determined her to quit England for Italy and the South of France, where she remained till shortly before her death in 1762. Her letters from Constantinople were first published in the following year.]

[5] II. Contrarieties in the *Soft-natur'd.* P.

Fine by defect, and delicately weak,
Their happy Spots the nice admirer take,[1]
'T was thus Calypso once each heart alarm'd,[2]   45
Aw'd without Virtue, without Beauty charm'd;
Her Tongue bewitch'd as oddly as her Eyes,
Less Wit than Mimic, more a Wit than wise;
Strange graces still, and stranger flights she had,
Was just not ugly, and was just not mad;   50
Yet ne'er so sure our passion to create,
As when she touch'd the brink of all we hate.

Narcissa's[3] nature, tolerably mild,[4]
To make a wash, would hardly stew a child;
Has ev'n been prov'd to grant a Lover's pray'r,   55
And paid a Tradesman once to make him stare;
Gave alms at Easter, in a Christian trim,
And made a Widow happy, for a whim.
Why then declare Good-nature is her scorn,
When 't is by that alone she can be borne?   60
Why pique all mortals, yet affect a name?
A fool to Pleasure, yet a slave to Fame:
Now deep in Taylor and the Book of Martyrs,[5]
Now drinking citron with his Grace and Chartres:[6]
Now Conscience chills her, and now Passion burns;   65
And Atheism and Religion take their turns;
A very Heathen in the carnal part,
Yet still a sad, good Christian at her heart.

See Sin in State, majestically drunk;[7]
Proud as a Peeress, prouder as a Punk;   70
Chaste to her Husband, frank to all beside,
A teeming Mistress, but a barren Bride.
What then? let Blood and Body bear the fault,
Her Head 's untouch'd, that noble Seat of Thought:
Such this day's doctrine— in another fit   75
She sins with Poets thro' pure Love of Wit.
What has not fir'd her bosom or her brain?
Cæsar and Tall-boy,[8] Charles and Charlemagne.

As Helluo, late Dictator of the Feast,
The Nose of Hautgoût, and the Tip of Taste,   80
Critic'd your wine, and analys'd your meat,
Yet on plain Pudding deign'd at home to eat;

---

[1] [Alluding to the 'beauty-spots' or *mouches* then in fashion.]

[2] III. Contrarieties in the *Cunning* and *Artful*. P.

[3] I have been informed, on good authority, that this character was designed for the then Duchess of Hamilton. *Warton*. [These lines were originally published, in a somewhat different form, under the title of *Sylvia, a Fragment*, in the *Miscellanies* of 1727.] See p. 526.

[4] IV. In the *Whimsical*. P.

[5] [Jeremy Taylor's devotional works and Fox's Book of Martyrs.]

[6] [For Chartres see Pope's note to Ep. III. v. 20.]

[7] V. In the *Lewd* and *Vicious*. P.

[8] [According to Carruthers, a character in the *Jovial Crew*. But I cannot find the character in that brutal farce.]

MORAL ESSAYS.

So Philomedé,[1] lect'ring all mankind
On the soft Passion, and the Taste refin'd,
Th' Address, the Delicacy— stoops at once,   85
And makes her hearty meal upon a Dunce.
    Flavia 's a Wit, has too much sense to Pray;[2]
To Toast our wants and wishes, is her way;
Nor asks of God, but of her Stars, to give
The mighty blessing, "while we live, to live."   90
Then all for Death, that Opiate of the soul!
Lucretia's dagger, Rosamonda's[3] bowl.
Say, what can cause such impotence of mind?
A Spark too fickle, or a Spouse too kind.
Wise Wretch! with Pleasures too refin'd to please;   95
With too much Spirit to be e'er at ease;
With too much Quickness ever to be taught;
With too much Thinking to have common Thought:
You purchase Pain with all that Joy can give,
And die of nothing but a Rage to live.   100
    Turn then from Wits; and look on Simo's Mate,
No Ass so meek, no Ass so obstinate.
Or her, that owns her Faults, but never mends,
Because she 's honest, and the best of Friends.
Or her, whose life the Church and Scandal share,   105
For ever in a Passion, or a Pray'r.
Or her, who laughs at Hell, but (like her Grace)[4]
Cries, "Ah! how charming, if there 's no such place!"
Or who in sweet vicissitude appears
Of Mirth and Opium, Ratafie[5] and Tears,   110
The daily Anodyne, and nightly Draught,
To kill those foes to Fair ones, Time and Thought.
Woman and Fool are two hard things to hit;
For true No-meaning puzzles more than Wit.
    But what are these to great Atossa's mind?[6]   115

---

[1] Design'd for the Duchess of Marlborough who so much admired Congreve. *Warton.* [Not the famous Duchess Sarah, but her daughter Henrietta, who was Duchess of Marlborough in her own right, and married the Earl of Godolphin.]

[2] VI. Contrarieties in the *Witty* and *Refin'd*. P.

[3] [The Fair Rosamond of Henry II. In Addison's Opera of *Rosamond* the heroine demands 'the deadly bowl' instead of the dagger offered by Queen Elinor.]

[4] The Duchess of Montagu. *Warton.* [She was an intimate friend of Lady Mary Wortley Montagu's, who speaks of her 'tender esteem' for the Duchess.]

[5] [A kind of *liqueur*.]

[6] [The Duchess of Marlborough. See note on p. 240. Her maiden name was Sarah Jennings; and Colonel Churchill was her third husband. As Lady Churchill she acquired an irresistible influence over the Princess Anne, to whom she was appointed First Lady of the Bedchamber, and with whom for twenty years she carried on a correspondence under the loving pseudonym of Mrs. Freeman. It was through her that Churchill rose to power and place and became Earl of Marlborough. After Queen Anne's accession the influence of Marlborough (created Duke in 1702) became for a time absolute; and was imperiously maintained at home by his Duchess while he was gaining laurels abroad. It was at last successfully undermined by Harley and his instrument Abigail Hill, a relative of the Duchess and bedchamber-woman to the Queen; and in 1712, Marlborough was dismissed from all his employments. The Duchess survived his death (in 1722) for 22

Scarce once herself, by turns all Womankind!
Who, with herself, or others, from her birth
Finds all her life one warfare upon earth:
Shines in exposing Knaves, and painting Fools,
Yet is, whate'er she hates and ridicules.   120
No Thought advances, but her Eddy Brain
Whisks it about, and down it goes again.[1]
Full sixty years the World has been her Trade,
The wisest Fool much Time has ever made.
From loveless youth to unrespected age,   125
No Passion gratify'd except her Rage.
So much the Fury still out-ran the Wit,
The Pleasure miss'd her, and the Scandal hit.
Who breaks with her, provokes Revenge from Hell,
But he's a bolder man who dares be well.   130
Her ev'ry turn with Violence pursu'd,
Nor more a storm her Hate than Gratitude:
To that each Passion turns, or soon or late;
Love, if it makes her yield, must make her hate:
Superiors? death! and Equals? what a curse!   135
But an Inferior not dependant? worse.
Offend her, and she knows not to forgive;
Oblige her, and she'll hate you while you live:
But die, and she'll adore you — Then the Bust
And Temple rise — then fall again to dust.[2]   140
Last night, her Lord was all that's good and great;
A Knave this morning, and his Will a Cheat.
Strange! by the Means defeated of the Ends,
By Spirit robb'd of Pow'r, by Warmth of Friends,
By Wealth of Follow'rs! without one distress   145
Sick of herself thro' very selfishness!
Atossa, curs'd with ev'ry granted pray'r,
Childless with all her Children, wants an Heir.[3]
To Heirs unknown descends th' unguarded store,
Or wanders, Heav'n-directed, to the Poor.[4]   150
  Pictures like these, dear Madam, to design,

years; and in her *Vindications* of his conduct and her own has left materials for modifying some at least among the extravagant charges brought against both. With Pope's caustic references to every doubtful point in her career and character should be compared the equally unmerciful prose attacks of Swift in the *Examiner*, Nos. 16, 19, 49, &c. It may be added that the name of Atossa, the ambitious daughter of Cyrus and mother of Xerxes, is admirably chosen.]

[1] After v. 122, in the MS.
'Oppress'd with wealth and wit, abundance sad!
One makes her poor, the other makes her mad.'
Warburton.

[2] This alludes to a temple she erected with a bust of Queen Anne in it, which mouldered away in a few years. *Wilkes.*

[3] After v. 148, in the MS.
'This Death decides, nor lets the blessing fall
On any one she hates, but on them all.
Curs'd chance! this only could afflict her more,
If any part should wander to the poor.'
Warburton.

[4] [Pitt (the elder) was then one of the poor; and to him Heaven directed a portion of the wealth of the haughty Dowager. *Macaulay.*]

Asks no firm hand, and no unerring line;
Some wand'ring touches, some reflected light,
Some flying stroke alone can hit 'em right:
For how should equal Colours do the knack?   155
Chameleons who can paint in white and black?
" Yet Chloe¹ sure was form'd without a spot " —
Nature in her then err'd not, but forgot.
" With ev'ry pleasing, ev'ry prudent part,
Say, what can Chloe want? " — She wants a Heart.   160
She speaks, behaves, and acts just as she ought;
But never, never, reach'd one gen'rous Thought.
Virtue she finds too painful an endeavour,
Content to dwell in Decencies for ever.
So very reasonable, so unmov'd,   165
As never yet to love, or to be lov'd.
She, while her Lover pants upon her breast,
Can mark the figures on an Indian chest;
And when she sees her Friend in deep despair,
Observes how much a Chintz exceeds Mohair.²   170
Forbid it Heav'n, a Favour or a Debt
She e'er should cancel — but she may forget.
Safe is your Secret still in Chloe's ear;
But none of Chloe's shall you ever hear.
Of all her Dears she never slander'd one,   175
But cares not if a thousand are undone.
Would Chloe know if you're alive or dead?
She bids her Footman put it in her head.
Chloe is prudent — Would you too be wise?
Then never break your heart when Chloe dies.   180
   One certain Portrait may (I grant) be seen,
Which Heav'n has varnish'd out, and made a *Queen:*
THE SAME FOR EVER! and describ'd by all
With Truth and Goodness, as with Crown and Ball.
Poets heap Virtues, Painters Gems at will,   185
And shew their zeal, and hide their want of skill.
'T is well — but, Artists! who can paint or write,
To draw the Naked is your true delight.
That robe of Quality so struts and swells,
None see what Parts of Nature it conceals: 190
Th' exactest traits of Body or of Mind,
We owe to models of an humble kind.
If QUEENSBURY³ to strip there's no compelling,

---

[1] Lady Suffolk. *Warton.* [This great lady, whose friendship was courted by Swift, Pope, Arbuthnot and Gay, is described by Lord Stanhope as 'placid, good-natured, and kind-hearted, but very deaf, and not remarkable for wit.' She was the mistress of George II.]

[2] [*Mohair,* a stuff made of camel's or other uncommon hair.]

[3] [The Duchess of Queensbury, the correspondent of Swift and the untiring patroness of Gay. Her commanding position as a leader of fashion is illustrated by an amusing anecdote of Lady Mary Wortley Montagu's, who speaks of the Duchess at the head of a tribe of dames insisting upon admission to the House of Lords on an occasion when for want of room ladies had been excluded from the Chamber.]

'T is from a Handmaid we must take a Helen,
From Peer or Bishop 't is no easy thing   195
To draw the man who loves his God, or King:
Alas! I copy (or my draught would fail)
From honest Mah'met,[1] or plain Parson Hale.[2]
  But grant, in Public Men sometimes are shown,[3]
A Woman 's seen in Private life alone: 200
Our bolder Talents in full light display'd;
Your virtues open fairest in the shade.
Bred to disguise, in Public 't is you hide;
There, none distinguish 'twixt your Shame or Pride,
Weakness or Delicacy; all so nice,   205
That each may seem a Virtue, or a Vice.[4]
  In Men, we various Ruling Passions find;[5]
In Women, two almost divide the kind;
Those, only fix'd, they first or last obey,
The Love of Pleasure, and the Love of Sway.   210
  That, Nature gives; and where the lesson taught[6]
Is but to please, can Pleasure seem a fault?
Experience, this; by Man's oppression curst,
They seek the second not to loose the first.
  Men, some to Bus'ness, some to Pleasure take;   215
But every Woman is at heart a Rake:
Men, some to Quiet, some to public Strife;
But ev'ry Lady would be Queen for life.
  Yet mark the fate of a whole Sex of Queens![7]
Pow'r all their end, but Beauty all the means: 220
In Youth they conquer, with so wild a rage,
As leaves them scarce a subject in their Age:
For foreign glory, foreign joy, they roam;
No thought of peace or happiness at home.
But Wisdom's triumph is well-tim'd Retreat,   225
As hard a science to the Fair as Great!
Beauties, like Tyrants, old and friendless grown,

---

[1] *Mah'met*, servant to the late King [George I.], said to be the son of a Turkish Bassa, whom he took at the Siege of Buda, and constantly kept about his person. P.

[2] Dr. *Stephen Hale*, not more estimable for his useful discoveries as a natural philosopher, than for his exemplary Life and Pastoral Charity as a Parish Priest. P.

[3] *But grant, in Public, &c.*] In the former Editions, between this and the foregoing lines, a want of Connexion might be perceived, occasioned by the omission of certain *Examples* and *Illustrations* to the Maxims laid down; and tho' some of these have since been found, viz. the Characters of *Philomedè, Atossa, Chloe*, and some verses following, others are still wanting, nor can we answer that these are exactly inserted. P.

[4] *That each may seem a Virtue, or a Vice.*] For Women are taught Virtue so artificially, and Vice so naturally, that, in the nice exercise of them, they may be easily mistaken for one another. *Scriblerus*.

[5] The former part having shewn, that the *particular Characters* of Women are more various than those of Men, it is nevertheless observed, that the *general* Characteristic of the sex, as to the *ruling Passion*, is more uniform. P.

[6] This is occasioned partly by their *Nature*, partly their *Education*, and in some degree by *Necessity*. P.

[7] What are the *Aims* and the *Fate* of this Sex?—I. As to *Power*. P.

MORAL ESSAYS.

Yet hate repose, and dread to be alone,
Worn out in public, weary ev'ry eye,
Nor leave one sigh behind them when they die.[1]   230
    Pleasures the sex, as children Birds, pursue,[2]
Still out of reach, yet never out of view;
Sure, if they catch, to spoil the Toy at most,
To covet flying, and regret when lost:
At last, to follies Youth could scarce defend,   235
It grows their Age's prudence to pretend;
Asham'd to own they gave delight before,
Reduc'd to feign it, when they give no more:
As Hags hold Sabbaths,[3] less for joy than spite,
So these their merry, miserable Night;   240
Still round and round the Ghosts of Beauty glide,
And haunt the places where their Honour died.
    See how the World its Veterans rewards!
A Youth of Frolics, an old Age of Cards;
Fair to no purpose, artful to no end,   245
Young without Lovers, old without a Friend;
A Fop their Passion, but their Prize a Sot;
Alive, ridiculous, and dead, forgot![4]
    Ah! Friend! to dazzle let the Vain design;[5]
To raise the Thought, and touch the Heart be thine!   250
That Charm shall grow, while what fatigues the Ring,[6]
Flaunts and goes down, an unregarded thing:
So when the Sun's broad beam has tir'd the sight,
All mild ascends the Moon's more sober light,
Serene in Virgin Modesty she shines,   255
And unobserv'd the glaring Orb declines.[7]
    Oh! blest with Temper, whose unclouded ray
Can make to-morrow cheerful as to-day;
She, who can love a Sister's charms, or hear
Sighs for a daughter with unwounded ear;   260
She, who ne'er answers till a Husband cools,
Or if she rules him never shews she rules;
Charms by accepting, by submitting sways,
Yet has her humour most, when she obeys;
Let Fops or Fortune fly which way they will;   265
Disdains all loss of Tickets, or Codille:[8]

---

[1] Copied from Young, Satire V. *Warton.*
[2] II. As to *Pleasure.* P.
[3] [The Hags' or Witches' Sabbath is properly the Walpurgis-night, preceding May-day.]
[4] [For the history of these lines see note to lines *To Martha Blount on her birthday* in the *Miscellaneous Poems.*]
[5] Advice for their true Interest. P.
[6] [The fashionable promenade in the Park, made in the reign of Charles I. and partially destroyed at the time of the formation of the Serpentine by order of Queen Caroline.]
[7] [These four lines were originally addressed to Miss Judith Cowper, preceded by this triplet;
'Though sprightly Sappho force our love and praise,
A softer wonder my pleas'd soul surveys:
The mild Erinna blushing in her bays.']
See Carruthers's *Life.*
[8] [*Codille:* cf. *Rape of the Lock*, Canto III. v. 92.]

Spleen, Vapours, or Small-pox, above them all,
And Mistress of herself, tho' China fall.[1]
   And yet, believe me, good as well as ill,
Woman's at best a Contradiction still.   270
Heav'n, when it strives to polish all it can
Its last best work, but forms a softer Man;
Picks from each sex, to make the Fav'rite blest,
Your love of Pleasure, or desire of Rest:
Blends, in exception to all gen'ral rules,   275
Your Taste of Follies, with our Scorn of Fools:
Reserve with Frankness, Art with Truth ally'd,
Courage with Softness, Modesty with Pride;
Fix'd Principles, with Fancy ever new;
Shakes all together, and produces — You.[2]   280
   Be this a Woman's Fame: with this unblest,
Toasts live a scorn, and Queens may die a jest.
This Phœbus promis'd (I forget the year)
When those blue eyes first open'd on the sphere;
Ascendant Phœbus watch'd that hour with care,   285
Averted half your Parents' simple Pray'r;
And gave you Beauty, but deny'd the Pelf
That buys your sex a Tyrant o'er itself.
The gen'rous God, who Wit and Gold refines,
And ripens Spirits as he ripens Mines,   290
Kept Dross for Duchesses, the world shall know it,[3]
To you gave Sense, Good-humour, and a Poet.

EPISTLE III.[4]

To Allen Lord Bathurst.[5]

ARGUMENT.

Of the Use of RICHES.

THAT it is known to few, most falling into one of the extremes, Avarice *or* Profusion, v. 1, &c. *The point discuss'd, whether the invention of Money has been more commodious or pernicious to Mankind,* v. 21 to 77. *That Riches, either to the* Avaricious *or the*

---

[1] Addison has touched this subject with his usual exquisite humour in the *Lover,* No. 10, quoting Epictetus, to comfort a Lady that labours under this heavy calamity. *Warton.*

[2] [Warton compares Swift's:
'Jove mix'd up all, and his best clay employ'd,
Then call'd the happy composition — Floyd.']

[3] [Yet it was for Martha Blount, to whom these compliments are addressed, that Pope seems to have taken the dross of the Duchess of Marlborough. V. *ante.*]

[4] This Epistle was written after a violent outcry against our Author, on a supposition that he had ridiculed a worthy nobleman merely for his wrong taste. He justified himself upon that article in a letter to the Earl of Burlington; at the end of which are these words: "I have learnt that there are some who would rather be wicked than ridiculous: and therefore it may be safer to attack vices than follies. I will therefore leave my betters in the quiet possession of their idols, their groves, and their high places; and change my subject from their pride to their meanness, from their vanities to their miseries; and as the only certain way to avoid misconstructions, to lessen offence, and not to multiply ill-natured applications, I may probably, in my next, make use of real names instead of fictitious ones." P.

[5] [Allen Apsley Lord Bathurst, a Tory peer, was one of the most intimate of Pope's friends

MORAL ESSAYS. 249

Prodigal, *cannot afford Happiness, scarcely Necessaries*, v. 89–160. *That Avarice is an absolute Frenzy, without an End or Purpose*, v. 113, &c. 152. *Conjectures about the Motives of Avaricious men*, v. 121 to 153. *That the conduct of men, with respect to Riches, can only be accounted for by the* ORDER OF PROVIDENCE, *which works the general Good out of Extremes, and brings all to its great End by perpetual Revolutions*, v. 161 to 178. *How a* Miser *acts upon Principles which appear to him reasonable*, v. 179. *How a* Prodigal *does the same*, v. 199. *The due Medium, and true use of Riches*, v. 219. *The* Man *of* Ross, v. 250. *The fate of the* Profuse *and the* Covetous, *in two examples; both miserable in Life and in Death*, v. 300, &c. *The Story of Sir* Balaam, v. 339 to the end.

P. WHO shall decide, when Doctors disagree,
And soundest Casuists doubt, like you and me?
You hold the word, from Jove to Momus[1] giv'n
That Man was made the standing jest of Heav'n;
And Gold but sent to keep the fools in play,   5
For some to heap, and some to throw away.
    But I, who think more highly of our kind,
(And surely, Heav'n and I are of a mind)
Opine, that Nature, as in duty bound,
Deep hid the shining mischief under ground: 10
But when by Man's audacious labour won,
Flam'd forth this rival to its Sire, the Sun,
Then careful Heav'n supply'd two sorts of Men,
To squander These, and Those to hide again.
    Like Doctors thus, when much dispute has past,   15
We find our tenets just the same at last.
Both fairly owing Riches, in effect,
No grace of Heav'n or token of th' Elect;
Giv'n to the Fool, the Mad, the Vain, the Evil,
To Ward,[2] to Waters,[2] Chartres,[2] and the Devil.[2]   20

and associates. 'He united,' says Carruthers, 'a sort of French vivacity' ['Bathurst impetuous, whom you and I strive who shall love the most,' is the mention of him in Gay's catalogue of Pope's friends] 'to English principles, and mingled freely in society till past ninety, living to walk under the shade of lofty trees which Pope and he had planted, and to see his son Lord Chancellor of England.' He died in the year 1774, at the age of 91.]

[1] [Momus (derisive blame) is personified as a god in the Theogony of Hesiod.]

[2] John Ward, of Hackney, Esq.; Member of Parliament, being prosecuted by the Duchess of Buckingham, and convicted of Forgery, was first expelled the House, and then stood in the Pillory on the 17th of March, 1727. He was suspected of joining in a conveyance with Sir John Blunt, to secrete fifty thousand pounds of that Director's Estate, forfeited to the South-Sea Company by Act of Parliament. The company recovered the fifty thousand pounds against Ward; but he set up prior conveyances of his real estate to his brother and son, and conceal'd all his personal, which was computed to be one hundred and fifty thousand pounds. These conveyances being also set aside by a bill in Chancery, Ward was imprisoned, and hazarded the forfeiture of his life, by not giving in his effects till the last day, which was that of his examination. During his confinement, his amusement was to give poison to dogs and cats, and to see them expire by slower or quicker torments. To sum up the *worth* of this gentleman, at the several æra's of his life, At his standing in the Pillory he was *worth above two hundred thousand pounds;* at his commitment to Prison, he was *worth one hundred and fifty thousand;* but has been since so far diminished in his reputation, as to be thought a *worse man* by *fifty or sixty thousand*. P. [From Pope's intimate acquaintance with Mr. Ward's career, it might almost be suspected that he is the same who is enumerated among Pope's friends in Gay's poem.]

Mr. Waters, the third of these worthies, was a man no way resembling the former in his

B. What nature wants, commodious[1] Gold bestows,
'T is thus we eat the bread another sows.
P. But how unequal it bestows, observe,
'T is thus we riot, while, who sow it, starve:
What Nature wants (a phrase I much distrust)   25
Extends to Luxury, extends to Lust:
Useful, I grant, it serves what life requires,
But, dreadful too, the dark Assassin hires:
B. Trade it may help, Society extend.
P. But lures the Pirate, and corrupts the Friend.   30
B. It raises Armies in a Nation's aid.
P. But bribes a Senate, and the Land's betray'd.
In vain may Heroes fight, and Patriots rave;
If secret Gold sap on from knave to knave.[2]

military, but extremely so in his civil capacity; his great fortune having been rais'd by the like diligent attendance on the necessities of others. But this gentleman's history must be deferred till his death, when his *worth* may be known more certainly. P.

Fr. Chartres, a man infamous for all manner of vices. When he was an ensign in the army, he was drumm'd out of the regiment for a cheat; he was next banish'd Brussels, and drumm'd out of Ghent on the same account. After a hundred tricks at the gaming tables, he took to lending of money at exorbitant interest and on great penalties, accumulating premium, interest, and capital into a new capital, and seizing to a minute when the payments became due; in a word, by a constant attention to the vices, wants, and follies of mankind, he acquired an immense fortune. His house was a perpetual bawdy-house. He was twice condemn'd for rapes, and pardoned: but the last time not without imprisonment in Newgate, and large confiscations. He died in Scotland in 1731, aged 62. The populace at his funeral rais'd a great riot, almost tore the body out of the coffin, and cast dead dogs, &c, into the grave along with it. The following Epitaph contains his character very justly drawn by Dr. Arbuthnot;

HERE continueth to rot
The Body of FRANCIS CHARTRES,
Who with an INFLEXIBLE CONSTANCY,
and INIMITABLE UNIFORMITY of Life,
PERSISTED,
In spite of AGE and INFIRMITIES,
In the Practice of EVERY HUMAN VICE;
Excepting PRODIGALITY and HYPOCRISY:
His insatiable AVARICE exempted him from the first,
His matchless IMPUDENCE from the second.
Nor was he more singular
in the undeviating *Pravity* of his *Manners*
. Than successful
in *Accumulating* WEALTH.
For, without TRADE or PROFESSION,
Without TRUST of PUBLIC MONEY,
And without BRIBE-WORTHY Service,
He acquired, or more properly created,
A MINISTERIAL ESTATE.
He was the only Person of his Time,
Who could CHEAT without the Mask of HONESTY,
Retain his Primeval MEANNESS
When possess'd of TEN THOUSAND a YEAR,
And having daily deserved the GIBBET for what he *did*,
Was at last condemn'd to it for what he *could not do*.
Oh Indignant Reader!
Think not his Life useless to Mankind!
PROVIDENCE conniv'd at his execrable Designs,
To give to After-ages
A conspicuous PROOF and EXAMPLE,
Of how small Estimation is EXORBITANT WEALTH
in the Sight of GOD,
By his bestowing it on the most UNWORTHY of ALL MORTALS.

This Gentleman was *worth seven thousand pounds a year* estate in Land, and about *one hundred thousand* in Money. P.

and the Devil.] Alluding to the vulgar opinion, that all mines of metal and subterraneous treasures are in the guard of the Devil: which seems to have taken its rise from the pagan fable of Plutus the God of Riches. *Warburton.* [The name of Pluton, given to the God beneath the surface who sends forth the wealth of corn, probably originated in the Eleusinian Mysteries.]

[1] *Commodious*, i.e. accommodating.]
[2] *If secret Gold* sap *on from knave to knave.*] The expression is fine, and gives us

MORAL ESSAYS. 251

Once, we confess, beneath the Patriot's cloak,[1] 35
From the crack'd bag the dropping Guinea spoke,
And jingling down the back-stairs, told the crew,
"Old Cato is as great a Rogue as you."
Blest paper-credit! last and best supply![2]
That lends Corruption lighter wings to fly! 40
Gold imp'd[3] by thee, can compass hardest things,
Can pocket States, can fetch or carry Kings;[4]
A single leaf shall waft an Army o'er,
Or ship off Senates to a distant Shore;[5]
A leaf, like Sibyl's, scatter to and fro 45
Our fates and fortunes, as the winds shall blow:
Pregnant with thousands flits the Scrap unseen,
And silent sells a King, or buys a Queen.[6]
 Oh! that such bulky Bribes as all might see,
Still, as of old, encumber'd Villainy![7] 50
Could France or Rome divert our brave designs,
With all their brandies or with all their wines?
What could they more than Knights and Squires confound,
Or water all the Quorum[8] ten miles round?
A Stateman's slumbers how this speech would spoil! 55
" Sir, Spain has sent a thousand jars of oil;
Huge bales of British cloth blockade the door;
A hundred oxen at your levee roar."
 Poor Avarice one torment more would find;
Nor could Profusion squander all in kind. 60

the image of a place invested, where the approaches are made by communications which support each other; as the connexions amongst knaves, after they have been taken in by a state engineer, serve to screen and encourage one another's private corruptions.

[1] —*beneath the Patriot's cloak,*] This is a true story, which happened in the reign of William III. to an unsuspected old Patriot, who coming out at the back-door from having been closeted by the King, where he had receiv'd a large bag of Guineas, the bursting of the bag discovered his business there. P. [According to Warburton, quoting Burnet, this was Sir Christopher Musgrave, who as a leader of opposition was induced by King William III. to give up many points of importance at the critical minute, in return for payments amounting in the total to £12,000.]

[2] *paper-credit.* [In 1733 the privileges of the Bank of England were renewed. In the same year, in spite of the opposition of Barnard and others, Walpole openly availed himself of the Sinking Fund, and before 1737 had mortgaged and alienated its entire produce.]

[3] *Imp'd* [i.e. fresh-winged. *To imp* is a term of falconry, used of the repairing of the falcon's wings by new feathers. (Cf. the German *impfen*, to engraft.)]

[4] —*fetch or carry Kings;*] In our author's time, many Princes had been sent about the world, and great changes of Kings projected in Europe. The partition-treaty had disposed of Spain; France had set up a King for England, who was sent to Scotland, and back again; King Stanislaus was sent to Poland, and back again; the Duke of Anjou was sent to Spain, and Don Carlos to Italy. P.

[5] *Or ship off Senates to a distant Shore;*] Alludes to several Ministers, Counsellors, and Patriots banished in our times to Siberia, and to that MORE GLORIOUS FATE of the PARLIAMENT OF PARIS, banished to Pontoise in the year 1720. P.

[6] [The allusion seems to be to the Pretender 'King James III.' and to Queen Caroline. There are no grounds for such an imputation upon the latter; but the taunt might be applied with much force to her unhappy later namesake.]

[7] After v. 50, in the MS.
'To break a trust were Peter brib'd with wine,
Peter! 't would pose as wise a head as thine.'

[8] [i.e. every justice of peace.]

Astride his cheese¹ Sir Morgan might we meet;
And Worldly crying coals from street to street,²
Whom with a wig so wild, and mien so maz'd,
Pity mistakes for some poor tradesman craz'd.
Had Colepepper's³ whole wealth been hops and hogs,　　　65
Could he himself have sent it to the dogs?
His Grace will game: to White's⁴ a Bull be led,
With spurning heels and with a butting head.
To White's be carry'd, as to ancient games,
Fair Coursers, Vases, and alluring Dames.　　　70
Shall then Uxorio, if the stakes he sweep,
Bear home six Whores, and make his Lady weep?
Or soft Adonis, so perfum'd and fine,
Drive to St. James's a whole herd of swine?
Oh filthy check on all industrious skill,　　　75
To spoil the nation's last great trade, Quadrille!⁵
Since then, my Lord, on such a World we fall,
What say you? B.　Say?　Why take it, Gold and all.
P.　What Riches give us let us then enquire:
Meat, Fire, and Clothes. B. What more? P. Meat, Clothes,
　　and Fire.　　　80
Is this too little? would you more than live?
Alas! 't is more than Turner⁶ finds they give.
Alas! 't is more than (all his Visions past)
Unhappy Wharton,⁷ waking, found at last!
What can they give? to dying Hopkins,⁸ Heirs;　　　85

---

¹ [As a Welshman attached to a cheap national delicacy.]

² Some Misers of great wealth, proprietors of the coal-mines, had entered at this time into an association to keep up coals to an extravagant price, whereby the poor were reduced almost to starve, till one of them taking the advantage of underselling the rest, defeated the design. One of these Misers was *worth ten thousand*, another *seven thousand* a year. P.

³ *Colepepper*] Sir William Colepepper, Bart., a person of an ancient family, and ample fortune, without one other quality of a Gentleman, who, after ruining himself at the Gaming-table, past the rest of his days in sitting there to see the ruin of others; preferring to subsist upon borrowing and begging, rather than to enter into any reputable method of life, and refusing a post in the army which was offered him. P.

⁴ [The famous Club-house in St. James' Street, where games of chance were played for the highest stakes.]

⁵ [The game of *Quadrille*, which is a species of *Ombre*, soon came to surpass the latter in popularity.]

⁶ *Turner*] One, who, being possessed of three hundred thousand pounds, laid down his Coach, because Interest was reduced from five to four *per cent.* and then put seventy thousand into the Charitable Corporation for better interest; which sum having lost, he took it so much to heart, that he kept his chamber ever after. It is thought he would not have outlived it, but that he was heir to another considerable estate, which he daily expected, and that by this course of life he saved both cloaths and all other expenses. P.

⁷ *Unhappy Wharton*,] A Nobleman of great qualities, but as unfortunate in the application of them, as if they had been vices and follies. See his Character in the first Epistle. P. [v. 179.]

⁸ *Hopkins*,] A Citizen, whose rapacity obtained him the name of *Vulture Hopkins*. He lived worthless, but died *worth three hundred thousand pounds*, which he would give to no person living, but left it so as not to be inherited till after the second generation. His counsel representing to him how many years it must be, before this could take effect, and that his money could only lie at interest all that time, he expressed great joy thereat, and said, "They would then be as long in spending, as he had been in getting it." But the Chancery afterwards set aside the will, and gave it to the heir at law. P.

MORAL ESSAYS. 253

To Chartres, Vigour; Japhet, Nose and Ears?[1]
Can they, in gems bid pallid Hippia glow,
In Fulvia's buckle ease the throbs below;
Or heal, old Narses, thy obscener ail,
With all th' embroid'ry plaister'd at thy tail?   90
They might (were Harpax not too wise to spend)
Give Harpax' self the blessing of a friend;
Or find some Doctor that would save the life
Of wretched Shylock, spite of Shylock's Wife:
But thousands die, without or this or that,   95
Die, and endow a College, or a Cat.[2]
To some indeed, Heav'n grants the happier fate,
T' enrich a Bastard, or a Son they hate.
  Perhaps you think the Poor might have their part?
Bond damns the Poor, and hates them from his heart:[3]   100
The grave Sir Gilbert[4] holds it for a rule,
That "ev'ry man in want is knave or fool:
God cannot love (says Blunt, with tearless eyes)
The wretch he starves"—and piously denies:
But the good Bishop,[5] with a meeker air,   105
Admits, and leaves them, Providence's care.
  Yet, to be just to these poor men of pelf,
Each does but hate his neighbour as himself:
Damn'd to the Mines, an equal fate betides
The Slave that digs it, and the Slave that hides.   110
  B. Who suffer thus, mere Charity should own,

---

[1] *Japhet, Nose and Ears?*] Japhet Crook, alias Sir *Peter Stranger*, was punished with the loss of those parts, for having forged a conveyance of an Estate to himself, upon which he took up several thousand pounds. He was at the same time sued in Chancery for having fraudulently obtained a Will, by which he possessed another considerable Estate, in wrong of the brother of the deceased. By these means he was *worth* a great sum, which (in reward for the small loss of his ears) he enjoyed in prison till his death, and quietly left to his executor. P.

[2] *Die, and endow a College, or a Cat.*] A famous Dutchess of Richmond in her last will left considerable legacies and annuities to her Cats. P. [Warton more than vindicates the memory of this famous beauty of Charles II.'s court from Pope's taunt by stating that she left annuities to certain poor ladies of her acquaintance, with the burden of maintaining some of her cats; this proviso being intended to disguise the charitable character of the bequests. In Hamburgh, an annuity was not long ago left to the Swans which adorn the famous Alster-lake in that city.]

[3] *Bond damns the Poor, &c.*] This epistle was written in the year 1730, when a corporation was established to lend money to the poor upon pledges, by the name of the *Charitable Corporation;* but the whole was turned only to an iniquitous method of enriching particular people, to the ruin of such numbers, that it became a parliamentary concern to endeavour the relief of those unhappy sufferers, and three of the managers, who were members of the house, were expell'd. By the report of the committee, appointed to enquire into that iniquitous affair, it appears, that when it was objected to the intended removal of the office, that the Poor, for whose use it was erected, would be hurt by it, Bond, one of the Directors, replied, *Damn the Poor.* That "God hates the poor," and, "That every man in want is knave or fool," &c. were the genuine apothegms of some of the persons here mentioned. P. [Dennis Bond, a member of Parliament, died in 1747. *Carruthers.*]

[4] [Sir Gilbert Heathcote, director of the Bank of England, and one of the richest men of his day.]

[5] [The imaginary Bishop was at Warburton's request substituted for the name of a real person of whose virtual innocence in the matter Warburton felt convinced.]

Must act on motives pow'rful, tho' unknown.
P. Some War, some Plague, or Famine they foresee,
Some Revelation hid from you and me.
Why Shylock wants a meal, the cause is found, 115
He thinks a Loaf will rise to fifty pound.
What made Directors cheat in South-sea year?[1]
To live on Ven'son when it sold so dear.[2]
Ask you why Phryne the whole Auction buys?[3]
Phryne foresees a general Excise.[4] 120
Why she and Sappho[5] raise that monstrous sum?
Alas! they fear a man will cost a plum.
   Wise Peter[6] sees the World's respect for Gold,
And therefore hopes this Nation may be sold:
Glorious Ambition! Peter, swell thy store, 125
And be what Rome's great Didius[7] was before.
   The Crown of Poland, venal twice an age,[8]
To just three millions stinted modest Gage.[9]
But nobler scenes Maria's dreams unfold,

---

[1] [*South-sea year:* 1720; in August the stock of the South Sea Company had risen to 1000; by the end of September it had fallen to 300; and the news of the failure of Law's Mississippi scheme in Paris completed the crash which reduced thousands of families to beggary. Pope himself told Atterbury that after the bursting of the bubble he remained with ' half what he imagined he had,' probably meaning half his gains, as there is every reason to believe that he sold out in time.]

[2] *To live on Ven'son*] In the extravagance and luxury of the South-sea year, the price of a haunch of Venison was from three to five pounds. P.

[3] [Sir Robert Walpole's scheme of the year 1733 for bringing the tobacco- and wine-duties under the laws of excise, was magnified by report into the design of a general excise upon all articles of consumption. The popular ferment which the proposal aroused led to its abandonment. See Lord Stanhope's *History of England*, Chap. xvi.]

[4] —*general Excise*] Many people about the year 1733 had a conceit that such a thing was intended, of which it is not improbable this lady might have some intimation. P. [In 1733 Walpole contemplated a comprehensive measure for adding to the excise-duties, and reforming the whole administration of the revenue: a cry was set up against the measure by the Opposition, and the country, terrified by the bugbear of a general excise. Pulteney headed the opposition in Parliament, while the prejudices of the public were worked upon in the *Craftsman*. Walpole was forced to withdraw his excellent proposal.]

[5] [Pope himself advised Lady M. W. Montagu to purchase South-sea stock in August 1720.]

[6] *Wise Peter*] Peter Walter, a person not only eminent in the wisdom of his profession, as a dextrous attorney, but allowed to be a good, if not a safe conveyancer; extremely respected by the Nobility of this land, tho' free from all manner of luxury and ostentation: his Wealth was never seen, and his bounty never heard of, except to his own son, for whom he procured an employment of considerable profit, of which he gave him as much as was *necessary*. Therefore the taxing this gentleman with any Ambition, is certainly a great wrong to him. P. [The 'Waters' of v. 20.]

[7] *Rome's great Didius*] A Roman Lawyer, so rich as to purchase the Empire when it was set to sale upon the death of Pertinax. P. [Didius Julianus A.D. 193. The vendors were the Prætorian Guards.]

[8] *The Crown of Poland, &c.*] The two persons here mentioned were of Quality, each of whom in the Mississippi despis'd to realize above *three hundred thousand pounds;* the Gentleman with a view to the purchase of the Crown of Poland, the Lady on a vision of the like royal nature. They since retired into Spain, where they are still in search of gold in the mines of the Asturies. P.

[9] A Mr. Gage, of the ancient Suffolk Catholic family of that name: and Lady Mary Herbert, daughter of the Marquess of Powis and of a natural daughter of James II.; whence the phrase ' *hereditary* realms.' *Bowles.*

Hereditary Realms, and worlds of Gold.   130
Congenial souls! whose life one Av'rice joins,
And one fate buries in th' Asturian Mines.
  Much injur'd Blunt![1] why bears he Britain's hate?
A wizard told him in these words our fate:
"At length Corruption, like a gen'ral flood,   135
(So long by watchful Ministers withstood)
Shall deluge all; and Av'rice, creeping on,
Spread like a low-born mist, and blot the Sun;
Statesman and Patriot ply alike the stocks,
Peeress and Butler share alike the Box,   140
And Judges job, and Bishops bite the town,
And mighty Dukes pack Cards for half a crown.
See Britain sunk in lucre's sordid charms,
And France reveng'd of ANNE's and EDWARD's arms?"
'T was no Court-badge, great Scriv'ner! fir'd thy brain,   145
Nor lordly Luxury, nor City Gain:
No, 't was thy righteous end, asham'd to see
Senates degen'rate, Patriots disagree,
And, nobly wishing Party-rage to cease,
To buy both sides, and give thy Country peace.   150
  "All this is madness," cries a sober sage:
But who, my friend, has reason in his rage?
"The ruling Passion, be it what it will,
The ruling Passion conquers Reason still."
Less mad the wildest whimsey we can frame,   155
Than ev'n that Passion, if it has no Aim;
For tho' such motives Folly you may call,
The Folly's greater to have none at all.[2]
  Hear then the truth: "'T is Heav'n each Passion sends,
And diff'rent men directs to diff'rent ends.   160
Extremes in Nature equal good produce,
Extremes in Man concur to gen'ral use."
Ask we what makes one keep, and one bestow?
That POW'R who bids the Ocean ebb and flow,
Bids seed-time, harvest, equal course maintain,   165
Thro' reconcil'd extremes of drought and rain,
Builds life on Death, on Change Duration founds,
And gives th' eternal wheels to know their rounds.
  Riches, like insects, when conceal'd they lie,

---

[1] *Much injur'd Blunt!*] Sir John Blunt, originally a scrivener, was one of the first projectors of the South-sea Company, and afterwards one of the directors and chief managers of the famous scheme in 1720. He was also one of those who suffer'd most severely by the bill of pains and penalties on the said directors. He was a Dissenter of a most religious deportment and professed to be a greater believer. Whether he did really credit the prophecy here mentioned is not certain, but it was constantly in this very style he declaimed against the corruption and luxury of the age, the partiality of Parliaments, and the misery of party-spirit. He was particularly eloquent against *Avarice* in great and noble persons, of which he had indeed lived to see many miserable examples. He died in the year 1732. P.

[2] Verbatim from Rochefoucault. *Warton.*

Wait but for Wings, and in their season fly. 170
Who see pale Mammon pine amidst his store,
Sees but a backward steward for the Poor;
This year a Reservoir, to keep and spare;[1]
The next, a Fountain, spouting thro' his Heir,
In lavish streams to quench a Country's thirst, 175
And men and dogs shall drink him till they burst.

    Old Cotta[2] sham'd his fortune and his birth,
Yet was not Cotta void of wit or worth:
What tho' (the use of barb'rous spits forgot)
His kitchen vied in coolness with his grot?[3] 180
His court with nettles, moats with cresses stor'd,
With soups unbought[4] and salads bless'd his board?
If Cotta liv'd on pulse, it was no more
Than Brahmins, Saints, and Sages did before;
To cram the Rich was prodigal expense, 185
And who would take the Poor from Providence?
Like some lone Chartreux[5] stands the good old Hall,
Silence without, and Fasts within the wall;
No rafter'd roofs with dance and tabor sound,
No noontide-bell invites the country round; 190
Tenants with sighs the smokeless tow'rs survey,
And turn th' unwilling steeds another way;
Benighted wanderers, the forest o'er,
Curse the sav'd candle, and unop'ning door;
While the gaunt mastiff growling at the gate, 195
Affrights the beggar whom he longs to eat.

    Not so his Son; he mark'd this oversight,
And then mistook reverse of wrong for right.
(For what to shun will no great knowledge need;
But what to follow, is a task indeed.) 200
Yet sure, of qualities deserving praise,
More go to ruin Fortunes, than to raise.
What slaughter'd hecatombs, what floods of wine,
Fill the capacious Squire, and deep Divine!
Yet no mean motive this profusion draws, 205
His oxen perish in his country's cause;
'T is GEORGE and LIBERTY that crowns the cup,
And Zeal for that great House[6] which eats him up.
The woods recede around the naked seat;
The Sylvans groan — no matter — for the Fleet; 210
Next goes his Wool — to clothe our valiant bands;

---

[1] Taken from Fuller's *Church History*, p. 28. *Warton.*

[2] [Supposed to be the Duke of Newcastle, who died in 1711; and his son, the well-known peer of that name, who afterwards became prime minister. *Carruthers.* [See Macaulay's portrait of the son in his Essay on Chatham.]

[3] ['Cool was his kitchen, though his brains were hot.' Dryden, *Absalom and Achitophel.* I.]

[4] *With soups unbought*]
— dapibus mensas onerabat inemptis. Virg. P. [*Georg.* IV. 133.]

[5] [Carthusian monastery.]

[6] [Of Hanover.]

Last, for his Country's love, he sells his Lands.
To town he comes, completes the nation's hope,
And heads the bold Train-bands,[1] and burns a Pope.
And shall not Britain now reward his toils, 215
Britain, that pays her Patriots with her Spoils?
In vain at Court the Bankrupt pleads his cause,
His thankless Country leaves him to her Laws.[2]
    The Sense to value Riches, with the Art
T' enjoy them, and the Virtue to impart, 220
Not meanly, nor ambitiously pursu'd,
Not sunk by sloth, nor rais'd by servitude;
To balance Fortune by a just expense,
Join with Economy, Magnificence;
With Splendour, Charity; with Plenty, Health; 225
O teach us, BATHURST! yet unspoil'd by wealth![3]
That secret rare, between th' extremes to move
Of mad Good-nature, and of mean Self-love.
    B. To Worth or Want well-weigh'd, be Bounty giv'n,
And ease, or emulate, the care of Heav'n; 230
(Whose measure full o'erflows on human race)
Mend Fortune's fault, and justify her grace.
Wealth in the gross is death, but life diffus'd;
As Poison heals, in just proportion us'd:
In heaps, like Ambergrise, a stink it lies, 235
But well-dispers'd, is Incense to the Skies.
    P. Who starves by Nobles, or with Nobles eats?
The Wretch that trusts them, and the Rogue that cheats.
Is there a Lord, who knows a cheerful noon
Without a Fiddler, Flatt'rer, or Buffoon? 240
Whose table, Wit, or modest Merit share,
Unelbow'd by a Gamester, Pimp, or Play'r?
Who copies Your's or OXFORD'S better part,[4]
To ease th' oppress'd, and raise the sinking heart?
Where-e'er he shines, oh Fortune, gild the scene, 245
And Angels guard him in the golden Mean!
There, English Bounty yet awhile may stand,
And Honour linger ere it leaves the land.
    But all our praises why should Lords engross?

---

[1] [The demonstrative Protestantism of the Metropolis is the subject of Dryden's *Medal*.]

[2] After v. 218 in the MS.
'Where one lean herring furnish'd Cotta's board,
And nettles grew, fit porridge for their Lord;
Where mad good-natured bounty misapply'd,
In lavish Curio blaz'd awhile and dy'd;
Their Providence once more shall shift the scene,
And shewing H—y, teach the Golden mean.'
    Warburton.
[H—y may stand for Harley.]

[3] After v. 226 in the MS.
'That secret rare, with affluence hardly join'd,
Which W—n lost, yet B—y ne'er could find;
Still miss'd by Vice, and scarce by Virtue hit,
By G—'s goodness, or by S—'s Wit.'
[Possibly Wharton, Bingley, Granville, Sheffield.]

[4] OXFORD'S *better part*,] Edward Harley, Earl of Oxford. The son of Robert, created Earl of Oxford and Earl Mortimer by Queen Anne. This nobleman died regretted by all men of letters, great numbers of whom had experienced his benefits. He left behind him one of the most noble Libraries in Europe. P.

Rise, honest Muse! and sing the MAN of ROSS:[1]　　　250
Pleas'd Vaga[2] echoes thro' her winding bounds,
And rapid Severn hoarse applause resounds.
Who hung with woods yon mountain's sultry brow?
From the dry rock who bade the waters flow?
Not to the skies in useless columns tost,　　　255
Or in proud falls magnificently lost,
But clear and artless, pouring thro' the plain
Health to the sick, and solace to the swain.
Whose Cause-way parts the vale with shady rows?
Whose Seats the weary Traveller repose?　　　260
Who taught that heav'n-directed spire to rise?
"The MAN of Ross," each lisping babe replies.
Behold the Market-place with poor o'erspread!
The MAN of Ross divides the weekly bread;
He feeds yon Alms-house, neat, but void of state,　　　265
Where Age and Want sit smiling at the gate;
Him portion'd maids, apprentic'd orphans blest,
The young who labour, and the old who rest.
Is any sick? the MAN of ROSS relieves,
Prescribes, attends, the med'cine makes, and gives.　　　270
Is there a variance; enter but his door,
Balk'd are the Courts, and contest is no more.
Despairing Quacks with curses fled the place,
And vile Attorneys, now an useless race.
　　B.　Thrice happy man! enabled to pursue　　　275
What all so wish, but want the pow'r to do!
Oh say, what sums that gen'rous hand supply?
What mines, to swell that boundless charity?
　　P.　Of Debts, and Taxes, Wife and Children clear,
This man possest — five hundred pounds a year.　　　280
Blush, Grandeur, blush! proud Courts, withdraw your blaze!
Ye little Stars! hide your diminish'd rays.
　　B.　And what? no monument, inscription, stone?[3]
His race, his form, his name almost unknown?
　　P.　Who builds a Church to God, and not to Fame,　　　285

---

[1] *The* MAN *of* ROSS:] The person here celebrated, who with a small Estate actually performed all these good works, and whose true name was almost lost (partly by the title of the *Man of Ross* given him by way of eminence, and partly by being buried without so much as an inscription), was called Mr. John Kyrle. He died in the year 1724, aged 90, and lies interred in the chancel of the church of Ross in Herefordshire. P.

We must understand what is here said, of *actually performing*, to mean by the contributions which the *Man of Ross*, by his assiduity and interest, collected in his neighbourhood.
　　　　　　　　　　Warburton.

[Johnson, in his life of Pope, accordingly censures this passage as in vain recommending what is unattainable, inasmuch as the Man of Ross did not do the wonders ascribed to him with his five hundred pounds a year.]

After v. 250 in the MS.
' Trace humble worth beyond Sabrina's shore,
Who sings not him, oh may he sing no more!'
　　　　　　　　　　Warburton.

[2] [*Vaga* is Latin name of the river Wye.]

[3] [This deficiency was afterwards supplied by the Earl of Kinnoul, a connexion of the family of the Man of Ross.]

MORAL ESSAYS.

Will never mark the marble with his Name:
Go, search it there,[1] where to be born and die,[2]
Of rich and poor makes all the history;
Enough, that Virtue fill'd the space between;
Prov'd, by the ends of being, to have been.   290
When Hopkins dies,[3] a thousand lights attend
The wretch, who living sav'd a candle's end:
Should'ring God's altar a vile image stands,
Belies his features, nay extends his hands;
That live-long wig which Gorgon's self might own,   295
Eternal buckle takes in Parian stone.[4]
Behold what blessings Wealth to life can lend!
And see, what comfort it affords our end.
   In the worst inn's worst room, with mat half-hung,
The floors of plaister, and the walls of dung,   300
On once a flock-bed, but repair'd with straw,
With tape-ty'd curtains, never meant to draw,
The George and Garter dangling from that bed
Where tawdry yellow strove with dirty red,
Great Villiers lies[5]— alas! how chang'd from him, 305
That life of pleasure, and that soul of whim!
Gallant and gay, in Cliveden's[6] proud alcove,
The bow'r of wanton Shrewsbury[7] and love;
Or just as gay, at Council, in a ring
Of mimic'd Statesmen, and their merry King.   310
No Wit to flatter left of all his store!
No Fool to laugh at, which he valu'd more.
There, Victor of his health, of fortune, friends,
And fame, this lord of useless thousands ends.

---

[1] *Go, search it there,*] The Parish-register. *Warburton.*

[2] Ver. 287 thus in the MS.
' The Register inrolls him with his Poor,
Tells he was born and dy'd, and tells no more.
Just as he ought, he fill'd the Space between;
Then stole to rest, unheeded and unseen.'
Warburton.

[3] Edmund Boulter, Esq., executor to Vulture Hopkins, made so splendid a funeral for him, that the expenses amounted to £7666. *Bowles.*

[4] *Eternal buckle takes in Parian stone.*] The poet ridicules the wretched taste of carving large perriwigs on bustos, of which there are several vile examples in the tombs at Westminster and elsewhere. P.

[5] *Great Villiers lies —*] This Lord, yet more famous for his vices than his misfortunes, after having been possess'd of about £50,000 a year, and passed thro' many of the highest posts in the kingdom, died in the Year 1687, in a remote inn in Yorkshire, reduced to the utmost misery. P.

[George Villiers Duke of Buckingham, the son of the first Duke (the favourite and minister of James I. and Charles I.) was born in 1637. He lost his estates as a royalist, but recovered them by his marriage with the daughter of Lord Fairfax. He is the Zimri of the Absalom and Achitophel of Dryden, whom he had ridiculed as Bayes in the burlesque play of the *Rehearsal.* Thus we have portraits of this typical hero of the Restoration period by Dryden and Pope, as well as by Burnet and Butler, Count Grammont and Horace Walpole. The tenant's house at which he died (in 1687) was at Kirby Moor Side, near Helmsly in Yorkshire.]

[6] *Cliveden*] A delightful palace, on the banks of the Thames, built by the D. of Buckingham. P.

[7] *Shrewsbury*] The Countess of Shrewsbury, a woman abandoned to gallantries. The Earl her husband was kill'd by the Duke of Buckingham in a duel; and it has been said, that during the combat she held the Duke's horses in the habit of a page. P.

His Grace's fate sage Cutler[1] could foresee, 315
And well (he thought) advis'd him, "Live like me."
As well his Grace reply'd, "Like you, Sir John?
"That I can do, when all I have is gone."
Resolve me, Reason, which of these is worse,
Want with a full, or with an empty purse? 320
Thy life more wretched, Cutler, was confess'd,
Arise, and tell me, was thy death more bless'd?
Cutler saw tenants break, and houses fall,
For very want; he could not build a wall.
His only daughter in a stranger's pow'r, 325
For very want; he could not pay a dow'r.
A few grey hairs his rev'rend temples crown'd,
'T was very want that sold them for two pound.
What ev'n deny'd a cordial at his end,
Banish'd the doctor, and expell'd the friend? 330
What but a want, which you perhaps think mad,
Yet numbers feel the want of what he had!
Cutler and Brutus, dying both exclaim,
"Virtue! and Wealth! what are ye but a name!"[2]
  Say, for such worth are other worlds prepar'd? 335
Or are they both, in this their own reward?
A knotty point! to which we now proceed.
But you are tir'd — I'll tell a tale — B. Agreed.
  P. Where London's column,[3] pointing at the skies,
Like a tall bully, lifts the head, and lies; 340
There dwelt a Citizen of sober fame,
A plain good man, and Balaam was his name;
Religious, punctual, frugal, and so forth;
His word would pass for more than he was worth.
One solid dish his week-day meal affords, 345
An added pudding solemniz'd the Lord's:
Constant at Church, and Change; his gains were sure,
His givings rare, save farthings to the poor.
  The Dev'l was piqu'd such saintship to behold,
And long'd to tempt him like good Job of old: 350
But Satan now is wiser than of yore,
And tempts by making rich, not making poor.
  Rous'd by the Prince of Air, the whirlwinds sweep
The surge, and plunge his Father in the deep;
Then full against his Cornish[4] lands they roar, 355

---

[1] [Sir John Cutler, a wealthy citizen of the Restoration period, accused of rapacity on account of a large claim made by his executors against the College of Physicians which he had aided by a loan. *Carruthers.*]

[2] [Wakefield refers to the account of Brutus' death. Dion Cassius (XLVII. 49).]

[3] *Where London's column,*] The Monument, on Fish Street Hill, built in memory of the fire of London, of 1666, with an inscription, importing that city to have been burnt by the Papists. P.

[4] *Cornish*] The author has placed the scene of these shipwrecks in Cornwall, not only from their frequency on that coast, but from the inhumanity of the inhabitants to those to whom that misfortune arrives. When a ship happens to be stranded there, they have been known to bore holes in it, to prevent its getting off; to plunder, and sometimes even to massacre the People: nor has the Parliament of England been yet able wholly to suppress these barbarities. P.

And two rich ship-wrecks bless the lucky shore.
    Sir Balaam now, he lives like other folks,
He takes his chirping pint, and cracks his jokes:
"Live like yourself," was soon my Lady's word;
And lo! two puddings smok'd upon the board.   360
    Asleep and naked as an Indian lay,
An honest factor stole a Gem away:[1]
He pledg'd it to the knight; the knight had wit,
So kept the Di'mond, and the rogue was bit.
Some scruple rose, but thus he eas'd his thought,   365
"I'll now give six-pence where I gave a groat;
"Where once I went to Church, I'll now go twice—
"And am so clear too of all other vice."
    The Tempter saw his time; the work he ply'd;
Stocks and Subscriptions pour on ev'ry side,   370
'Till all the Demon makes his full descent
In one abundant show'r of Cent per Cent,
Sinks deep within him, and possesses whole,
Then dubs Director, and secures his soul.
    Behold Sir Balaam, now a man of spirit,   375
Ascribes his gettings to his parts and merit;
What late he call'd a Blessing, now was Wit,
And God's good Providence, a lucky Hit.
Things change their titles, as our manners turn:
His Counting-house employ'd the Sunday-morn;   380
Seldom at Church ('t was such a busy life)
But duly sent his family and wife.
There (so the Dev'l ordain'd) one Christmas-tide
My good old Lady catch'd a cold, and died.
    A Nymph of Quality admires our Knight;   385
He marries, bows at Court, and grows polite:
Leaves the dull Cits, and joins (to please the fair)
The well-bred cuckolds in St. James's air:
First, for his Son a gay commission buys,
Who drinks, whores, fights, and in a duel dies: 390
His daughter flaunts a Viscount's tawdry wife;
She bears a Coronet and P—x for life.
In Britain's Senate he a seat obtains,
And one more Pensioner St. Stephen gains.[2]
My Lady falls to play; so bad her chance,   395
He must repair it; takes a bribe from France;
The House impeach him; Coningsby harangues;[3]
The Court forsake him, and Sir Balaam hangs:
Wife, son, and daughter, Satan! are thy own,

---

[1] Pope was supposed to allude here to the Pitt diamond, a gem brought to England by Thomas Pitt, Governor of Madras, about 1700. Mr. Pitt purchased this celebrated diamond, which goes by his name, for £20,400, and sold it to the King of France for more than five times that sum. It was then reckoned the largest jewel in Europe, and weighed 127 carats. *Carruthers.*

[2] *And one more Pensioner St. Stephen [gains.]*
— atque unum civem donare *Sibyllæ*.
Juv. [III. 3.] *Warburton.*

[3] [The impeachment of Oxford in 1715 was moved by Lord Coningsby.]

His wealth, yet dearer, forfeit to the Crown: 400
The Devil and the King divide the prize,
And sad Sir Balaam curses God and dies.

EPISTLE IV.

To Richard Boyle, Earl of Burlington.[1]

ARGUMENT.

Of the Use of RICHES.

The Vanity of Expence in People of Wealth and Quality. The abuse of the word Taste, v. 13. *That the first principle and foundation, in this as in every thing else, is* Good Sense, v. 40. *The chief proof of it is to* follow Nature *even in works of mere Luxury and Elegance. Instanced in* Architecture *and* Gardening, *where all must be adapted to the Genius and* Use *of the Place, and the Beauties not forced into it, but resulting from it*, v. 50. *How men are disappointed in their most expensive undertakings, for want of this true Foundation, without which nothing can please long, if at all; and the best Examples and* Rules *will but be perverted into something* burdensome *or ridiculous*, v. 65, &c. to 92. *A description of the* false Taste *of* Magnificence; *the first grand Error of which is to imagine that* Greatness *consists in the* Size *and* Dimension, *instead of the* Proportion *and* Harmony *of the* whole, v. 97, *and the second, either in joining together* Parts incoherent, *or too* minutely resembling, *or in the* Repetition *of the same too frequently*, v. 105, &c. *A word or two of false Taste in* Books, *in* Music, *in* Painting, *even in* Preaching *and* Prayer, *and lastly in* Entertainments, v. 133, &c. *Yet* PROVIDENCE *is justified in giving Wealth to be squandered in this manner, since it is dispersed to the Poor and Laborious part of mankind*, v. 169 [*recurring to what is laid down in the first book, Ep.* ii. *and in the Epistle preceding this*, v. 159, &c.]. *What are the proper Objects of Magnificence, and a proper field for the Expence of Great Men*, v. 177, &c., *and finally, the Great and Public Works which become a* Prince, v. 191, *to the end.*

'TIS strange, the Miser should his Cares employ
To gain those Riches he can ne'er enjoy:
Is it less strange, the Prodigal should waste
His wealth, to purchase what he ne'er can taste?
Not for himself he sees, or hears, or eats; 5
Artists must choose his Pictures, Music, Meats:
He buys for Topham,[2] Drawings and Designs,
For Pembroke,[3] Statues, dirty Gods, and Coins;
Rare monkish Manuscripts for Hearne[4] alone,

---

[1] [Richard Boyle third Earl of Burlington born in 1695 died in 1753. He took no prominent part in politics, although his high rank obtained for him a great post at court and the order of the Garter. But he obtained wide fame by his taste in architecture, inspired by a natural love of art and educated by studies in Italy. Horace Walpole says of him that he 'had every quality of genius and artist, except envy.' It has been doubted whether the architect Kent, who long lived with him, did not owe more to his patron, than the latter owed to the artist. The designs of many notable buildings were made by Lord Burlington; among these the Colonnade of Burlington-house (the house itself was built by his father).]

[2] A Gentleman famous for a judicious collection of Drawings. P.

[3] [Henry Earl of Pembroke, under whom the ancient family seat of Wilton, already adorned by the art of Holbein, Inigo Jones and Vandyke, received its last touches of beauty. See *Warton's* Note.]

[4] [Thomas Hearne, the well-known antiquary;

MORAL ESSAYS. 263

And Books for Mead, and Butterflies for Sloane.[1]   10
Think we all these are for himself? no more
Than his fine Wife, alas! or finer Whore.
    For what has Virro painted, built, and planted?
Only to show, how many Tastes he wanted.
What brought Sir Visto's ill got wealth to waste?   15
Some Dæmon whisper'd, "Visto! have a Taste."
Heav'n visits with a Taste the wealthy fool,
And needs no Rod but Ripley[2] with a Rule.
See! sportive fate, to punish awkward pride,
Bids Bubo[3] build, and sends him such a Guide: 20
A standing sermon, at each year's expense,
That never Coxcomb reach'd Magnificence![4]
    You show us, Rome was glorious, not profuse,[5]
And pompous buildings once were things of Use.
Yet shall, my Lord, your just, your noble rules   25
Fill half the land with Imitating-Fools;
Who random drawings from your sheets shall take,
And of one beauty many blunders make;
Load some vain Church with old Theatric state,
Turn Arcs of triumph to a Garden-gate;   30
Reverse your Ornaments, and hang them all
On some patch'd dog-hole ek'd with ends of wall;
Then clap four slices of Pilaster on 't,
That, lac'd with bits of rustic, makes a Front.
Shall call the winds thro' long arcades to roar,   35
Proud to catch cold at a Venetian door;[6]
Conscious they act a true Palladian part,

who revenged himself for the sarcastic reference to him in the Dunciad by ill-natured reflexions on Pope's parentage and education in his Diary. See Carruthers's *Life of Pope*, p. 14, note.]

[1] *And Books for Mead, and Butterflies for Sloane.*] Two eminent Physicians; the one had an excellent Library, the other the finest collection in Europe of natural curiosities; both men of great learning and humanity. P. [Dr. Mead, physician to George II. and the most noted practitioner of his day, was born in 1675 and died in 1754, bequeathing the greater part of his famous Library to the College of Physicians. He was, however, the reverse of a bookworm; for Johnson says of him (Boswell *ad ann.* 1778) that 'he lived more in the broad sunshine of life than almost any man.' Sir John or Hans Sloane (*b.* 1660), the well-known botanist and physician, in his will offered his collections to the nation at a sum one quarter of their estimated value. His Natural History cabinet now forms part of the national collections in the British Museum; his pictures &c. are in Lincoln's Inn Fields.]

[2] *Ripley*] This man was a carpenter, employed by a first Minister, who raised him to an Architect, without any genius in the art; and after some wretched proofs of his insufficiency in public Buildings, made him Comptroller of the Board of works. P. Mr. [Horace] Walpole speaks more favourably of this architect. *Warton*. [He was a protégé of Sir Robert Walpole's, and built his house at Houghton.]

[3] [Bubb Doddington. See *Epistle to Arbuthnot*, ver. 280.]

[4] After v. 22, in the MS.
'Must Bishops, Lawyers, Statesmen, have the skill
To build, to plant, judge paintings, what you will?
Then why not Kent as well our treaties draw, Bridgman explain the Gospel, Gibbs the Law?'

[5] The Earl of Burlington was then publishing the Designs of Inigo Jones, and the Antiquities of Rome by Palladio. P.

[6] A door or window so called, from being much practised at Venice, by Palladio and others. P.

And, if they starve, they starve by rules of art.
Oft have you hinted to your brother Peer
A certain truth, which many buy too dear: 40
Something there is more needful than Expense,
And something previous ev'n to Taste — 't is Sense:
Good Sense, which only is the gift of Heav'n,
And tho' no Science, fairly worth the seven:[1]
A Light, which in yourself you must perceive; 45
Jones[2] and Le Nôtre[3] have it not to give.

To build, to plant, whatever you intend,
To rear the Column, or the Arch to bend,
To swell the Terrace, or to sink the Grot;
In all, let Nature never be forgot. 50
But treat the Goddess like a modest fair,
Nor over-dress, nor leave her wholly bare;
Let not each beauty ev'rywhere be spy'd,
Where half the skill is decently to hide.
He gains all points, who pleasingly confounds, 55
Surprises, varies, and conceals the Bounds.
Consult the Genius of the Place in all;
That tells the Waters or to rise, or fall;
Or helps th' ambitious Hill the heav'ns to scale,
Or scoops in circling theatres the Vale; 60
Calls in the Country, catches op'ning glades,
Joins willing woods, and varies shades from shades;
Now breaks, or now directs, th' intending Lines;
Paints as you plant, and, as you work, designs.

Still follow Sense, of ev'ry Art the Soul, 65
Parts answ'ring parts shall slide into a whole,
Spontaneous beauties all around advance,
Start ev'n from Difficulty, strike from Chance;
Nature shall join you; Time shall make it grow
A Work to wonder at — perhaps a STOWE.[4] 70

Without it, proud Versailles! thy glory falls;
And Nero's Terraces desert their walls:[5]
The vast Parterres a thousand hands shall make,
Lo! COBHAM comes, and floats them with a Lake:

---

[1] [The seven sciences of the scholastic *trivium* and *quadrivium*.]

[2] [Inigo Jones the architect of the Banqueting House of Whitehall, the 'English Palladio,' died in 1653. He had originally risen into fame by designing Rosenborg, the Luxembourg of Copenhagen, for Christian IV., the brother-in-law of James I.]

[3] Inigo Jones, the celebrated Architect, and M. le Nôtre, the designer of the best gardens of France. P. [André Le Nôtre, the favourite landscape-gardener of Louis XIV., was born in 1613, and died in 1700. It was he who introduced into France the taste for the so-called 'jardins Anglais,' which he exemplified at all the royal residences, and especially at Versailles.]

[4] The seat and gardens of the Lord Viscount Cobham in Buckinghamshire. P.

[5] [i.e. are utterly subverted. Warton truly remarks that every instance of false taste and false magnificence is to be found at Versailles — and, it may be added, in the hundred copies of Versailles in Germany. Of Nero's Golden House, probably the most colossal effort architecture and landscape gardening ever made, a good short account will be found in Dyer's *History of the City of Rome*, Sect. IV.]

MORAL ESSAYS.

Or cut wide views thro' Mountains to the Plain, 75
You 'll wish your hill or shelter'd seat again.[1]
Ev'n in an ornament its place remark,
Nor in an Hermitage set Dr. Clarke.[2]
Behold Villario's ten years' toil complete;
His Quincunx darkens, his Espaliers meet; 80
The Wood supports the Plain, the parts unite,
And strength of Shade contends with strength of Light;
A waving Glow the bloomy beds display,
Blushing in bright diversities of day,
With silver-quiv'ring rills mæander'd o'er — 85
Enjoy them, you! Villario can no more;
Tir'd of the scene Parterres and Fountains yield,
He finds at last he better likes a Field.
Thro' his young Woods how pleas'd Sabinus stray'd,
Or sat delighted in the thick'ning shade, 90
With annual joy the redd'ning shoots to greet,
Or see the stretching branches long to meet!
His Son's fine Taste an op'ner Vista loves,
Foe to the Dryads of his Father's groves;
One boundless Green, or flourish'd Carpet views,[3] 95
With all the mournful family of Yews;[4]
The thriving plants ignoble broomsticks made,
Now sweep those Alleys they were born to shade.
At Timon's Villa[5] let us pass a day,
Where all cry out, "What sums are thrown away!" 100
So proud, so grand; of that stupendous air,
Soft and Agreeable come never there.
Greatness, with Timon, dwells in such a draught
As brings all Brobdignag[6] before your thought.
To compass this, his building is a Town, 105

[1] *Or cut wide views thro' Mountains to the Plain, You 'll wish your hill or shelter'd seat again.*] This was done in Hertfordshire, by a wealthy citizen, at the expense of above £5000, by which means (merely to overlook a dead plain) he let in the north-wind upon his house and parterre, which were before adorned and defended by beautiful woods. P.

[2] — *set Dr. Clarke.*] Dr. S. Clarke's busto placed by the Queen in the Hermitage, while the Dr. duly frequented the Court. P. [Dr. Clarke, one of Queen Caroline's chaplains, and the author of *Evidences of Religion*, and *Prayers and Meditations*, was charged with Arian opinions. See Boswell's *Life of Johnson*. On Pope's visit to Oxford in 1716, Dr. Clarke in vain endeavoured to engage him in controversy on theological subjects.]

[3] The two extremes in parterres, which are equally faulty; a *boundless Green*, large and naked as a field, or a *flourished Carpet*, where the greatness and nobleness of the piece is lessened by being divided into too many parts, with scroll'd works and beds, of which the examples are frequent. P.

[4] — *mournful family of Yews;*] Touches upon the ill taste of those who are so fond of Evergreens (particularly Yews, which are the most tonsile) as to destroy the nobler Forest-trees, to make way for such little ornaments as Pyramids of dark-green continually repeated, not unlike a Funeral procession. P.

[5] *At Timon's Villa*] This description is intended to comprize the principles of a false Taste of Magnificence, and to exemplify what was said before, that nothing but Good Sense can attain it. P. [As to the allusion in these lines to Canons, the seat of the Duke of Chandos, see Note on *Moral Essays, Ep.* 1. v. 54.]

[6] — *all Brobdignag*] A region of giants, in the satires of *Gulliver*. Warburton.

His pond an Ocean, his parterre a Down:
Who but must laugh, the Master when he sees,
A puny insect, shiv'ring at a breeze!
Lo, what huge heaps of littleness around![1]
The whole, a labour'd Quarry above ground;   110
Two Cupids squirt before; a Lake behind
Improves the keenness of the Northern wind.
His Gardens next your admiration call,
On ev'ry side you look, behold the Wall!
No pleasing Intricacies intervene,   115
No artful wildness to perplex the scene;
Grove nods at grove, each Alley has a brother,
And half the platform just reflects the other.
The suff'ring eye inverted Nature sees,
Trees cut to Statues, Statues thick as trees;   120
With here a Fountain, never to be play'd;
And there a Summer-house, that knows no shade;
Here Amphitrite sails thro' myrtle bow'rs;
There Gladiators[2] fight, or die in flow'rs;
Un-watered see the drooping sea-horse mourn,   125
And swallows roost in Nilus' dusty Urn.

 My Lord advances with majestic mien,
Smit with the mighty pleasure, to be seen:
But soft,—by regular approach,—not yet,—
First thro' the length of yon hot Terrace sweat;[3]   130
And when up ten steep slopes you've dragg'd your thighs,
Just at his Study-door he'll bless your eyes.

 His Study! with what Authors is it stor'd?[4]
In Books, not Authors, curious is my Lord;
To all their dated Backs he turns you round: 135
These Aldus[5] printed, those Du Sueil has bound.
Lo, some are Vellum, and the rest as good
For all his Lordship knows, but they are Wood.[6]
For Locke or Milton 't is in vain to look,
These shelves admit not any modern book.   140
 And now the Chapel's silver bell you hear,

---

[1] *Lo, what huge heaps of littleness around!*] *Grandeur* in building, as in the human frame, takes not its denomination from the *body*, but the *soul* of the work: when the soul therefore is lost or encumber'd in its invelope, the unanimated parts, how *huge* soever, are not members of grandeur, but mere *heaps of littleness*.

[2] The two Statues of the *Gladiator pugnans* and *Gladiator moriens*. P.

[3] The *Approaches* and *Communication* of house with garden, or of one part with another, ill judged, and inconvenient. P.

[4] *His Study! &c.*] The false Taste in Books; a satire on the vanity in collecting them, more frequent in men of Fortune than the study to understand them. Many delight chiefly in the elegance of the print, or of the binding; some have carried it so far, as to cause the upper shelves to be filled with painted books of wood; others pique themselves so much upon books in a language they do not understand, as to exclude the most useful in one they do. P.

[5] [Aldo Manutio, who established his famous printing-press at Venice about 1490.]

[6] [i.e. as if they were wood. Warton compares to Pope's disadvantage Young's passage on the same subject in *Universal Passion*, Sat. III.]

MORAL ESSAYS.   267

That summons you to all the Pride of Pray'r:[1]
Light quirks of Music, broken and uneven,
Make the soul dance upon a Jig to Heav'n.
On painted Ceilings[2] you devoutly stare,   145
Where sprawl the Saints of Verrio or Laguerre,[3]
On gilded clouds in fair expansion lie,
And bring all Paradise before your eye.
To rest, the Cushion and soft Dean invite,
Who never mentions Hell to ears polite.[4]   150
  But hark! the chiming Clocks to dinner call;
A hundred footsteps scrape the marble Hall:
The rich Buffet well-colour'd Serpents grace,[5]
And gaping Tritons spew to wash your face.
Is this a dinner? this a Genial room?   155
No, 't is a Temple, and a Hecatomb.[6]
A solemn Sacrifice, perform'd in state,
You drink by measure, and to minutes eat.
So quick retires each flying course, you 'd swear
Sancho's dread Doctor and his Wand were there.[7]   160
Between each Act the trembling salvers ring,
From soup to sweet-wine, and God bless the King.
In plenty starving, tantaliz'd in state,
And complaisantly help'd to all I hate,
Treated, caress'd, and tir'd, I take my leave,   165
Sick of his civil Pride from Morn to Eve;
I curse such lavish cost, and little skill,
And swear no Day was ever past so ill.
  Yet hence the Poor are cloth'd, the Hungry fed;[8]
Health to himself, and to his Infants bread   170
The Lab'rer bears: What his hard Heart denies,

---

[1] The false Taste in *Music*, improper to the subjects, as of light airs in churches, often practised by the organists, &c. P.

[2] — And in *Painting* (from which even Italy is not free) of naked figures in Churches, &c. which has obliged some Popes to put draperies on some of those of the best masters. P.

[3] *Verrio or Laguerre.*] Verrio (Antonio) painted many ceilings, &c. at Windsor, Hampton-court, &c. and Laguerre at Blenheim-castle, and other places. P. [Verrio's ceilings at Windsor are referred to in *Windsor Forest*, v. 305. The line in the text was said exactly to describe the ceilings at Canons; but Pope in a letter to Aaron Hill (Feb. 3, 1732) asserts that the frescoes there were not by the painters mentioned and that the rest of the description was equally inapplicable. See Roscoe's *Life*.]

[4] *Who never mentions Hell to ears polite.*] This is a fact; a reverend Dean preaching at Court, threatened the sinner with punishment in "a place which he thought it not decent to name in so polite an assembly." P.

[5] Taxes the incongruity of *Ornaments* (tho' sometimes practised by the ancients) where an open mouth ejects the water into a fountain, or where the shocking images of serpents, &c. are introduced in Grottos or Buffets. P.

[6] *Is this a dinner, &c.*] The proud Festivals of some men are here set forth to ridicule, where pride destroys the ease, and formal regularity all the pleasurable enjoyment of the entertainment. P.

[7] *Sancho's dread Doctor*] See Don Quixote, chap. xlvii. P.

[8] *Yet hence the Poor, &c.*] The *Moral* of the whole, where PROVIDENCE is justified in giving Wealth to those who squander it in this manner. A bad Taste employs more hands, and diffuses Expence more than a good one. This recurs to what is laid down in Book i. Epist. II. v. 230-7, and in the Epistle preceding this, v. 161, &c. P.

His charitable Vanity supplies.
    Another age shall see the golden Ear [1]
Embrown the Slope, and nod on the Parterre,
Deep Harvests bury all his pride has plann'd,
And laughing Ceres re-assume the land.
    Who then shall grace, or who improve the Soil?
Who plants like BATHURST, or who builds like BOYLE.
'T is Use alone that sanctifies Expense,
And Splendour borrows all her rays from Sense.   180
    His Father's Acres who enjoys in peace,
Or makes his Neighbours glad, if he increase:
Whose cheerful Tenants bless their yearly toil,
Yet to their Lord owe more than to the soil;
Whose ample Lawns are not asham'd to feed   185
The milky heifer and deserving steed;
Whose rising Forests, not for pride or show,
But future Buildings, future Navies, grow:
Let his plantations stretch from down to down,
First shade a Country, and then raise a Town.   190
    You too proceed! make falling Arts your care,
Erect new wonders, and the old repair;
Jones [2] and Palladio [3] to themselves restore,
And be whate'er Vitruvius [4] was before:
'Till Kings call forth th' Ideas of your mind,   195
(Proud to accomplish what such hands designed,)
Bid Harbours open,[5] public Ways extend,
Bid Temples, worthier of the God, ascend;
Bid the broad Arch the dang'rous Flood contain,

---

[1] *Another age, &c.*] Had the Poet lived but three Years longer, he had seen this prophecy fulfilled. *Warburton*. [This note, as Warton points out, was judiciously generalised by Warburton in a later edition, to avoid the plain reference to Canons.]

[2] [*Jones*, v. ante line 46.]

[3] [Palladio was born at Vicenza, where the Basilica della Ragione was his first work. He ultimately settled at Venice where most of his masterpieces were undertaken. He died in 1580.]

[4] [M. Vitruvius Pollio, celebrated for his work *de Architectura*, was born about the year 80 B.C.]

[5] *'Till Kings — Bid Harbours open, &c.*] The poet after having touched upon the proper objects of Magnificence and Expense, in the private works of great men, comes to those great and public works which become a prince. This Poem was published in the year 1732, when some of the new-built Churches, by the act of Queen Anne, were ready to fall, being founded in boggy land (which is satirically alluded to in our author's imitation of Horace, Lib. ii. Sat. 2,

Shall half the new-built Churches round thee fall;

others were vilely executed, thro' fraudulent cabals between undertakers, officers, &c. Dagenham-breach had done very great mischiefs; many of the Highways throughout England were hardly passable; and most of those which were repaired by Turnpikes were made jobs for private lucre, and infamously executed, even to the entrances of London itself: The proposal of building a Bridge at Westminster had been petition'd against and rejected; but in two years after the publication of this poem, an Act for building a Bridge pass'd thro' both houses. After many debates in the committee, the execution was left to the carpenter above-mentioned, who would have made it a wooden one: to which our author alludes in these lines,

Who builds a Bridge that never drove a pile?
Should Ripley venture, all the world would smile.

See the notes on that place. P. [The two lines quoted are from Epistle to Augustus, l. 186, p. 316, but Pope had no notes to either passage. Am. Ed.]

ADDISON.
(From a picture, copied by J. Thurston.)

The Mole projected break the roaring Main; 200
Back to his bounds their subject Sea command,
And roll obedient Rivers thro' the Land:
These Honours Peace to happy Britain brings,
These are Imperial Works, and worthy Kings.[1]

EPISTLE V.

TO MR. ADDISON.

Occasioned by his Dialogues on MEDALS.

THIS was originally written in the year 1715, when Mr. Addison intended to publish his book of medals; it was sometime before he was secretary of State; but not published till Mr. Tickell's Edition of his works; at which time the verses on Mr. Craggs, which conclude the poem, were added, viz. in 1720. P. [The materials for these Dialogues were collected by Addison during his travels in Italy, and the book itself was begun to be written at Vienna as early as 1702. Though known to and favourably esteemed by many scholars of note, it was never published in his lifetime; for he died in 1719. Concerning Pope's relations with Addison see *Introductory Memoir*, p. xv. f.

The following is Warburton's attempt to connect the revised version of Pope's lines to Addison with the series of *Moral Essays*:

'As the third Epistle treated of the extremes of *Avarice* and *Profusion;* and the 'fourth took up one particular branch of the latter, namely, the *vanity of expence* in 'people of wealth and quality, and was therefore a corollary to the third; so this treats 'of one circumstance of that Vanity, as it appears in the common collectors of old 'coins; and is, therefore, a corollary to the fourth.']

SEE the wild Waste of all-devouring years!
How Rome her own sad Sepulchre appears,[2]
With nodding arches, broken temples spread!
The very Tombs now vanish'd like their dead!
Imperial wonders rais'd on Nations spoil'd, 5
Where mix'd with Slaves the groaning Martyr toil'd:[3]
Huge Theatres, that now unpeopled Woods,
Now drain'd a distant country of her Floods:
Fanes, which admiring Gods with pride survey,
Statues of Men, scarce less alive than they! 10
Some felt the silent stroke of mould'ring age,
Some hostile fury, some religious rage.
Barbarian blindness, Christian zeal conspire,
And Papal piety, and Gothic fire.
Perhaps, by its own ruins sav'd from flame, 15
Some bury'd marble half preserves a name;
That Name the learn'd with fierce disputes pursue,
And give to Titus old Vespasian's due.

---

[1] [Carruthers refers to Dryden's free translation of Æn. VI. 853-4:
'These are imperial arts and worthy thine.']

[2] St. Jerome calls Rome 'quondam orbis caput, postea populi Romani sepulcrum.' *Warton*.

[3] [According to an ancient tradition, the Christians were forced to labour at the construction of the famous Baths of Diocletian.]

MORAL ESSAYS.

    Ambition sigh'd: She found it vain to trust
The faithless Column and the crumbling Bust: 20
Huge moles, whose shadow stretch'd from shore to shore,
Their ruins perish'd, and their place no more!
Convinc'd, she now contracts her vast design,
And all her triumphs shrink into a Coin.
A narrow orb each crowded conquest keeps;   25
Beneath her Palm here sad Judæa weeps;[1]
Now scantier limits the proud Arch[2] confine,
And scarce are seen the prostrate Nile or Rhine;[3]
A small Euphrates thro' the piece is roll'd,
And little Eagles wave their wings in gold.   30
    The Medal, faithful to its charge of fame,
Thro' climes and ages bears each form and name:
In one short view subjected to our eye
Gods, Emp'rors, Heroes, Sages, Beauties, lie.
With sharpen'd sight[4] pale Antiquaries pore,   35
Th' inscription value, but the rust adore.
This the blue varnish, that the green endears,[5]
The sacred rust of twice ten hundred years!
To gain Pescennius[6] one employs his schemes,
One grasps a Cecrops in ecstatic[7] dreams.   40
Poor Vadius,[8] long with learned spleen devour'd,
Can taste no pleasure since his Shield was scour'd;
And Curio, restless by the Fair-one's side,
Sighs for an Otho, and neglects his bride.[9]
    Theirs is the Vanity, the Learning thine: 45
Touch'd by thy hand, again Rome's glories shine;
Her Gods, and god-like Heroes rise to view,
And all her faded garlands bloom anew.
Nor blush, these studies thy regard engage;
These pleas'd the Fathers of poetic rage;   50
The verse and sculpture bore an equal part,
And Art reflected images to Art.
    Oh when shall Britain, conscious of her claim,[10]
Stand emulous of Greek and Roman fame?

---

[1] ['Judæa Capta' on a reverse of Vespasian.]

[2] —*the proud Arch*] i.e. The triumphal Arch, which was generally an enormous mass of building. *Warburton.*

[3] [A small figure of the conquered province frequently occurs on medals struck on the occasion of a triumph.]

[4] [i.e. with the aid of microscopes.]

[5] *This the blue varnish, that the green endears,*] i.e. This a collector of silver; that, of brass coins. *Warburton.*

[6] Pescennius Niger assumed the purple in Syria in 131, but was speedily worsted by Septimius Severus.]

[7] [Ecstatic, because of course no such medals exist.]

[8] *Poor Vadius,*] See his history, and that of his Shield, in the *Memoirs of Scriblerus*. *Warburton.* [Aimed at Dr. Woodward the eminent physician and naturalist, who wrote a dissertation on an ancient shield which he possessed. *Carruthers.*]

[9] Charles Patin was banished from the Court because he sold Louis XIV. an Otho that was not genuine. *Warton.* [A very remarkable Otho is given by Addison.]

[10] *Oh when shall Britain, &c.*] A compliment to one of Mr. Addison's papers in the Spectator on this subject. *Warburton.*

MORAL ESSAYS.

In living medals see her wars enroll'd, 55
And vanquish'd realms supply recording gold?
Here, rising bold, the Patriot's honest face;
There Warriors frowning in historic brass?
Then future ages with delight shall see
How Plato's, Bacon's, Newton's looks agree; 60
Or in fair series laurell'd Bards be shown,
A Virgil there, and here an Addison.[1]
Then shall thy CRAGGS[2] (and let me call him mine)
On the cast ore, another Pollio, shine;
With aspect open, shall erect his head, 65
And round the orb in lasting notes be read,
" Statesman, yet friend to Truth! of soul sincere,[3]
" In action faithful, and in honour clear;
" Who broke no promise, serv'd no private end,
" Who gain'd no title, and who lost no friend; 70
" Ennobled by himself, by all approv'd,
" And prais'd, unenvy'd, by the Muse he lov'd."[4]

---

[1] Copied evidently from Tickell to Addison on his *Rosamond:* 'Which gain'd a Virgil and an Addison.' *Warton.* [Asinius Pollio, on the birth of whose son Vergil wrote the Eclogue paraphrased in Pope's *Messiah.*]

[2] [*Craggs.* See note to Pope's *Epitaph* IV.]

[3] *Statesman, yet friend to truth! &c.*] It should be remembered that this poem was written to be printed before Mr. Addison's *Discourse on Medals,* in which there is the following censure of long legends upon coins: "The first "fault I find with a modern legend is its diffu-"siveness. You have sometimes the whole side "of a medal over-run with it. One would fancy "the Author had a Design of being Ciceronian "— but it is not only the tediousness of these "inscriptions that I find fault with; supposing "them of a moderate length, why must they be "in verse? We should be surprized to see the "title of a serious book in rhyme." — Dial. iii.

[4] *And prais'd, unenvy'd, by the Muse he lov'd.*] It was not likely that men acting in so different spheres as were those of Mr. Craggs and Mr. Pope, should have their friendship disturbed by Envy. We must suppose then that some circumstances in the friendship of Mr. Pope and Mr. Addison are hinted at in this place. *Warburton.*

www.ingramcontent.com/pod-product-compliance
Lightning Source LLC
Chambersburg PA
CBHW031940080426
42735CB00007B/209